W9-BYA-795

# .NET Framework Standard Library Annotated Reference
## Volume 1

## Microsoft .NET Development Series

John Montgomery, *Series Advisor*
Don Box, *Series Advisor*
Martin Heller, *Series Editor*

The **Microsoft .NET Development Series** is supported and developed by the leaders and experts of Microsoft development technologies including Microsoft architects and DevelopMentor instructors. The books in this series provide a core resource of information and understanding every developer needs in order to write effective applications and managed code. Learn from the leaders how to maximize your use of the .NET Framework and its programming languages.

## Titles in the Series

Brad Abrams, *.NET Framework Standard Library Annotated Reference Volume 1*, 0-321-15489-4

Keith Ballinger, *.NET Web Services: Architecture and Implementation*, 0-321-11359-4

Don Box with Chris Sells, *Essential .NET, Volume 1: The Common Language Runtime*, 0-201-73411-7

Mahesh Chand, *Graphics Programming with GDI+*, 0-321-16077-0

Anders Hejlsberg, Scott Wiltamuth, Peter Golde, *The C# Programming Language*, 0-321-15491-6

Alex Homer, Dave Sussman, Mark Fussell, *A First Look at ADO.NET and System.Xml v. 2.0*, 0-321-22839-1

Alex Homer, Dave Sussman, Rob Howard, *A First Look at ASP.NET v. 2.0*, 0-321-22896-0

James S. Miller and Susann Ragsdale, *The Common Language Infrastructure Annotated Standard*, 0-321-15493-2

Fritz Onion, *Essential ASP.NET with Examples in C#*, 0-201-76040-1

Fritz Onion, *Essential ASP.NET with Examples in Visual Basic .NET*, 0-201-76039-8

Ted Pattison and Dr. Joe Hummel, *Building Applications and Components with Visual Basic .NET*, 0-201-73495-8

Chris Sells, *Windows Forms Programming in C#*, 0-321-11620-8

Chris Sells and Justin Gehtland, *Windows Forms Programming in Visual Basic .NET*, 0-321-12519-3

Paul Vick, *The Visual Basic .NET Programming Language*, 0-321-16951-4

Damien Watkins, Mark Hammond, Brad Abrams, *Programming in the .NET Environment*, 0-201-77018-0

Shawn Wildermuth, *Pragmatic ADO.NET: Data Access for the Internet World*, 0-201-74568-2

**www.awprofessional.com/msdotnetseries/**

# .NET Framework Standard Library Annotated Reference Volume 1

*Base Class Library and Extended Numerics Library*

Brad Abrams

Addison-Wesley

Boston • San Francisco • New York • Toronto • Montreal
London • Munich • Paris • Madrid
Capetown • Sydney • Tokyo • Singapore • Mexico City

The publisher offers discounts on this book when ordered in quantity for special sales. For more information, please contact:

U.S. Corporate and Government Sales
(800) 382-3419
corpsales@pearsontechgroup.com

For sales outside of the U.S., please contact:

International Sales
(317) 581-3793
international@pearsontechgroup.com

Visit Addison-Wesley on the Web: www.awprofessional.com

*Library of Congress Cataloging-in-Publication Data*
Abrams, Brad.
.NET framework standard library annotated reference volume 1: base class library and extended numerics library / Brad Abrams.
p. cm.
ISBN 0-321-15489-4 (hardcover : alk. paper)
1. Microsoft .NET Framework. I. Title.

QA76.76.M52A27 2004
005.2'768—dc22 2003024327



Pearson Education, Inc.
Rights and Contracts Department
75 Arlington Street, Suite 300
Boston, MA 02116
Fax: (617) 848-7047

ISBN 0-321-15489-4
Text printed on recycled paper
1 2 3 4 5 6 7 8 9 10—CRW—0807060504
First printing, March 2004

*To the two most important things in my life:*
*My God and my family.*

# Contents

*Foreword xiii*
*Preface xvii*

## Part I Namespace Overviews 1

System 3
System.Collections 11
System.Diagnostics 14
System.Globalization 15
System.IO 17
System.Security 21
System.Text 25
System.Threading 27

## Part II Class Libraries 31

System.ApplicationException 33
System.ArgumentException 35
System.ArgumentNullException 37
System.ArgumentOutOfRangeException 40
System.ArithmeticException 42
System.Array 44
System.Collections.ArrayList 52
System.ArrayTypeMismatchException 57
System.Text.ASCIIEncoding 59
System.AsyncCallback Delegate 61
System.Attribute 63

System.AttributeTargets Enum 68
System.AttributeUsageAttribute 71

System.Boolean Structure 75
System.Byte Structure 77

System.Char Structure 81
System.CharEnumerator 85
System.CLSCompliantAttribute 88
System.Security.CodeAccessPermission 90
System.Security.Permissions.CodeAccessSecurityAttribute 94
System.Collections.Comparer 96
System.Diagnostics.ConditionalAttribute 97
System.Console 100
System.Convert 104

System.DateTime Structure 115
System.Globalization.DateTimeFormatInfo 121
System.Globalization.DateTimeStyles Enum 131
System.Decimal Structure 133
System.Text.Decoder 140
System.Delegate 142
System.Collections.DictionaryEntry Structure 146
System.IO.Directory 148
System.IO.DirectoryNotFoundException 151
System.DivideByZeroException 153
System.Double Structure 155
System.DuplicateWaitObjectException 160

System.Text.Encoder 163
System.Text.Encoding 164
System.IO.EndOfStreamException 170
System.Enum 172
System.Environment 177
System.Security.Permissions.EnvironmentPermission 180
System.Security.Permissions.EnvironmentPermissionAccess Enum 183
System.Security.Permissions.EnvironmentPermissionAttribute 185

System.EventArgs 187
System.EventHandler Delegate 190
System.Exception 192
System.ExecutionEngineException 198

System.IO.File 201
System.IO.FileAccess Enum 204
System.Security.Permissions.FileIOPermission 206
System.Security.Permissions.FileIOPermissionAccess Enum 211
System.Security.Permissions.FileIOPermissionAttribute 213
System.IO.FileLoadException 215
System.IO.FileMode Enum 218
System.IO.FileNotFoundException 220
System.IO.FileShare Enum 223
System.IO.FileStream 225
System.FlagsAttribute 231
System.FormatException 233

System.GC 235

System.Collections.Hashtable 239

System.IAsyncResult Interface 245
System.ICloneable Interface 248
System.Collections.ICollection Interface 251
System.IComparable Interface 254
System.Collections.IComparer Interface 258
System.Collections.IDictionary Interface 260
System.Collections.IDictionaryEnumerator Interface 262
System.IDisposable Interface 264
System.Collections.IEnumerable Interface 267
System.Collections.IEnumerator Interface 269
System.IFormatProvider Interface 271
System.IFormattable Interface 273
System.Collections.IHashCodeProvider Interface 283
System.Collections.IList Interface 286
System.IndexOutOfRangeException 292

System.Int16 Structure 294
System.Int32 Structure 297
System.Int64 Structure 301
System.Threading.Interlocked 304
System.InvalidCastException 307
System.InvalidOperationException 309
System.InvalidProgramException 311
System.IO.IOException 312
System.Security.IPermission Interface 314

System.MarshalByRefObject 317
System.Math 319
System.IO.MemoryStream 321
System.Threading.Monitor 325

System.NotFiniteNumberException 331
System.NotImplementedException 333
System.NotSupportedException 335
System.NullReferenceException 337
System.Globalization.NumberFormatInfo 339
System.Globalization.NumberStyles Enum 343

System.Object 347
System.ObjectDisposedException 350
System.ObsoleteAttribute 352
System.OutOfMemoryException 354
System.OverflowException 356

System.IO.Path 359
System.IO.PathTooLongException 365
System.Security.PermissionSet 367
System.Security.Permissions.PermissionState Enum 373

System.Random 375
System.RankException 378

System.SByte Structure 381
System.Security.Permissions.SecurityAction Enum 384

System.Security.Permissions.SecurityAttribute 386
System.Security.SecurityElement 388
System.Security.SecurityException 390
System.Security.Permissions.SecurityPermission 392
System.Security.Permissions.SecurityPermissionAttribute 395
System.Security.Permissions.SecurityPermissionFlag Enum 398
System.IO.SeekOrigin Enum 400
System.Single Structure 402
System.StackOverflowException 406
System.IO.Stream 408
System.IO.StreamReader 414
System.IO.StreamWriter 417
System.String 420
System.Text.StringBuilder 429
System.IO.StringReader 434
System.IO.StringWriter 436
System.Threading.SynchronizationLockException 438
System.SystemException 440
System.IO.TextReader 443
System.IO.TextWriter 445
System.Threading.Thread 448
System.Threading.ThreadAbortException 452
System.Threading.ThreadPriority Enum 454
System.Threading.ThreadStart Delegate 456
System.Threading.ThreadState Enum 458
System.Threading.ThreadStateException 461
System.Threading.Timeout 463
System.Threading.Timer 465
System.Threading.TimerCallback Delegate 468
System.TimeSpan Structure 470
System.Type 474
System.TypeInitializationException 484
System.UInt16 Structure 487
System.UInt32 Structure 490

System.UInt64 Structure 493
System.UnauthorizedAccessException 496
System.Globalization.UnicodeCategory Enum 498
System.Text.UnicodeEncoding 500
System.Text.UTF8Encoding 503

System.ValueType 507
System.Security.VerificationException 510
System.Version 512

System.Threading.WaitHandle 515

*Annotations Index 519*
*Index 521*

# Foreword

When I began my standards "career" back in August 2000, "ECMA" and "ISO" meant as much to me as the sequence of letters in the daily newspaper jumble. I hadn't a clue on how the standards process actually worked, from either a technical or a political perspective. Now, as I write this, I am chair of the ECMA committee that oversees the standardization of programming and scripting languages. In addition, I am convener of the task group within the committee that is responsible for the standardization of the CLI, on which, of course, the content of this book is based.

In 2000, Microsoft publicly introduced its .NET vision. A key component of this vision is the .NET Framework, which includes a set of class libraries and a virtual machine ("runtime engine") to execute next-generation applications.

In September 2000, Microsoft, co-sponsored by Intel and Hewlett-Packard, formally submitted a core subset of the .NET Framework to ECMA International, a renowned international standards organization. The submission was entitled the Common Language Infrastructure, or CLI. The meeting was held in Bristol, England, with representatives from companies such as IBM and Sun Microsystems. Microsoft presented the CLI to ECMA's Programming and Scripting Languages Technical Committee, or TC39. It was decided by unanimous consent that the CLI would be added to the program of work for TC39 and that a new task group, called the TG3, would be responsible for the standardization effort. One might ask what happened to TG1 and TG2. Before the submission of the CLI, the TC39 was responsible for the standardization of only ECMAScript. There were no task groups, per se. When the CLI was approved for work, ECMAScript was moved to a newly formed TG1. C#, which was submitted at the same time as the CLI, introduced the TG2. The TG3 was reserved for the CLI. There is now even a TG4 responsible for the standardization of the Eiffel programming language and a TG5 chartered to standardize a binding between ISO C++ and the CLI.

There are two primary facets to the CLI standardization process within ECMA, the virtual machine and the class libraries. The virtual machine provides the environment necessary to execute applications written for the CLI. The class libraries provide the core infrastructure to enable developers to create libraries and applications for execution on top of the virtual machine.

I am involved in both facets of the standardization process, but I have enjoyed the class library aspect the most. This is primarily because I have a better understanding of that level of the development stack than I do the lower layers, such as where the virtual machine would lie. And since Brad Abrams was the Microsoft lead in the class library standardization effort, my good relationship with him began.

The set of class libraries submitted to ECMA International are, from a .NET Framework perspective, relatively small. However, they definitely provide the foundation upon which all other class libraries are built. The class library was segmented into what the standard calls "profiles." The kernel profile consists of the base types that would be expected to exist in modern programming languages (as well as types to assist compilers for those languages). `String` and `Int32` are examples of such types. The kernel profile must be implemented in order to claim conformance to the standard. The compact profile consists of the kernel profile, plus some types necessary to implement basic Web services-type applications while maintaining a small enough footprint to fit on standard compact, connected devices. Then there are some types that do not fit any profile, but can be implemented as part of any profile. These include types dealing with floating point numbers and multidimensional arrays. Brad's book concentrates on the base types that are part of the kernel profile, as well as the extended numerics (e.g., floating point and decimal). For information on the concept behind the segmentation of the class libraries into profiles, see Partition IV of the ECMA Standard ECMA-335, also published as ISO/IEC 23271. The ECMA Standard can be downloaded—and freely copied—free of charge from http://www.ecma-international.org.

The process by which we standardized the base types associated with kernel profile was systematic, and yet churned out some very interesting and heated discussion. There was an initial cursory review of all of the libraries in order to weed out any obvious errors and missing data. Then came the detailed reviews. We started with the type of all types, `System.Object`. This served as the model of the process we would use to do the rest of the detailed reviews. The task group members would work offline and formulate individual comments on the type. Then at the meeting we would go page by page, method by method, property by property to see if there were any comments. Brad, who managed the editing process at Microsoft, took the comments back and incorporated them. Finally, the task group would review the type again with the incorporated changes and consider it final. Of course, if the task group just reviewed one type per meeting, we would still be reviewing the class libraries. After `System.Object`, the base types were divided into relatively equal parts, and at each meeting the task group would review one of those parts. To expedite the process, a subgroup of people were assigned as primary reviewers for certain types. Thus, committee members weren't overwhelmed by having to do detailed analysis and commentary on all types.

If all we did at the meetings were editorial reviews of the types—fixing punctuation here and changing a word there—they would have been quite boring. (Actually, come to think of it, it would have been amazing if that were the case—no substantial changes were needed to the class libraries because they were already perfect!) I mentioned that some interesting and heated discussion occurred during the reviews of the class libraries. This was because they were, of course, *not* perfect, and thus illustrate the benefit and relevance of the standardization process. You will see many annotations in this book that are examples of cool discussion, so I won't dive into it much here, but one instance definitely sticks out as a whopper. It was within the `System.Decimal` structure, where the original specification of the `ToString()` method did not preserve the scale (trailing zeros) during conversion (even though it maintained scale internally, it was not exposed through conversions back and forth from `String`). For example, given a decimal value of 134.320000, it can be noted that this has a scale of 6. Calling the `ToString()` method would produce a string with the characters 134.32, making a decimal value with a scale of 2. This was deemed the wrong thing to do. Now one must remember that the .NET Framework 1.0 had already been shipped to millions of customers. Even so, the change was made to the specification and, even more important, Microsoft staff agreed to this change even though it would break code. They knew, however, it was the right thing to do. Indeed, standardization can be quite interesting!

The class library specifications were submitted to ECMA International, but not as the Microsoft Word or Adobe PDF documentation that one would expect. Instead they were submitted in XML format. This was done for various reasons, but the primary one was so that implementers could create documentation in any form they chose (HTML, Word, PDF, etc.) using well-known XSLT techniques and other mechanisms. It allowed for a lot of freedom in the documentation. Of course, no one (at least no one of sound mind) is going to read 10 MB of raw XML, let alone use it as the means to review the types. Thus a way to convert the XML to Word was needed. A managed code-based tool was developed by one of the task group members using XSLT and COM Interop to access the Word APIs (I am usually very humble, so I won't mention the tool author by name, but... ☺). This turned out to be very valuable because it produced human-readable documentation. It also saved months of manual editing and formatting because the tool allowed edits to be made to the XML only, and then it would take care of the rest. The tool was also versatile. It did not just generate Word documents. For example, the type, method, and property signatures you see in this book—even those in the C# standard—are based on the running of the conversion tool. It was actually quite fun to develop. Not everyone was convinced of the benefits of the XML, and there was some controversy regarding the submission of the class libraries in that format (although ECMA had already developed another standard in this format); it even caused one delegation within ISO to vote against accepting the standard at first. After discussion, however, the XML format was accepted as an appropriate submission mechanism. The tool, and the results it produces, is published as ECMA TR/84, which is also freely available from the ECMA Web site.

Some people may ask why the CLI was submitted for standardization in the first place. Yes, it's true that the current standard CLI specification alone will not allow developers to implement a majority of real-world applications (e.g., I doubt Quake could be etched out of the standard library set). However, it is, in my mind, a near-perfect base to begin such an implementation. Also, the industry has accepted the standard. Intel's Open Class Libraries (OCL), as well as other public projects, are based on what the standard has to offer (the licensing arrangements for the standard are very kind, which helps here, but I won't get into that). It provides a cookbook for researchers to do work in the area of managed runtime environments, knowing that this cookbook is based on a high-quality and widely used commercial implementation. It also provides a foundation for future technologies to be added to the standard, which is already evident in the work happening to the next edition of the standard.

The first edition of the standard was ratified by ECMA in December 2001, and approved by ISO in October 2002 (which became Edition 2 of the ECMA standard in December 2002 because minor edits were made during the ISO review process). Work on Edition 3 is occurring as I write this, and some interesting libraries are being considered in the area of generics and threading.

The specification itself, while important in implementing the CLI class libraries, could be construed as very dry reading. It is, after all, primarily a cookbook specifying what must be included in a successful class library recipe. *.NET Framework Standard Library Annotated Reference, Volume 1,* adds some pizzazz to the standard. Annotations are not typically an official part of a standard, and rightly so, as a standard must be as clear and concise as possible, only providing necessary information for implementation. However, if I were a developer using the CLI class libraries (heck, even if I were an *implementer* of the libraries), this book would be my primary tool. Why? Because it provides you with all the information of the official standard, but also includes firsthand insight, examples, and occasionally a little humor by those who developed it. And those added extras could answer a lot of the "Why was this done that way?" questions that many developers have.

Some quick praise for the author of this book, Brad Abrams: It is obvious that he is a content guru. In addition, it was his leadership in producing the specifications, accepting (most of the time ☺) and incorporating changes, and reproducing the results in a timely manner, that enabled this standard to be produced in the time frame it was.

For me, the journey from alphabet soup to where we are today has been an interesting ride. I like to think my hard work during the process and my passion for what was being standardized led me to the ECMA positions I hold today. But if it weren't for the dedication of people like Brad, who was instrumental in getting the first edition of the standard out the door, I am not sure there would *be* such positions in the first place.

Step into the minds of the people who actually made the standard class libraries happen, and enjoy the book.

Joel Marcey
Intel Corporation
Chair of TC39
Convener of TG3[1]

1. The views expressed in this Foreword do not necessarily reflect the views of Intel Corporation, its affiliates, its subsidiaries, or its employees.

# Preface

This book is intended for anyone building applications using the .NET Framework. It is meant to be a dictionary-style reference to the core types in the Framework.

The .NET Framework is huge. The amount of time that would be required (and the physical constraints of binding a book) limits our ability to cover the entire .NET Framework in the depth it deserves. As a result, we have focused the scope of this book on the most important, widely used types in the Framework. Luckily, such a subset was already created in the standardization process of the Common Language Runtime and the C# Programming Language. This book covers the first half of that subset (Volume 2 will pick up the second half). In the printed portion of this volume you will find all the type-level information for these types. Both the type-level information and member-level information are available in electronic form on the CD.

To make the standard more accessible, this book includes the following features:

- Annotations from key folks involved in the design of the .NET Framework
- Namespace overviews
- Type descriptions
- Sample code to illustrate type uses
- A fully searchable CD that includes all source code, descriptions, annotations, and examples
- A fold-out poster containing a detailed inheritance diagram for all types covered in this volume.

These features not only bring the standard to life, but more importantly, they serve as a convenient, informative reference to the most used types in the .NET Framework.

## The Standard

At the Professional Developer's Conference in October 2001, Microsoft, in partnership with HP and Intel, began the ECMA standardization process of three core parts of its new developer platform: the Common Language Infrastructure (CLI), the C# programming language, and a subset of the .NET Framework that is included in the CLI and referenced in the C# specification.

The CLI and the C# programming language are covered in other books in this series. Jim Miller's *The Common Language Infrastructure Annotated Standard* covers the CLI, which includes the metadata file format, IL Instruction set, and the type system. *The C# Programming Language* by Anders Hejlsberg, Scott Wiltamuth, and Peter Golde covers the C# programming language specification.

This book covers the first half of the .NET Framework as standardized in ECMA 335 and ISO 23271. The standards break the .NET Framework into seven different libraries to allow conformant implementations in resource-constrained environments. Those libraries are as follows:

**Base Class Library**—A simple runtime library for modern programming languages. It serves as the standard for the runtime library for the language C#, as well as one of the CLI standard libraries. It provides types to represent the built-in data types of the CLI, simple file access, custom attributes, security attributes, string manipulation, formatting, streams, collections, and so forth.

**Extended Numerics Library**—Provides the support for floating-point (`System.Single`, `System.Double`) and extended-precision (`System.Decimal`) data types. Like the Base Class Library, this library is directly referenced by the C# standard.

**Network Library**—Provides simple networking services, including direct access to network ports and HTTP support.

**Reflection Library**—Provides the ability to examine the structure of types, create instances of types, and invoke methods on types, all based on a description of the type.

**XML Library**—Provides a simple "pull-style" parser for XML. It is designed for resource-constrained devices, yet provides a simple user model.

**Runtime Infrastructure Library**—Provides the services needed by a compiler to target the CLI and the facilities needed to dynamically load types from a stream in the file format specified. For example, it provides `System.BadImageFormatException`, which is thrown when a stream that does not have the correct format is loaded.

**Extended Array Library**—Provides support for non-vector arrays, that is, arrays that have more than one dimension and arrays that have non-zero lower bounds.

This volume completely covers the Base Class Library and the Extended Numerics Library, as well as Microsoft-specific members on those types. It is our intention to cover the remaining libraries in future volumes.

## Namespace Overviews

To facilitate reader understanding, we provide an overview of each namespace we cover that describes the functionality and the inheritance hierarchy of types defined in that namespace. At the end of the namespace overview section we include a complete inheritance hierarchy for all the types covered in this volume. In the diagrams we differentiate the various kinds of types that make up the framework as follows:

- For classes, we use a rectangle:

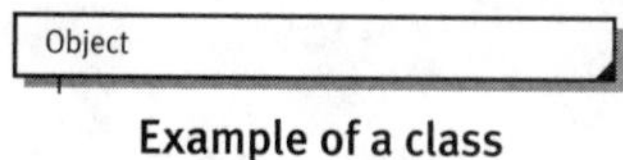


**Example of a class**

- For interfaces, we use a rounded rectangle:

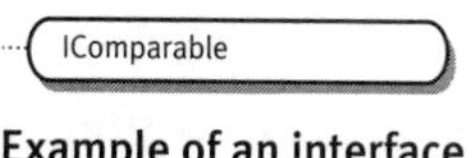


**Example of an interface**

- Abstract types are indicated with an "A":

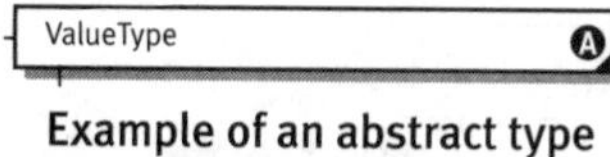


**Example of an abstract type**

- Enums are indicated with an "E":

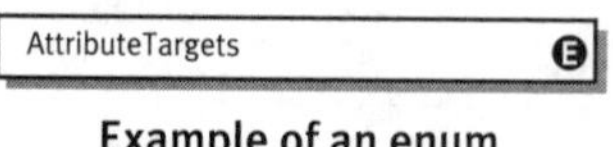


**Example of an enum**

- All other value types are indicated with a "V":

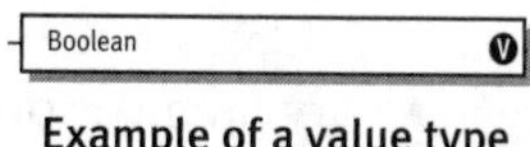


**Example of a value type**

- Types in the Extended Numerics Library and those that are not standardized are specifically called out. If not otherwise noted, a type belongs to the Base Class Library.

**Example of a type in the Extended Numerics Library**

## Type Chapters

Types are described in their own chapters, which are organized alphabetically by type name.

*Header*

The header contains the namespace name (1), the type name (2), and the library name from the ECMA\ISO Standard (3).

*Type Hierarchy*

Under the header we include a diagram representing the full inheritance hierarchy for this type (1), subclasses of this type found in this volume (2), and any interfaces they implement (3). The type being described is shown with a gray background (4).

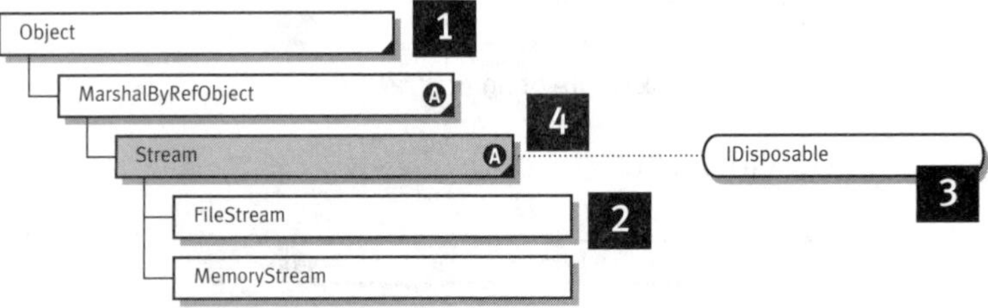


**Example of type hierarchy for the `Stream` class.**

*Type Summary*

This section contains the C# declaration syntax for all members defined on this type. It is meant to provide a quick reference in a very familiar format to what is in the type. In this summary we highlight certain attributes of these members.

- ~~**CF**~~ Indicates the member is not available in the .NET Compact Framework. If not included the member is available.
- ***MS*** Indicates that the member is not included in the ECMA\ISO standard.
- *1.1* Indicates that the member is new in V1.1 of the .NET Framework.

Most of these attributes are shown below.

```
  public sealed class Environment
  {
    // Properties
    CF public static string CommandLine { get; }
 MS CF public static string CurrentDirectory { set; get; }
    CF public static int ExitCode { set; get; }
CF 1.1 public static bool HasShutdownStarted { get; }
 MS CF public static string MachineName { get; }
    CF public static string NewLine { get; }
    MS public static OperatingSystem OSVersion { get; }
    CF public static string StackTrace { get; }
 MS CF public static string SystemDirectory { get; }
       public static int TickCount { get; }
 MS CF public static string UserDomainName { get; }
 MS CF public static bool UserInteractive { get; }
 MS CF public static string UserName { get; }
       public static Version Version { get; }
 MS CF public static long WorkingSet { get; }

    // Methods
    CF public static void Exit (int exitCode);
 MS CF public static string ExpandEnvironmentVariables (string name);
    CF public static string[] GetCommandLineArgs ();
    CF public static string GetEnvironmentVariable (string variable);
    CF public static IDictionary GetEnvironmentVariables ();
 MS CF public static string GetFolderPath (SpecialFolder folder);
 MS CF public static string[] GetLogicalDrives ();
  }
```

### *Type Description*

This section contains a detailed description of how this type is to be used. For the most part this text is taken directly from the standard.

### *Annotations*

Throughout this section we provide annotations from key members of the design team at Microsoft and members of the ECMA standardization committee. The comments in this section vary widely, and include notes on everything from common issues to the history of the class design or standardization process to areas where, in retrospect, the designers feel they could have done better.

Here's an example of an annotation from Anders Hejlsberg on the `String` class:

> **AH** While it may seem obvious, one of the big advantages of .NET is that it defines a single representation for strings. During its evolution, the Windows platform has accrued quite a collection of string representations: ANSI strings, Unicode strings, `null` terminated strings, length prefixed strings, etc. Unifying all of those has made .NET a much simpler and safer place to program.

Each annotation is attributed to individuals by their initials. In this volume you will find annotations from:

**BA—Brad Abrams** is a Lead Program Manager on the .NET Framework team at Microsoft, where he has been designing the Framework Class Libraries since 1997. Brad graduated with a B.A. in computer science from North Carolina State University. He is the primary author of the .NET Framework Design Guidelines, the Common Language Specification, and the class libraries for the ECMA\ISO CLI standard and C# language standard.

**KC—Krzysztof Cwalina** is a program manager on the .NET Framework team at Microsoft. He graduated in 1999 with an M.A. in computer science from the University of Iowa, specializing in software engineering. He has participated in the design and implementation of the first release of the .NET Framework. He is also a member of a working group developing the .NET Framework Design Guidelines.

**KG—Kit George** is a program manager on the Common Language Runtime team at Microsoft. He graduated in 1995 with a B.A. in psychology, philosophy, and mathematics from Victoria University of Wellington (New Zealand). Prior to joining Microsoft, he worked as a technical trainer, primarily in Visual Basic. He participated in the design and implementation of the first two releases of the framework for the last two years.

**BG—Brian Grunkemeyer** has been a software design engineer on the .NET Framework team at Microsoft for more than five years. He graduated in 1998 with a B.S. in computer science (and a double major in cognitive science) from Carnegie Mellon University. He has implemented a large portion of the Framework Class Libraries and contributed to the details of many classes in the ECMA\ISO CLI standard. He is currently working on future versions of the .NET Framework, including areas such as generic collections and managed code reliability.

**AH—Anders Hejlsberg** is a Distinguished Engineer in the Developer Division for Microsoft. He is the chief designer of the C# programming language and a key participant in the development of the Microsoft .NET Framework. Hejlsberg has also represented Microsoft in ECMA, where C# and the .NET Framework have been submitted by Microsoft for standardization. Before his work on C# and the .NET Framework, Hejlsberg was an architect for the Visual J++ development system and the Windows Foundation Classes. Before joining Microsoft, Hejlsberg was one of the first employees of Borland International Inc. As principal engineer, he was the original author of Turbo Pascal and later worked as the chief architect of the Delphi product line. Anders studied engineering at the Technical University of Denmark.

**YL—Yung-Shin Lin** is a development lead on the Windows Globalization team at Microsoft. He participated in the design and implemented most of the functionality in the `System.Globalization` namespace.

**JM—Joel Marcey** is a senior software engineer at Intel Corporation in Folsom, California. He has been with Intel for six years. He graduated in 1997 with a B.S. in computer engineering from North Carolina State University. He is currently doing research and development in the area of managed runtime execution environments. He is also a key member and technical contributor to the CLI standardization process within ECMA. He is the elected chair of ECMA TC39 and the elected convener of the TC39 TG3 for the 2003 calendar year.

**JR—Jeffrey Richter** is a co-founder of Wintellect (www.Wintellect.com), a training, debugging, and consulting firm dedicated to helping companies build better software, faster. He is the author of *Applied Microsoft .NET Framework Programming* (Microsoft Press) and several Windows programming books. Jeffrey is also a contributing editor to *MSDN Magazine*, where he writes the .NET column. Jeff has been consulting with Microsoft's .NET Framework team since October 1999 and has been involved in the standardization process of the CLI.

### *Type Examples*

In this section we provide sample code illustrating use of the type. Some samples are from the standard, but we added many more to facilitate a deeper and quicker understanding of the use of the type. All the samples we provide are fully compilable programs (1) and include selected output (2).

Example using `System;`

```
namespace Samples
{
  public class ObjectSample
  {
   public static void Main()
   {
     Object o = new Object();
     Console.WriteLine("Are they equal: {0}",
     o.Equals(new Object()));
     Console.WriteLine("Are they equal: {0}",
              o.Equals(o));
     Console.WriteLine("GetHashcode yields {0}",
              o.GetHashCode());                       1
     Console.WriteLine("GetHashcode yields {0}",
              new Object().GetHashCode());
     Console.WriteLine("o.ToString(): {0}", o.ToString());
   }
  }
}
```

The output is

```
Are they equal: False
Are they equal: True          2
GetHashcode yields 3
GetHashcode yields 5
o.ToString(): System.Object
```

All of these samples have been tested with V1.0 and V1.1 of the .NET Framework and the appropriate ones have been tested on the .NET Compact Framework.

Complete source code for the samples is available at www.awprofessional.com/titles/0321154894 and on the CD that is included in the back of the book.

### *Type Members*

The detailed descriptions of the members are included in the electronic version of the book on the CD. To facilitate easy look-ups, the member descriptions appear in the same order as the type summary sections. Each member contains some or all of the following fields:

**Syntax**—C# declaration syntax is provided for familiar reference. ILASM syntax is provided for completeness.

**Summary**—Short description of the member's purpose.

**Parameters**—Table of parameters accepted by this member and their meaning.

**Description**—A complete description of this member.

**Return Value**—The value and range returned by this method.

**Property Value**—The value of this property.

**Exceptions**—Table of the common exceptions thrown by this member.

**Permissions**—Table of the code access permissions demanded by this method.

**Example**—An example using this member following the same pattern as the type samples.

## Conventions Used in This Book

`Courier` is used for all source code blocks, including syntax declarations, class names, and member names.

## Additional Features

In addition to including the content from the ISO CLI standard, this book includes a number of other features:

- For every type covered in the book we include all the members as defined in V1.1 of the .NET Framework. Many members were left out of the ECMA standard to streamline platform work because types in the signature were not in the standard or because of scheduling reasons. As this book is primarily targeted at developers using the .NET Framework, we elected to include all the members of the types we cover, not just those that are standardized.
- Nearly every type contains annotations from key members of the design team at Microsoft and members of the ECMA standards group. These annotations bring rationale, history, and other interesting notes about the types covered.
- We added more than 1,000 samples to the book. Nearly every member has a working sample with output included. All of the samples can be found on the CD.

## Acknowledgments

Many people contributed to making this book possible. We would like to thank:

Martin Heller, editor, for his technical guidance as well has coordinating a myriad of details involved in creating the book.

Stephane Thomas from Addison-Wesley for her constant support and for keeping us on schedule.

David Platt for producing the excellent namespace overviews provided here.

Damien Watkins for writing (and re-writing) hundreds of samples.

Tamara Abrams for her painstaking review and copy edit of the entire work.

Joel Marcey for providing technical support in working with the Xml doc format used in the ECMA standard and for providing thoughtful and lighthearted annotations.

Jeffrey Richter for advisory services and for providing insightful annotations.

Yung-Shin Lin, Anders Hejlsberg, Brian Grunkemeyer, Kit George, and Krzysztof Cwalina for providing additional annotations.

The contributing members of ECMA TC-39 TG1 and TG2 for formalizing the CLI and C# Standards on which this book is based.

Susan Radke-Sproull, my manager here at Microsoft, for allowing me the time to contribute this work.

Tyrrell Albaugh and Reuben Kantor, the real unsung heroes of this project, who put up with countless changes through the project. Their efforts resulted in a much better book.

Brad Abrams
Lead Program Manager, .NET Framework Team
Microsoft Corporation
February 2004

# PART I
## Namespace Overviews

# System



The `System` namespace is the root of all namespaces in the .NET Framework, containing all other namespaces as subordinates. It also contains the types that we felt to be the most fundamental and frequently used.

## Basic Variable Types

The class `Object` is the root of the inheritance hierarchy in the .NET Framework. Every class in the .NET Framework ultimately derives from this class. If you define a class without specifying any other inheritance, `Object` is the implied base class. It provides the most basic methods and properties that all objects need to support, such as returning an identifying string, returning a `Type` object (think of it as a class descriptor) to use for runtime discovery of the object's contents, and providing a location for a garbage collection finalizer.

The .NET Framework provides two kinds of types, value types and reference types. Instances of value types are allocated on the stack or inline inside an object, which incurs a lower overhead than using the managed heap. Value types are most often used for small, lightweight variables accessed primarily for a single data value, while still allowing them to be treated as objects in the inheritance hierarchy (for example, having methods). All value types must derive from the abstract base class `ValueType`. Table 1 lists the value types in the System namespace.

**TABLE 1**

| Name | Represents |
|---|---|
| `Boolean` | Boolean value (true or false). |
| `Byte` | 8-bit unsigned integer. |
| `Char` | UTF-16 code point. |
| `DateTime` | An instant in time, typically expressed as a date and time of day. |
| `Decimal` | Decimal number. |
| `Double` | Double-precision floating-point number. |
| `Enum` | Base class for enumerations. |
| `Int16` | 16-bit signed integer. |
| `Int32` | 32-bit signed integer. |

TABLE 1 *(continued)*

| Name | Represents |
|---|---|
| `Int64` | 64-bit signed integer. |
| `SByte` | 8-bit signed integer. |
| `Single` | Single-precision floating-point number. |
| `TimeSpan` | Time interval. |
| `UInt16` | 16-bit unsigned integer. |
| `UInt32` | 32-bit unsigned integer. |
| `UInt64` | 64-bit unsigned integer. |

All objects that are not value types are by definition reference types. Creating an instance of a reference type allocates the new object from the managed heap and returns a reference to it, hence the name. Most objects are reference types. The class `String` is a reference type that represents an immutable series of characters. The class `CharEnumerator` supports iterating over a `String` and reading its individual characters.

The `System` namespace also contains the abstract base class `Array`, which represents a fixed-size, ordered series of objects accessed by index. It contains methods for creating, manipulating, and searching for elements within the array. Programmers will generally not use this class directly. Instead, their programming language will provide an abstraction of it.

## Attributes

The .NET Framework makes extensive use of attributes, descriptive pieces of read-only information that a programmer can place in an object's metadata. Attributes can be read by any interested piece of code that has the required level of permission. Many attributes are provided and used by the system. Others are defined by programmers and used for their own purposes. All attributes derive from the abstract base class `System.Attribute`. The attributes in Table 2 were felt to be common enough to occupy the `System` namespace. Many other subordinate namespaces also define more specialized attributes.

TABLE 2

| Attributes | Meaning |
|---|---|
| `AttributeUsageAttribute` | Used in the definition of other attribute classes, specifying the target types to which the other attribute class can be applied (assembly, class, method, some combination, etc.). Uses `AttributeTargets` enumeration. |
| `CLSCompliantAttribute` | Indicates whether a program element is compliant with the Common Language Specification (CLS). |
| `FlagsAttribute` | Indicates that an enumeration can be treated as a bit field; that is, a set of flags. |
| `ObsoleteAttribute` | Marks the program elements that are no longer in use. |



## Utility Objects

The class `Console` provides functions for performing input and output to a console window. It's useful for debugging and development, and any functionality for which a full Windows interface is overkill.

The class `Convert` provides static methods for converting a variable of one base type into another base type, such as `Int32` to `Double`.

The class `GC` provides a connection to the garbage collector in the automatic memory management system. It contains methods such as `Collect`, which forces an immediate garbage collection.

The utility class `Environment` provides access to environment variables, and other environment properties such as machine name.

The class `MarshalByRefObject` is the abstract base class for objects that communicate across application domain boundaries by exchanging messages using a proxy. Classes must inherit from `MarshalByRefObject` when the type is used across application domain boundaries, and the state of the object must not be copied because the members of the object are not usable outside the application domain where they were created.

The class `Math` provides access to mathematical operations such as trigonometric and logarithmic functions.

The class `Random` provides methods that generate a sequence of random numbers, starting from a specified seed. You should use specialized cryptographic functionality (in the `System.Security.Cryptography` namespace) for random number generation for cryptographic purposes.

The class `Type` is the basis for all reflection operations. Think of it as a class descriptor.

The class `Version` represents a dotted quad version number (major, minor, build, revision). It is used in the utility functions that specify versioning behavior of assemblies.

## Interfaces

The System namespace defines a number of interfaces. An interface is a set of pure virtual function definitions, which a class can choose to implement. You define an interface to enforce a common design pattern among classes that are not hierarchically related. For example, the IDisposable interface contains the method Dispose, used for deterministic finalization. This provides a way to force an object to perform its cleanup code immediately instead of when the garbage collector feels like getting around to it. Any class anywhere in any inheritance hierarchy might reasonably need this behavior. However, most classes won't need this behavior, so it wouldn't make sense to put it in the System.Object base class and force all objects to implement it whether they needed it or not. Instead, a class that needs this behavior implements the interface, ensuring that it follows the same syntactic rules as all other objects that do so, without disturbing its inheritance relationships with its base classes. The interfaces in Table 3 were felt to be common enough to occupy the System namespace. Many other subordinate namespaces also define more specialized interfaces.

TABLE 3

| Interface | Meaning |
|---|---|
| IAsyncResult | Represents the status of an asynchronous operation. |
| ICloneable | Supports cloning, which creates a new instance of a class with the same value as an existing instance. |
| IComparable | Defines a generalized comparison method that a value type or class implements to create a type-specific comparison method. |
| IDisposable | Defines a method to release allocated unmanaged resources. |
| IFormatProvider | Provides a mechanism for retrieving an object to control formatting. |
| IFormattable | Provides functionality to format the value of an object into a string representation. |

## Delegates

The .NET Framework supports callbacks from one object to another by means of the class Delegate. A Delegate represents a pointer to an individual object method or to a static class method. You generally will not use the Delegate class directly, but instead will use the wrapper provided by your programming language. The .NET Framework event system uses delegates. The object wanting to receive the event provides the sender with a delegate, and the sender calls the function on the delegate to signal the event.

The .NET Framework supports asynchronous method invocation for any method on any object. The caller can either poll for completion, or pass a delegate of the AsyncCallback class to be notified of completion by an asynchronous callback.

## Exceptions

In order to provide a common, rich, easily programmed and difficult to ignore way of signaling and handling errors, the .NET Framework supports structured exception handling. A caller places an exception handler on the stack at the point at which he wants to catch the error, using the try–catch syntax of his programming language. A called function wanting to signal an error creates an object of class `System.Exception` (or one derived from it) containing information about the error and throws it. The CLR searches up the call stack until it finds a handler for the type of exception that was thrown, at which time the stack is unwound and control transferred to the catch block, which contains the error-handling code.

The class `System.Exception` is the base class from which all exception objects derive. It contains such basic information as a message provided by the thrower and the stack trace at which the exception took place. The class `System.SystemException` derives from it, and all system-provided exceptions derive from that. This allows a programmer to differentiate between system-provided and programmer-built exceptions. The system-provided exceptions in Table 4 were felt to be common enough to occupy the base `System` namespace. Many more specialized exception classes live in subordinate namespaces.

TABLE 4

| Exception | Meaning |
|---|---|
| `ApplicationException` | A non-fatal application error occurred. |
| `ArgumentException` | One of the arguments provided to a method is not valid. |
| `ArgumentNullException` | A `null` reference is passed to a member that does not accept it as a valid argument. |
| `ArgumentOutOfRange-Exception` | The value of an argument is outside the allowable range of values as defined by the invoked member. |
| `ArithmeticException` | Error in an arithmetic, casting, or conversion operation. |
| `ArrayTypeMismatch-Exception` | An attempt is made to store an element of the wrong type within an array. |
| `DivideByZeroException` | An attempt was made to divide an integral or decimal value by zero. |
| `DuplicateWaitObject-Exception` | An object appears more than once in an array of synchronization objects. |
| `ExecutionEngineException` | An internal error occurred in the execution engine of the common language runtime. |

TABLE 4 *(continued)*

| Exception | Meaning |
| --- | --- |
| `FormatException` | The format of an argument does not meet the parameter specifications of the invoked method. |
| `IndexOutOfRangeException` | An attempt is made to access an element of an array with an index that is outside the bounds of the array. |
| `InvalidCastException` | Invalid casting or explicit conversion. |
| `InvalidOperationException` | A method call is invalid for the object's current state. |
| `InvalidProgramException` | A program contains invalid Microsoft intermediate language (MSIL) or metadata. Generally this indicates a bug in a compiler. |
| `NotFiniteNumberException` | A floating-point value is positive infinity, negative infinity, or Not-a-Number (NaN). |
| `NotSupportedException` | An invoked method is not supported or not supported in the current mode of operation. |
| `NullReferenceException` | An attempt to dereference a `null` object reference. |
| `ObjectDisposedException` | An operation is performed on a disposed object. |
| `OutOfMemoryException` | There is not enough memory to continue the execution of a program. |
| `OverflowException` | An arithmetic, casting, or conversion operation in a checked context results in an overflow. |
| `RankException` | An array with the wrong number of dimensions is passed to a method. |
| `StackOverflowException` | The execution stack overflows by having too many pending method calls. |
| `TypeInitialization-Exception` | A wrapper around the exception thrown by the type initializer. |
| `UnauthorizedAccess-Exception` | The operating system denies access because of an I/O error or a specific type of security error. |

## Diagram

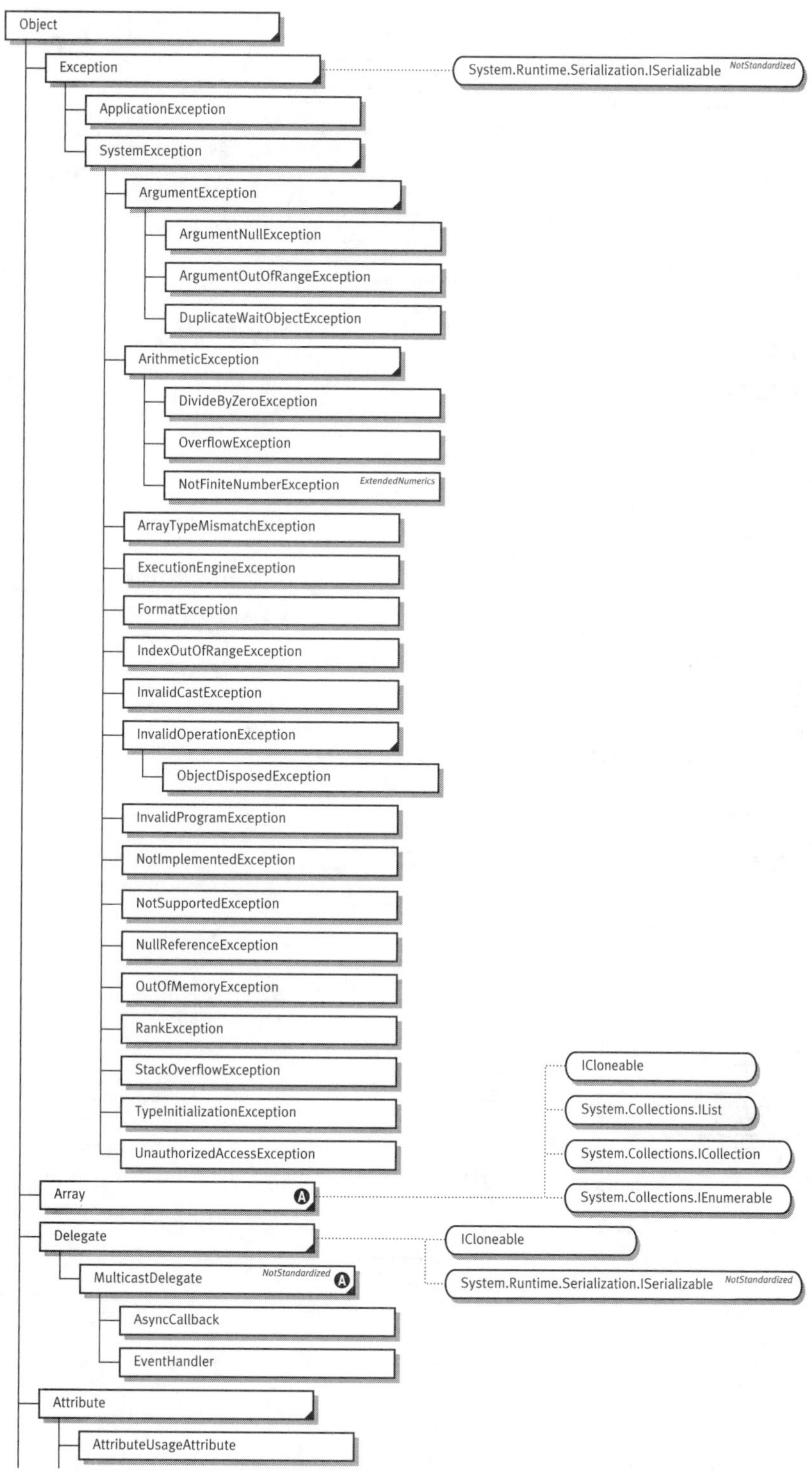
Object
Exception
System.Runtime.Serialization.ISerializable NotStandardized
ApplicationException
SystemException
ArgumentException
ArgumentNullException
ArgumentOutOfRangeException
DuplicateWaitObjectException
ArithmeticException
DivideByZeroException
OverflowException
NotFiniteNumberException ExtendedNumerics
ArrayTypeMismatchException
ExecutionEngineException
FormatException
IndexOutOfRangeException
InvalidCastException
InvalidOperationException
ObjectDisposedException
InvalidProgramException
NotImplementedException
NotSupportedException
NullReferenceException
OutOfMemoryException
RankException
StackOverflowException
TypeInitializationException
UnauthorizedAccessException
Array
ICloneable
System.Collections.IList
System.Collections.ICollection
System.Collections.IEnumerable
Delegate
ICloneable
System.Runtime.Serialization.ISerializable NotStandardized
MulticastDelegate NotStandardized
AsyncCallback
EventHandler
Attribute
AttributeUsageAttribute

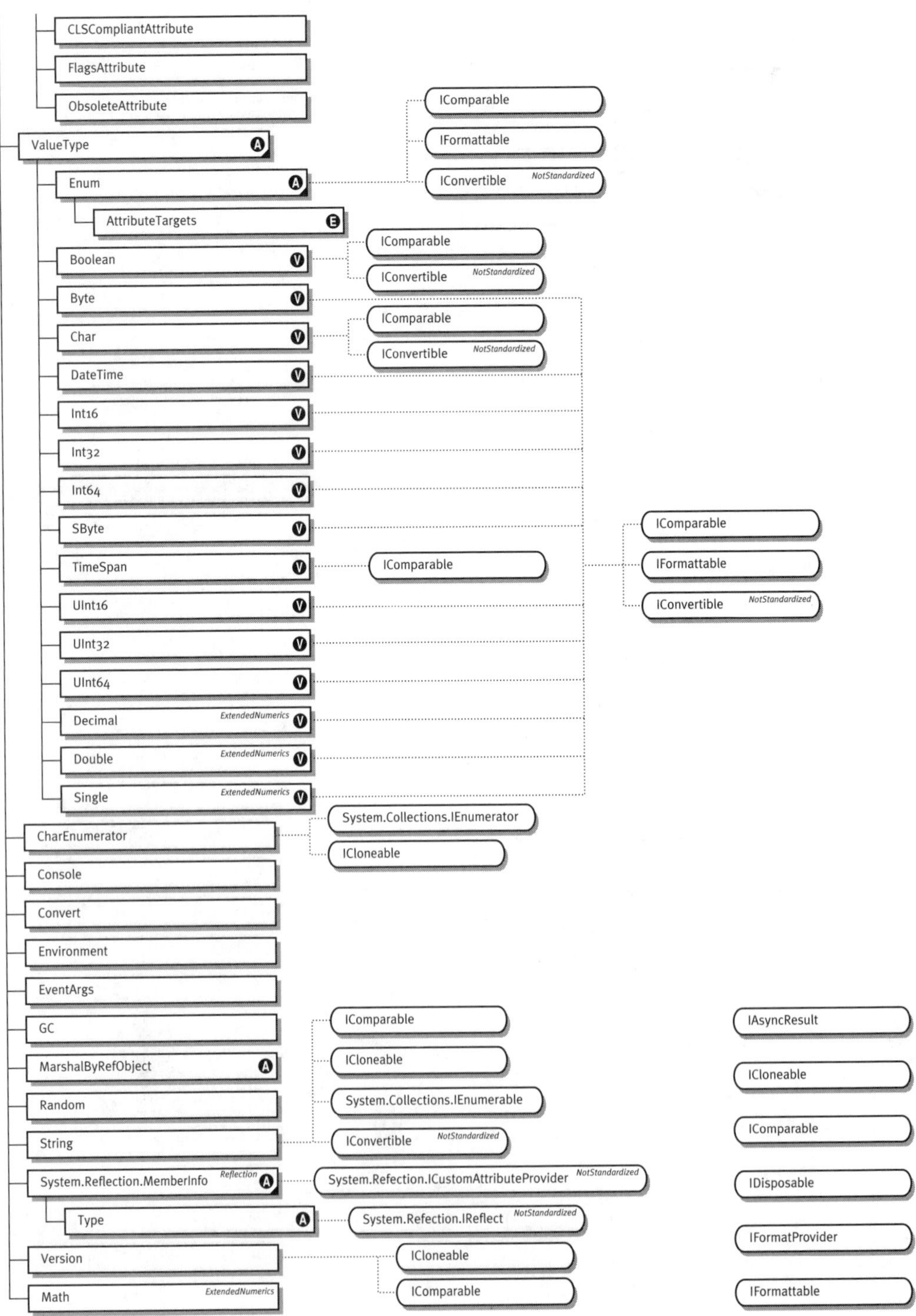
CLSCompliantAttribute
FlagsAttribute
ObsoleteAttribute
ValueType
Enum
AttributeTargets
Boolean
Byte
Char
DateTime
Int16
Int32
Int64
SByte
TimeSpan
UInt16
UInt32
UInt64
Decimal ExtendedNumerics
Double ExtendedNumerics
Single ExtendedNumerics
CharEnumerator
Console
Convert
Environment
EventArgs
GC
MarshalByRefObject
Random
String
System.Reflection.MemberInfo Reflection
Type
Version
Math ExtendedNumerics
IComparable
IFormattable
IConvertible NotStandardized
System.Collections.IEnumerator
ICloneable
System.Collections.IEnumerable
System.Refection.ICustomAttributeProvider NotStandardized
System.Refection.IReflect NotStandardized
IAsyncResult
IDisposable
IFormatProvider

# System.Collections



Organizing collections of objects is a vital but boring task that operating system designers have historically left to language implementers. Naturally, every language's and every vendor's implementation of collections varied drastically, making it essentially impossible for different applications to exchange, say, an array of objects without having intimate knowledge of each other's internal workings.

With the `System.Collections` namespace, Microsoft has brought the common implementation philosophy to the mundane task of organizing collections of objects. Rather than depend on individual languages to implement such common concepts as arrays and hash tables, Microsoft decided to bring them into the .NET Framework, thereby standardizing them for all applications. This namespace contains classes that are used to organize collections of objects, and also the interfaces that you can use to write your own collection classes while still retaining a common interface to callers.

The two main classes of collection are `ArrayList` and `Hashtable`. Each is dynamically sizable and can hold any type of object, even mixing contained object types within the same collection object. They differ in their organization strategies. The `ArrayList` is an ordered, numerically indexed collection of objects. When you place an object into an `ArrayList` or fetch an object from it, you specify which element location to put it in or fetch it from ("Put this object in slot 2," "Get the object from slot 5"). Think of it as a set of pigeonholes. It differs from the basic array class `System.Array` by being dynamically sizable. The architects felt that the basic fixed-size array was fundamental enough to join the most basic types in the `System` namespace.

A `Hashtable` is an unordered collection in which objects are identified by keys. When you place an object in a `Hashtable`, you specify the key that you want used to identify it. When you fetch an object from a `Hashtable`, you provide the key and the `Hashtable` returns the object that the key identifies. The key is most often a string, but it can be any type of object.

As you examine the individual member functions, you will notice that the collection classes share many common methods. For example, the `ArrayList` and `Hashtable` classes each contain the method `GetEnumerator`. These common behaviors ease the tasks of implementers and consumers alike. The collection classes obtain this commonality of behavior by implementing standardized interfaces. You probably want to do the same with your derived classes. The standardized interfaces, and their usages in the collection classes, are shown in Table 5.

Note that a number of the interfaces are not implemented directly on the collection classes that I've listed. For example, the `IEnumerator` interface is not implemented directly on `ArrayList` or `Hashtable` object, but instead is returned by the `IEnumerable` interface, which is. Also note that the collection classes listed implement interfaces from other namespaces, such as `System.ICloneable`.

TABLE 5

| Interface | Description | ArrayList | HashTable |
|---|---|---|---|
| `ICollection` | Defines size, enumerators and synchronization methods for all collections. | Y | Y |
| `IComparer` | Exposes a method that compares two objects. | | |
| `IDictionary` | Represents a collection of key-and-value pairs. | | Y |
| `IDictionaryEnumerator` | Enumerates the elements of a dictionary. | | |
| `IEnumerable` | Exposes the enumerator, which supports a simple iteration over a collection. | Y | Y |
| `IEnumerator` | Supports a simple iteration over a collection. | | |
| `IHashCodeProvider` | Supplies a hash code for an object, using a custom hash function. | | |
| `IList` | Represents a collection of objects that can be individually accessed by index. | Y | |

## Diagram

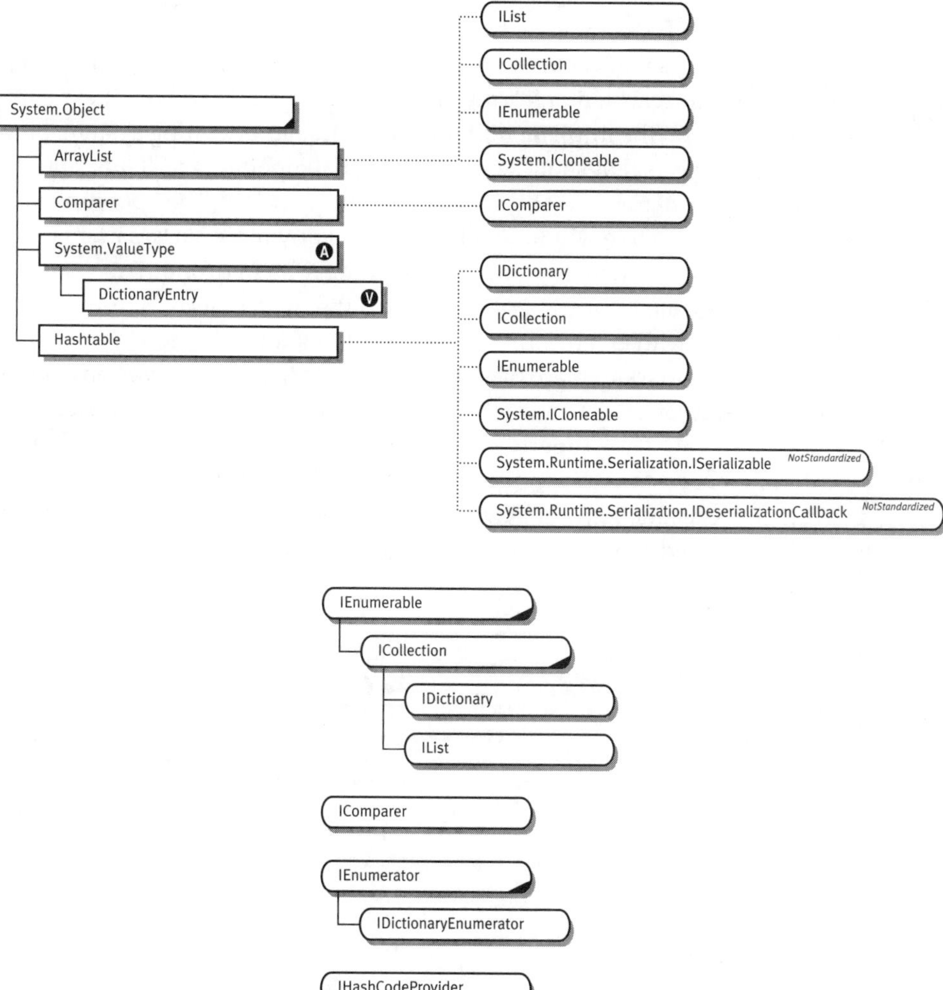
System.Object
ArrayList
Comparer
System.ValueType
DictionaryEntry
Hashtable
IList
ICollection
IEnumerable
System.ICloneable
IComparer
IDictionary
ICollection
IEnumerable
System.ICloneable
System.Runtime.Serialization.ISerializable NotStandardized
System.Runtime.Serialization.IDeserializationCallback NotStandardized
IEnumerable
ICollection
IDictionary
IList
IComparer
IEnumerator
IDictionaryEnumerator
IHashCodeProvider

# System.Diagnostics

The System.Diagnostics namespace was designed to contain classes that allow a program to do profiling, performance monitoring, and error logging. However, these sorts of features depend critically on the implementation of a particular operating system. Since the Standard describes objects that should be common to all operating systems, and diagnostic objects by their very nature can't be, it contains only one class. The operating system for which you actually write code will probably provide many more classes in this namespace, but these will vary widely from one operating system to another.

The common class is called ConditionalAttribute, which derives from System.Attribute. As with all attributes, it represents a read-only piece of metadata with which a programmer marks a piece of code. When this attribute appears on a method, it tells the compiler that it can omit calls to the method unless a compilation variable is defined at the site of the call. The property ConditionString specifies the name of the variable and the value that it must have. It's an easy way to implement features such as tracing in a debugging executable while having them automatically disappear from the release executable generated from the same code base.

## Diagram

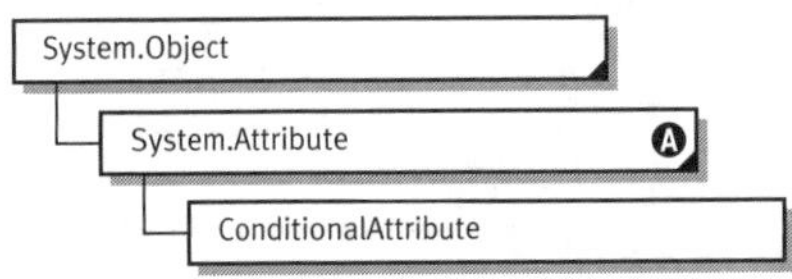

# System.Globalization



The global reach of the Internet, which essentially connects every intelligent box in the universe to every other intelligent box in the universe, means that essentially any application can be used by a native speaker of essentially any human language. Presenting numbers and dates in the manner that each user expects and immediately understands is not a matter of cultural sensitivity. It is a critical piece of communication necessary to avoid expensive errors. When you buy your non-refundable airline ticket online, does the departure date of 6-5-02 represent May 6 or June 5? The `System.Globalization` namespace in the .NET Framework contains classes that provide prefabricated functionality allowing a programmer to write programs that adjust to the language of its user, particularly in the area of formatting dates and numbers.

The class `DateTimeFormatInfo` provides methods and properties that assist with the formatting of DateTime objects in accordance with a particular culture (a language and optionally a country, such as English and optionally US or Canada). For example, the methods `Parse` and `ParseExact` convert input strings into `DateTime` objects. You fetch the `DateTimeFormatInfo` for the calling thread's current culture via the static property `CurrentInfo`, or you can create them directly via the constructor. The `DateTimeFormatInfo` class implements the interface `System.IFormatProvider`, which returns the proper date format pattern according to the culture for use in string formatting. You pass the `DateTimeFormatInfo` to the method `DateTime.ToString` when you want to format a date. The enumeration `DateTimeStyles` customizes how the `DateTime.Parse` and `DateTime.ParseExact` methods parse a string, for example, specifying whether whitespace is or isn't allowed in the input string.

The class `NumberFormatInfo` provides methods and properties that assist with the formatting of numeric values according to culture. For example, the property `CurrencySymbol` returns the currency symbol in the culture associated with a particular `NumberFormatInfo` object instance. You fetch the `NumberFormatInfo` for the calling thread's current culture via the static property `CurrentInfo`, or you can create them directly via the class constructor. The `NumberFormatInfo` class implements the interface `System.IFormatProvider`, which returns the proper number format pattern according to the culture for use in string formatting. You pass the `NumberFormatInfo` to the method `ToString` when you want to format a number. The enumeration `NumberStyles` customizes how the `Parse` methods of individual numeric types (for example, `Int32.Parse`) parse a string, for example, whether or not to allow an exponent.

The enumeration `UnicodeCategory` contains values that denote the various categories of Unicode characters that exist, for example, uppercase letter or lowercase letter. It is the return type of the method `System.Char.GetUnicodeCategory`.

## Diagram

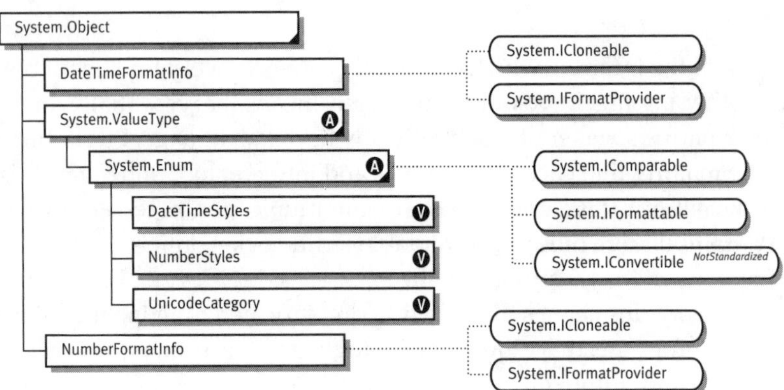
System.Object
DateTimeFormatInfo
System.ValueType
System.Enum
DateTimeStyles
NumberStyles
UnicodeCategory
NumberFormatInfo
System.ICloneable
System.IFormatProvider
System.IComparable
System.IFormattable
System.IConvertible
NotStandardized
System.ICloneable
System.IFormatProvider

# System.IO



The modern operating system as we know it was first developed to provide applications with prefabricated I/O operations on the (at the time) newfangled things called disks. Providing programmers with a logically contiguous stream of bytes called a "file", regardless of the underlying hardware, was an enormous advance and saved programmers a great deal of time. The extra system overhead was a small price to pay. The `System.IO` namespace contains classes that provide low-level file system I/O operations.

The cornerstone of the I/O system is the abstract base class `Stream`, which represents a logically contiguous sequence of bytes. All actual I/O operations use classes that derive from `Stream`. This base class defines abstract methods for common stream operations, such as `Read`, `Write`, and `Seek`, which an implementer overrides to provide functionality in the derived class. All `Stream`-derived classes will thus contain the same access methods and parameters regardless of the storage medium to which the `Stream` mediates access.

The base class itself does not provide or specify any particular storage medium backing to the stream. It is up to the implementer of the derived class to marry the `Stream`-based functions to a particular storage medium. Table 6 lists the classes in this namespace derived from `Stream`.

TABLE 6

| Class | Meaning |
|---|---|
| `FileStream` | `Stream` whose backing is a file. |
| `MemoryStream` | `Stream` whose backing store is memory. |

You usually create a `Stream`-based object directly from its own constructor. Alternatively, the `File` class allows you to create a `FileStream` from a `File`.

Once you have a stream, you generally want to read from it or write to it. If the stream contains binary data, you can do this directly from the `Stream` object's methods. However, if the stream contains text, reading directly from the `Stream` object would force you to deal manually with the various character encodings that the stream's contents might use, a waste of valuable developer time. To make this task easier, the .NET Framework provides the abstract base classes `TextReader` and `TextWriter`. These classes enforce a common programmatic interface for reading and writing text on their descendants, taking into account character encodings and other features of textual data such as newline characters. The `TextReader` and `TextWriter` classes do not provide or specify a backing medium, in the same manner as `StreamReader` and `StreamWriter`.

The classes StreamReader and StreamWriter provide an implementation of the TextReader and TextWriter that works with any class derived from Stream. You associate a StreamReader or StreamWriter with a stream by passing the stream in the StreamReader or StreamWriter constructor. You can also directly instantiate a StreamReader or StreamWriter directly from a file's path name. The classes StringReader and StringWriter provide an implementation of the TextReader and TextWriter on variables of class System.String. Several other namespaces contain other classes that derive from TextReader and TextWriter, implementing their philosophy on other types of media.

Files live in directories, and directories are organized hierarchically. The class Directory contains static methods (those which do not require an individual directory instance) for creating, moving, and searching among file system directories. You identify the directory on which you want to operate by passing its path string. In the same manner, the class File provides static methods for creating, destroying, copying, and opening files. You identify the file on which you want to operate by passing its path string.

The utility class Path performs handy operations on path strings, such as extracting a file name or an extension. It's handy.

It is quite common for file system operations to fail, for example, when you try to open a file that doesn't exist. As with all parts of the .NET Framework, file system objects signal failed operations by throwing exceptions. The System.IO namespace contains a number of different exception classes that are listed in Table 7, which signal specific types of file system-related failure. Note that objects in the System.IO namespace are not limited to throwing the exceptions that live in this namespace.

TABLE 7

| Exception | Meaning |
|---|---|
| DirectoryNotFound-Exception | Exception thrown when part of a file or directory cannot be found. |
| EndOfStreamException | Exception thrown when reading is attempted past the end of a stream. |
| FileLoadException | Exception thrown when a file is found but cannot be loaded. |
| FileNotFoundException | Exception thrown when an attempt to access a file that does not exist on disk fails. |
| IOException | Exception thrown when an I/O error occurs. |
| PathTooLongException | Exception thrown when a pathname or filename is longer than the system-defined maximum length. |

This namespace also contains several enumerations that are used for making choices among discrete sets of properties used in various functions. Table 8 lists the enumerations.

TABLE 8

| Enumeration | Meaning |
|---|---|
| `FileAccess` | Constants signifying file access permission, such as read, write, or read/write. |
| `FileMode` | Constants signifying how the operating system should open a file, such as append, open, create, etc. |
| `SeekOrigin` | Constants signifying reference points in streams for seeking, such as begin, current, and end. |

## Diagram

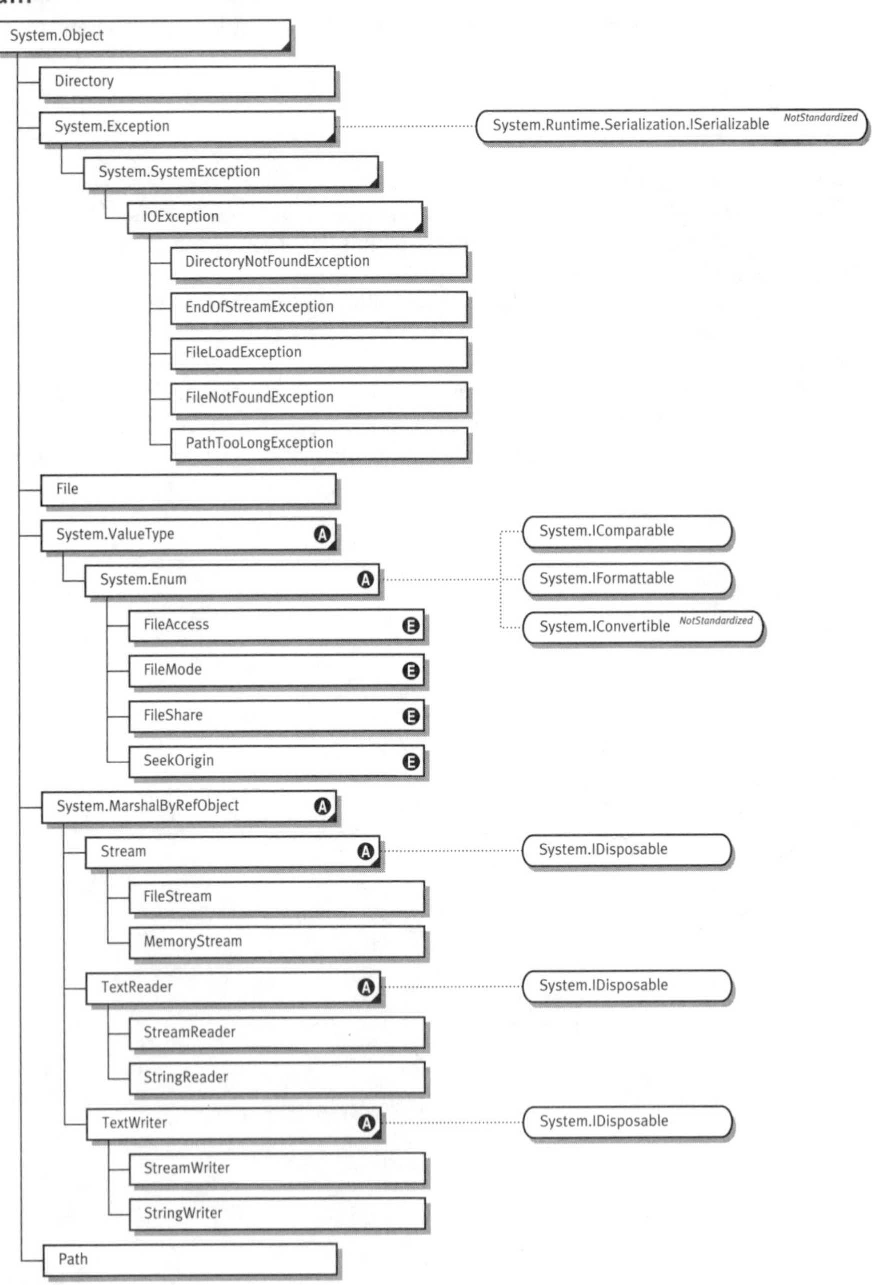
System.Object
Directory
System.Exception
System.Runtime.Serialization.ISerializable
NotStandardized
System.SystemException
IOException
DirectoryNotFoundException
EndOfStreamException
FileLoadException
FileNotFoundException
PathTooLongException
File
System.ValueType
System.Enum
System.IComparable
System.IFormattable
System.IConvertible
NotStandardized
FileAccess
FileMode
FileShare
SeekOrigin
System.MarshalByRefObject
Stream
System.IDisposable
FileStream
MemoryStream
TextReader
System.IDisposable
StreamReader
StringReader
TextWriter
System.IDisposable
StreamWriter
StringWriter
Path

# System.Security



Code that runs in modern operating systems comes from many different sources. Some assemblies might be installed from a shrink-wrapped CD-ROM, others downloaded from local intranets or the global Internet, still others may come in the form of e-mail documents. Many runtime systems prior to the .NET Framework ran all code on an all-or-nothing privilege level, allowing an administrator no choices except to let installed code do anything it wanted or not to install it at all. However, it is essentially impossible for a human user to correctly determine in every case which pieces of code are worthy of this high level of trust and which are not. The .NET Framework therefore provides the Code Access Security mechanism, which allows administrators to restrict the operations that individual assemblies may perform on protected resources. This allows an operating system to run assemblies with different levels of trust. For example, an administrator might configure the system so that Assembly A is allowed to read and write a certain file, but Assembly B is only allowed to read it and Assembly C can't interact with the file system in any manner. These privileges can be based on individual code modules, or on such properties as a code module's author or the location from which it came. The `System.Security` namespace contains classes that allow a programmer to interact with the code access security system.

Each secured operation that can be granted or denied to a program is represented by an object called a permission, many of which live in the `System.Security.Permissions` namespace. Because each type of protected resource requires its own type of description such as, for example, the location of a file or the name of an environment variable, each type of protected resource permission is represented by its own class of object. The abstract base class `CodeAccessPermission` is the base for all permissions and implements the `IPermission` interface. This interface contains such methods as Demand, which tells the CLR to walk the call stack and ensure that all callers of an object contain the specified permission, throwing an exception if any of them don't.

The `PermissionSet` class is a collection that can contain any number of permission objects (that is, objects derived from `CodeAccessPermission`). The `PermissionSet` contains methods that allow you to demand or deny permissions as a group instead of individually. It also contains methods to calculate its union and intersection with other `PermissionSet` objects.

Security descriptors often need to serialize themselves into and out of XML for storage in administrative files. This happens in the case of declarative security, as described in the `System.Security.Permissions` namespace. The class `SecurityElement` is a helper class developed to make this process easier. It's a lightweight XML element that contains a collection of attributes.

As with all .NET Framework methods, security operations throw exceptions when they fail. The class `SecurityException` signals a permission failure, such as trying to open a file for which your application does not have permission. It tells you which permission caused the exception, and the permission's state at the time the exception was thrown.

The CLR performs verification of code as part of its just-in-time compilation. The verification process ensures that objects are accessed in a type-safe manner, for example, accessing objects only at the specified offsets of public members, instead of any arbitrary numeric offset that could lead to a security violation. The CLR throws the `VerificationException` if the code fails the type safety check.



## Diagram

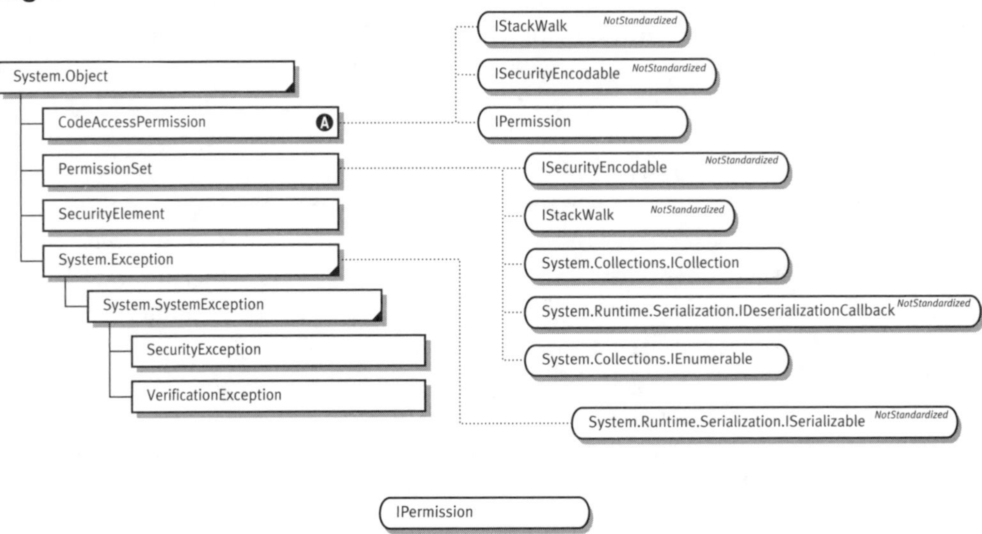


## System.Security.Permissions

A permission is an object that specifies security rules for access to a protected resource. Permissions come in two flavors, programmatic and declarative. In the former case, the permission class (e.g., `EnvironmentPermission`), derives from `CodeAccessPermission`. You write code that creates these objects, sets their properties, and calls their methods in the usual way. You will need this technique when your security operations can vary dynamically at runtime.

Alternatively, many programmers like to specify their permissions declaratively by marking their code with attributes. The attributes tell the CLR which security permissions the code needs to do its job, in the same way that calling methods on a permission object would do. When a caller attempts to access the marked code, the CLR checks if the caller has the permissions that the code requires and throws an exception if it doesn't. This allows security permission failures (say, your caller doesn't have permission to use the file system) to be detected when code is first loaded instead of later in the runtime session (say, after the user has done a lot of work and needs to save it in a file). Specifying security requirements declaratively also allows an administrator using a viewer program to see which permissions your code requires, so she can either (a) grant them ahead of time and avoid the fuss, or (b) refuse to grant them and understand why the code, or at least certain portions of it, won't work. Specifying permissions declaratively is usually easier than doing it programmatically provided that you know your permission needs at development time.

The class `SecurityAttribute` (deriving from `System.Attribute`) contains a member variable called `Action`, which contains a member of the `SecurityAction` enumeration. This specifies the type of action to be taken (demand a permission, deny a permission) that the attribute specifies. The attribute `CodeAccessSecurityAttribute` derives from `SecurityAttribute`, and is the abstract base class for all code access security attributes.

The permission classes, their corresponding attribute classes, and the protected resources to which they control access are listed in Table 9.

TABLE 9

| Permission | Attribute | Controls Access to |
|---|---|---|
| `EnvironmentPermission` | `EnvironmentPermissionAttribute` | System and user environment variables |
| `FileIOPermission` | `FileIOPermissionAttribute` | Files and folders |
| `SecurityPermission` | `SecurityPermissionAttribute` | Miscellaneous operations listed in `SecurityPermissionFlag` enumeration |

A permission object can contain its own fine-grained subdivisions of permissions. For example, a `FileIOPermission` object does not have to grant permission to do anything to any file anywhere in the system, and generally will not. Each permission class has its own enumeration specifying the sub-privileges that a piece of code may ask for, as listed in Table 10.

In addition to the fine-grained permission states listed above, the `PermissionState` enumeration contains the values "None" and "Unrestricted," which can be used in any of the permissions.

TABLE 10

| Enumeration | Meaning |
| --- | --- |
| `EnvironmentPermission-Access` | Type of access requested, such as `Read` or `Write`. |
| `FileIOPermissionAccess` | Type of file access requested, such as `Read` or `Write` or `Append`. |
| `SecurityPermissionFlag` | Miscellaneous security permissions, such as skipping type safety verification or accessing unmanaged code. Often powerful, use with caution. |

## Diagram

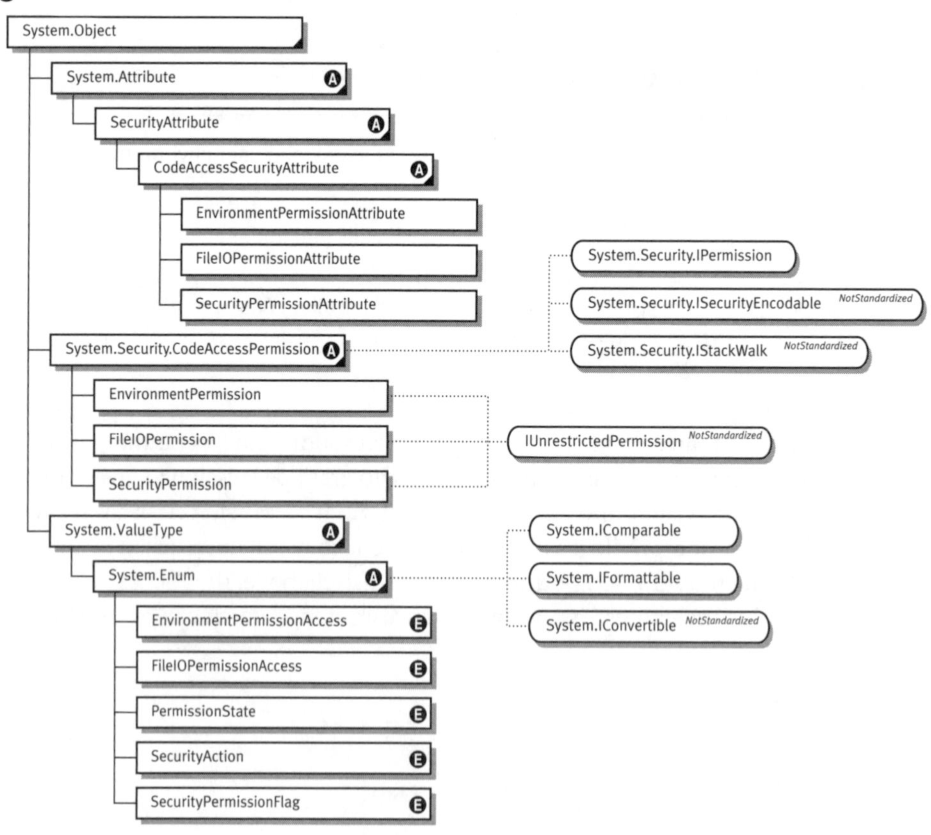

# System.Text



The character set used within a text string is an important design decision in any development project. Within the .NET Framework it's quite simple, as all text strings use the same Unicode character set. However, your programs will often need to use other character sets when you exchange strings or files with other non-.NET Framework systems and programs. The namespace `System.Text` contains classes that assist you in converting from one character set to another.

An encoding is an object that converts text to or from a particular character set. The abstract base class `Encoding` defines a common set of methods and properties that all classes deriving from it must implement, thereby providing a common programmatic interface for all character set conversions. For example, the method `GetBytes` converts characters from Unicode into the character set of the derived class. The classes `ASCIIEncoding`, `UnicodeEncoding`, and `UTF8Encoding` derive from Encoding, converting characters to and from the character sets as listed in Table 11.

TABLE 11

| Class | Character Set |
|---|---|
| `ASCIIEncoding` | 7-bit ASCII characters. |
| `UnicodeEncoding` | Unicode character set, 16 bits per character. |
| `UTF8Encoding` | Unicode character set, 8 or 16 bits per character depending on character. |

Each encoding contains internal objects that implement the abstract base class `Encoder` and `Decoder`, which perform the actual conversion respectively out of and into the encoding's character set. For large or repetitive conversions, it is sometimes more efficient to fetch these objects from the encoding and deal with them directly rather than going through the additional layer of the encoding.

A `StringBuilder` is a mutable (changeable) string. Adding characters to a standard `System.String` object creates a new instance of a string. Adding characters to a `StringBuilder` modifies the existing `StringBuilder` without creating a new one. This can yield a large performance gain in certain cases, such as adding a small amount of new data to a large existing string.

## Diagram

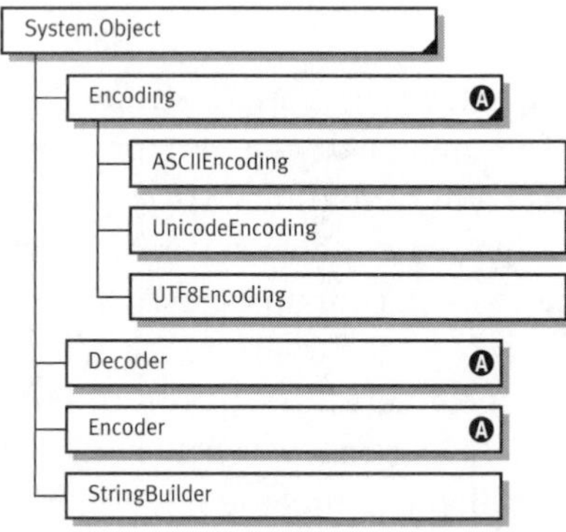
System.Object
Encoding
ASCIIEncoding
UnicodeEncoding
UTF8Encoding
Decoder
Encoder
StringBuilder

# System.Threading



Modern operating systems handle many independent programs at once, and the programs themselves often contain many independent tasks. Logically segregating these tasks for efficient development, and sharing the computer's processor(s) among them for efficient operation, is such an important concept that the functionality for doing it comes built into the modern operating system. Programmers divide their program's functionality into threads. A thread is an object within a process that executes code, and a process is a virtual address space. You can think of a process as a garage and a thread as an engine within the garage. Every process gets created with one thread. A programmer may explicitly create more threads in order to accomplish the program's work, for example, one thread to handle a user interface and another to handle background printing. Some CLR operations, such as garbage collection or asynchronous method invocation, may cause the operating system to create and use additional threads behind the scenes. So your programs live in a multithreaded environment whether they think about it or not.

The operating system preemptively multitasks the threads of all applications. The OS maintains a list of all the threads in the entire computer that are ready, willing, and able to run. Every 10 milliseconds or so (an interval known as the *timeslice*), the OS performs an interrupt and checks to see which thread should have the CPU. Each thread has a priority, and the scheduler picks the highest priority thread in the computer-wide ready list to run. If several threads share the highest priority level, the scheduler alternates them in a round-robin fashion. If the machine contains more than one CPU, each CPU is assigned a thread from the ready list, working from the highest priority downward. The register values of the currently running thread are saved in memory ("swapped out"), and those of the incoming thread placed into the CPU ("swapped in"), which then starts running the incoming thread at the point where it was swapped out the last time. A thread doesn't know when it is swapped in or out. As far as it knows, it's simply executing to completion at a speed over which it has no control.

Not all threads in the system are in the ready state, squabbling with each other over CPU cycles; in fact most of them usually aren't. One of the most useful features of threads is that they can be made to wait, without consuming CPU cycles, for various external events to happen. For example, a Windows Forms application's main thread is generally waiting to receive a message from the operating system announcing that the user has clicked the mouse or pressed a key. A thread in this waiting state is said to be *blocked*. Think of this thread as a car waiting at a stoplight. It's more efficient than that, however, as the thread doesn't have its own engine, so it's not wasting gas sitting there idling. Other threads can use the CPU while the blocked thread waits. When the block clears, the thread goes back into the ready list to compete for CPU time with the rest of the threads.

The class `Thread` represents a thread in the .NET Framework. The methods on this object allow a programmer to start a thread's operation, suspend it, resume it, abort it, or set its priority. Creating a new object of this class creates a new thread within the caller's process.

You must pass its constructor a delegate that implements that `ThreadStart` design pattern. This delegate contains the code that the thread will execute when it starts to run.

The `Timer` class uses a background thread to provide callbacks to your program at specified intervals. You create an object of this class, passing its constructor a delegate that implements the `TimerCallback` design pattern. The timer will call the delegate's code on a thread from the pool at the specified interval.

As with all parts of the .NET Framework, threading operations throw exceptions when they encounter errors. The namespace includes classes for signaling these exceptions. Table 12 lists these classes.

TABLE 12

| Exception | Meaning |
|---|---|
| `ThreadAbortException` | Thrown when a call is made to the `Abort` method. |
| `ThreadStateException` | Thrown when a `Thread` is in an invalid `ThreadState` for a method call made on it. |

Using threads looks relatively simple, but this appearance is deceptive. The operating system swaps running threads in and out of the CPU without regard to where a thread is in the course of its work. Writing good multithreaded code is primarily about dealing with the interactions of the various threads swapping in and out at times you can't control. The main problem in multithreaded code arises when one thread modifies data that another thread is using. Think of two children sharing one set of watercolor paints, or two programmers working on the same file.

Consider the code snippet `N = N + 1`. Most programmers can't imagine anything simpler, easier, and safer. And indeed, every thread has its own stack, so if *N* is a stack (automatic) variable or a function parameter, each thread that executes the code has its own copy and we have no problem. But if two threads try to share the same copy of *N*, we're looking at a nasty, hard-to-find bug waiting to happen. They will occasionally mix each other up and produce the wrong result. Such a mix-up can occur if *N* is a global variable (or a shared class variable, which is just a politically correct form of global) and two threads access it simultaneously. It can also occur if *N* is an object member variable and two threads access the same object simultaneously.

How could such a simple piece of code as `N = N + 1` possibly screw up? Look at Figure 1, which shows the assembler instructions to which the source line compiles: move the contents of the variable's memory location to a processor register, increment the value in the register, and move the result back to the variable's memory location.

```
mov   AX, [N]      ; move variable memory location to CPU register
add   AX, 1        ; add 1 to contents of register
mov   [N], AX      ; move contents of register back to memory location
```

Figure 1: **Assembler listing of simple variable increment**

The problem happens if threads get swapped at the wrong time. Suppose the memory location of the variable *N* contains the value 4. Suppose Thread A executes the first two statements—moves 4 into the AX register, adds 1 to it to get 5—but further suppose that it reaches this code near the end of its timeslice, so it gets swapped out before it can execute the last statement, which would have stored the result. This isn't immediately a problem. The operating system retains the values of Thread A's registers in its own memory along with other administrative information about Thread A, so it doesn't get lost. But now suppose that Thread B gets swapped in and starts executing the same code—it fetches 4 from memory (because Thread A hasn't had time to store its result), adds 1, and moves 5 back to memory. At some future time, Thread B exhausts its timeslice and the operating system swaps in Thread A, restoring the value of 5 to register AX. Thread A picks up where it left off, and moves 5 into the memory location. The variable *N* now contains an incorrect value of 5, whereas if Thread A had been allowed to complete its operation before Thread B ran, *N* would contain the correct value of 6. We lost one of our increments because thread swapping happened at the wrong moment. This is the most difficult, frustrating kind of bug to track down that I've ever encountered because, as you can see, it is devilishly hard to reproduce. It only happens when the threads get swapped in and out at exactly the wrong moments, and any instrumentation you add to detect it will likely change that timing. If Thread A had finished its operation before getting swapped out, or hadn't started it, or Thread B executed some other code during its timeslice, we wouldn't have encountered this problem. This is the kind of bug that causes programmers to smash their keyboards and take up goat herding.

We need to ensure that Thread B doesn't mess with any operations that Thread A has started but hasn't yet finished. We need to make any access to shared resources *atomic* with respect to threads. We do this by using the synchronization objects provided by the .NET Framework. The most common way of doing this generically is by using the class `Monitor`, which provides methods that ensure that only one thread can execute a block of code at a time. You can use this class directly if you want, but more commonly your programming language will wrap this class up in a language construct where you don't see it directly. The lock statement in C# uses this class internally. The first thread to enter the monitored region is granted ownership of it. Subsequent threads attempting to enter the region will block until the first thread leaves it. The `Monitor` throws an exception of class `SynchronizationLockException` if someone tries to bypass it.

A faster alternative for very simple operations is to use the class `Interlocked`, which contains static methods for incrementing, decrementing, or exchanging two values. These methods are thread-safe but incur a lower overhead cost than does the use of a `Monitor` object.

A programmer may want to develop other synchronization objects to provide different waiting and blocking behavior than the mutual exclusion offered by the `Monitor` or `Interlocked` classes. The .NET Framework contains the class `WaitHandle` in order to provide a common design pattern for developing these types of objects. For example, Microsoft's implementation of the .NET Framework contains the class `Mutex`, which derives from `WaitHandle` and provides `Monitor`-like behavior across different processes. `WaitHandle` contains methods that cause the calling thread to block, with an optional timeout, until the synchronization object's conditions for unblocking are met. The calling thread can wait on one synchronization object, or any or all of a collection of them.

## Diagram

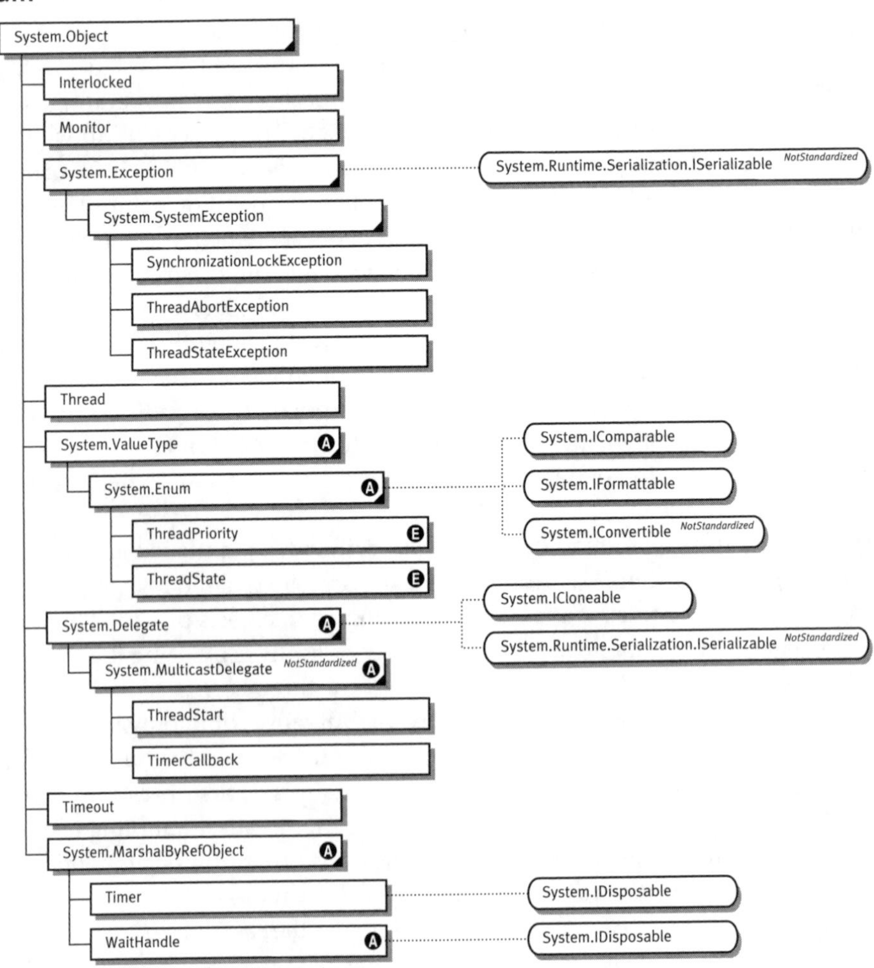

# PART II
## Class Libraries

# System ApplicationException

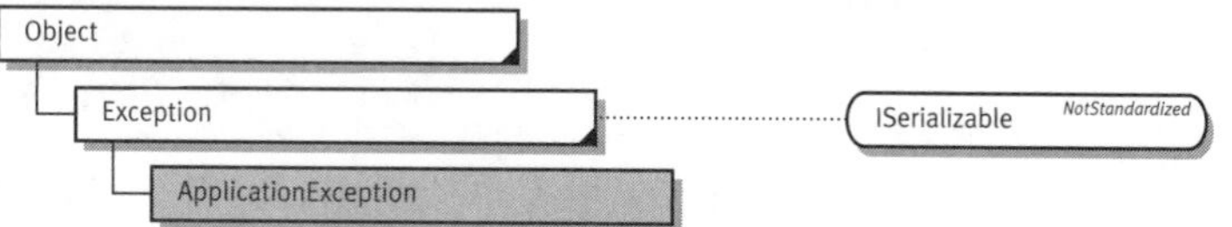


## Summary

`System.ApplicationException` is the base class for all exceptions defined by applications.

## Type Summary

```
public class ApplicationException : Exception
{
  // Constructors
     public ApplicationException ();
     public ApplicationException (string message);
     public ApplicationException (string message,
                                  Exception innerException);
MS CF protected ApplicationException (SerializationInfo info,
                                     StreamingContext context);
}
```

**KC** Designing exception hierarchies is tricky. Well-designed exception hierarchies are wide, not very deep, and contain only those exceptions for which there is a programmating scenario for catching. We added `ApplicationException` thinking it would add value by grouping exceptions declared outside of the .NET Framework, but there is no scenario for catching `ApplicationException` and it only adds unnecessary depth to the hierarchy.

**JR** You should not define new exception classes derived from `ApplicationException`; use Exception instead. In addition, you should not write code that catches `ApplicationException`.

## Description

This class represents application-defined errors detected during the execution of an application. It is provided as means to differentiate between exceptions defined by applications versus exceptions defined by the system. [*Note:* For more information on exceptions defined by the system, see `System.SystemException`.]

[*Note:* `System.ApplicationException` does not provide information as to the cause of the exception. In most scenarios, instances of this class should not be thrown. In cases where this class is instantiated, a human-readable message describing the error should be passed to the constructor.]



## Example

The following example demonstrates catching an exception type that derives from `ApplicationException`. There is, however, no valid scenerio for catching an `ApplicationException` type.

```
using System;
using System.Reflection;

namespace Samples
{
  public class ApplicationExceptionSample
  {
    public static void Main()
    {
      try
      {
        Type t = typeof(string);
        MethodInfo m = t.GetMethod("EndsWith");
        string s = "Hello world!";
        object[] arguments = {"world!", "!"};
        Console.WriteLine(m.Invoke(s, arguments));
      }
      catch(ApplicationException e)
      {
        Console.WriteLine("Exception: {0}", e);
      }
    }
  }
}
```

The output is

```
Exception: System.Reflection.TargetParameterCountException: Parameter count mismatch.
   at System.Reflection.RuntimeMethodInfo.InternalInvoke(Object obj, BindingFlags
invokeAttr, Binder binder, Object[] parameters, CultureInfo culture, Boolean
isBinderDefault, Assembly caller, Boolean verifyAccess)
   at System.Reflection.RuntimeMethodInfo.InternalInvoke(Object obj, BindingFlags
invokeAttr, Binder binder, Object[] parameters, CultureInfo culture, Boolean
verifyAccess)
   at System.Reflection.RuntimeMethodInfo.Invoke(Object obj, BindingFlags
invokeAttr, Binder binder, Object[] parameters, CultureInfo culture)
   at System.Reflection.MethodBase.Invoke(Object obj, Object[] parameters)
   at Samples.ApplicationExceptionSample.Main() in C:\Books\BCL\Samples\System\
ApplicationException\ApplicationException.cs:line 16
```

# System
# ArgumentException

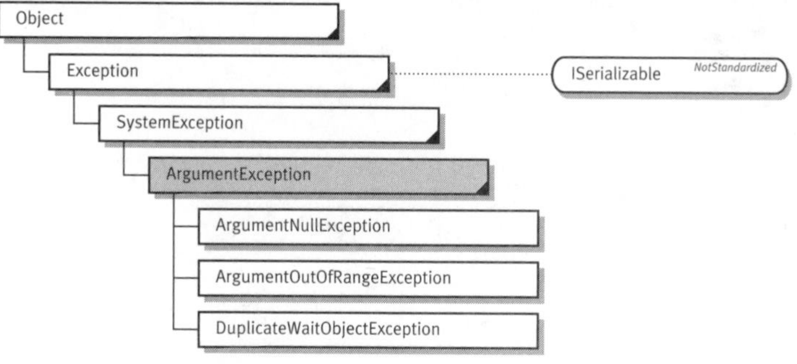


A B C D E F G H I J K L M N O P Q R S T U V W X Y Z

## Summary

Represents the error that occurs when an argument passed to a method is invalid.

## Type Summary

```
public class ArgumentException : SystemException,
                                 ISerializable
{
  // Constructors
     public ArgumentException ();
     public ArgumentException (string message);
     public ArgumentException (string message,
                               string paramName);
  CF public ArgumentException (string message,
                               string paramName,
                               Exception innerException);
     public ArgumentException (string message,
                               Exception innerException);
MS CF protected ArgumentException (SerializationInfo info,
                                   StreamingContext context);

  // Properties
MS CF public override string Message { get; }
   CF public virtual string ParamName { get; }

  // Methods
MS CF public override void GetObjectData (SerializationInfo info,
                                          StreamingContext context);
}
```

## Description

`System.ArgumentException` is thrown when a method is invoked and at least one of the passed arguments does not meet the method's parameter specification.

[*Note:* The Base Class Library includes three derived types: When appropriate, use these types instead of System.ArgumentException.]

A B C D E F G H I J K L M N O P Q R S T U V W X Y Z

## Example

```
using System;

namespace Samples
{
  public class ArgumentExceptionSample
  {
    public static void Main()
    {
      try
      {
        string s = "one";
        s.CompareTo(1);
      }
      catch(ArgumentException e)
      {
        Console.WriteLine("Exception: {0}", e);
      }
    }
  }
}
```

The output is

```
Exception: System.ArgumentException: Object must be of type String.
   at System.String.CompareTo(Object value)
   at Samples.ArgumentExceptionSample.Main() in C:\Books\BCL\Samples\System\
ArgumentException\ArgumentException.cs:line 12
```

# System ArgumentNullException

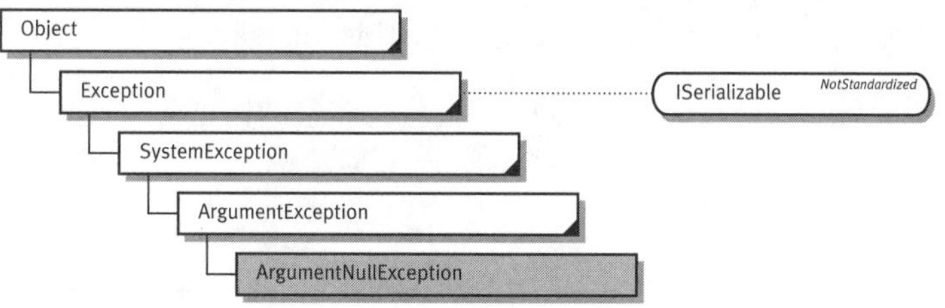


A B C D E F G H I J K L M N O P Q R S T U V W X Y Z

## Summary

Represents the error that occurs when an argument passed to a method is invalid because it is `null`.

## Type Summary

```
public class ArgumentNullException : ArgumentException
{
  // Constructors
     public ArgumentNullException ();
     public ArgumentNullException (string paramName);
     public ArgumentNullException (string paramName,
                                   string message);
MS CF protected ArgumentNullException (SerializationInfo info,
                                      StreamingContext context);
}
```

**BA** This class goes down in the API design hall of shame. `ArgumentNullException` does not follow the exception constructor pattern given in the Design Guidelines Specification, which says the constructor overloads should include at least:

```
public XxxException ();
public XxxException (string message);
public XxxException (string message, Exception inner);
```

The rationale for violating this guideline was that the parameter name would be much more commonly specified than the message text. However, because nearly every

*CONTINUED*

other exception in the system *does* follow the pattern, the usual result is that the force of habit wins out. Developers commonly make this mistake:

```
throw new ArgumentNullException ("must pass an employee name");
```

Rather than:

```
throw new ArgumentNullException ("Name", "must pass an employee name");
```

This mistake means that we end up with an error message such as this one:

```
Unhandled Exception: System.ArgumentNullException: Value cannot be null.
Parameter name: "must pass employee name"
```

Lesson learned: Just follow the pattern.

**JR** In addition to Brad's comments, a properly designed exception class should also allow for serializability. Specifically, this means that the class should have the `System.SerializableAttribute` applied to it and the class should implement the ISerializable interface with its `GetObjectData` method and special constructor. These two methods should serialize/deserialize any fields in the class and be sure to call the base class methods so that any fields in the base class are also serialized/deserialized. If the exception class is sealed, the constructor can be marked private; otherwise, mark the constructor as protected. Since `GetObjectData` is an interface method, mark it as public.

## Description

[*Note:* `System.ArgumentNullException` is thrown when a method is invoked and at least one of the passed arguments is `null` and should never be `null`. `System.ArgumentNullException` behaves identically to `System.ArgumentException`. It is provided so that application code can differentiate between exceptions caused by `null` arguments and exceptions caused by non-`null` arguments. For errors caused by non-`null` arguments, see `System.ArgumentOutOfRangeException`.]

## Example

```
using System;

namespace Samples
{
  class ArgumentNullExceptionSample
  {
    public static void Main()
    {
      String[] strings = null;
      String separator  = " ";
      try
      {
        String s = String.Join(separator, strings);
      }
      catch(ArgumentNullException e)
      {
        Console.WriteLine("Exception: {0}", e);
      }
    }
  }
}
```

The output is

```
Exception: System.ArgumentNullException: Value cannot be null.
Parameter name: value
   at System.String.Join(String separator, String[] value)
   at Samples.ArgumentNullExceptionSample.Main() in C:\Books\BCL\Samples\System\
ArgumentNullException\ArgumentNullException.cs:line 13
```

# System ArgumentOutOfRangeException





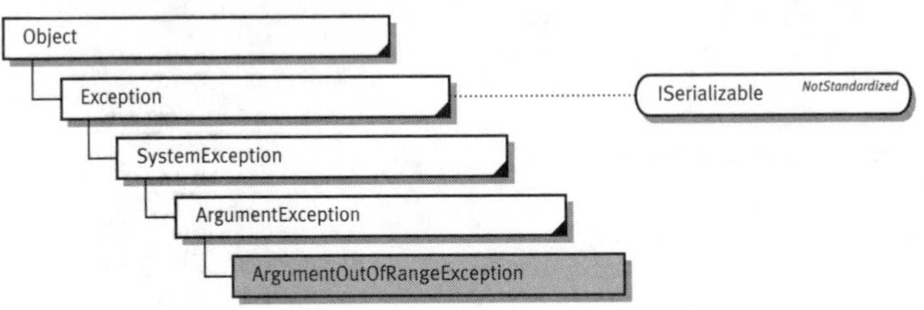


## Summary

Represents the error that occurs when an argument passed to a method is invalid because it is outside the allowable range of values as specified by the method.

## Type Summary

```
public class ArgumentOutOfRangeException : ArgumentException,
                                          ISerializable
{
  // Constructors
     public ArgumentOutOfRangeException ();
     public ArgumentOutOfRangeException (string paramName);
  CF public ArgumentOutOfRangeException (string paramName,
                                         object actualValue,
                                         string message);
  CF public ArgumentOutOfRangeException (string paramName,
                                         string message);
MS CF protected ArgumentOutOfRangeException (SerializationInfo info,
                                            StreamingContext context);

  // Properties
  CF public virtual object ActualValue { get; }
MS CF public override string Message { get; }

  // Methods
MS CF public override void GetObjectData (SerializationInfo info,
                                         StreamingContext context);
}
```

> **BA** Please see my comments in `ArgumentNullException`.

## Description

[*Note:* `System.ArgumentOutOfRangeException` is thrown when a method is invoked and at least one of the arguments passed to the method is not `null` and does not contain a valid value. `System.ArgumentOutOfRangeException` behaves identically to `System.ArgumentException`. It is provided so that application code can differentiate between exceptions caused by invalid arguments that are not `null`, and exceptions caused by `null` arguments. For errors caused by `null` arguments, see `System.ArgumentNullException`.]

## Example

```
using System;

namespace Samples
{
  class ArgumentOutOfRangeExceptionSample
  {
    public static void Main()
    {
      int[] array1 = {42, 42};
      int[] array2 = {0, 0};
      try
      {
        Array.Copy(array1, array2, -1);
      }
      catch(ArgumentOutOfRangeException e)
      {
        Console.WriteLine(e);
      }
    }
  }
}
```

The output is

```
System.ArgumentOutOfRangeException: Non-negative number required.
Parameter name: length
   at System.Array.Copy(Array sourceArray, Int32 sourceIndex, Array
destinationArray, Int32 destinationIndex, Int32 length)
   at System.Array.Copy(Array sourceArray, Array destinationArray, Int32 length)
   at Samples.ArgumentOutOfRangeExceptionSample.Main() in C:\Books\BCL\Samples\
System\ArgumentOutOfRangeException\ArgumentOutOfRangeException.cs:line 13
```

# System ArithmeticException

BCL



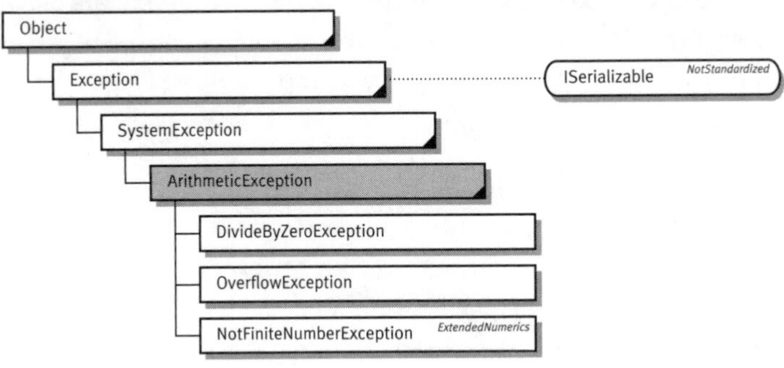


## Summary

Represents an error caused by an arithmetic operation.

## Type Summary

```
public class ArithmeticException : SystemException
{
  // Constructors
     public ArithmeticException ();
     public ArithmeticException (string message);
     public ArithmeticException (string message,
                                 Exception innerException);
MS CF protected ArithmeticException (SerializationInfo info,
                                     StreamingContext context);
}
```

## Description

[*Note:* The Base Class Library includes two types derived from `System.ArithmeticException`: When appropriate, use these types instead of `System.ArithmeticException`.]

## Example

```
using System;

namespace Samples
{
  class ArithmeticExceptionSample
  {
    public static void Main()
    {
      try
      {
        Math.Sign(Double.NaN);
```

```
      }
      catch(ArithmeticException e)
      {
        Console.WriteLine("Exception: {0}", e);
      }
    }
  }
}
```

The output is

```
Exception: System.ArithmeticException: Function does not accept floating point
Not-a-Number values.
   at System.Math.Sign(Double value)
   at Samples.ArithmeticExceptionSample.Main() in C:\Books\BCL\Samples\System\
ArithmeticException\ArithmeticException.cs:line 11
```

# System
# Array



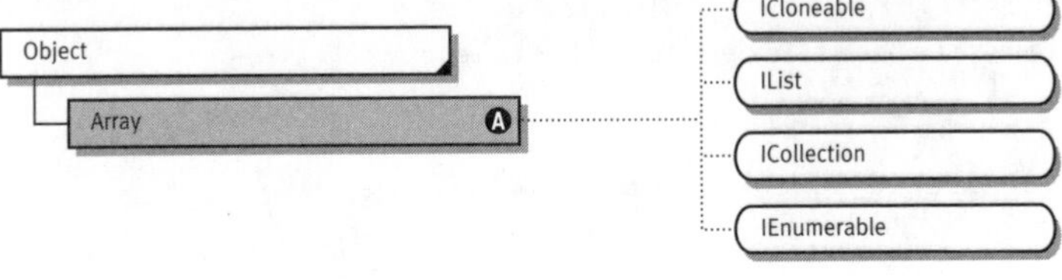


## Summary

Serves as the base class for arrays. Provides methods for creating, copying, manipulating, searching, and sorting arrays.

## Type Summary

```
public abstract class Array : ICloneable, IList,
                              ICollection, IEnumerable
{
    // Constructors
       protected Array();

    // Properties
    MS public virtual bool IsFixedSize { get; }
    MS public virtual bool IsReadOnly { get; }
    MS public virtual bool IsSynchronized { get; }
       public int Length { get; }
CF 1.1 public long LongLength { get; }
       public int Rank { get; }
    MS public virtual object SyncRoot { get; }

    // Methods
    CF public static int BinarySearch (Array array,
                                       int index,
                                       int length,
                                       object value);
       public static int BinarySearch (Array array,
                                       int index,
                                       int length,
                                       object value,
                                       IComparer comparer);
       public static int BinarySearch (Array array,
                                       object value);
    CF public static int BinarySearch (Array array,
                                       object value,
                                       IComparer comparer);
       public static void Clear (Array array, int index,
                                 int length);
```

```
           public virtual object Clone ();
           public static void Copy (Array sourceArray,
                                    int sourceIndex,
                                    Array destinationArray,
                                    int destinationIndex,
                                    int length);
MS CF 1.1  public static void Copy (Array sourceArray,
                                    long sourceIndex,
                                    Array destinationArray,
                                    long destinationIndex,
                                    long length);
       CF  public static void Copy (Array sourceArray,
                                    Array destinationArray,
                                    int length);
MS CF 1.1  public static void Copy (Array sourceArray,
                                         Array destinationArray,
                                         long length);
           public virtual void CopyTo (Array array, int index);
MS CF 1.1  public virtual void CopyTo (Array array, long index);
           public static Array CreateInstance (Type elementType,
                                               int length);
       CF  public static Array CreateInstance (Type elementType,
                                               int length1,
                                               int length2);
       CF  public static Array CreateInstance (Type elementType,
                                               int length1,
                                               int length2,
                                               int length3);
           public static Array CreateInstance (Type elementType,
                                               params int[] lengths);
       CF  public static Array CreateInstance (Type elementType,
                                               int[] lengths,
                                               int[] lowerBounds);
MS CF 1.1  public static Array CreateInstance (Type elementType,
                                               params long[] lengths);
           public virtual IEnumerator GetEnumerator ();
       MS  public int GetLength (int dimension);
MS CF 1.1  public long GetLongLength (int dimension);
           public int GetLowerBound (int dimension);
           public int GetUpperBound (int dimension);
           public object GetValue (int index);
       CF  public object GetValue (int index1, int index2);
       CF  public object GetValue (int index1, int index2,
                                   int index3);
           public object GetValue (params int[] indices);
MS CF 1.1  public object GetValue (long index);
MS CF 1.1  public object GetValue (long index1,
                                   long index2);
```

A B C D E F G H I J K L M N O P Q R S T U V W X Y Z

```
MS CF 1.1 public object GetValue (long index1,
                                  long index2,
                                  long index3);
MS CF 1.1 public object GetValue (params long[] indices);
       CF public static int IndexOf (Array array,
                                     object value);
       CF public static int IndexOf (Array array,
                                     object value,
                                     int startIndex);
          public static int IndexOf (Array array,
                                     object value,
                                     int startIndex,
                                     int count);
          public void Initialize ();
       CF public static int LastIndexOf (Array array,
                                         object value);
       CF public static int LastIndexOf (Array array,
                                         object value,
                                         int startIndex);
          public static int LastIndexOf (Array array,
                                         object value,
                                         int startIndex,
                                         int count);
       CF public static void Reverse (Array array);
          public static void Reverse (Array array,
                                      int index, int length);
          public void SetValue (object value, int index);
       CF public void SetValue (object value, int index1,
                                int index2);
       CF public void SetValue (object value, int index1,
                                int index2, int index3);
          public void SetValue (object value, params int[] indices);
MS CF 1.1 public void SetValue (object value, long index);
MS CF 1.1 public void SetValue (object value,
                                long index1,
                                long index2);
MS CF 1.1 public void SetValue (object value,
                                long index1,
                                long index2,
                                long index3);
MS CF 1.1 public void SetValue (object value,
                                params long[] indices);
          public static void Sort (Array array);
       CF public static void Sort (Array array, int index,
                                   int length);
          public static void Sort (Array array, int index,
                                   int length, IComparer comparer);
       CF public static void Sort (Array keys, Array items);
```

```
   CF public static void Sort (Array keys, Array items,
                               int index, int length);
      public static void Sort (Array keys, Array items,
                               int index, int length,
                               IComparer comparer);
   CF public static void Sort (Array keys, Array items,
                               IComparer comparer);
   CF public static void Sort (Array array, IComparer comparer);

   // Explicit Interface Members
   CF int IList.Add(object value);
   CF void IList.Clear();
   CF bool IList.Contains(object value);
   CF int IList.IndexOf(object value);
   CF void IList.Insert(int index, object value);
   CF void IList.Remove(object value);
   CF void IList.RemoveAt(int index);
   CF int ICollection.Count { get; };
   CF object IList.this [int index] {get; set;}
}
```



**BA** Notice the heavy use of 32-bit integer values for indices in this class. In the standardization process we spent hours discussing how this class moves to the 64-bit world. There were arguments that suggested we will rarely need arrays bigger than 2,147,483,647 values (this is the largest integer value). In the end we decided to offer a LongLength property which returns the length as a 64-bit value. We decided it was prudent to wait and add all the other support for 64-bit indices once there was a demonstrable customer requirement.

Notice that we used signed values for the indices in the `Array` class. Some people may feel this is an odd choice as the negative values are always invalid for indices. There are two reasons for this. First, the Common Language Specification lacks support for unsigned 32-bit integrals, which means some languages would not be able to consume these members. Second, unsigned numbers are just harder to work with. Many domains naturally return values as signed numbers, so using unsigned indices here would lead to uglier code with more casts.

Notice that the `Array` class implements the `IList` interface. We did that to support databinding and other generic mechanisms such as the "foreach" language construct in C#.

*CONTINUED*

Accessing elements through the IList interface on an array is significantly more expensive than accessing elements directly, because the JIT can, for example, recognize code patterns and host bounds checks. Luckily, the C# compiler generates special case code for arrays that the JIT is able to recognize and optimize. For example, look at the code the C# compiler generates for this:

```
int [] arr = new int[] {1,2,3,4};
foreach (int i in arr) {
    Console.WriteLine (i)
}
```

Rather than going through the enumerator the C# compiler generates code as if you had written:

```
int [] arr = new int[] {1,2,3,4};
for (int i = 0; i < arr.Length; i++){
    Console.WriteLine (i)
}
```

Notice that we used explicit method implementation to hide many of the methods from the IList interface that do not make much sense on Array. This keeps the Array class clean but still allows arrays to be plugged into generic services such as databinding.

**JM** In the original submission of this class for standardization, the Clear() method was not specified as precisely as it is now. Before it was specified as just zeroing out an array. But for Booleans and reference types it needs to be false and null, respectively. The change was indeed made during the standardization process.

**BG** Looking forward, as we add generic collections into the picture, one might imagine making all array instances implement a generic IList<T> interface (i.e., Int32[] would implement IList<Int32>). This would facilitate writing generic algorithms without requiring an STL-style iterator. A clever CLI implementation might potentially avoid performance hits when accessing an array through this generic interface, with sufficient complexity in the JIT.

Providing a base class for all arrays is one of our subtler but more notable advances. Most notably it allows all arrays to implement the IList interface, meaning that you can write one method that consumes a collection and also works with arrays, because our arrays *are* collections. Note that this duality allows us and our users to write APIs

CONTINUED

that accept *any* collection instead of just an enumerator. This gives developers more flexibility than STL's iterator-centric approach.

`Array::Copy` is a very interesting method, supporting all the conversions that we can prove will always work (i.e., upcasting, downcasting particular instances, boxing, unboxing, and primitive widening). Most people do not realize how useful this method can be when dealing with arrays of various primitive types.

**JR** The `CreateInstance` method can be used for all kinds of interesting things. I have used it to create a method that can redimension any kind of array. Here is a simple example showing how to redimension a single-dimension array:

```
static Array Redim(Array origArray, Int32 desiredSize) {
   Type t = origArray.GetType().GetElementType();
   Array newArray = Array.CreateInstance(t, desiredSize);
   Array.Copy(origArray, 0, newArray, 0,
              Math.Min(origArray.Length, desiredSize));
   return newArray;
}
```

I've also used `CreateInstance` to create arrays whose lower bounds are not `0`:

```
// I want a two-dimensional array [1995..2004][1..4]

Int32[] lowerBounds = { 1995, 1 };
Int32[] lengths = { 10, 4 };
Decimal[,] quarterlyRevenue =
   (Decimal[,])    Array.CreateInstance(typeof(Decimal), lengths, lower-
Bounds);
...
Console.WriteLine("The quarterly revenue for the 2nd quarter of 1998 is: "
   + quarterlyRevenue[1998][2]);
```

You can pass an `IComparable` object to `Array's Sort` and `BinarySearch` methods. If your object's `CompareTo` method throws an exception (any exception), `Sort` and `BinarySearch` catch the exception and throw an `InvalidOperationException`. This is not ideal; the exception thrown should not have been caught and allowed to propagate the call stack.

## Description

This class is intended to be used as a base class by language implementations that support arrays. Only the system can derive from this type: derived classes of `System.Array` are not to be created by the developer.

[*Note:* An array is a collection of identically typed data *elements* that are accessed and referenced by sets of integral *indices*. The *rank* of an array is the number of dimensions in the array. Each dimension has its own set of indices. An array with a rank greater than one can have a different lower bound and a different number of elements for each dimension. Multidimensional arrays (i.e., arrays with a rank greater than one) are processed in row-major order. The *lower bound* of a dimension is the starting index of that dimension. The *length* of an array is the total number of elements contained in all of its dimensions. A *vector* is a one-dimensional array with a *lower bound* of "0". If the implementer creates a derived class of `System.Array`, expected `System.Array` behavior cannot be guaranteed. For information on array-like objects with increased functionality, see the `System.Collections.IList` interface. For more information regarding the use of arrays versus the use of collections, see Partition V of the CLI Specification.] Every specific `System.Array` type has three instance methods defined on it. While some programming languages allow direct access to these methods, they are primarily intended to be called by the output of compilers based on language syntax that deals with arrays.

- `Get`: Takes as many `System.Int32` arguments as the array has dimensions and returns the value stored at the given index. It throws a `System.IndexOutOfRangeException` exception for invalid indices.
- `Set`: Takes as many `System.Int32` arguments as the array has dimensions, plus one additional argument (the last argument), which has the same type as an array element. It stores the final value in the specified index of the array. It throws a `System.IndexOutOfRangeException` exception for invalid indices.
- `Address`: Takes as many `System.Int32` arguments as the array has dimensions and returns the address of the element at the given index. It throws a `System.IndexOutOfRangeException` exception for invalid indices.

In addition, every specific `System.Array` type has a constructor on it that takes as many positive `System.Int32` arguments as the array has dimensions. The arguments specify the number of elements in each dimension, and a lower bound of 0. Thus, a two-dimensional array of `System.Int32` objects would have a constructor that could be called with `(2, 4)` as its arguments to create an array of eight zeros with the first dimension indexed with 0 and 1 and the second dimension indexed with 0, 1, 2, and 3.

For all specific array types except vectors (i.e., those permitted to have non-zero lower bounds and those with more than one dimension) there is an additional constructor. It takes twice as many arguments as the array has dimensions. The arguments are considered in pairs, with the first of the pair specifying the lower bound for that dimension and the second specifying the total number of elements in that dimension. Thus, a two-dimensional array of `System.Int32` objects would also have a constructor that could be called with `(-1, 2, 1, 3)` as its arguments, specifying an array of 6 zeros, with the first dimension indexed by –1 and 0, and the second dimension indexed by 1, 2, and 3.

## Example

```
using System;
using System.Collections;

namespace Samples
{
  public class ArraySample
  {
    public class MyReverseComparer: IComparer
    {
      public int Compare(Object a, Object b)
      {
        return -((IComparable)a).CompareTo(b);
      }
    }
    public static void Main()
    {
      string[] strings = {"one", "two", "three"};
      Console.WriteLine("Array elements: ");
      Display(strings);
      Array.Reverse(strings);
      Display(strings);
      Array.Sort(strings);
      Display(strings);
      Array.Sort(strings, new MyReverseComparer());
      Display(strings);
    }
    public static void Display(Array a)
    {
      foreach(object o in a)
        Console.Write("{0} ", o);
      Console.WriteLine();
    }
  }
}
```

The output is

```
Array elements:
one two three
three two one
one three two
two three one
```

# System.Collections ArrayList

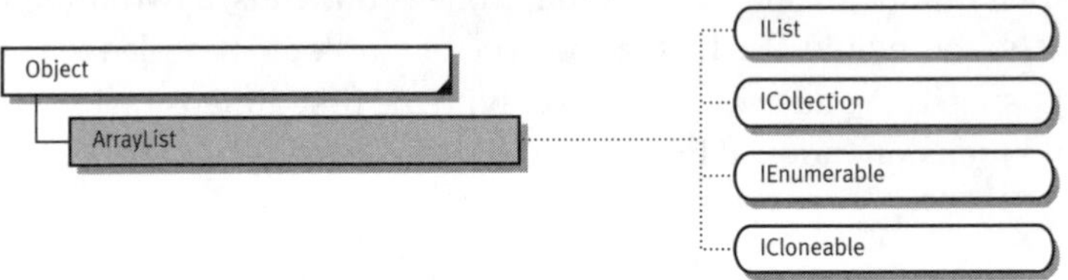




## Summary

Implements a variable-size `System.Collections.IList` that uses an array of objects to store its elements.

## Type Summary

```
public class ArrayList : IList, ICollection,
                         IEnumerable, ICloneable
{
  // Constructors
     public ArrayList ();
     public ArrayList (int capacity);
     public ArrayList (ICollection c);

  // Properties
     public virtual int Capacity { set; get; }
     public virtual int Count { get; }
     public virtual bool IsFixedSize { get; }
     public virtual bool IsReadOnly { get; }
     public virtual bool IsSynchronized { get; }
     public virtual object this[int index] { set; get; }
     public virtual object SyncRoot { get; }

  // Methods
  CF public static ArrayList Adapter (IList list);
     public virtual int Add (object value);
     public virtual void AddRange (ICollection c);
     public virtual int BinarySearch (int index,
                                      int count,
                                      object value,
                                      IComparer comparer);
  CF public virtual int BinarySearch (object value);
  CF public virtual int BinarySearch (object value,
                                      IComparer comparer);
     public virtual void Clear ();
     public virtual object Clone ();
     public virtual bool Contains (object item);
     public virtual void CopyTo (int index, Array array,
                                 int arrayIndex,
                                 int count);
```

```
      public virtual void CopyTo (Array array);
      public virtual void CopyTo (Array array,
                                  int arrayIndex);
   CF public static ArrayList FixedSize (ArrayList list);
MS CF public static IList FixedSize (IList list);
      public virtual IEnumerator GetEnumerator ();
   CF public virtual IEnumerator GetEnumerator (int index,
                                              int count);
   CF public virtual ArrayList GetRange (int index,
                                        int count);
      public virtual int IndexOf (object value);
   CF public virtual int IndexOf (object value,
                                 int startIndex);
      public virtual int IndexOf (object value,
                                 int startIndex,
                                 int count);
      public virtual void Insert (int index, object value);
      public virtual void InsertRange (int index,
                                      ICollection c);
   CF public virtual int LastIndexOf (object value);
   CF public virtual int LastIndexOf (object value,
                                     int startIndex);
   CF public virtual int LastIndexOf (object value,
                                     int startIndex,
                                     int count);
   CF public static ArrayList ReadOnly (ArrayList list);
MS CF public static IList ReadOnly (IList list);
      public virtual void Remove (object obj);
      public virtual void RemoveAt (int index);
      public virtual void RemoveRange (int index,
                                      int count);
   CF public static ArrayList Repeat (object value,
                                     int count);
      public virtual void Reverse ();
      public virtual void Reverse (int index,
                                  int count);
   CF public virtual void SetRange (int index,
                                   ICollection c);
      public virtual void Sort ();
      public virtual void Sort (int index, int count,
                               IComparer comparer);
      public virtual void Sort (IComparer comparer);
      public static ArrayList Synchronized (ArrayList list);
MS CF public static IList Synchronized (IList list);
      public virtual object[] ToArray ();
      public virtual Array ToArray (Type type);
      public virtual void TrimToSize ();
   }
```

**JM** The `IndexOf(string, int, int)` method used to have as its last parameter the name "lastIndex." This name caused confusion regarding whether the index was included in the search or not (inclusive or exclusive). Thus, as part of the standardization process the name got changed to "count" to avoid that confusion.

**BG** Note the heavy use of wrapper collections on `ArrayList` to add in functionality like thread safety or making a list read-only. This is very useful in that it allows users to write their code using `ArrayList` and then add in thread safety without having to change more than one line of code. At least, that was the original goal. However, there are two drawbacks with this approach. One is a subtle performance penalty—every method call on `ArrayList` is virtual, meaning it cannot be inlined and is therefore slower than it could be. The second is that the design isn't quite what people need, at least for synchronization. Sometimes users may want code that does two operations with an `ArrayList` in a consistent state, like this:

```
ArrayList list = ArrayList.Synchronized(someOtherArrayList);
if (list.Count > 0)
    Object node = list[0];
```

At this point, our threadsafe wrapper will not work as expected. True, the `Count` property will be accessed in a thread-safe way, as will the first element of the `ArrayList`. However, the way our design for the threadsafe wrapper works requires that we take a lock when calling each method, then release the lock after calling each method. Therefore, after we have retrieved the `Count` property, another thread could add or remove an element from the list, meaning that the next line might fail. The correct way to write code like this would be to use the `SyncRoot` property:

```
lock(list.SyncRoot) {
    if (list.Count > 0)
        Object node = list[0];
}
```

This code is correct and has the added benefit of taking the lock only once, instead of twice. Note the thread-safe wrapper collections are expected to use the `SyncRoot` property (defined on `ICollection`) to implement their thread-safety guarantees, so doing this in one part of your code is fully compatible with using a thread-safe wrapper in a different section of your code.

*CONTINUED*

A B C D E F G H I J K L M N O P Q R S T U V W X Y Z

For these reasons, the SyncRoot property is a great idea and the idea of a thread-safe wrapper is less appealing than you'd like to believe. If we were designing collections over again, we might not allow subclasses of our collections for performance reasons and because they don't add a lot of value. The IList interface should be rich enough for most users, and if it isn't, the correct approach is to write another interface. Classes implementing that interface are free to use ArrayList internally for their own implementation details if necessary.

**JR** Since an ArrayList is simply a wrapper on top of an Array, my comment about Array's Sort and BinarySearch methods and exceptions applies to ArrayList as well.

## Description

System.Collections.ArrayList implements a variable-size System.Collections.IList that uses an array of objects to store the elements. A System.Collections.ArrayList has a System.Collections.ArrayList.Capacity, which is the allocated length of the internal array. The total number of elements contained by a list is its System.Collections.ArrayList.Count. As elements are added to a list, its capacity is automatically increased as required by reallocating the internal array.

## Example

```
using System;
using System.Collections;

namespace Samples
{
  public class ArrayListSamples
  {
    public static void Main()
    {
      ArrayList a = new ArrayList();
      a.Add("damien");
      a.Add(42);
      a.Add(new object());
      Console.WriteLine("-- ArrayList --" );
      Console.WriteLine("Count: {0}", a.Count);
      Console.WriteLine("Capacity: {0}", a.Capacity );
      Console.Write("Values:");
      PrintElements(a);
      a.Reverse();
      Console.Write("Values:");
      PrintElements(a);
      a.Remove(new object());
```

```
        a.Remove("damien");
        Console.Write("Values:");
        PrintElements(a);
      }
      public static void PrintElements(IEnumerable ie)
      {
        IEnumerator e = ie.GetEnumerator();
        while(e.MoveNext())
          Console.Write(" {0}", e.Current );
        Console.WriteLine();
      }
    }
  }
```

The output is

```
-- ArrayList --
Count: 3
Capacity: 16
Values: damien 42 System.Object
Values: System.Object 42 damien
Values: System.Object 42
```

# System ArrayTypeMismatchException

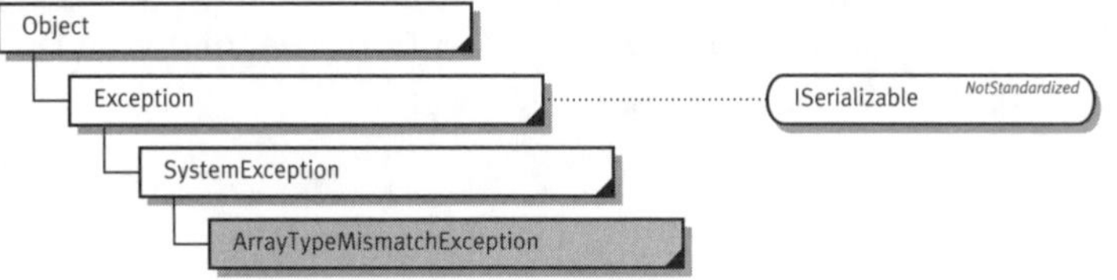




## Summary

Represents the error that occurs when an attempt is made to store an element of the wrong type in an array.

## Type Summary

```
public class ArrayTypeMismatchException : SystemException
{
  // Constructors
     public ArrayTypeMismatchException ();
     public ArrayTypeMismatchException (string message);
     public ArrayTypeMismatchException (string message,
                                        Exception innerException);
MS CF protected ArrayTypeMismatchException (SerializationInfo info,
                                        StreamingContext context);
}
```

**BA** It is interesting to look at the exceptions that are only thrown by the runtime, such as `ArrayTypeMismatchException`, `NullReferenceException`, and `ExecutionEngionException`. Even though we did not expect these exceptions to be thrown by user code, we included the standard constructors. We believe that consistency is the overriding principle in this case; therefore, we did not force ourselves to come up with clear scenarios that require these constructors. That said, we do see developers throwing them explicitly in code designed to test exception handling.

## Description

`System.ArrayTypeMismatchException` is thrown when the system cannot convert the element to the type declared for the array. [*Note:* This exception will not be thrown if the element can be converted to the type declared for the array. For example, an element of type `System.Byte` can be stored in an array declared to store `System.Int32` values, but an element of type `System.String` cannot be stored in a `System.Int32` array because conversion between these types is not supported.]

[*Note:* This exception is thrown by the `System.Array.Copy` method if a widening conversion cannot be performed on the operand to convert it to the array type. It is generally unnecessary for applications to throw this exception. The following IL instructions throw `System.ArrayTypeMismatchException`.]

A
B
C
D
E
F
G
H
I
J
K
L
M
N
O
P
Q
R
S
T
U
V
W
X
Y
Z

## Example

```
using System;

namespace Samples
{
  public class ArrayTypeMisMatch
  {
    public static void Main()
    {
      string[] strings = {"one", "two", "three"};
      int[] ints = {1, 2, 3};
      try
      {
        Array.Copy(strings, ints, 3);
      }
      catch(ArrayTypeMismatchException e)
      {
        Console.WriteLine("Exception: {0}", e);
      }
    }
  }
}
```

The output is

```
Exception: System.ArrayTypeMismatchException: Source array type cannot be assigned
to destination array type.
   at System.Array.Copy(Array sourceArray, Int32 sourceIndex, Array
destinationArray, Int32 destinationIndex, Int32 length)
   at System.Array.Copy(Array sourceArray, Array destinationArray, Int32 length)
   at Samples.ArrayTypeMisMatch.Main() in C:\Books\BCL\Samples\System\
ArrayTypeMismatchException\ArrayTypeMismatchException.cs:line 13
```

# System.Text ASCIIEncoding

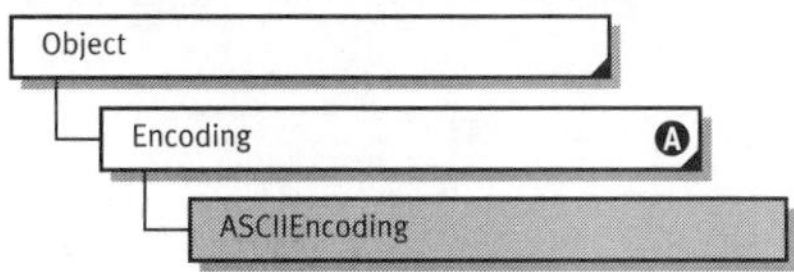


## Summary

Represents an ASCII character implementation of `System.Text.Encoding`.

## Type Summary

```
public class ASCIIEncoding : Encoding
{
  // Constructors
     public ASCIIEncoding ();

  // Methods
     public override int GetByteCount (char[] chars,
                                       int index,
                                       int count);
     public override int GetByteCount (string chars);
     public override int GetBytes (char[] chars,
                                   int charIndex,
                                   int charCount,
                                   byte[] bytes,
                                   int byteIndex);
     public override int GetBytes (string chars,
                                   int charIndex,
                                   int charCount,
                                   byte[] bytes,
                                   int byteIndex);
     public override int GetCharCount (byte[] bytes,
                                       int index,
                                       int count);
     public override int GetChars (byte[] bytes,
                                   int byteIndex,
                                   int byteCount,
                                   char[] chars,
                                   int charIndex);
     public override int GetMaxByteCount (intcharCount);
     public override int GetMaxCharCount (int byteCount);
  CF public override string GetString (byte[] bytes);
  CF public override string GetString (byte[] bytes,
                                       int byteIndex,
                                       int byteCount);
}
```

A B C D E F G H I J K L M N O P Q R S T U V W X Y Z

**BA** Regrettably, the `ASCIIEncoding` class does not follow the standard naming convention: it should really be called `AsciiEncoding`. We settled on the naming convention for abbreviations too late in the cycle to fix this.

**BG** We hope that users will not choose ASCII for persisting data in files when they can control the file format. We have fully shifted to Unicode, and our recommended text transfer format is UTF-8, which is as compact as ASCII for US English text, yet also supports all Unicode characters.

**JR** Normally, there is no need for your application code to construct an `Encoding`-derived object (such as `ASCIIEncoding`). Instead, you normally obtain an `Encoding`-derived object by calling one of `Encoding` class's static, read-only properties. Here is an example:

```
ASCIIEncoding asciiEncoding = Encoding.ASCII;
```

This is more efficient because it returns a reference to a single `ASCIIEncoding` object rather than creating new `ASCIIEncoding` objects.

## Description

`System.Text.ASCIIEncoding` encodes characters as single 7-bit ASCII characters. This encoding supports Unicode code points between U+0000 and U+007F, inclusive.

[*Note:* The limited range of code points supported by `System.Text.ASCIIEncoding` makes ASCII inadequate for many internationalized applications. `System.Text.UTF8Encoding` and `System.Text.UnicodeEncoding` provide encodings that are more suitable for internationalized applications.]

# System AsyncCallback Delegate

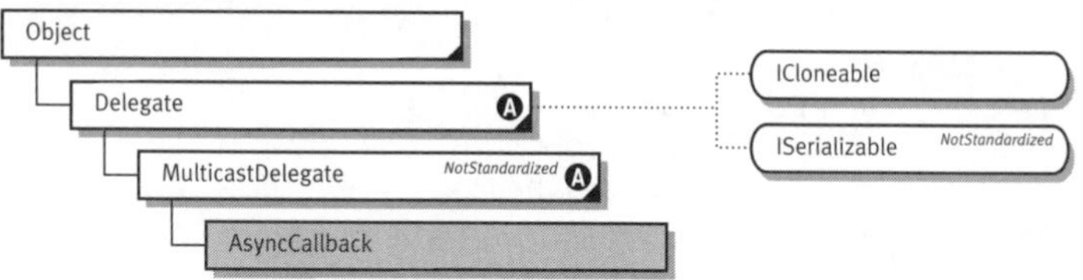



## Summary

References one or more methods called when an asynchronous operation completes.


## Type Summary

```
public delegate void AsyncCallback (IAsyncResult ar);
```

> **JR** I like the asynchronous programming model a lot and I recommend that everyone learn to apply it where appropriate to improve the performance and scalability of their applications.

## Parameters

| Parameter | Description |
|---|---|
| ar | A `System.IAsyncResult` object containing information about the asynchronous operation that has completed. |

## Example

```
using System;
using System.IO;
using System.Text;
using System.Threading;

namespace Samples
{
  public class AsyncCallBackSample
  {
    const int limit = 512;
    const int readlimit = 15;
    public class StateHolder
    {
      public byte[] bytes ;
      public FileStream fs ;
```

```
      }
      public static void Main()
      {
        string s = "filestream.txt";
        FileStream fs = new FileStream(s,
                                FileMode.Open,
                                FileAccess.Read);
        StateHolder sh = new StateHolder();
        sh.fs = fs;
        sh.bytes = new Byte[limit];
        AsyncCallback ac = new AsyncCallback(CallMe);
        fs.BeginRead(sh.bytes, 0, readlimit, ac, sh);
        Thread.Sleep(2000);
        Console.WriteLine();
        Console.WriteLine("Finishing Main()");
      }
      public static void CallMe(IAsyncResult asyncResult)
      {
        StateHolder sh = (StateHolder) asyncResult.AsyncState;
        FileStream fs = sh.fs;
        int count = fs.EndRead(asyncResult);
        Console.Write("Bytes read: {0} ", count);
        if(count != 0)
        {
          Decoder d = Encoding.UTF8.GetDecoder();
          char[] chars = null;
          int i = d.GetCharCount(sh.bytes, 0, count);
          chars = new Char[i];
          count = d.GetChars(sh.bytes, 0, count, chars, 0);
          Console.WriteLine(new string(chars));
          fs.BeginRead(sh.bytes, 0, readlimit,
                      new AsyncCallback(CallMe), sh);
        }
        else
        {
          fs.Close() ;
        }
      }
    }
  }
```

The output is

```
Bytes read: 15 Hello world..

Bytes read: 15 Goodbye world

Bytes read: 5 ...

Bytes read: 0
Finishing Main()
```

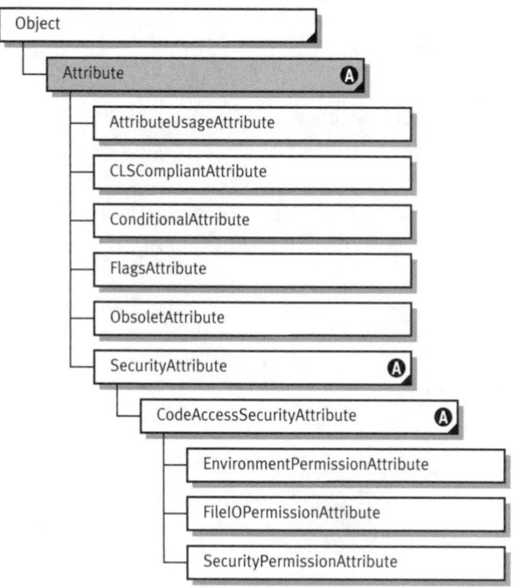


## Summary

Serves as the base class for custom attributes.

## Type Summary

```
  public abstract class Attribute
  {
    // Constructors
       protected Attribute ();

    // Properties
MS CF  public virtual object TypeId { get; }

    // Methods
       public override bool Equals (object obj);
       public static Attribute GetCustomAttribute (Assembly element,
                                                   Type attributeType);
    MS public static Attribute GetCustomAttribute (Assembly element,
                                                   Type attributeType,
                                                   bool inherit);
       public static Attribute GetCustomAttribute (MemberInfo element,
                                                   Type attributeType);
    MS public static Attribute GetCustomAttribute (MemberInfo element,
                                                   Type attributeType,
                                                   bool inherit);
       public static Attribute GetCustomAttribute (Module element,
                                                   Type attributeType);
```

```
MS public static Attribute GetCustomAttribute (Module element,
                                                Type attributeType,
                                                bool inherit);
   public static Attribute GetCustomAttribute (ParameterInfo element,
                                                Type attributeType);
MS public static Attribute GetCustomAttribute (ParameterInfo element,
                                                Type attributeType,
                                                bool inherit);
   public static Attribute[] GetCustomAttributes (Assembly element);
MS public static Attribute[] GetCustomAttributes (Assembly element,
                                                   bool inherit);
   public static Attribute[] GetCustomAttributes (Assembly element,
                                                   Type attributeType);
MS public static Attribute[] GetCustomAttributes (Assembly element,
                                                   Type attributeType,
                                                   bool inherit);
   public static Attribute[] GetCustomAttributes (MemberInfo element);
MS public static Attribute[] GetCustomAttributes (MemberInfo element,
                                                   bool inherit);
   public static Attribute[] GetCustomAttributes (MemberInfo element,
                                                   Type type);
MS public static Attribute[] GetCustomAttributes (MemberInfo element,
                                                   Type type,
                                                   bool inherit);
   public static Attribute[] GetCustomAttributes (Module element);
MS public static Attribute[] GetCustomAttributes (Module element,
                                                   bool inherit);
   public static Attribute[] GetCustomAttributes (Module element,
                                                   Type attributeType);
MS public static Attribute[] GetCustomAttributes (Module element,
                                                   Type attributeType,
                                                   bool inherit);
   public static Attribute[] GetCustomAttributes (ParameterInfo element);
MS public static Attribute[] GetCustomAttributes (ParameterInfo element,
                                                   bool inherit);
   public static Attribute[] GetCustomAttributes (ParameterInfo element,
                                                   Type attributeType);
MS public static Attribute[] GetCustomAttributes (ParameterInfo element,
                                                   Type attributeType,
                                                   bool inherit);
   public override int GetHashCode ();
MS CF public virtual bool IsDefaultAttribute ();
   public static bool IsDefined (Assembly element,
                                 Type attributeType);
MS public static bool IsDefined (Assembly element,
                                 Type attributeType,
                                 bool inherit);
```

```
    public static bool IsDefined (MemberInfo element,
                                  Type attributeType);
 MS public static bool IsDefined (MemberInfo element,
                                  Type attributeType,
                                  bool inherit);
    public static bool IsDefined (Module element,
                                  Type attributeType);
 MS public static bool IsDefined (Module element,
                                  Type attributeType,
                                  bool inherit);
    public static bool IsDefined (ParameterInfo element,
                                  Type attributeType);
 MS public static bool IsDefined (ParameterInfo element,
                                  Type attributeType,
                                  bool inherit);
 MS public virtual bool Match (object obj);
}
```

**BA** The ability to extend the metadata format in a structured way is an important advance of the CLI. The development community has always had a need to add declarative information to code. With the advent of custom attributes, we are no longer limited to the glacially slow pace of adding new keywords to languages or the ugly and error-prone pre-processor support for adding declarative markup to code.

**JR** I agree with Brad. Custom attributes is an incredibly useful and innovative feature. I'm constantly coming up with new ways to apply them. For example, I've created my own custom attribute to help me with command-line argument parsing. I define a structure with fields and apply an instance of my attribute to each field. The attribute indicates the command-line switch letter and I implemented a method that can parse command-line arguments and set the appropriate fields in the structure. Then, the rest of my code just accesses the structure's fields. Adding new command-line switches is a breeze. I've also used attributes to localize strings for enum values and for defining strings to present for a user that correspond with programmatic values. Creative use of custom attributes can greatly simplify development effort and improve extensibility.

## Description

All attributes, whether built-in or user-defined, derive directly or indirectly from `System.Attribute`. Attributes inherit certain default behaviors: the attribute may be associated with any target element (see `System.AttributeTargets`); may or may not be inherited by a derived element; and multiple instances may or may not be allowed on the same target element. These behaviors are specified using `System.AttributeUsageAttribute`.

[*Note:* An attribute is an annotation that may be placed on an element of source code and used to store application-specific information at compile time. This information is stored in the metadata and can be accessed either during application execution, through a process known as reflection, or when another tool reads the metadata. Attributes might change the behavior of the application during execution, provide transaction information about an object, or convey organizational information to a designer.]

The CLI predefines some attribute types and uses them to control runtime behavior. Some languages predefine attribute types to represent language features not directly represented in the Common Language Specification (CLS). User-defined attribute classes, inheriting from `System.Attribute`, may also be created. The definition of such a class includes the name of the attribute, its default behavior, and the information to be stored.

## Example

```
using System;
using System.Reflection;

namespace Samples
{
  [AttributeUsage(AttributeTargets.All,
                 AllowMultiple = true,
                 Inherited = true)]
  public class AuthorAttribute: Attribute
  {
    private string familyName;
    private string givenName;
    public AuthorAttribute(string familyName)
    {
      this.familyName = familyName;
    }
    public override String ToString()
    {
      return String.Format("Author: {0} {1}",
                           familyName, givenName);
    }
    public string FamilyName
    {
      get {return familyName;}
    }
    public string GivenName
    {
      get {return givenName;}
      set {givenName = value;}
    }
  }
```

```
  [Author("Watkins", GivenName = "Damien")]
  [Author("Abrams")]
  public class AttributeSample
  {
    [Author("Abrams", GivenName = "Brad")]
    public static void Main()
    {
      Type t = typeof(AttributeSample);
      Attribute[] attributes =
           Attribute.GetCustomAttributes(t);
      foreach(Attribute a in attributes)
      {
        if(a is AuthorAttribute)
        {
          AuthorAttribute at = a as AuthorAttribute;
          Console.WriteLine("Given Name: {0}", at.GivenName);
          Console.WriteLine("Family Name: {0}", at.FamilyName);
          Console.WriteLine("------------------------------");
        }
      }
    }
  }
}
```

The output is

```
Given Name:
Family Name: Abrams
------------------------------
Given Name: Damien
Family Name: Watkins
------------------------------
```

# System AttributeTargets Enum

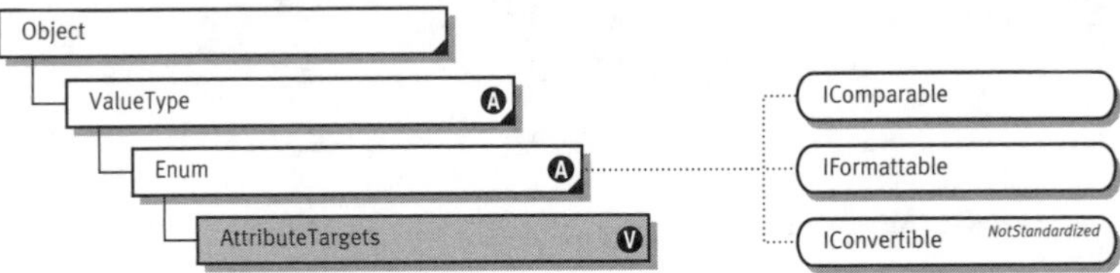


A B C D E F G H I J K L M N O P Q R S T U V W X Y Z

## Summary

Enumerates the application elements to which it is valid to attach an attribute.

## Type Summary

```
public enum AttributeTargets {
    All = Assembly | 0x2 | Class | Struct | Enum | Constructor | Method | Property |
          Field | Event | Interface | Parameter | Delegate | ReturnValue,
    Assembly = 0x1,
    Class = 0x4,
    Constructor = 0x20,
    Delegate = 0x1000,
    Enum = 0x10,
    Event = 0x200,
    Field = 0x100,
    Interface = 0x400,
    Method = 0x40,
    Module = 0x2,
    Parameter = 0x800,
    Property = 0x80,
    ReturnValue = 0x2000,
    Struct = 0x8,
}
```

**BA** This enum is intended allow members to be combined via the bitwise OR operation such that you can indicate a custom attribute on `Classes` or `Enums`; for example:

```
AttributeTargets.Class | AttributeTargets.Enum
```

You can recognize enums that were designed for this style of usage by noticing the enum name is plural (`AttributeTargets` rather than `AttributeTarget`) and by the `FlagAttribute` custom attribute applied to the type.

You might wonder why we put the hard-wired `0x2` in the `All` field. We left it in for binary compatibility with the Microsoft .NET Framework, which defines an

*CONTINUED*

enum member called `Module` with that value. The `Module` member is not required in the standard because we wanted to emphasize assembly as the smallest unit of encapsulation.

**JR** When defining your own custom attribute, be sure to apply the `AttributeUsage` attribute to it, setting the `AttributeTargets` value.

A B C D E F G H I J K L M N O P Q R S T U V W X Y Z

## Description

`System.AttributeTargets` is used as a parameter for `System.AttributeUsageAttribute` to enable an attribute to be associated with one or more kinds of application elements.

## Example

For brevity, the program only checks for the existence of one custom attibute, but for completeness, attributes are applied to most targets in the source code. The value `AttributeTargets.All` could also have been used in the following program instead of using individual values.

```
using System;
using System.Reflection;

[assembly: Samples.MyCustom]
[module: Samples.MyCustom]

namespace Samples
{
  [AttributeUsage(AttributeTargets.Assembly |
                  AttributeTargets.Class |
                  AttributeTargets.Constructor |
                  AttributeTargets.Delegate |
                  AttributeTargets.Enum |
                  AttributeTargets.Event |
                  AttributeTargets.Field |
                  AttributeTargets.Interface |
                  AttributeTargets.Module |
                  AttributeTargets.Method |
                  AttributeTargets.Parameter |
                  AttributeTargets.Property |
                  AttributeTargets.ReturnValue |
                  AttributeTargets.Struct,
          AllowMultiple = false,
          Inherited = false)]
  public class MyCustomAttribute: Attribute {}

  [AttributeUsage(AttributeTargets.Class,
```

## AttributeTargets Enum

```
        AllowMultiple = true,
        Inherited = false)]
  public class MyOtherCustomAttribute: Attribute{}

  public class Foo {}

  public interface IFoo
  {
    [MyCustom]
    int age { get;}
  }

  [MyCustom]
  public struct Bar {}

  [MyCustom, MyOtherCustom, MyOtherCustom]
  public class AttributeTargetsSample
  {
    [MyCustom]
    enum Color {black, white}
    [MyCustom]
    public delegate int D();
    [MyCustom]
    public event D MyD;
    [MyCustom]
    private int i;
    [MyCustom]
    public static void Main()
    {
      Assembly e = Assembly.GetExecutingAssembly();
      Console.WriteLine("Name: {0} ", e.FullName);
      if(Attribute.IsDefined(e, typeof(MyCustomAttribute)))
        Console.WriteLine("MyCustom attribute defined");
      else
        Console.WriteLine("MyCustom attribute not defined");
    }
    [return: MyCustom]
    public static int MyMethod([MyCustom] Foo f)
    {
      return 42;
    }
  }
}
```

The output is

```
Name: AttributeTargets, Version=0.0.0.0, Culture=neutral, PublicKeyToken=null
MyCustom attribute defined
```

# System AttributeUsageAttribute

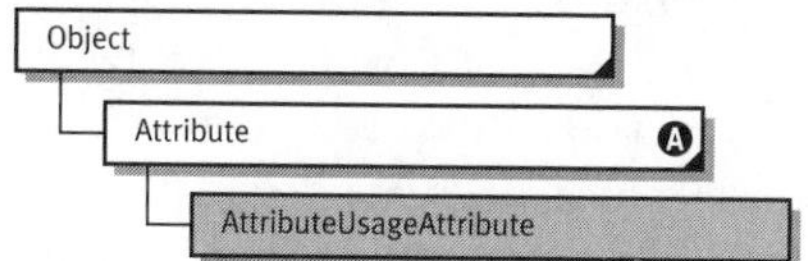




## Summary

Specifies the behavior of a custom attribute when that attribute is defined.

## Type Summary

```
public sealed class AttributeUsageAttribute : Attribute
{
  // Constructors
     public AttributeUsageAttribute (AttributeTargets validOn);

  // Properties
     public bool AllowMultiple { set; get; }
     public bool Inherited { set; get; }
     public AttributeTargets ValidOn { get; }
}
```

## Description

[*Note:* Custom attributes may be applied to various application ("target") elements, such as classes, parameters, and structures (see `System.AttributeTargets` for the full list). The `System.AttributeUsageAttribute` class contains three properties that govern custom attribute behavior: the kinds of application elements the attribute may be associated with; whether the attribute may or may not be inherited by derived elements; and whether multiple instances of the attribute may or may not be allowed on the same target element.]

A B C D E F G H I J K L M N O P Q R S T U V W X Y Z

**BA** Notice that this custom attribute is sealed. In general I am not a big fan of randomly sealing classes to prevent extensibility. (I prefer non-virtual methods for that purpose.) However, for custom attributes it is a good practice. In the .NET Framework, the reflection code path that looks up custom attributes from members is slightly faster if it does not have to consider subclasses of the target attribute.

**BG** In general, sealing a class or making members non-virtual (when appropriate) can help a JIT to inline methods. Inlining has always been a powerful optimization, but virtual methods can prevent inlining. Sealing members or leaving them non-virtual also allows you more flexibility in changing your class's implementation in the future, by limiting users' points of customization. Non-virtual members definitely have an appropriate place both as a design point and as an implementation detail for better performance.

Users defining their own custom attributes should specify the `AttributeTargetAttribute` at all times. Like this:

```
[AttributeUsage (AttributeTargets.Methods |
                AttributeTargets.Properites,
                AllowMultiple=false)]
public class MyNewAttribute : Attribute
{
    public MyNewAttribute () {}
}
```

We begrudgingly added the `AttributeTargetAttribute` to the `Attribute` class so that people subclassing `Attribute` didn't need to understand another custom attribute when creating their own custom attribute. However, this allows people using that new attribute to put the attribute in potentially surprising places. If you define an attribute to function as a marker on an assembly, your program might not work as expected if you happen to find the custom attribute applied to the return value of a method. Class library authors really need to understand and use this attribute.

## Example

For brevity, the program only checks for the existence of one custom attribute, but for completeness attributes are applied to most targets in the source code.

```
using System;
using System.Reflection;

[assembly: Samples.MyCustom]
[module: Samples.MyCustom]

namespace Samples
{
  [AttributeUsage(AttributeTargets.All,
                  AllowMultiple = false,
                  Inherited = false)]
  public class MyCustomAttribute: Attribute {}

  public class Foo {}

  public interface IFoo
  {
    [MyCustom]
    int age { get;}
  }

  [MyCustom]
  public struct Bar {}

  [MyCustom]
  public class AttributeUsageSample
  {
    [MyCustom]
    enum Color {black, white}
    [MyCustom]
    public delegate int D();
    [MyCustom]
    public event D MyD;
    [MyCustom]
    private int i;
    [MyCustom]
    public static void Main()
    {
      Assembly e = Assembly.GetExecutingAssembly();
      Console.WriteLine("Name: {0} ", e.FullName);
      if(Attribute.IsDefined(e, typeof(MyCustomAttribute)))
        Console.WriteLine("MyCustom attribute defined");
      else
```

```
        Console.WriteLine("MyCustom attribute not defined");
    }
    [return: MyCustom]
    public static int MyMethod([MyCustom] Foo f)
    {
      return 42;
    }
  }
}
```

The output is

```
Name: AttributeUsageAttribute, Version=0.0.0.0, Culture=neutral,
PublicKeyToken=null
MyCustom attribute defined
```

# System
# Boolean Structure

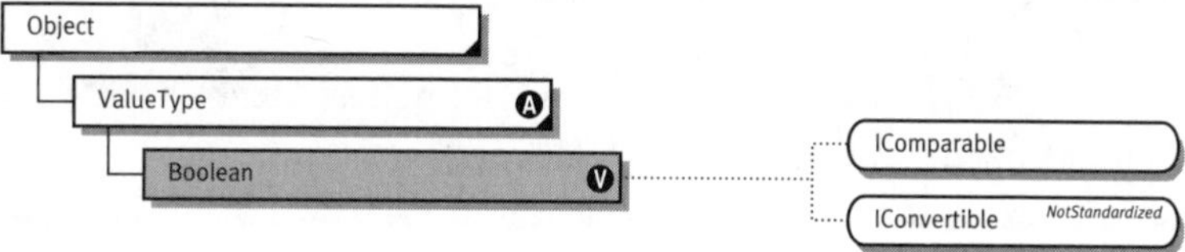


A B C D E F G H I J K L M N O P Q R S T U V W X Y Z

## Summary

Represents a Boolean value.

## Type Summary

```
public struct Boolean : IComparable, IConvertible
{
  // Fields
     public static readonly string FalseString = "False";
     public static readonly string TrueString = "True";

  // Methods
     public int CompareTo (object obj);
     public override bool Equals (object obj);
     public override int GetHashCode ();
  MS public TypeCode GetTypeCode ();
     public static bool Parse (string value);
     public override string ToString ();
     public string ToString (IFormatProvider provider);

  // Explicit Interface Members
  MS bool IConvertible.ToBoolean(IFormatProvider provider);
  MS byte IConvertible.ToByte(IFormatProvider provider);
  MS char IConvertible.ToChar(IFormatProvider provider);
  MS DateTime IConvertible.ToDateTime(IFormatProvider provider);
  MS decimal IConvertible.ToDecimal(IFormatProvider provider);
  MS double IConvertible.ToDouble(IFormatProvider provider);
  MS short IConvertible.ToInt16(IFormatProvider provider);
  MS int IConvertible.ToInt32(IFormatProvider provider);
  MS long IConvertible.ToInt64(IFormatProvider provider);
  MS sbyte IConvertible.ToSByte(IFormatProvider provider);
  MS float IConvertible.ToSingle(IFormatProvider provider);
  MS object IConvertible.ToType(Type type,IFormatProvider provider);
  MS ushort IConvertible.ToUInt16(IFormatProvider provider);
  MS uint IConvertible.ToUInt32(IFormatProvider provider);
  MS ulong IConvertible.ToUInt64(IFormatProvider provider);
}
```

Boolean Structure

JR Note that Parse performs a case-insensitive comparison against "true" or "false."

Note that FalseString and TrueString are defined as "True" and "False"; the strings are not localized.



## Description

The System.Boolean value type represents the logical values true and false.

## Example

```
using System;

namespace Samples
{
  public class BooleanSample
  {
    public static void Main()
    {
      Boolean b = true;
      if(b)
        Console.WriteLine("'b' is true");
      b = false;
      if(!b)
        Console.WriteLine("'b' is not true now");
    }
  }
}
```

The output is

```
'b' is true
'b' is not true now
```

# System
# Byte Structure

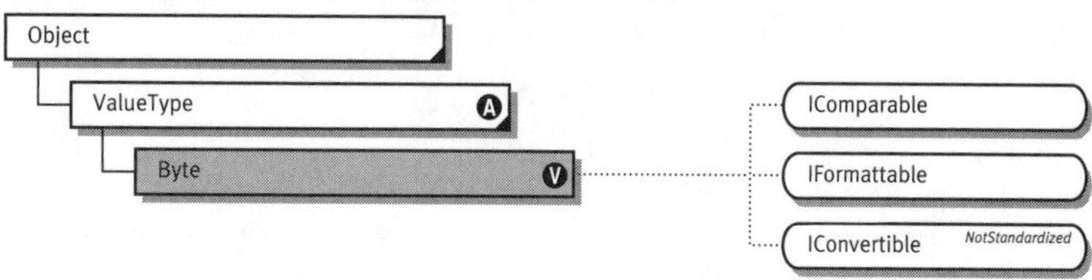


## Summary

Represents an 8-bit unsigned integer.

## Type Summary

```
public struct Byte : IComparable, IFormattable,
                     IConvertible
{
  // Fields
     public const byte MaxValue = 255;
     public const byte MinValue = 0;

  // Methods
     public int CompareTo (object value);
     public override bool Equals (object obj);
     public override int GetHashCode ();
  MS public TypeCode GetTypeCode ();
     public static byte Parse (string s);
     public static byte Parse (string s, NumberStyles style);
     public static byte Parse (string s, NumberStyles style,
                               IFormatProvider provider);
  CF public static byte Parse (string s, IFormatProvider provider);
     public override string ToString ();
     public string ToString (string format);
     public string ToString (string format, IFormatProvider provider);
     public string ToString (IFormatProvider provider);

  // Explicit Interface Members
  MS bool IConvertible.ToBoolean(IFormatProvider provider);
  MS byte IConvertible.ToByte(IFormatProvider provider);
  MS char IConvertible.ToChar(IFormatProvider provider);
  MS DateTime IConvertible.ToDateTime(IFormatProvider provider);
  MS decimal IConvertible.ToDecimal(IFormatProvider provider);
  MS double IConvertible.ToDouble(IFormatProvider provider);
  MS short IConvertible.ToInt16(IFormatProvider provider);
  MS int IConvertible.ToInt32(IFormatProvider provider);
  MS long IConvertible.ToInt64(IFormatProvider provider);
  MS sbyte IConvertible.ToSByte(IFormatProvider provider);
  MS float IConvertible.ToSingle(IFormatProvider provider);
```

Byte Structure

```
    MS object IConvertible.ToType(Type type,IFormatProvider provider);
    MS ushort IConvertible.ToUInt16(IFormatProvider provider);
    MS uint IConvertible.ToUInt32(IFormatProvider provider);
    MS ulong IConvertible.ToUInt64(IFormatProvider provider);
  }
```

**BA** The naming of this class diverges from our pattern for naming integral base types. Strictly following the pattern would have led us to naming this class `UInt8`. How ugly that would have been for such a commonly used type! After much debate we decided that bytes are so commonly mentioned in our APIs (`ReadByte`, `WriteByte` on `Stream`, for example) that it warranted having a good name for the base type even though it meant breaking the naming pattern. Similarly we include `Byte` rather than `SByte` in the Common Language Specification because it is much more common to view bytes as unsigned 0..255 values than –128..127 values.

## Description

The `System.Byte` data type represents integer values ranging from 0 to positive 255 (hexadecimal 0xFF).

## Example

```
using System;

namespace Samples
{
  public class ByteSample
  {
    public static void Main()
    {
      byte b = Byte.MaxValue;
      Console.WriteLine("MaxValue is {0}", b);
      Console.WriteLine("MaxValue.GetHashCode is {0}",
                        b.GetHashCode());
      b = Byte.MinValue;
      Console.WriteLine("MinValue is {0}", b);
      Console.WriteLine("MinValue.GetHashCode is {0}",
                        b.GetHashCode());
      string s = Byte.MaxValue.ToString();
      b = Byte.Parse(s);
      Console.WriteLine(b);
    }
  }
}
```

Byte Structure

The output is

```
MaxValue is 255
MaxValue.GetHashCode is 255
MinValue is 0
MinValue.GetHashCode is 0
255
```

BCL

# System
# Char Structure

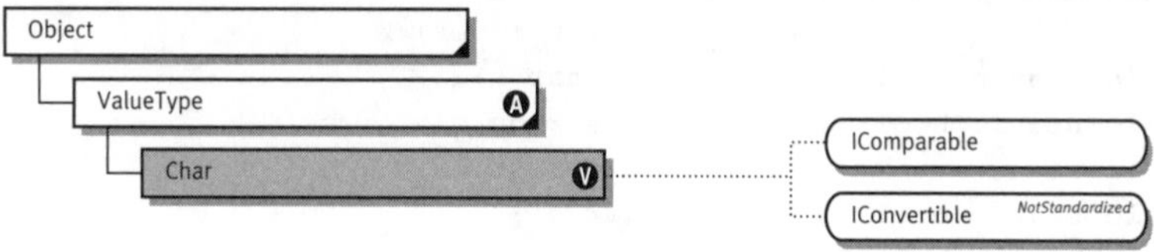


A B C D E F G H I J K L M N O P Q R S T U V W X Y Z

## Summary

Represents a Unicode character.

## Type Summary

```
public struct Char : IComparable, IConvertible
{
  // Fields
     public const char MaxValue = = (char)0xFFFF
     public const char MinValue = = (char)0x0

  // Methods
     public int CompareTo (object value);
     public override bool Equals (object obj);
     public override int GetHashCode ();
     public static double GetNumericValue (char c);
  CF public static double GetNumericValue (string s,
                                           int index);
  MS public TypeCode GetTypeCode ();
     public static UnicodeCategory GetUnicodeCategory (char c);
  CF public static UnicodeCategory GetUnicodeCategory (string s,
                                                       int index);
     public static bool IsControl (char c);
  CF public static bool IsControl (string s,
                                   int index);
     public static bool IsDigit (char c);
  CF public static bool IsDigit (string s, int index);
     public static bool IsLetter (char c);
  CF public static bool IsLetter (string s, int index);
     public static bool IsLetterOrDigit (char c);
  CF public static bool IsLetterOrDigit (string s,
                                         int index);
     public static bool IsLower (char c);
  CF public static bool IsLower (string s, int index);
     public static bool IsNumber (char c);
     public static bool IsNumber (string s, int index);
     public static bool IsPunctuation (char c);
  CF public static bool IsPunctuation (string s,
                                       int index);
```

Char Structure

```
CF public static bool IsSeparator (char c);
CF public static bool IsSeparator (string s,
                                   int index);
CF public static bool IsSurrogate (char c);
CF public static bool IsSurrogate (string s,
                                   int index);
CF public static bool IsSymbol (char c);
CF public static bool IsSymbol (string s, int index);
   public static bool IsUpper (char c);
CF public static bool IsUpper (string s, int index);
   public static bool IsWhiteSpace (char c);
CF public static bool IsWhiteSpace (string s,
                                    int index);
CF public static char Parse (string s);
   public static char ToLower (char c);
MS public static char ToLower (char c, CultureInfo culture);
   public override string ToString ();
MS public static string ToString (char c);
   public string ToString (IFormatProvider provider);
   public static char ToUpper (char c);
MS public static char ToUpper (char c, CultureInfo culture);

// Explicit Interface Members
MS bool IConvertible.ToBoolean(IFormatProvider provider);
MS byte IConvertible.ToByte(IFormatProvider provider);
MS char IConvertible.ToChar(IFormatProvider provider);
MS DateTime IConvertible.ToDateTime(IFormatProvider provider);
MS decimal IConvertible.ToDecimal(IFormatProvider provider);
MS double IConvertible.ToDouble(IFormatProvider provider);
MS short IConvertible.ToInt16(IFormatProvider provider);
MS int IConvertible.ToInt32(IFormatProvider provider);
MS long IConvertible.ToInt64(IFormatProvider provider);
MS sbyte IConvertible.ToSByte(IFormatProvider provider);
MS float IConvertible.ToSingle(IFormatProvider provider);
MS object IConvertible.ToType(Type type,IFormatProvider provider);
MS ushort IConvertible.ToUInt16(IFormatProvider provider);
MS uint IConvertible.ToUInt32(IFormatProvider provider);
MS ulong IConvertible.ToUInt64(IFormatProvider provider);
}
```

Char Structure

> **BA** In the design of this type we debated having all the predicates (IsXxx methods) in this class, versus putting them in another class. In the end we felt the simplicity of having just one class for all these operations made it worthwhile.
>
> **JR** Note that `Char` is not the most accurate name for this type. A `Char` is really a UTF-16 code point, which will be a character unless the code point represents a high or low surrogate value. A string is really a set of UTF-16 code points. To properly traverse the characters of a string, you should use the `System.Globalization.StringInfo` class's methods.



## Description

The `System.Char` value type represents Unicode characters, with code points ranging from 0 to 65,535. [*Note:* The *code point* of a Unicode character is that character's 2-byte, encoded value.]

[*Note:* The `System.Globalization.UnicodeCategory` enumeration describes the categories that a Unicode character can be mapped to. For information on mapping specific Unicode characters to Unicode categories, see the UnicodeData.txt file in the Unicode Character Database at http://www.unicode.org/Public/UNIDATA/UnicodeCharacterDatabase.html. The UnicodeData.txt file format is described at http://www.unicode.org/Public/3.1-Update/UnicodeData-3.1.0.html.]

## Example

```
using System;

namespace Samples
{
  public class CharSample
  {
    public static void Main()
    {
      Console.WriteLine("Char.MaxValue is {0}",
                        (int) Char.MaxValue);
      Console.WriteLine("MaxValue hash code {0}",
                        Char.MaxValue.GetHashCode());
      Console.WriteLine("Char.MinValue is {0}",
                        (int) Char.MinValue);
      Console.WriteLine("MinValue hash code {0}",
                        Char.MinValue.GetHashCode());
      Char c = '3';
      double d = Char.GetNumericValue(c);
      Console.WriteLine("Char '{0}' has numeric value: {1}",
                        c, d);
```

Char Structure

```
            c = Convert.ToChar(0X00BC);
            d = Char.GetNumericValue(c);
            Console.WriteLine("Char '{0}' has numeric value: {1}",
                              c, d);
            c = 'A';
            d = Char.GetNumericValue(c);
            Console.WriteLine("Char '{0}' has numeric value: {1}",
                              c, d);
            c = '3';
            Console.WriteLine("Char '{0}' is a digit: {1}",
                              c, Char.IsDigit(c));
            c = 'B';
            Console.WriteLine("Char '{0}' is a digit: {1}",
                              c, Char.IsDigit(c));
        }
    }
}
```

The output is

```
Char.MaxValue is 65535
MaxValue hash code -1
Char.MinValue is 0
MinValue hash code 0
Char '3' has numeric value: 3
Char '¼' has numeric value: 0.25
Char 'A' has numeric value: -1
Char '3' is a digit: True
Char 'B' is a digit: False
```

# System CharEnumerator

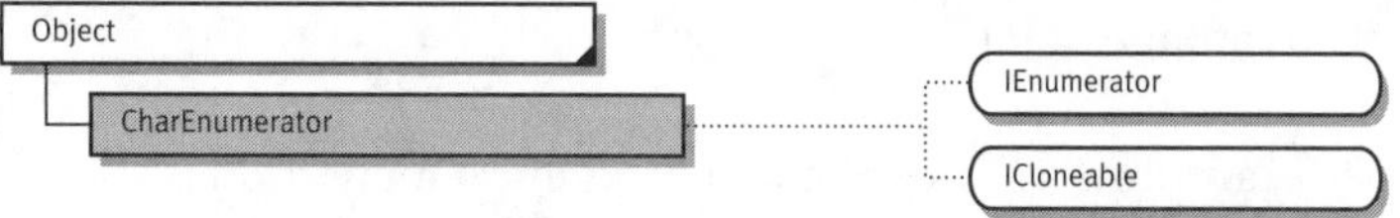




## Summary

Supports iteration over and provides read-only access to the individual characters in a `System.String`.

## Type Summary

```
public sealed class CharEnumerator : IEnumerator,
                                     ICloneable
{
  // Properties
     public char Current { get; }

  // Methods
     public object Clone ();
     public bool MoveNext ();
     public void Reset ();

  // Explicit Interface Members
     object IEnumerator.Current { get; }
}
```

**BA** Our reason for adding this class to the BCL was not that we felt there was a huge demand for enumerating characters. It was required to enable efficient support for applying `foreach` over strings. Simply using `IEnumerator` would have caused a boxing operation for each character accessed out of the string.

```
string s = "John Smith";
foreach (char c in  s) {
   Console.WriteLine ("{0}-", c);
}
```

A side note on this is that the C# compiler now does not even use this class. It special-cases `foreach` over strings and generates very efficient code for accessing a string that not only avoids the boxing operation, but is also as good as you could do with a

*CONTINUED*

A B C D E F G H I J K L M N O P Q R S T U V W X Y Z

for loop. In particular it does not pay the cost of another allocation for the enumerator, and takes full advantage of JIT optimizations.

This is a classic example of why explicit method implementation is such an important feature. Notice that we have both:

```
object IEnumerator.Current { get; }
public char Current { get; }
```

We needed to have `Current` property return `Object` to satisfy the `IEnumerator` interface. But we also wanted to have a `Current` property that returned a `char` such that usage of this type would not force a boxing operation for each access and to make usage easier (no ugly casts). However in C# (and the CLS) it is not possible to differ only by return type. So we explicitly implement the `Object` version such that the property is only there when cast to the interface.

**BG** The key point to understand about private interface implementation (using the C# terminology although it is more properly a subset of the CLI feature we call `methodimpls`) is that it allows you to override an interface method based on its return type. While it also allows you to provide different method implementations for two different versions of a method coming from different interfaces, in practice most people try to avoid problems like this. Multiple inheritance of interfaces, but not classes, seems to make the classic diamond inheritance pattern rarer, or at least significantly less confusing.

## Description

[*Note:* `System.CharEnumerator` is used to support the `foreach` statement of the C# programming language. Several independent instances of `System.CharEnumerator` across one or more threads can have access to a single instance of `System.String`. For more information regarding the use of an enumerator, see `System.Collections.IEnumerator`.]

## Example

```
using System;

namespace Samples
{
  public class CharEnumeratorSample
  {
    public static void Main()
    {
      string s = "Hello world!";
```

```
      CharEnumerator e = s.GetEnumerator();
      while(e.MoveNext())
        Console.Write(e.Current);
      Console.WriteLine();
    }
  }
}
```

The output is

```
Hello world!
```

# System CLSCompliantAttribute

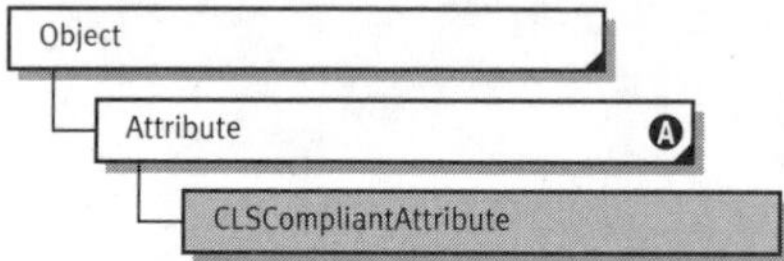




## Summary

Indicates whether the target of the current attribute complies with the Common Language Specification (CLS).

## Type Summary

```
public sealed class CLSCompliantAttribute : Attribute
{
  // Constructors
     public CLSCompliantAttribute (bool isCompliant);

  // Properties
     public bool IsCompliant { get; }
}
```

**BA** Unfortunately, we codified the naming convention for acronyms too late to fix this one. It should have been `ClsCompliantAttribute` rather than `CLSCompliantAttribute`.

Notice that this attribute is just a marker intended for compilers to enforce. The runtime does enforce any CLS-compliance rules.

**JR** Note that the CLS only applies to publicly exposed members so compilers generally only check CLS-compliance of types and members that are exposed outside of an assembly. Internal types and private methods, for example, are not checked for CLS compliance.

## Description

If no `System.CLSCompliantAttribute` is associated with a given assembly, that assembly is assumed not to be CLS-compliant.

A type is assumed to be CLS-compliant if and only if its enclosing type (for nested types) or assembly (for top-level types) is CLS-compliant. Other members (methods, fields, properties, and events) are CLS-compliant if and only if the type in which they are defined is CLS-compliant.

[*Note:* The CLS is a subset of CLI features that is supported by a broad set of compliant languages and tools. CLS-compliant languages and tools are guaranteed to interoperate with other CLS-compliant languages and tools. Because the CLS defines the rules for language interoperability, its rules apply only to "externally visible" items. The CLS assumes that language interoperability is important only across the assembly boundary — that is, within a single assembly there are no restrictions as to the programming techniques that are used. Thus, the CLS rules apply only to items that are visible outside of their defining assembly and have public, family, or family-or-assembly accessibility. For more information on CLS-compliance, see Partition I of the CLI Specification. This attribute can be applied to any valid attribute target. For a complete list of valid targets, see `System.AttributeTargets`.]



## Example

```
using System;

[assembly: CLSCompliant(true)]

namespace Samples
{
  public class CLSCompliantSample
  {
    public static void Main()
    {
    }
    public static uint Method1(uint i)
    {
      return i;
    }
  }
}
```

The compiler output is

```
Microsoft (R) Program Maintenance Utility Version 7.00.9466
Copyright (C) Microsoft Corporation.  All rights reserved.

        csc /debug CLSCompliantAttribute.cs
Microsoft (R) Visual C# .NET Compiler version 7.00.9466
for Microsoft (R) .NET Framework version 1.0.3705
Copyright (C) Microsoft Corporation 2001. All rights reserved.

CLSCompliantAttribute.cs(12,32): error CS3001: Argument type 'uint' is not
        CLS-compliant
CLSCompliantAttribute.cs(12,19): error CS3002: Return type of
        'Samples.CLSCompliantSample.Method1(uint)' is not CLS-compliant
NMAKE : fatal error U1077: 'csc' : return code '0x1'
Stop.
```

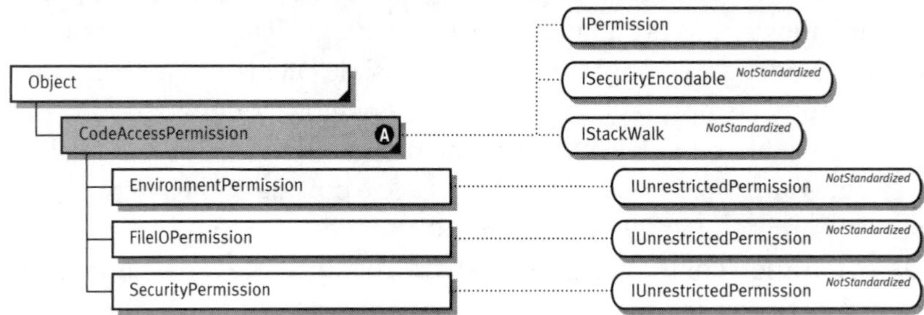


## Summary

Serves as the base class for all code access permissions.

## Type Summary

```
   CF public abstract class CodeAccessPermission : IPermission,
                                                    ISecurityEncodable,
                                                    IStackWalk
   {
     // Constructors
     CF protected CodeAccessPermission ();

     // Methods
     CF public void Assert ();
     CF public abstract IPermission Copy ();
     CF public void Demand ();
     CF public void Deny ();
     CF public abstract void FromXml (SecurityElement elem);
     CF public abstract IPermission Intersect (IPermission target);
     CF public abstract bool IsSubsetOf (IPermission target);
  MS CF public void PermitOnly ();
  MS CF public static void RevertAll ();
  MS CF public static void RevertAssert ();
  MS CF public static void RevertDeny ();
  MS CF public static void RevertPermitOnly ();
     CF public override string ToString ();
     CF public abstract SecurityElement ToXml ();
     CF public virtual IPermission Union (IPermission other);
   }
```

**BA** Notice the use of `SecurityElement` in this class. We did not use `System.Xml.XmlElement` because it is defined in a different assembly, and the base MSCorlib assembly is not allowed to make references to any other assembly.

**AH** Our basic XML APIs should have been in mscorlib from day one. XML is core to almost everything we do in the platform and not being able to use them in the lowest level of the library has been a problem.

A B C D E F G H I J K L M N O P Q R S T U V W X Y Z

## Description

[*Note:* Classes derived from `System.Security.CodeAccessPermission` are required to override the following methods of the `System.Security.CodeAccessPermission` class. In addition, classes derived from `System.Security.CodeAccessPermission` are required to implement a constructor that takes a `System.Security.Permissions.PermissionState` as its only parameter.]

The XML encoding of a `System.Security.CodeAccessPermission` instance is defined below in EBNF format. The following conventions are used:

- All non-literals in the grammar below are shown in normal type.
- All literals are in bold font.
- The following meta-language symbols are used:
  - '*' represents a meta-language symbol suffixing an expression that can appear zero or more times.
  - '?' represents a meta-language symbol suffixing an expression that can appear zero or one time.
  - '+' represents a meta-language symbol suffixing an expression that can appear one or more times.
  - '(',')' is used to group literals, non-literals, or a mixture of literals and non-literals.
  - '|' denotes an exclusive disjunction between two expressions.
  - '::= ' denotes a production rule where a left-hand non-literal is replaced by a right-hand expression containing literals, non-literals, or both.
- ClassName is the name of the class implementing the permission, such as `System.Security.Permissions.EnvironmentPermission`.
- AssemblyName is the name of the assembly that contains the class implementing the permission, such as mscorlib.
- Version is the three-part version number indicating the version of the assembly implementing the permission, such as 1.0.1.
- StrongNamePublicKeyToken is the strong name public key token constituting the strong name of the assembly that implements the permission.

- PermissionAttributes is any attribute and attribute value on the `System.Security.IPermission` element used by the permission to represent a particular permission state, for example, unrestricted "`true`".
- PermissionXML is any valid XML used by the permission to represent permission state.

The XML encoding of a `System.Security.CodeAccessPermission` instance is as follows:

```
CodeAccessPermissionXML::=
<IPermission class="
ClassName,
AssemblyName,
Version=Version,
Culture=neutral,
PublicKeyToken=StrongNamePublicKeyToken"
version="1"
(PermissionAttributes)*
>
(PermissionXML)?
</IPermission>
```

## Example

`CodeAccessPermission` is an abstract class, see derived classes for more examples.

```
using System;
using System.Security;
using System.Security.Permissions;

namespace Samples
{
  public class CodeAccessPermissionSample
  {
    public static void Main()
    {
      string ev = "USERNAME";
      EnvironmentPermission p =
             new EnvironmentPermission(
                     EnvironmentPermissionAccess.Read,
                     ev);
      p.Assert();
      TestAccess(ev);
      CodeAccessPermission.RevertAssert();
      p.Deny();
      TestAccess(ev);
      CodeAccessPermission.RevertDeny();
      p.PermitOnly();
```

```
      TestAccess(ev);
    }
    public static void TestAccess(string s)
    {
      try
      {
         Console.WriteLine("Variable {0} Value: {1}", s,
                 Environment.GetEnvironmentVariable(s));
      }
      catch(Exception)
      {
        Console.WriteLine("Variable {0} cannot be read", s);
      }
    }
  }
}
```

The output is

```
Variable USERNAME Value: damien
Variable USERNAME cannot be read
Variable USERNAME Value: damien
```

# System.Security.Permissions CodeAccessSecurityAttribute

BCL

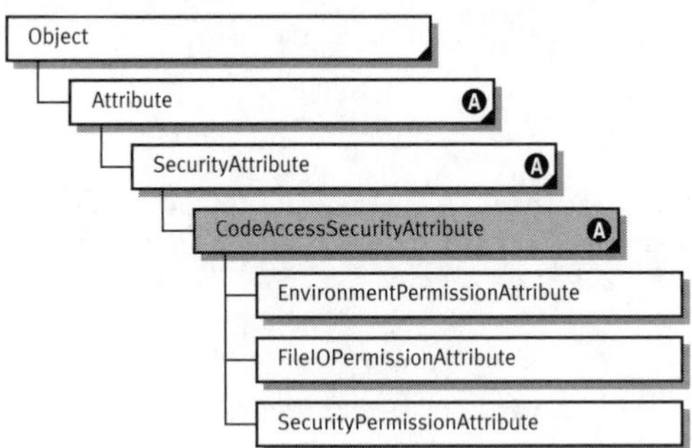


A B C D E F G H I J K L M N O P Q R S T U V W X Y Z

## Summary

This is the base class for code access security attributes.

## Type Summary

```
CF public abstract class CodeAccessSecurityAttribute : SecurityAttribute
   {
   // Constructors
   CF public CodeAccessSecurityAttribute (SecurityAction action);
   }
```

## Description

[*Note:* The types that derive from `System.Security.Permissions.CodeAccessSecurityAttribute` are used to secure access to resources or securable operations. The security information declared by a security attribute is stored in the metadata of the attribute target, and is accessed by the system at runtime. Security attributes are used for declarative security only. Use the corresponding permission class derived from `System.Security.CodeAccessPermission` for imperative security.]

## Example

`CodeAccessSecurityAttribute` is an abstract class; see derived classes for more examples.

```
using System;
using System.Security;
using System.Security.Permissions;

[assembly:EnvironmentPermissionAttribute(
            SecurityAction.RequestMinimum,
            Read="COMPUTERNAME;USERNAME")]
```

```
namespace Samples
{
  public class EnvironmentPermissionAttributeSample
  {
    public static void Main()
    {
      string[] v = {"USERNAME", "COMPUTERNAME"};
      foreach(string s in v)
        Console.WriteLine("Variable {0} Value: {1}",
                  s,
                  Environment.GetEnvironmentVariable(s));
    }
  }
}
```

The output is

```
Variable USERNAME Value: damien
Variable COMPUTERNAME Value: PROJECT42
```

# System.Collections
# Comparer

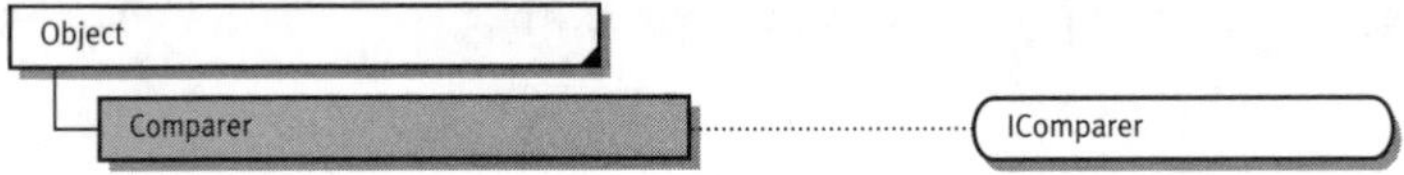




## Summary

Provides the default implementation of the `System.Collections.IComparer` interface.

## Type Summary

```
public sealed class Comparer : IComparer
{
  // Constructors
  MS public Comparer(CultureInfo culture);

  // Fields
     public static readonly Comparer Default;
  MS public static readonly Comparer DefaultInvariant;

  // Methods
     public int Compare(object a,object b);
}
```

## Example

```
using System;
using System.Collections;

namespace Samples
{
  public class ComparerSamples
  {
    public static void Main()
    {
      Comparer c = Comparer.Default;
      string a = "apples", o = "oranges";
      Console.WriteLine(
        "Comparing {0} to {1} returns {2}",
        a, o, c.Compare(a, o));
    }
  }
}
```

The output is

```
Comparing apples to oranges returns -1
```

# System.Diagnostics ConditionalAttribute

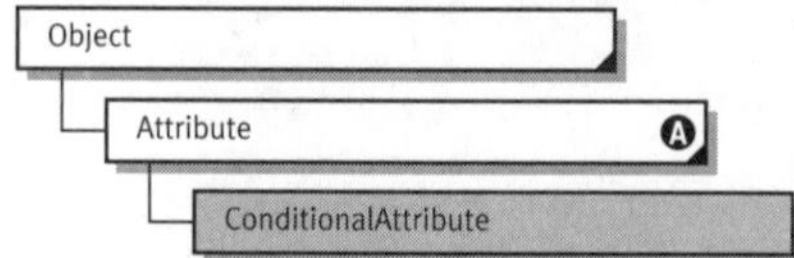


A B C D E F G H I J K L M N O P Q R S T U V W X Y Z

## Summary

Indicates to compilers that a method is callable if and only if a specified pre-processing identifier has been defined on the method.

## Type Summary

```
public sealed class ConditionalAttribute : Attribute
{
  // Constructors
     public ConditionalAttribute (string conditionString);

  // Properties
     public string ConditionString { get; }
}
```

**BA** There is a common misconception with usage of this custom attribute. By applying the `ConditionalAttribute` on a method you indicate that calls to that method should be removed by the compiler if the `conditionString` is defined. However, the method body is always compiled into the assembly regardless of whether the `conditionString` is defined or not.

**BG** This is another clever custom attribute, which works similarly to C-style pre-processor directives but in reverse. Calls to methods with this attribute are conditionally compiled into source code, depending on whether the given symbol is defined at compile time. For debugging or tracing code, this means you simply add this attribute to the method you want to call conditionally, instead of putting `#if FOO` ... `#endif` all throughout your code.

**JR** The `ConditionalAttribute` can be applied to methods that return `void` only.

Note that any expressions that are evaluated when calling a conditional method are not evaluated if the method is not called. For example, in the following code, `GetString` *and* `Foo` are not called if "xx" is not defined:

CONTINUED

```
using System;
using System.Diagnostics;

class App {
   static void Main() {
      Foo(GetString());
   }

   static String GetString() { return "Jeff"; }

   [Conditional("xx")]
   static void Foo(String s) { Console.WriteLine(s); }
}
```

If you examined the IL produced by the compiler for `Main`, you'd see that it contains just one IL instruction: `ret`.

## Description

[*Note:* A `System.Diagnostics.ConditionalAttribute`, which has an associated condition `System.Diagnostics.ConditionalAttribute.ConditionString`, can be attached to the definition of a method, creating a *conditionalmethod*. Thereafter, when a compiler encounters a call to that method, it may choose to ignore the call unless a compilation variable is defined at the site of the call, with a value that matches in a case-sensitive manner the `System.Diagnostics.ConditionalAttribute.ConditionString` supplied to the `System.Diagnostics.ConditionalAttribute`. Note that compilers may provide several techniques to define such compilation variables, such as: CLS-Compliant compilers are permitted to ignore uses of the `System.Diagnostics.ConditionalAttribute`.]

## Example

```
#undef A

using System;
using System.Diagnostics;

namespace Samples
{
  public class MyClass
  {
    [ConditionalAttribute("A")]
    public static void Display()
    {
```

```
      Console.WriteLine("A was defined");
    }
  }
  public class ConditionalAttributeSample
  {
    public static void Main()
    {
      MyClass.Display();
      Console.WriteLine("Done");
    }
  }
}
```

The output is

```
Done
```

# System Console

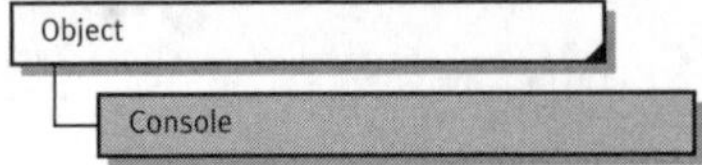




## Summary

Represents the standard input, output, and error streams for console applications.

## Type Summary

```
public sealed class Console
{
  // Properties
  CF public static TextWriter Error { get; }
  CF public static TextReader In { get; }
  CF public static TextWriter Out { get; }

  // Methods
  CF public static Stream OpenStandardError ();
  CF public static Stream OpenStandardError (int bufferSize);
  CF public static Stream OpenStandardInput ();
  CF public static Stream OpenStandardInput (int bufferSize);
  CF public static Stream OpenStandardOutput ();
  CF public static Stream OpenStandardOutput (int bufferSize);
  CF public static int Read ();
     public static string ReadLine ();
  CF public static void SetError (TextWriter newError);
  CF public static void SetIn (TextReader newIn);
  CF public static void SetOut (TextWriter newOut);
  CF public static void Write (bool value);
     public static void Write (char value);
     public static void Write (char[] buffer);
     public static void Write (char[] buffer,
                               int index, int count);
  CF public static void Write (decimal value);
  CF public static void Write (double value);
  CF public static void Write (float value);
     public static void Write (int value);
  CF public static void Write (long value);
     public static void Write (object value);
     public static void Write (string value);
     public static void Write (string format,
                               object arg0);
     public static void Write (string format,
                               object arg0, object arg1);
     public static void Write (string format,
                               object arg0, object arg1,
```

```
                                    object arg2);
      public static void Write (string format,
                                    params object[] arg);
   CF public static void Write (uint value);
   CF public static void Write (ulong value);
      public static void WriteLine ();
   CF public static void WriteLine (bool value);
      public static void WriteLine (char value);
      public static void WriteLine (char[] buffer);
   CF public static void WriteLine (char[] buffer,
                                    int index,
                                    int count);
   CF public static void WriteLine (decimal value);
   CF public static void WriteLine (double value);
   CF public static void WriteLine (float value);
      public static void WriteLine (int value);
   CF public static void WriteLine (long value);
      public static void WriteLine (object value);
      public static void WriteLine (string value);
      public static void WriteLine (string format,
                                    object arg0);
      public static void WriteLine (string format,
                                    object arg0,
                                    object arg1);
      public static void WriteLine (string format,
                                    object arg0,
                                    object arg1,
                                    object arg2);
      public static void WriteLine (string format,
                                    params object[] arg);
   CF public static void WriteLine (uint value);
   CF public static void WriteLine (ulong value);
}
```

**BA** Notice the heavy use of method overloading in this class. We special-case each of the primitive types in order to avoid boxing overhead. We could have gotten away with just having the overload that takes the object, but then calls such as these would cause an extra allocation for the coercion to object:

```
Console.WriteLine (42);
```

and

```
Console.WriteLine ('c');
```

*CONTINUED*

In general this kind of special casing is not necessary, but for a class that is likely to be used in a tight loop it can be very helpful.

This class is a classic example of "design in reverse." Before we designed this class we knew what we wanted the Hello World example to look like:

```
Console.WriteLine ("Hello World");
```

We then created this class to make that sample code a reality. Even in the face of the full complexity of a well-factored I/O system, we kept the simple things simple.

**AH** It is interesting to note that all of the `Console.WriteXxx()` methods are just shorthand for `Console.Out.WriteXxx()`. Likewise, `Console.ReadXxx()` is shorthand for `Console.In.ReadXxx()`. This design enables the `In` and `Out` streams to be available directly in the rare cases where they are needed but does not complicate the simple usage with them.

**BG** The `OpenStandardXxx` methods that take an integer for the buffer size are really rather useless. We eventually decided that supporting buffering on the streams used for `Console` is a silly notion, especially since classes like `StreamReader` and `StreamWriter` may internally do their own buffering.

**KG** Note that there is no easy way for a user to get a single key press: Return has to be pressed before `Read` or `ReadLine` complete. This did not seem like a critical scenario when we designed this class originally, but it is interesting to note that this has been one of our top requests for the `Console` class since Version 1 was released.

## Description

The `System.Console` class provides basic input and output support for applications that read from and write characters to the console. If the console does not exist, as in a GUI application, writing to the console produces no result, and no exception is raised.

The standard input, output, and error streams are represented by properties, and are automatically associated with the console when the application starts. Applications can redirect these properties to other streams; for example, streams associated with files instead of the console. [*Note:* For additional information see the `System.Console.SetIn`, `System.Console.SetOut`, and `System.Console.SetError` methods.] By default, the read methods in this class use the standard input stream and the write methods use the standard output stream.

The write methods support writing data with or without automatically appending carriage return and linefeed characters. This enables the writing of strings, formatted strings, arrays of characters, instances of primitive types, and arbitrary objects without first having to convert them to strings.

This class uses synchronized `System.IO.TextReader` and `System.IO.TextWriter` instances. Multiple threads can concurrently read from and/or write to an instance of this type.

## Example

```
using System;

namespace Samples
{
  public class ConsoleSample
  {
    public static void Main()
    {
      Console.WriteLine("Write a string {0}",
                        "Hello world!");
      Console.WriteLine("Write a number {0}", 42);
      Console.WriteLine("Please enter your name:");
      string name = Console.ReadLine();
      Console.WriteLine("Hello {0}", name);
      Console.Error.WriteLine("Errors go here by default");
      Console.WriteLine("Date: {0:dd/MM/yy}", DateTime.Now);
      int i = -42;
      Console.WriteLine("{0:0000}, {1, -20}, {2, 20}.", i, i, i);
      Console.WriteLine("{0:X}, {1:C}, {2:G}.", i, i, i);
    }
  }
}
```

The output is

```
Write a string Hello world!
Write a number 42
Please enter your name:
damien
Hello damien
Errors go here by default
Date: 05/06/03
-0042, -42                  ,                   -42.
FFFFFFD6, -$42.00, -42.
```

# System
# Convert

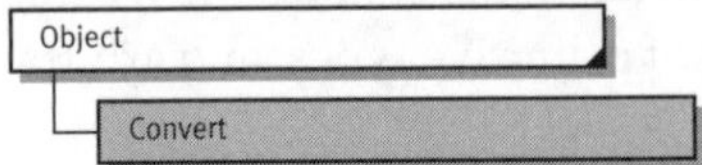


A B C D E F G H I J K L M N O P Q R S T U V W X Y Z

## Summary

Performs conversions between base data types.

## Type Summary

```
public sealed class Convert
{
  // Fields
  MS public static readonly object DBNull = DBNull.Value;

  // Methods
MS CF public static object ChangeType (object value,
                                       TypeCode typeCode);
  MS public static object ChangeType (object value,
                                       TypeCode typeCode,
                                       IFormatProvider provider);
MS CF public static object ChangeType (object value,
                                       Type conversionType);
  MS public static object ChangeType (object value,
                                       Type conversionType,
                                       IFormatProvider provider);
  MS public static byte[] FromBase64CharArray (char[] inArray,
                                                int offset,
                                                int length);
  MS public static byte[] FromBase64String (string s);
  MS public static TypeCode GetTypeCode (object value);
  MS public static bool IsDBNull (object value);
  MS public static int ToBase64CharArray (byte[] inArray,
                                          int offsetIn,
                                          int length,
                                          char[] outArray,
                                          int offsetOut);
MS CF public static string ToBase64String (byte[] inArray);
  MS public static string ToBase64String (byte[] inArray,
                                          int offset,
                                          int length);
     public static bool ToBoolean (bool value);
     public static bool ToBoolean (byte value);
  MS public static bool ToBoolean (char value);
     public static bool ToBoolean (decimal value);
     public static bool ToBoolean (double value);
```

```
      public static bool ToBoolean (float value);
      public static bool ToBoolean (int value);
      public static bool ToBoolean (long value);
   MS public static bool ToBoolean (object value);
   MS public static bool ToBoolean (object value,
                                    IFormatProvider provider);
      public static bool ToBoolean (sbyte value);
      public static bool ToBoolean (short value);
      public static bool ToBoolean (string value);
   MS public static bool ToBoolean (string value,
                                    IFormatProvider provider);
MS CF public static bool ToBoolean (DateTime value);
      public static bool ToBoolean (uint value);
      public static bool ToBoolean (ulong value);
      public static bool ToBoolean (ushort value);
      public static byte ToByte (bool value);
      public static byte ToByte (byte value);
      public static byte ToByte (char value);
      public static byte ToByte (decimal value);
      public static byte ToByte (double value);
      public static byte ToByte (float value);
      public static byte ToByte (int value);
      public static byte ToByte (long value);
MS CF public static byte ToByte (object value);
   MS public static byte ToByte (object value,
                                 IFormatProvider provider);
      public static byte ToByte (sbyte value);
      public static byte ToByte (short value);
      public static byte ToByte (string value);
   MS public static byte ToByte (string value,
                                 int fromBase);
      public static byte ToByte (string value,
                                 IFormatProvider provider);
MS CF public static byte ToByte (DateTime value);
      public static byte ToByte (uint value);
      public static byte ToByte (ulong value);
      public static byte ToByte (ushort value);
MS CF public static char ToChar (bool value);
      public static char ToChar (byte value);
      public static char ToChar (char value);
   MS public static char ToChar (decimal value);
   MS public static char ToChar (double value);
   MS public static char ToChar (float value);
      public static char ToChar (int value);
      public static char ToChar (long value);
   MS public static char ToChar (object value);
   MS public static char ToChar (object value,
                                 IFormatProvider provider);
```

Convert Class



```
         public static char ToChar (sbyte value);
         public static char ToChar (short value);
         public static char ToChar (string value);
      MS public static char ToChar (string value,
                                    IFormatProvider provider);
   MS CF public static char ToChar (DateTime value);
         public static char ToChar (uint value);
         public static char ToChar (ulong value);
         public static char ToChar (ushort value);
   MS CF public static DateTime ToDateTime (bool value);
   MS CF public static DateTime ToDateTime (byte value);
   MS CF public static DateTime ToDateTime (char value);
   MS CF public static DateTime ToDateTime (decimal value);
   MS CF public static DateTime ToDateTime (double value);
   MS CF public static DateTime ToDateTime (float value);
   MS CF public static DateTime ToDateTime (int value);
   MS CF public static DateTime ToDateTime (long value);
      MS public static DateTime ToDateTime (object value);
      MS public static DateTime ToDateTime (object value,
                                            IFormatProvider provider);
   MS CF public static DateTime ToDateTime (sbyte value);
   MS CF public static DateTime ToDateTime (short value);
         public static DateTime ToDateTime (string value);
         public static DateTime ToDateTime (string value,
                                            IFormatProvider provider);
      CF public static DateTime ToDateTime (DateTime value);
   MS CF public static DateTime ToDateTime (uint value);
   MS CF public static DateTime ToDateTime (ulong value);
   MS CF public static DateTime ToDateTime (ushort value);
         public static decimal ToDecimal (bool value);
         public static decimal ToDecimal (byte value);
      MS public static decimal ToDecimal (char value);
         public static decimal ToDecimal (decimal value);
         public static decimal ToDecimal (double value);
         public static decimal ToDecimal (float value);
         public static decimal ToDecimal (int value);
         public static decimal ToDecimal (long value);
      MS public static decimal ToDecimal (object value);
   MS CF public static decimal ToDecimal (object value,
                                          IFormatProvider provider);
         public static decimal ToDecimal (sbyte value);
         public static decimal ToDecimal (short value);
         public static decimal ToDecimal (string value);
         public static decimal ToDecimal (string value,
                                          IFormatProvider provider);
      MS public static decimal ToDecimal (DateTime value);
         public static decimal ToDecimal (uint value);
         public static decimal ToDecimal (ulong value);
```

```
      public static decimal ToDecimal (ushort value);
      public static double ToDouble (bool value);
      public static double ToDouble (byte value);
   MS public static double ToDouble (char value);
      public static double ToDouble (decimal value);
      public static double ToDouble (double value);
      public static double ToDouble (float value);
      public static double ToDouble (int value);
      public static double ToDouble (long value);
   MS public static double ToDouble (object value);
MS CF public static double ToDouble (object value,
                                     IFormatProvider provider);
      public static double ToDouble (sbyte value);
      public static double ToDouble (short value);
      public static double ToDouble (string value);
      public static double ToDouble (string value,
                                     IFormatProvider isop);
MS CF public static double ToDouble (DateTime value);
      public static double ToDouble (uint value);
      public static double ToDouble (ulong value);
      public static double ToDouble (ushort value);
      public static short ToInt16(bool value);
      public static short ToInt16(byte value);
      public static short ToInt16(char value);
      public static short ToInt16(decimal value);
      public static short ToInt16(double value);
      public static short ToInt16(float value);
      public static short ToInt16(int value);
      public static short ToInt16(long value);
MS CF public static short ToInt16(object value);
   MS public static short ToInt16(object value,
                                  IFormatProvider provider);
      public static short ToInt16(sbyte value);
      public static short ToInt16(short value);
      public static short ToInt16(string value);
   MS public static short ToInt16(string value,
                                  int fromBase);
      public static short ToInt16(string value,
                                  IFormatProvider provider);
MS CF public static short ToInt16(DateTime value);
      public static short ToInt16(uint value);
      public static short ToInt16(ulong value);
      public static short ToInt16(ushort value);
      public static int ToInt32(bool value);
      public static int ToInt32(byte value);
      public static int ToInt32(char value);
      public static int ToInt32(decimal value);
      public static int ToInt32(double value);
```

```
      public static int ToInt32(float value);
      public static int ToInt32(int value);
      public static int ToInt32(long value);
   MS public static int ToInt32(object value);
MS CF public static int ToInt32(object value,
                                 IFormatProvider provider);
      public static int ToInt32(sbyte value);
      public static int ToInt32(short value);
      public static int ToInt32(string value);
   MS public static int ToInt32(string value,
                                 int fromBase);
      public static int ToInt32(string value,
                                 IFormatProvider provider);
MS CF public static int ToInt32(DateTime value);
      public static int ToInt32(uint value);
      public static int ToInt32(ulong value);
      public static int ToInt32(ushort value);
      public static long ToInt64(bool value);
      public static long ToInt64(byte value);
      public static long ToInt64(char value);
      public static long ToInt64(decimal value);
      public static long ToInt64(double value);
      public static long ToInt64(float value);
      public static long ToInt64(int value);
      public static long ToInt64(long value);
   MS public static long ToInt64(object value);
MS CF public static long ToInt64(object value,
                                  IFormatProvider provider);
      public static long ToInt64(sbyte value);
      public static long ToInt64(short value);
      public static long ToInt64(string value);
   MS public static long ToInt64(string value,
                                  int fromBase);
      public static long ToInt64(string value,
                                  IFormatProvider provider);
MS CF public static long ToInt64(DateTime value);
      public static long ToInt64(uint value);
      public static long ToInt64(ulong value);
      public static long ToInt64(ushort value);
      public static sbyte ToSByte (bool value);
      public static sbyte ToSByte (byte value);
      public static sbyte ToSByte (char value);
      public static sbyte ToSByte (decimal value);
      public static sbyte ToSByte (double value);
      public static sbyte ToSByte (float value);
      public static sbyte ToSByte (int value);
      public static sbyte ToSByte (long value);
MS CF public static sbyte ToSByte (object value);
```

```
MS    public static sbyte ToSByte (object value,
                                   IFormatProvider provider);
      public static sbyte ToSByte (sbyte value);
      public static sbyte ToSByte (short value);
      public static sbyte ToSByte (string value);
MS    public static sbyte ToSByte (string value,
                                   int fromBase);
      public static sbyte ToSByte (string value,
                                   IFormatProvider provider);
MS CF public static sbyte ToSByte (DateTime value);
      public static sbyte ToSByte (uint value);
      public static sbyte ToSByte (ulong value);
      public static sbyte ToSByte (ushort value);
      public static float ToSingle (bool value);
      public static float ToSingle (byte value);
MS    public static float ToSingle (char value);
      public static float ToSingle (decimal value);
      public static float ToSingle (double value);
      public static float ToSingle (float value);
      public static float ToSingle (int value);
      public static float ToSingle (long value);
MS    public static float ToSingle (object value);
MS CF public static float ToSingle (object value,
                                    IFormatProvider provider);
      public static float ToSingle (sbyte value);
      public static float ToSingle (short value);
      public static float ToSingle (string value);
      public static float ToSingle (string value,
                                    IFormatProvider isop);
MS CF public static float ToSingle (DateTime value);
      public static float ToSingle (uint value);
      public static float ToSingle (ulong value);
      public static float ToSingle (ushort value);
      public static string ToString (bool value);
MS CF public static string ToString (bool value,
                                     IFormatProvider provider);
      public static string ToString (byte value);
MS    public static string ToString (byte value,
                                     int toBase);
   CF public static string ToString (byte value,
                                     IFormatProvider provider);
      public static string ToString (char value);
MS CF public static string ToString (char value,
                                     IFormatProvider provider);
      public static string ToString (decimal value);
      public static string ToString (decimal value,
                                     IFormatProvider isop);
      public static string ToString (double value);
```

```
      public static string ToString (double value,
                                     IFormatProvider isop);
      public static string ToString (float value);
      public static string ToString (float value,
                                     IFormatProvider isop);
      public static string ToString (int value);
   MS public static string ToString (int value,
                                     int toBase);
   CF public static string ToString (int value,
                                     IFormatProvider provider);
      public static string ToString (long value);
   MS public static string ToString (long value,
                                     int toBase);
   CF public static string ToString (long value,
                                     IFormatProvider provider);
   MS public static string ToString (object value);
MS CF public static string ToString (object value,
                                     IFormatProvider provider);
      public static string ToString (sbyte value);
   CF public static string ToString (sbyte value,
                                     IFormatProvider provider);
      public static string ToString (short value);
   MS public static string ToString (short value,
                                     int toBase);
   CF public static string ToString (short value,
                                     IFormatProvider provider);
   CF public static string ToString (string value);
MS CF public static string ToString (string value,
                                     IFormatProvider provider);
      public static string ToString (DateTime value);
   CF public static string ToString (DateTime value,
                                     IFormatProvider provider);
      public static string ToString (uint value);
   CF public static string ToString (uint value,
                                     IFormatProvider provider);
      public static string ToString (ulong value);
   CF public static string ToString (ulong value,
                                     IFormatProvider provider);
      public static string ToString (ushort value);
   CF public static string ToString (ushort value,
                                     IFormatProvider provider);
      public static ushort ToUInt16(bool value);
      public static ushort ToUInt16(byte value);
      public static ushort ToUInt16(char value);
      public static ushort ToUInt16(decimal value);
      public static ushort ToUInt16(double value);
      public static ushort ToUInt16(float value);
      public static ushort ToUInt16(int value);
```

```
      public static ushort ToUInt16(long value);
   MS public static ushort ToUInt16(object value);
MS CF public static ushort ToUInt16(object value,
                                    IFormatProvider provider);
      public static ushort ToUInt16(sbyte value);
      public static ushort ToUInt16(short value);
      public static ushort ToUInt16(string value);
   MS public static ushort ToUInt16(string value,
                                    int fromBase);
      public static ushort ToUInt16(string value,
                                    IFormatProvider provider);
MS CF public static ushort ToUInt16(DateTime value);
      public static ushort ToUInt16(uint value);
      public static ushort ToUInt16(ulong value);
      public static ushort ToUInt16(ushort value);
      public static uint ToUInt32(bool value);
      public static uint ToUInt32(byte value);
      public static uint ToUInt32(char value);
      public static uint ToUInt32(decimal value);
      public static uint ToUInt32(double value);
      public static uint ToUInt32(float value);
      public static uint ToUInt32(int value);
      public static uint ToUInt32(long value);
   MS public static uint ToUInt32(object value);
MS CF public static uint ToUInt32(object value,
                                  IFormatProvider provider);
      public static uint ToUInt32(sbyte value);
      public static uint ToUInt32(short value);
      public static uint ToUInt32(string value);
   MS public static uint ToUInt32(string value,
                                  int fromBase);
      public static uint ToUInt32(string value,
                                  IFormatProvider provider);
MS CF public static uint ToUInt32(DateTime value);
      public static uint ToUInt32(uint value);
      public static uint ToUInt32(ulong value);
      public static uint ToUInt32(ushort value);
      public static ulong ToUInt64(bool value);
      public static ulong ToUInt64(byte value);
      public static ulong ToUInt64(char value);
      public static ulong ToUInt64(decimal value);
      public static ulong ToUInt64(double value);
      public static ulong ToUInt64(float value);
      public static ulong ToUInt64(int value);
      public static ulong ToUInt64(long value);
   MS public static ulong ToUInt64(object value);
MS CF public static ulong ToUInt64(object value,
                                   IFormatProvider provider);
```

```
            public static ulong ToUInt64(sbyte value);
            public static ulong ToUInt64(short value);
            public static ulong ToUInt64(string value);
         MS public static ulong ToUInt64(string value,
                                         int fromBase);
            public static ulong ToUInt64(string value,
                                         IFormatProvider provider);
      MS CF public static ulong ToUInt64(DateTime value);
            public static ulong ToUInt64(uint value);
            public static ulong ToUInt64(ulong value);
            public static ulong ToUInt64(ushort value);
    }
```

**BA** Early in the design of the BCL we went back and forth trying to decide how we wanted conversions to be supported in the library. Initially we wanted to distribute them as instance methods in each class:

```
int i = 10;
double d = Int32.ToDouble(i);
```

This design has the advantage of being more easily discoverable as it does not require an intermediate object. Later, we tried a different design that had a single object with all the conversions, so that the same conversion would be:

```
int i = 10;
double d = Convert.ToDouble(i);
```

We liked this approach because if the developer needs to change the type of the *i* variable to a long she would only have to change the declaration, not every usage:

```
long i = 10;
double d = Convert.ToDouble(i);
```

**AH** In the early days of .NET we had two types that could be used to represent dynamically typed values: `System.Object` and `System.Variant`. `System.Variant` was basically a managed wrapper for OLE Automation variants.

Having two ways of doing what amounts to the same thing caused tremendous confusion in the libraries. Some APIs would use `Object`, others would use `Variant`. Some even tried to support both, which introduced lots of ambiguities. We finally

*CONTINUED*

made the hard call to get rid of `Variant`. In retrospect, this was clearly the right decision. We can now say that "every piece of data in .NET is an object," which brings about tremendous conceptual simplification.

The types of operations that were traditionally provided by OLE Automation's variant support, such `VarChangeType()` that converts a variant from one type to another, is now provided by the `Convert` class and the `IConvertible` interface.

**KG** The great thing about `Convert` is that once you know about it, it is easy to learn the pattern, and use it for any base type conversions you need. In addition, if you're working in a particular language, you can easily use exactly the same mechanism in a different language. Because the conversion mechanism is not part of the classes themselves, discovering it for the first time is a little more difficult: that is the trade-off.

It is interesting to note that we have yet to develop the same central conversion mechanism for truncating numbers. `Convert` uses standard banker's rounding to convert numbers to and from strings, or each other (`Convert.ToInt32(22.5)` will result in a value of 22, for example) but to simply get the integer part of the number, for truncation I have to use language-specific functionality such as casting in C#, or the `Int()` or `Fix()` functions in Visual Basic. This seems to defeat a guiding principle of the framework: to provide language-neutral mechanisms for standard operations.

**KC** Type names should be noun phrases, not verb phrases. Probably a better name for this type would be `Converter`.

**JR** When you want to convert a numeric value from one type to another, you should try to use your language's casting syntax first. If your language doesn't allow the cast, then you should use the methods of the `Convert` class. For example, Visual Basic. NET doesn't allow casting syntax to convert a `UInt32` to be cast to an `Int32` but, Visual Basic. NET code can call `Convert`'s `ToInt32` method passing a `UInt32` value. Finally, some classes implement the `IConvertible` interface which defines methods that convert a value from one type to another. You should avoid the `IConvertible` methods since they usually require the object be boxed first, which adversely affects your application's performance.

## Description

The following table shows conversions from source types to destination types. The first column contains the source types. The remaining columns indicate the destination types the source may be converted to. An 'x' indicates the `System.Convert` class implements the conversion. [*Note:* The column headers correspond precisely, in order, to the source types in the first column, but have been abbreviated to fit.]

| Type | Bool | Byte | Char | DT | Dec | Dou | I16 | I32 | I64 | SBy | Sin | Str | UI16 | UI32 | UI64 |
|---|---|---|---|---|---|---|---|---|---|---|---|---|---|---|---|
| Boolean | X | X | | | X | X | X | X | X | X | X | X | X | X | X |
| Byte | X | X | X | | X | X | X | X | X | X | X | X | X | X | X |
| Char | | X | X | | | | X | X | X | X | | X | X | X | X |
| DateTime | | | | X | | | | | | | | X | | | |
| Decimal | X | X | | | X | X | X | X | X | X | X | X | X | X | X |
| Double | X | X | | | X | X | X | X | X | X | X | X | X | X | X |
| Int16 | X | X | X | | X | X | X | X | X | X | X | X | X | X | X |
| Int32 | X | X | X | | X | X | X | X | X | X | X | X | X | X | X |
| Int64 | X | X | X | | X | X | X | X | X | X | X | X | X | X | X |
| SByte | X | X | X | | X | X | X | X | X | X | X | X | X | X | X |
| Single | X | X | | | X | X | X | X | X | X | X | X | X | X | X |
| String | X | X | X | X | X | X | X | X | X | X | X | X | X | X | X |
| UInt16 | X | X | X | | X | X | X | X | X | X | X | X | X | X | X |
| UInt32 | X | X | X | | X | X | X | X | X | X | X | X | X | X | X |
| UInt64 | X | X | X | | X | X | X | X | X | X | X | X | X | X | X |

If the conversion of a numeric type results in a loss of precision, no exception is thrown. However, an exception is thrown if the conversion result is a value that is larger than that which can be represented by the destination type. For example, when a `System.Double` is converted to a `System.Single`, a loss of precision may occur but no exception is thrown. However, if the magnitude of the `System.Double` is too large to be represented by a `System.Single`, a `System.OverflowException` is thrown.

# System
# DateTime Structure

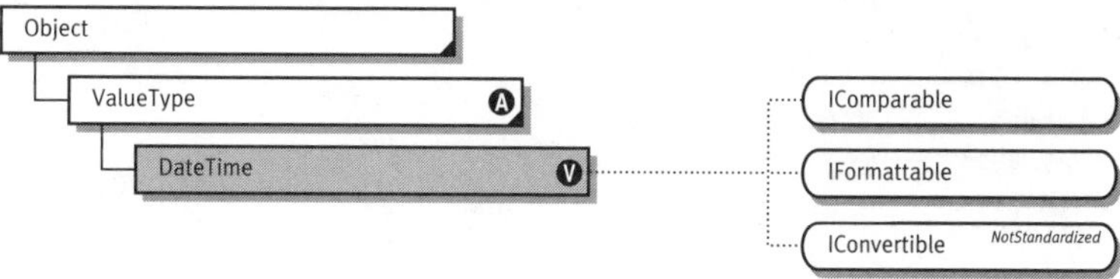




## Summary

Represents an instant in time, expressed as a date and time of day.

## Type Summary

```
public struct DateTime : IComparable, IFormattable,
                         IConvertible
{
  // Constructors
     public DateTime (int year, int month, int day);
     public DateTime (int year, int month, int day,
                      int hour, int minute, int second);
     public DateTime (int year, int month, int day,
                      int hour, int minute, int second,
                      int millisecond);
  MS public DateTime (int year, int month, int day,
                      int hour, int minute, int second,
                      int millisecond, Calendar calendar);
  MS public DateTime (int year, int month, int day,
                      int hour, int minute, int second,
                      Calendar calendar);
  MS public DateTime (int year, int month, int day,
                      Calendar calendar);
     public DateTime (long ticks);

  // Fields
     public static readonly DateTime MaxValue = new DateTime (3155378975999999999);
     public static readonly DateTime MinValue = new DateTime (0);

  // Properties
     public DateTime Date { get; }
     public int Day { get; }
  MS public DayOfWeek DayOfWeek { get; }
     public int DayOfYear { get; }
     public int Hour { get; }
     public int Millisecond { get; }
     public int Minute { get; }
     public int Month { get; }
```

DateTime Structure

```
      public static DateTime Now { get; }
      public int Second { get; }
      public long Ticks { get; }
      public TimeSpan TimeOfDay { get; }
      public static DateTime Today { get; }
      public static DateTime UtcNow { get; }
      public int Year { get; }

   // Methods
      public DateTime Add (TimeSpan value);
      public DateTime AddDays (double value);
      public DateTime AddHours (double value);
      public DateTime AddMilliseconds (double value);
      public DateTime AddMinutes (double value);
      public DateTime AddMonths (int months);
      public DateTime AddSeconds (double value);
      public DateTime AddTicks (long value);
      public DateTime AddYears (int value);
      public static int Compare (DateTime t1,
                                 DateTime t2);
      public int CompareTo (object value);
      public static int DaysInMonth (int year,
                                     int month);
      public override bool Equals (object value);
      public static bool Equals (DateTime t1,
                                 DateTime t2);
   MS public static DateTime FromFileTime (long fileTime);
MS 1.1 public static DateTime FromFileTimeUtc (long fileTime);
 MS CF public static DateTime FromOADate (double d);
   MS public string[] GetDateTimeFormats ();
   MS public string[] GetDateTimeFormats (char format);
   MS public string[] GetDateTimeFormats (char format,
                                          IFormatProvider provider);
   MS public string[] GetDateTimeFormats (IFormatProvider provider);
      public override int GetHashCode ();
   MS public TypeCode GetTypeCode ();
      public static bool IsLeapYear (int year);
      public static DateTime operator +(DateTime d,
                                        TimeSpan t);
      public static bool operator ==(DateTime d1,
                                     DateTime d2);
      public static bool operator >(DateTime t1,
                                    DateTime t2);
      public static bool operator >=(DateTime t1,
                                     DateTime t2);
      public static bool operator !=(DateTime d1,
                                     DateTime d2);
      public static bool operator <(DateTime t1,
```

DateTime Structure

```
                                       DateTime t2);
      public static bool operator <=(DateTime t1,
                                      DateTime t2);
      public static TimeSpan operator -(DateTime d1,
                                         DateTime d2);
      public static DateTime operator -(DateTime d,
                                         TimeSpan t);
      public static DateTime Parse (string s);
      public static DateTime Parse (string s,
                                    IFormatProvider provider);
      public static DateTime Parse (string s,
                                    IFormatProvider provider,
                                    DateTimeStyles styles);
      public static DateTime ParseExact (string s,
                                         string format,
                                         IFormatProvider provider);
      public static DateTime ParseExact (string s,
                                         string format,
                                         IFormatProvider provider,
                                         DateTimeStyles style);
      public static DateTime ParseExact (string s,
                                         string[] formats,
                                         IFormatProvider provider,
                                         DateTimeStyles style);
      public TimeSpan Subtract (DateTime value);
      public DateTime Subtract (TimeSpan value);
   MS public long ToFileTime ();
MS 1.1 public long ToFileTimeUtc ();
      public DateTime ToLocalTime ();
      public string ToLongDateString ();
      public string ToLongTimeString ();
 MS CF public double ToOADate ();
      public string ToShortDateString ();
      public string ToShortTimeString ();
      public override string ToString ();
      public string ToString (string format);
      public string ToString (string format, IFormatProvider provider);
      public string ToString (IFormatProvider provider);
      public DateTime ToUniversalTime ()

   // Explicit Interface Members
   MS bool IConvertible.ToBoolean(IFormatProvider provider);
   MS byte IConvertible.ToByte(IFormatProvider provider);
   MS char IConvertible.ToChar(IFormatProvider provider);
   MS DateTime IConvertible.ToDateTime(IFormatProvider provider);
   MS decimal IConvertible.ToDecimal(IFormatProvider provider);
   MS double IConvertible.ToDouble(IFormatProvider provider);
   MS short IConvertible.ToInt16(IFormatProvider provider);
```

DateTime Structure

```
    MS int IConvertible.ToInt32(IFormatProvider provider);
    MS long IConvertible.ToInt64(IFormatProvider provider);
    MS sbyte IConvertible.ToSByte(IFormatProvider provider);
    MS float IConvertible.ToSingle(IFormatProvider provider);
    MS object IConvertible.ToType(Type type,IFormatProvider provider);
    MS ushort IConvertible.ToUInt16(IFormatProvider provider);
    MS uint IConvertible.ToUInt32(IFormatProvider provider);
    MS ulong IConvertible.ToUInt64(IFormatProvider provider);
}
```



**BA** This is one of the few places in the library where we use operator overloading. Traditionally, operator overloading has been a much-abused feature—almost all proposed usages for it in the BCL were rejected. But this one, I believe, is completely legitimate. `DateTime` can be considered a built-in type on the order of `int` and `double`. It is stack allocated and is immutable. Our usage of operator overloading in this class is not overly creative. The >= operator does exactly what a developer would expect. No guessing is required.

Notice that we also provide nicely named methods for each of the operators for developers using languages that do not support operator overloading, since overloading is not required in the CLS.

**KG** It is surprising how difficult it can be to model a point in time. The `DateTime` type stores a point in time in Local or Universal Coordinated Time (abbreviated as UTC, a mix of the English and French acronyms). Just as we don't store units such as Kilometers or degrees Celsius with the Int32, we do not store the "units" with the `DateTime` type such as Local, or UTC. By default, the `DateTime` object assumes local time. We made this decision because most uses of `DateTime` are interesting only in the current time zone. The `DateTime` type does not internally store the time zone offset it is in. An implication of that is that if you perform these operations:

```
DateTime.Now.ToUniversalTime()
DateTime.Now.ToUniversalTime().ToUniversalTime()
```

you get different results as each operation on `DateTime` assumes the value starts out in Local time.

An outcome of this is that at the daylight savings time boundaries, times may not be represented accurately for the crossover hours. When using `DateTime` we suggest

*CONTINUED*

DateTime Structure

you use Universal Times for comparing `DateTime` values from different sources. Of course for display purposes Local time is still the best bet.

**JR** It's interesting to note that `DateTime`'s `Parse` method defines the `IFormat-Provider` parameter as the second parameter and its `DateTimeStyles` parameter as the third parameter. Contrast this to the `Parse` methods for `Byte`, `SByte`, `Int16`, `UInt16`, `Int32`, `UInt32`, `Int64`, `UInt64`, `Single`, `Double`, and `Decimal`. For the numeric types, their `Parse` methods define the `IFormatProvider` method as the third parameter and the `NumberStyles` parameter as the second parameter.

A B C D E F G H I J K L M N O P Q R S T U V W X Y Z

## Description

The `System.DateTime` value type represents dates and times with values ranging from 00:00:00, 1/1/0001 (Common Era) to 23:59:59 PM, 12/31/9999.

[*Note:* Time values are measured in 100-nanosecond units, *ticks*, and a particular date is the number of ticks since 12:00 Midnight, January 1, 1 in the Gregorian calendar. For example, a ticks value of 31241376000000000L represents the date, Friday, January 01, 0100 12:00:00 AM. Time values can be added to, or subtracted from, an instance of `System.DateTime`. Time values can be negative or positive, and expressed in units such as ticks, seconds, or instances of `System.TimeSpan`. Methods and properties in this value type take into account details such as leap years and the number of days in a month. 12:00:00 AM is Midnight.]

## Example

```
using System;
using System.Globalization;
namespace Samples
{
  public class DateTimeSample
  {
    public static void Main()
    {
      DateTime dt = DateTime.Now;
      string[] formats = {"d", "D",
              "f", "F", "g", "G", "m",
              "r", "s", "t", "T", "u", "U",
              "y", "dddd, MMMM dd yyyy",
              "ddd, MMM d \"'\"yy",
              "dddd, MMMM dd",
              "M/yy", "dd-MM-yy"};
     foreach(string format in formats)
      {
```

DateTime Structure

```
            Console.WriteLine("Displayed using format {0} is: {1}",
                              format,
                              dt.ToString(format,
                                 DateTimeFormatInfo.InvariantInfo));
          }
          DateTime d = new DateTime(1959, 9, 3);
          DateTime b = new DateTime(1973, 9, 25);
          Console.WriteLine("Today is {0:F}", dt);
          TimeSpan age = dt - d;
          Console.WriteLine("Damien is: {0:F}", age);
          Console.WriteLine("He has lived: {0,2:F} days",
                            age.TotalDays);
          age = dt - b;
          Console.WriteLine("Brad is: {0:F}", age);
          Console.WriteLine("He has lived: {0,2:F} days",
                            age.TotalDays);
        }
      }
    }
```

The output is

```
Displayed using format d is: 06/10/2003
Displayed using format D is: Tuesday, 10 June 2003
Displayed using format f is: Tuesday, 10 June 2003 09:00
Displayed using format F is: Tuesday, 10 June 2003 09:00:20
Displayed using format g is: 06/10/2003 09:00
Displayed using format G is: 06/10/2003 09:00:20
Displayed using format m is: June 10
Displayed using format r is: Tue, 10 Jun 2003 09:00:20 GMT
Displayed using format s is: 2003-06-10T09:00:20
Displayed using format t is: 09:00
Displayed using format T is: 09:00:20
Displayed using format u is: 2003-06-10 09:00:20Z
Displayed using format U is: Monday, 09 June 2003 23:00:20
Displayed using format y is: 2003 June
Displayed using format dddd, MMMM dd yyyy is: Tuesday, June 10 2003
Displayed using format ddd, MMM d "'"yy is: Tue, Jun 10 '03
Displayed using format dddd, MMMM dd is: Tuesday, June 10
Displayed using format M/yy is: 6/03
Displayed using format dd-MM-yy is: 10-06-03
Today is Tuesday, 10 June 2003 9:00:20 AM
Damien is: 15986.09:00:20.1009552
He has lived: 15986.38 days
Brad is: 10850.09:00:20.1009552
He has lived: 10850.38 days
```

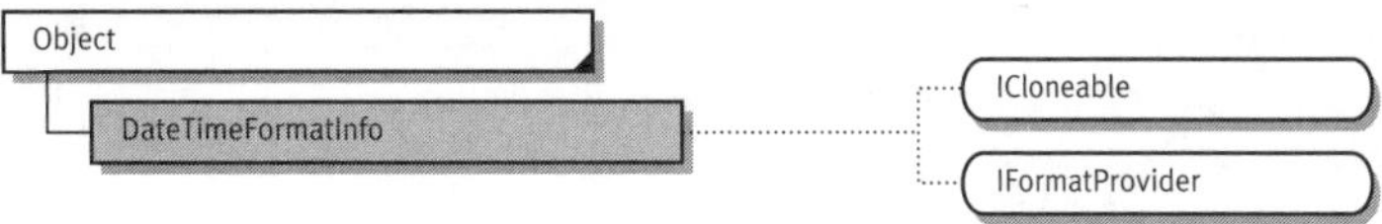


A B C D E F G H I J K L M N O P Q R S T U V W X Y Z

## Summary

Defines culture-specific formats and patterns for `System.DateTime` values.

## Type Summary

```
public sealed class DateTimeFormatInfo : ICloneable,
                                         IFormatProvider
{
  // Constructors
     public DateTimeFormatInfo ();

  // Properties
     public string[] AbbreviatedDayNames { set; get; }
     public string[] AbbreviatedMonthNames { set; get; }
     public string AMDesignator { set; get; }
  MS public Calendar Calendar { set; get; }
  MS public CalendarWeekRule CalendarWeekRule { set; get; }
     public static DateTimeFormatInfo CurrentInfo { get; }
     public string DateSeparator { set; get; }
     public string[] DayNames { set; get; }
  MS public DayOfWeek FirstDayOfWeek { set; get; }
     public string FullDateTimePattern { set; get; }
     public static DateTimeFormatInfo InvariantInfo { get; }
     public bool IsReadOnly { get; }
     public string LongDatePattern { set; get; }
     public string LongTimePattern { set; get; }
     public string MonthDayPattern { set; get; }
     public string[] MonthNames { set; get; }
     public string PMDesignator { set; get; }
  MS public string RFC1123Pattern { get; }
     public string ShortDatePattern { set; get; }
     public string ShortTimePattern { set; get; }
  MS public string SortableDateTimePattern { get; }
     public string TimeSeparator { set; get; }
  MS public string UniversalSortableDateTimePattern { get; }
     public string YearMonthPattern { set; get; }

  // Methods
     public object Clone ();
  MS public string GetAbbreviatedDayName (DayOfWeek dayofweek);
  MS public string GetAbbreviatedEraName (int era);
```

```
    public string GetAbbreviatedMonthName (int month);
 MS public string[] GetAllDateTimePatterns ();
 MS public string[] GetAllDateTimePatterns (char format);
 MS public string GetDayName (DayOfWeek dayofweek);
    public int GetEra (string eraName);
    public string GetEraName (int era);
    public object GetFormat (Type formatType);
 MS public static DateTimeFormatInfo GetInstance (IFormatProvider provider);
    public string GetMonthName (int month);
    public static DateTimeFormatInfo ReadOnly (DateTimeFormatInfo dtfi)
}
```

**BA** In general I am not a big fan of properties that return arrays; they are just too easy to get wrong. In this case, for example, in the early days of the .NET Framework we had a bug such that we were returning the internal instance from one of these properties which allowed a malicious or careless developer to change the names of the days of the week for the entire process!

Highly simplified code from the `DateTimeFormatInfo` with the bug:

```
private string[] dayNames = new string[]{"Monday", "Tuesday"};
public string[] DayNames {
   get {
     return dayNames;
   }
}
```

Code that exploits the bug:

```
DateTimeFormatInfo.InvariantInfo.DayNames[0] = "UpperDay";
Console.WriteLine (DateTimeFormatInfo.InvariantInfo.DayNames[0]);
```

From any process this will return "UpperDay".

The fix is simple:

```
public string[] DayNames {
   get {
     return (string[]) dayNames.Clone();
   }
}
```

*CONTINUED*

But then the down side is you create a copy of the array every time it is asked for. That may not be so bad in this example, but if the array is large it could be a big issue.

Consider the code:

```
for (int i = 0; i < DateTimeFormatInfo.InvariantInfo.DayNames.Length; i++){
Console.WriteLine (DateTimeFormatInfo.InvariantInfo.DayNames[i]);
}
```

It creates a copy of the array every time through the loop. Because of the property syntax that fact would be easy to miss in a code review. In general it would be better to return a collection from properties of this type, or turn the member into a method.

**BG** One note on this type of security bug—many people may incorrectly assume that the CLI's `initonly` keyword (exposed as C#'s `readonly` keyword) means that an array is not modifiable. They might try writing their code like this:

```
private readonly String[] dayNames = new String[]{"Monday", "Tuesday"};
```

That's not sufficient. This means the reference to the array is `readonly`, but arrays are always mutable. You can't assign a different array to the `dayNames` field, but you can call a method like `Array::Clear` on that array, or simply assign a different value to the array, like this:

```
dayNames[0] = "Yesterday";
```

## Description

`System.DateTime` values are formatted by the `System.DateTime.ParseExact` and `System.DateTime.ToString` methods according to standard or custom patterns stored in the properties of a `System.Globalization.DateTimeFormatInfo` instance. The standard patterns can be accessed and modified through the associated `System.Globalization.DateTimeFormatInfo` properties. [*Note:* The format patterns and properties of a read-only `System.Globalization.DateTimeFormatInfo` instance cannot be changed. To determine whether a `System.Globalization.DateTimeFormatInfo` instance is read-only, use the `System.Globalization.DateTimeFormatInfo.IsReadOnly` property.]

Date and time format patterns are specified using strings called *format specifiers*. A string is interpreted as a standard format specifier if it contains exactly one standard format specifier character. If the string contains a single character and that character is not one of the standard format specifiers, an exception is thrown. If the string contains two or more characters, even if the extra characters are white spaces, the string is interpreted as a custom format specifier. Format specifiers and format patterns are case-sensitive; for example, 'g' and 'G' represent different patterns.

The following table shows the standard format specifiers and the associated format pattern defined for the invariant culture. The exact pattern produced by a format specifier is influenced by culture-specific date and/or time settings on the current system; computers with different date and time settings might display different patterns. The asterisk at the end of a format pattern indicates that the preceding character may be repeated without changing the meaning of the pattern. For example, the pattern "HH*" indicates that the strings "HH", "HHH", "HHHH", and "HHHHH" produce the same result when used with `System.DateTime.ParseExact` and `System.DateTime.ToString` methods.

| Format Specifier | Format Pattern | Description |
|---|---|---|
| d | MM/dd/yyyy | The full date in numeric format (`System.Globalization.DateTimeFormatInfo.ShortDatePattern`). |
| D | dddd*, dd MMMM* yyyy | The full date including the day of the week and the name of the month (`System.Globalization.DateTimeFormatInfo.LongDatePattern`). |
| f | dddd*, dd MMMM* yyyy HH*:mm* | The full date and time, including the day of the week and the name of the month (`System.Globalization.DateTimeFormatInfo.LongDatePattern` combined with `System.Globalization.DateTimeFormatInfo.ShortTimePattern`). |
| F | dddd*, dd MMMM* yyyy HH*:mm*:ss* | The full date and time, including the seconds (`System.Globalization.DateTimeFormatInfo.FullDateTimePattern` equivalent to `System.Globalization.Date-Time-FormatInfo.LongDatePattern` combined with `System.Globalization.DateTimeFormatInfo.LongTimePattern`). |
| g | MM/dd/yyyy HH*:mm* | A general date pattern including the short time form (`System.Globalization.DateTimeFormatInfo.ShortDatePattern` combined with `System.Globalization.DateTimeFormatInfo.ShortTimePattern`). |
| G | MM/dd/yyyy HH*:mm*:ss* | A general date pattern including the long time form (`System.Globalization.DateTimeFormatInfo.ShortDatePattern` combined with `System.Globalization.DateTimeFormatInfo.LongTimePattern`). |

| Format Specifier | Format Pattern | Description |
|---|---|---|
| m, M | MMMM* dd | The full name of the month and the date (`System.Globalization.DateTimeFormatInfo.MonthDayPattern`). |
| t | HH*:mm* | The time in short format (`System.Globalization.DateTimeFormatInfo.ShortTimePattern`). |
| T | HH*:mm*:ss* | The time in long format (`System.Globalization.DateTimeFormatInfo.LongTimePattern`). |
| U | dddd*, dd MMMM* yyyy HH*:mm*:ss* | The full date and time, including the seconds, in the Gregorian calendar (`System.Globalization.DateTimeFormatInfo.FullDateTimePattern`). |
| y, Y | yyyy MMMM* | The full name of the month and the year in four-digit format (`System.Globalization.DateTimeFormatInfo.YearMonthPattern`). |

The following table lists custom format specifiers that can be combined to construct custom patterns. If the custom pattern contains white space characters, characters enclosed in single or double quotation marks, or characters not defined in the following table, these characters are considered literals and are included in the output string unchanged. [*Note:* See the `System.String` class for the list of white space characters.]

| Format Pattern | Description | Examples |
|---|---|---|
| d | The day of the month as a value in the range 1-31, inclusive. Single-digit days do not have a leading zero. | 1<br>22 |
| dd | The day of the month as a value in the range 1-31, inclusive. Single-digit days have a leading zero. | 01<br>22 |
| ddd | The abbreviated name of the day of the week, as defined in `System.Globalization.DateTimeFormatInfo.AbbreviatedDayNames`. | Mon |
| dddd* | The full name of the day of the week, as defined in `System.Globalization.DateTimeFormatInfo.DayNames`. | Monday |

| Format Pattern | Description | Examples |
|---|---|---|
| M | The numeric month as a value in the range 1-12, inclusive. Single-digit months do not have a leading zero. | 2<br>11 |
| MM | The numeric month as a value in the range 1-12, inclusive. Single-digit months have a leading zero. | 02<br>11 |
| MMM | The abbreviated name of the month, as defined in `System.Globalization.DateTimeFormatInfo.AbbreviatedMonthNames`. | Feb |
| MMMM* | The full name of the month, as defined in `System.Globalization.DateTimeFormatInfo.MonthNames`. | February |
| y | The year without the century (two-digit). If the value is less than 10, the year is displayed with no leading zero. | 0<br>3 |
| yy | The year without the century (two-digit). If the year without the century is less than 10, the year is displayed with a leading zero. | 00<br>03 |
| yyyy | The year including the century in four digits. | 2000<br>2003 |
| g* | The name of a period or era (such as "A.D." or "B.C."). This pattern is ignored if the date to be formatted does not have an associated period or era string. | A.D. |
| h | The hour within a 12-hour range as a value in the range 1-12, inclusive. Single-digit hours do not have a leading zero. [*Note:* The value represents whole hours passed since either midnight (12) or noon (12). To distinguish between values occurring before and after noon, include the "t" or "tt*" custom format specifier.] | 3<br>11 |
| hh* | The hour within a 12-hour range as a value in the range 1-12, inclusive. Single-digit hours have a leading zero. [*Note:* The value represents whole hours passed since either midnight (12) or noon (12). To distinguish between values occurring before and after noon, include the "t" or "tt*" custom format specifier.] | 03<br>11 |
| H | The hour as a value in the range 0-23, inclusive. Single-digit hours do not have a leading zero. [*Note:* The value represents whole hours passed since midnight.] | 3<br>13 |

| Format Pattern | Description | Examples |
|---|---|---|
| HH* | The hour as a value in the range 0 and 23, inclusive. Single-digit hours have a leading zero. [*Note:* The value represents whole hours passed since midnight.] | 03<br>13 |
| m | The minute as a value in the range 0-59, inclusive. Single-digit minutes do not have a leading zero. [*Note:* The value represents whole minutes passed since the last hour.] | 5<br>15 |
| mm* | The minute as a value in the range 0-59, inclusive. Single-digit minutes have a leading zero. [*Note:* The value represents whole minutes passed since the last hour.] | 05<br>15 |
| s | The second as a value in the range 0-59, inclusive. Single-digit seconds do not have a leading zero. [*Note:* The value represents whole seconds passed since the last minute.] | 1<br>30 |
| ss* | The second as a value in the range 0-59, inclusive. Single-digit seconds have a leading zero. [*Note:* The value represents whole seconds passed since the last minute.] | 01<br>30 |
| f | Displays fractional seconds represented in one digit. | 1 |
| ff | Displays fractional seconds represented in two digits. | 01 |
| fff | Displays fractional seconds represented in three digits. | 001 |
| ffff | Displays fractional seconds represented in four digits. | 0001 |
| fffff | Displays fractional seconds represented in five digits. | 00001 |
| ffffff | Displays fractional seconds represented in six digits. | 000001 |
| fffffff | Displays fractional seconds represented in seven digits. | 0000001 |
| t | The first character of the AM/PM designator defined in the `System.Globalization.DateTimeFormatInfo` property `System.Globalization.DateTimeFormatInfo.AMDesignator` or `System.Globalization.DateTimeFormatInfo.PMDesignator`. [*Note:* If the total number of hours passed since midnight is less than 12, the A.M. designator is used; otherwise the P.M. designator is used.] | A<br>P |

DateTimeFormatInfo Class

| Format Pattern | Description | Examples |
|---|---|---|
| tt* | The AM/PM designator defined in the `System.Globalization.DateTimeFormatInfo` property `System.Globalization.DateTimeFormatInfo.AMDesignator` or `System.Globalization.DateTimeFormatInfo.PMDesignator`. [*Note:* If the total number of hours passed since midnight is less than 12, the A.M. designator is used; otherwise the P.M. designator is used.] | AM<br>PM |
| z | The time zone offset (hour only) from the universal time coordinate (UTC) time (Greenwich Mean Time) as a value in the range –12 to +13, inclusive. Single-digit hours do not have a leading zero. [*Note:* The value always includes a leading sign (zero is '+0'), indicating hours ahead of UTC time (+) or hours behind UTC time (–). The offset takes Daylight Savings Time into account.] | –8 |
| zz | The time zone offset (hour only) from the UTC time (Greenwich Mean Time) as a value in the range –12 to +13, inclusive. Single-digit hours have a leading zero. [*Note:* The value always includes a leading sign (zero is '+0'), indicating hours ahead of UTC time (+) or hours behind UTC time (–). The offset takes Daylight Savings Time into account.] | –08 |
| zzz* | The full time zone offset (hour and minutes) from the UTC time (Greenwich Mean Time) as a value in the range –12:00 to +13:00, inclusive. Single-digit hours and minutes have leading zeros. [*Note:* The value always includes a leading sign (zero is '+0'), indicating hours ahead of UTC time (+) or hours behind UTC time (–). The offset takes Daylight Savings Time into account.] | –08:00 |
| : | The invariant culture time separator defined in `System.Globalization.DateTimeFormatInfo.TimeSeparator`. | : |
| / | The invariant culture date separator defined in the `System.Globalization.DateTimeFormatInfo.DateSeparator`. | / |

| Format Pattern | Description | Examples |
|---|---|---|
| %c | *c* represents a single custom format character. Produces the custom format pattern associated with the format character *c*. The %*c* specifier provides a mechanism for specifying a single custom format character and having it recognized as a custom specifier. This format is intended for characters that define both a custom and a standard format. Note that a format string containing exactly one such character will be interpreted as a standard format specifier unless prefaced with the %. [*Note:* For example, for the invariant culture, "%d" produces the single or double digit date, while "d" produces the date in "MM/dd/yyyy" format. Without the %, a format string containing one character would have to include leading or trailing white space to be interpreted as a custom specifier because custom formats are required to have two or more characters.] | "%y" produces a two-digit year without a leading zero, and not the "MMMM, yyyy" pattern. |
| \c | *c* represents any character predefined as part of a format specifier. Prevents the character from being interpreted as a format specifier (the character is treated as a literal). [*Note:* In programming languages where the backslash ('\') character is used to specify control sequences such as newline (\n), the backslash character is required to be specified twice. For example, in C#, "\d" is coded as "\\d".] | "\d" produces the character 'd', and not the day of the month. |
| '*xx*' or "*xx*" | *xx* represents a string of characters of any length. The characters are treated as literals. | "'d'" produces the character 'd', and not the day of the month. |

## Example

```
using System;
using System.Globalization;
namespace Samples
{
  public class DateTimeFormatInfoSample
  {
    public static void Main()
    {
      DateTime d = DateTime.Now;
      DateTimeFormatInfo i =
          new CultureInfo("fr-FR").DateTimeFormat;
      string[] f = i.GetAllDateTimePatterns();
      foreach(string s in f)
        Console.WriteLine("ToString(\"{0}\") yields: {1}",
```

```
                        s, d.ToString(s, i));
      i = new CultureInfo("en-AU").DateTimeFormat;
      f = i.GetAllDateTimePatterns();
      foreach(string s in f)
        Console.WriteLine("ToString(\"{0}\") yields: {1}",
                        s, d.ToString(s, i));
    }
  }
}
```

The output is

```
ToString("dd/MM/yyyy") yields: 10/06/2003
ToString("dd/MM/yy") yields: 10/06/03
ToString("dd.MM.yy") yields: 10.06.03
ToString("dd-MM-yy") yields: 10-06-03
ToString("yyyy-MM-dd") yields: 2003-06-10
ToString("dddd d MMMM yyyy") yields: mardi 10 juin 2003
ToString("d MMM yy") yields: 10 juin 03
ToString("d MMMM yyyy") yields: 10 juin 2003
ToString("dddd d MMMM yyyy HH:mm") yields: mardi 10 juin 2003 12:57
ToString("dddd d MMMM yyyy H:mm") yields: mardi 10 juin 2003 12:57
ToString("dddd d MMMM yyyy HH.mm") yields: mardi 10 juin 2003 12.57
ToString("dddd d MMMM yyyy HH' h 'mm") yields: mardi 10 juin 2003 12 h 57
...
ToString("d/MM/yyyy") yields: 10/06/2003
ToString("d/MM/yy") yields: 10/06/03
ToString("d/M/yy") yields: 10/6/03
ToString("d/M/yyyy") yields: 10/6/2003
ToString("dd/MM/yy") yields: 10/06/03
ToString("dd/MM/yyyy") yields: 10/06/2003
ToString("dd-MMM-yy") yields: 10-Jun-03
ToString("dd-MMMM-yyyy") yields: 10-June-2003
ToString("yyyy-MM-dd") yields: 2003-06-10
ToString("yy/MM/dd") yields: 03/06/10
ToString("yyyy/MM/dd") yields: 2003/06/10
ToString("dddd, d MMMM yyyy") yields: Tuesday, 10 June 2003
ToString("d MMMM yyyy") yields: 10 June 2003
ToString("dddd, d MMMM yyyy h:mm tt") yields: Tuesday, 10 June 2003 12:57 PM
ToString("dddd, d MMMM yyyy H:mm") yields: Tuesday, 10 June 2003 12:57
ToString("dddd, d MMMM yyyy HH:mm") yields: Tuesday, 10 June 2003 12:57
...
```

# System.Globalization DateTimeStyles Enum

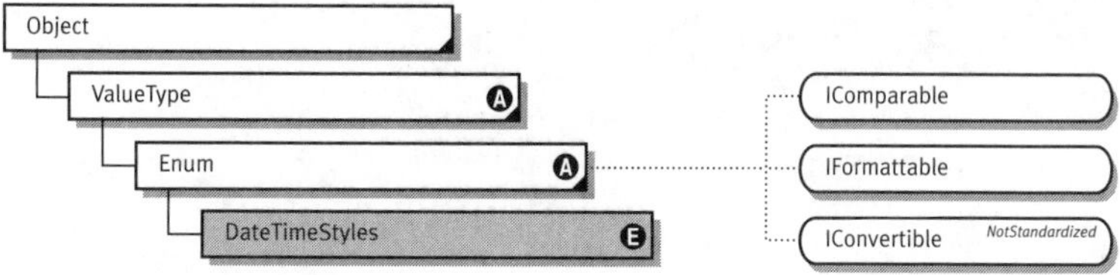




## Summary

Defines the formatting options that customize how the `System.DateTime.Parse` and `System.DateTime.ParseExact` methods parse a string.

## Type Summary

```
public enum DateTimeStyles  {
      AdjustToUniversal = 0x10,
      AllowInnerWhite = 0x4,
      AllowLeadingWhite = 0x1,
      AllowTrailingWhite = 0x2,
      AllowWhiteSpaces = AllowLeadingWhite | AllowTrailingWhite | AllowInnerWhite,
      NoCurrentDateDefault = 0x8,
      None = 0x0,
}
```

## Description

[*Note:* See the `System.String` class for the list of white space characters. Only the `System.Globalization.DateTimeStyles.NoCurrentDateDefault` option affects the `System.DateTime.Parse` method. `System.DateTime.Parse` always ignores leading, inner, and trailing white spaces.]

## Example

```
using System;
using System.Globalization;
namespace Samples
{
  public class DateTimeStylesSample
  {
    public static void Main()
    {
      IFormatProvider f = new CultureInfo("en-AU", true);
      string s = String.Format("\t  {0}  ",
                     DateTime.Now.ToString(f));
      DateTime d = DateTime.Parse(s, f,
```

```
                DateTimeStyles.AllowWhiteSpaces);
    Console.WriteLine("String: {0} yields date {1}", s, d);
    d = DateTime.Parse(s, f,
                DateTimeStyles.AllowLeadingWhite |
                DateTimeStyles.AllowInnerWhite |
                DateTimeStyles.AllowTrailingWhite);
    Console.WriteLine("String: {0} yields date {1}", s, d);
    s = String.Format("  {0}  \t",
                 DateTime.Now.ToString("T", f));
    d = DateTime.Parse(s, f,
                DateTimeStyles.NoCurrentDateDefault);
    Console.WriteLine("String: {0} yields date {1}", s, d);
   }
  }
}
```

The output is

```
String:   10/06/2003 1:30:25 PM   yields date 10/06/2003 1:30:25 PM
String:   10/06/2003 1:30:25 PM   yields date 10/06/2003 1:30:25 PM
String:   1:30:25 PM   yields date 1/01/0001 1:30:25 PM
```

# System
# Decimal Structure

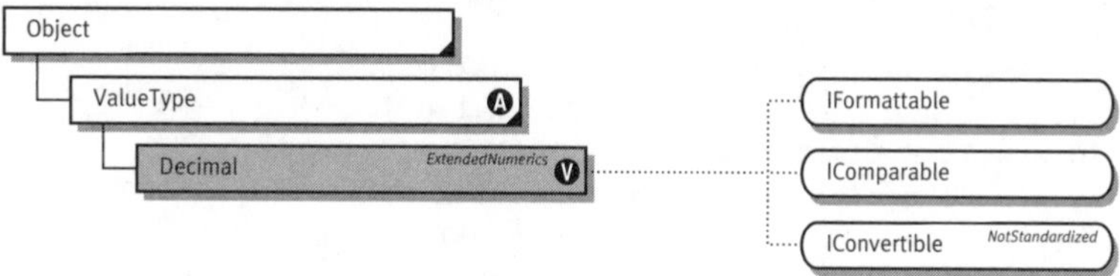


A
B
C
D
E
F
G
H
I
J
K
L
M
N
O
P
Q
R
S
T
U
V
W
X
Y
Z

## Summary

Represents a floating-point decimal data type with up to 29 significant digits, suitable for financial and commercial calculations.

## Type Summary

```
public struct Decimal : IFormattable, IComparable,
                        IConvertible
{
  // Constructors
     public Decimal (double value);
     public Decimal (float value);
     public Decimal (int value);
  MS public Decimal (int lo, int mid, int hi,
                     bool isNegative, byte scale);
     public Decimal (int[] bits);
     public Decimal (long value);
     public Decimal (uint value);
     public Decimal (ulong value);

  // Fields
     public static readonly decimal MaxValue =
            79228162514264337593543950335;
     public static readonly decimal MinusOne = -1;
     public static readonly decimal MinValue =
            -79228162514264337593543950335;
     public static readonly decimal One = 1;
     public static readonly decimal Zero = 0;

  // Methods
     public static decimal Add (decimal d1, decimal d2);
     public static int Compare (decimal d1, decimal d2);
     public int CompareTo (object value);
     public static decimal Divide (decimal d1,
                                   decimal d2);
     public static bool Equals (decimal d1, decimal d2);
     public override bool Equals (object value);
     public static decimal Floor (decimal d);
MS CF public static decimal FromOACurrency (long cy);
```

Decimal Structure

```
      public static int[] GetBits (decimal d);
      public override int GetHashCode ();
   MS public TypeCode GetTypeCode ();
      public static decimal Multiply (decimal d1,
                                      decimal d2);
      public static decimal Negate (decimal d);
      public static decimal operator +(decimal d1,
                                       decimal d2);
      public static decimal operator --(decimal d);
      public static decimal operator /(decimal d1,
                                       decimal d2);
      public static bool operator ==(decimal d1,
                                     decimal d2);
      public static explicit operator byte(decimal value);
      public static explicit operator char(decimal value);
      public static explicit operator decimal (double value);
      public static explicit operator decimal (float value);
      public static explicit operator double (decimal value);
      public static explicit operator float(decimal value);
      public static explicit operator int(decimal value);
      public static explicit operator long(decimal value);
      public static explicit operator sbyte(decimal value);
      public static explicit operator short(decimal value);
      public static explicit operator uint(decimal value);
      public static explicit operator ulong(decimal value);
      public static explicit operator ushort(decimal value);
      public static bool operator >(decimal d1,
                                    decimal d2);
      public static bool operator >=(decimal d1,
                                     decimal d2);
      public static implicit operator decimal (byte value);
      public static implicit operator decimal (char value);
      public static implicit operator decimal (int value);
      public static implicit operator decimal (long value);
      public static implicit operator decimal (sbyte value);
      public static implicit operator decimal (short value);
      public static implicit operator decimal (uint value);
      public static implicit operator decimal (ulong value);
      public static implicit operator decimal (ushort value);
      public static decimal operator ++(decimal d);
      public static bool operator !=(decimal d1,
                                     decimal d2);
      public static bool operator <(decimal d1,
                                    decimal d2);
      public static bool operator <=(decimal d1,
                                     decimal d2);
      public static decimal operator %(decimal d1,
                                       decimal d2);
      public static decimal operator *(decimal d1,
                                       decimal d2);
```

Decimal Structure

```
      public static decimal operator -(decimal d1,
                                       decimal d2);
      public static decimal operator -(decimal d);
      public static decimal operator +(decimal d);
      public static decimal Parse (string s);
      public static decimal Parse (string s, NumberStyles style);
      public static decimal Parse (string s, NumberStyles style,
                                   IFormatProvider provider);
      public static decimal Parse (string s, IFormatProvider provider);
      public static decimal Remainder (decimal d1,
                                       decimal d2);
      public static decimal Round (decimal d,
                                   int decimals);
      public static decimal Subtract (decimal d1,
                                      decimal d2);
   MS public static byte ToByte (decimal value);
   MS public static double ToDouble (decimal d);
   MS public static short ToInt16(decimal value);
   MS public static int ToInt32(decimal d);
   MS public static long ToInt64(decimal d);
MS CF public static long ToOACurrency (decimal value);
   MS public static sbyte ToSByte (decimal value);
   MS public static float ToSingle (decimal d);
      public override string ToString ();
      public string ToString (string format);
      public string ToString (string format, IFormatProvider provider);
      public string ToString (IFormatProvider provider);
   MS public static ushort ToUInt16(decimal value);
   MS public static uint ToUInt32(decimal d);
   MS public static ulong ToUInt64(decimal d);
      public static decimal Truncate (decimal d);

   // Explicit Interface Members
   MS bool IConvertible.ToBoolean(IFormatProvider provider);
   MS byte IConvertible.ToByte(IFormatProvider provider);
   MS char IConvertible.ToChar(IFormatProvider provider);
   MS DateTime IConvertible.ToDateTime(IFormatProvider provider);
   MS decimal IConvertible.ToDecimal(IFormatProvider provider);
   MS double IConvertible.ToDouble(IFormatProvider provider);
   MS short IConvertible.ToInt16(IFormatProvider provider);
   MS int IConvertible.ToInt32(IFormatProvider provider);
   MS long IConvertible.ToInt64(IFormatProvider provider);
   MS sbyte IConvertible.ToSByte(IFormatProvider provider);
   MS float IConvertible.ToSingle(IFormatProvider provider);
   MS object IConvertible.ToType(Type type,IFormatProvider provider);
   MS ushort IConvertible.ToUInt16(IFormatProvider provider);
   MS uint IConvertible.ToUInt32(IFormatProvider provider);
   MS ulong IConvertible.ToUInt64(IFormatProvider provider);
}
```

Decimal Structure

A B C D E F G H I J K L M N O P Q R S T U V W X Y Z

**BA** This is another good example of use of operator overloading. Clearly `Decimal` is a built-in type and it should behave that way. All the operators do exactly what you would expect. See `DateTime` for more notes on operator overloading.

Throughout the standardization process we were very fortunate to have the input of experts in their field. In the case of this decimal we benefited from having the world's leading expert assist us. Mike Cowlishaw, an IBM Fellow, has devoted much of his career to the study and implementation of `Decimal` on a wide range of systems. Although the debates around the changes to `Decimal` were at times heated, his input caused us to produce a better standard and better product. See more information on Mike's work with `Decimal` at http://www2.hursley.ibm.com/decimal.

**JM** Wow! `Decimal` sure drummed up some discussion and controversy. A code-breaking change in a certain implementation of the CLI was even made where the `ToString` method behavior was changed to preserve the scale, which is the right thing to do. This even had cross-task-group ramifications as the change affected the C# folks. Just goes to show that standardization can be exciting!

**KG** `Decimal` used to truncate trailing zeroes but the ECMA standardization process required that trailing zeroes be preserved on `Decimal` operations. So in version 1.1, we changed `Decimal` to preserve trailing zeroes. This has interesting serialization consequences for some scenarios (such as storing numeric information in a database), but the new behavior is far more appropriate for general situations.

**BG** Our original design for `Decimal` came straight from OLE Automation's `Decimal` type. About the only thing that changed was the behavior of `ToString` in some cases. In fact, the types have the same memory layout, which is convenient for COM Interop.

**JR** `Decimal` is a very interesting class. It is considered a primitive type by the C# compiler but it is not considered a primitive type by the CLI. This is why `Decimal` provides methods to add, subtract, multiple, and divide values. Notice that these methods do not exist for the other numeric types, such as `Int32`. So, when compiling code that adds two `Decimal` values together, the C# compiler emits code to call the overloaded operator methods but, when compiling code that adds two `Int32` values together, the C# compiler emits code that *knows* how to add two `Int32` values together—no method call is performed. Another side effect of this is that C#'s `checked` and `unchecked` code feature has no effect on `Decimal` values—operations on `Decimal` values are always `checked`.

Decimal Structure

## Description

The `System.Decimal` type can represent values from approximately $-7.9 \times 10^{28}$ to $7.9 \times 10^{28}$, with 28 or 29 significant digits. The `System.Decimal` data type is ideally suited to financial calculations that require a large number of significant digits and no round-off errors.

The finite set of values of type decimal are of the form $-1^s \times c \times 10^{-f}$, where the sign $s$ is 0 or 1, the coefficient $c$ is given by $0 <= c < 2^{96}$, and the scale f is such that $0 <= f <= 28$.

A `System.Decimal` is represented as a 96-bit integer scaled by a power of ten. For a `System.Decimal` with an absolute value less than 1.0, the value is exact to the $28^{th}$ decimal place, but no further. For a `System.Decimal` with an absolute value greater than or equal to 1.0, the value is exact to 28 or 29 digits.

The result of an operation on values of type `System.Decimal` is that which would result from calculating an exact result (preserving scale, as defined for each operator) and then rounding to fit the representation. That is, results are exact to 28 or 29 digits, but to no more than 28 decimal places. A zero result has a sign of 0 and a scale of 0.

Results are rounded to the nearest representable value, and, when a result is equally close to two representable values, to the value that has an even number in the least significant digit position (banker's rounding).

[*Note:* Unlike the `System.Single` and `System.Double` data types, decimal fractional numbers such as 0.1 can be represented exactly in the `System.Decimal` representation. In the `System.Single` and `System.Double` representations, such numbers are often infinite fractions, making those representations prone to round-off errors. Further, the `System.Decimal` representation preserves scale, so that 1.23 + 1.27 will give the answer 2.50, not 2.5.] If a `System.Decimal` arithmetic operation produces a value that is too small for the `System.Decimal` format after rounding, the result of the operation is zero. If a `System.Decimal` arithmetic operation produces a result that is too large for the `System.Decimal` format, a `System.OverflowException` is thrown.

[*Note:* The `System.Decimal` class implements implicit conversions from the `System.SByte`, `System.Byte`, `System.Int16`, `System.UInt16`, `System.Int32`, `System.UInt32`, `System.Int64`, and `System.UInt64` types to `System.Decimal`. These implicit conversions never lose information and never throw exceptions. The `System.Decimal` class also implements explicit conversions from `System.Decimal` to `System.Byte`, `System.SByte`, `System.Int16`, `System.UInt16`, `System.Int32`, `System.UInt32`, `System.Int64`, and `System.UInt64`. These explicit conversions round the `System.Decimal` value towards zero to the nearest integer, and then convert that integer to the destination type. A `System.OverflowException` is thrown if the result is not within the range of the destination type. The `System.Decimal` class provides narrowing conversions to and from the `System.Single` and `System.Double` types. A conversion from `System.Decimal` to `System.Single` or `System.Double` may lose precision, but will not lose information about the overall magnitude of the numeric value, and will never throw an exception. A conversion from `System.Single` or `System.Double` to `System.Decimal` throws a `System.OverflowException` if the value is not within the range of the `System.Decimal` type.]



## Example

```
using System;

namespace Samples
{
  public class DecimalSample
  {
    public static void Main()
    {
      Decimal max = Decimal.MaxValue,
              min = Decimal.MinValue;
      Console.WriteLine("MaxValue: {0}", max);
      Console.WriteLine("MinValue: {0}", min);
      Console.WriteLine("Is {0} equal to {1}: {2}",
                        max, max, max.Equals(max));
      Console.WriteLine("Is {0} equal to {1}: {2}",
                        max, min, max.Equals(min));
      Console.WriteLine("{0} has hashcode of: {1}",
                        max, max.GetHashCode());
      Console.WriteLine("{0} has hashcode of: {1}",
                        min, min.GetHashCode());
      string s = max.ToString();
      Console.WriteLine("\"{0}\" parsed from string yields: {1}",
                        s, Decimal.Parse(s));
      s = min.ToString();
      Console.WriteLine("\"{0}\" parsed from string yields: {1}",
                        s, Decimal.Parse(s));
      string[] formats = {"C","E","F","G","N","P"};
      foreach(string f in formats)
        Console.WriteLine("Format {0}: {1}", f, max.ToString(f));
    }
  }
}
```

The output is

```
MaxValue: 79228162514264337593543950335
MinValue: -79228162514264337593543950335
Is 79228162514264337593543950335 equal to 79228162514264337593543950335: True
Is 79228162514264337593543950335 equal to -79228162514264337593543950335: False
79228162514264337593543950335 has hashcode of: 1173356544
-79228162514264337593543950335 has hashcode of: -974127104
"79228162514264337593543950335" parsed from string yields:
79228162514264337593543950335
```

Decimal Structure

```
"-79228162514264337593543950335" parsed from string yields:
-79228162514264337593543950335
Format C: $79,228,162,514,264,337,593,543,950,335.00
Format E: 7.922816E+028
Format F: 79228162514264337593543950335.00
Format G: 79228162514264337593543950335
Format N: 79,228,162,514,264,337,593,543,950,335.00
Format P: 7,922,816,251,426,433,759,354,395,033,500.00 %
```

# System.Text
# Decoder

A B C D E F G H I J K L M N O P Q R S T U V W X Y Z

## Summary

Converts blocks of bytes into blocks of characters, maintaining state across successive calls for reading from a `System.IO.Stream`.

## Type Summary

```
public abstract class Decoder
{
  // Constructors
     protected Decoder ();

  // Methods
     public abstract int GetCharCount (byte[] bytes,
                                       int index,
                                       int count);
     public abstract int GetChars (byte[] bytes,
                                   int byteIndex,
                                   int byteCount,
                                   char[] chars,
                                   int charIndex);
}
```

## Description

[*Note:* Following instantiation of a decoder, sequential blocks of bytes are converted into blocks of characters through calls to the `System.Text.Decoder.GetChars` method. The decoder maintains state between the conversions, allowing it to correctly decode a character whose bytes span multiple blocks. This greatly assists decoding streams of bytes into characters. An instance of a specific implementation of the `System.Text.Decoder` class is typically obtained through a call to the `System.Text.Encoding.GetDecoder` method of a `System.Text.Encoding` object.]

## Example

The following example demonstrates using the `System.Text.UTF8Encoding` implementation of the `System.Text.Decoder` class to convert two byte arrays to a character array, where one character's bytes span multiple byte arrays. This demonstrates how to use a `System.Text.Decoder` in streaming-like situations.

```
using System;
using System.Text;
namespace Samples
{
  public class DecoderSample
  {
    public static void Main()
    {
      byte[] b1 = { 0x41, 0x23, 0xe2 };
      byte[] b2 = { 0x98, 0xa3 };
      Decoder d = Encoding.UTF8.GetDecoder();
      char[] chars = new char[3];
      int i = d.GetChars(b1, 0, b1.Length, chars, 0);
      i += d.GetChars(b2, 0, b2.Length, chars, i);
      foreach(char c in chars)
        Console.Write("U+{0:x} ", (ushort)c);
    }
  }
}
```

The output is

```
U+41 U+23 U+2623
```

# System
# Delegate



A B C D E F G H I J K L M N O P Q R S T U V W X Y Z

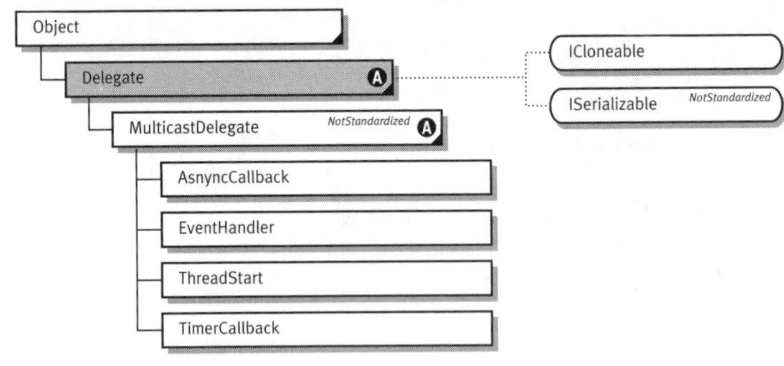


## Summary

A class used to create types that invoke methods.

## Type Summary

```
      public abstract class Delegate : ICloneable,
                                       ISerializable
      {
        // Constructors
   MS CF protected Delegate (object target, string method);
   MS CF protected Delegate (Type target, string method);

        // Properties
      CF public MethodInfo Method { get; }
      CF public object Target { get; }

        // Methods
      CF public virtual object Clone ();
      CF public static Delegate Combine (Delegate[] delegates);
         public static Delegate Combine (Delegate a,
                                         Delegate b);
      MS protected virtual Delegate CombineImpl (Delegate d);
      CF public static Delegate CreateDelegate (Type type,
                                                object target,
                                                string method);
   MS CF public static Delegate CreateDelegate (Type type,
                                                object target,
                                                string method,
                                                bool ignoreCase);
      CF public static Delegate CreateDelegate (Type type,
                                                MethodInfo method);
      CF public static Delegate CreateDelegate (Type type,
                                                Type target,
                                                string method);
```

```
    CF public object DynamicInvoke (object[] args);
 MS CF protected virtual object DynamicInvokeImpl (object[] args);
       public override bool Equals (object obj);
       public override int GetHashCode ();
       public virtual Delegate[] GetInvocationList ();
 MS CF protected virtual MethodInfo GetMethodImpl ();
 MS CF public virtual void GetObjectData (SerializationInfo info,
                                   StreamingContext context);
       public static bool operator ==(Delegate d1,
                                   Delegate d2);
       public static bool operator !=(Delegate d1,
                                   Delegate d2);
       public static Delegate Remove (Delegate source,
                                   Delegate value);
CF 1.1 public static Delegate RemoveAll (Delegate source,
                                   Delegate value);
    MS protected virtual Delegate RemoveImpl (Delegate d);
  }
```

**BA** One important design point about delegates is that they are immutable. Notice that the `Combine` and `Remove` operations return a new instance. This immutability constraint is important to maintain the thread safety of delegates.

**JR** Programmers usually have a difficult time learning about delegates because compilers typically offer abstractions over `Delegate`'s methods. For example, in C#, you can use the += and -= operators, which will call `Delegate`'s `Combine` and `Remove` methods, respectively.

## Description

Delegate types derive from the `System.Delegate` class. The declaration of a delegate type establishes a contract that specifies the signature of one or more methods. [*Note:* For an example of a delegate type declaration, see the examples at the end of this topic.]

Delegate types are implicitly sealed: it is not permissible to derive a new type from a delegate type. [*Note:* The `System.Delegate` class is not considered a delegate type; it is a class used to derive delegate types.]

[*Note:* For information on subclassing the `Delegate` class, see Partition II of the CLI Specification.]

A delegate is an instance of a delegate type. A non-`null` delegate references an *invocation list*, which is made up of one or more entries. Each entry consists of a pair of values: a non-`null` method and a corresponding object, called the *target*. If the method is static, the corresponding target is `null`; otherwise the target is the instance on which the method is to be called.

The signature of each method in the invocation list is required to exactly match the signature specified by the delegate's type.

When a delegate is invoked, the methods in the corresponding invocation list are invoked in the order in which they appear in that list. A delegate attempts to invoke every method in its invocation list, with duplicate methods being invoked once for each occurrence in that list.

Delegates are immutable; once created, the invocation list of a delegate does not change. Combining operations, such as `System.Delegate.Combine` and `System.Delegate.Remove`, cannot alter existing delegates. Instead, such operations result in the return of either a new delegate that contains the results of the operation, an existing delegate, or the `null` value. [*Note:* A combining operation returns the `null` value when the result of the operation is an empty invocation list. A combining operation returns an existing delegate when the requested operation has no effect (for example, if an attempt is made to remove a nonexistent entry).]

If an invoked method throws an exception, the method stops executing and the exception is passed back to the caller of the delegate. The delegate does not continue invoking methods from its invocation list. Catching the exception in the caller does not alter this behavior. It is possible that non-standard methods that implement combining operations allow the creation of delegates with different behavior. When this is the case, the non-standard methods are required to specify the behavior.

When the signature of the methods invoked by a delegate includes a return value, the delegate returns the return value of the last element in the invocation list. When the signature includes a parameter that is passed by reference, the final value of the parameter is the result of every method in the invocation list executing sequentially and updating the parameter's value.

## Example

```
using System;
namespace Samples
{
  public delegate string MyDelegate(string s);
  public class MyClass
  {
    public static string StaticMethod(string s)
    {
      Console.WriteLine("StaticMethod(\"{0}\")", s);
      return(s.ToUpper());
    }
    public string InstanceMethod(string s)
   {
      Console.WriteLine("InstanceMethod(\"{0}\")", s);
      return(s.ToLower());
    }
  }
```

```
  public class DelegateSample
  {
    public static void Main()
    {
      MyClass m = new MyClass();
      MyDelegate s =
           new MyDelegate(MyClass.StaticMethod);
      MyDelegate i =
           new MyDelegate(m.InstanceMethod);
      Console.WriteLine("Method is {0}", s.Method);
      Console.WriteLine("Method is {0}", i.Method);
      Console.WriteLine("Returns: {0}", s("Call 1"));
      Console.WriteLine("Returns: {0}", i("Call 2"));
      MyDelegate d = (MyDelegate)
                               Delegate.Combine(s, i);
      Console.WriteLine("Returns: {0}", d("Call 3"));
    }
  }
}
```

The output is

```
Method is System.String StaticMethod(System.String)
Method is System.String InstanceMethod(System.String)
StaticMethod("Call 1")
Returns: CALL 1
InstanceMethod("Call 2")
Returns: call 2
StaticMethod("Call 3")
InstanceMethod("Call 3")
Returns: call 3
```

# System.Collections DictionaryEntry Structure

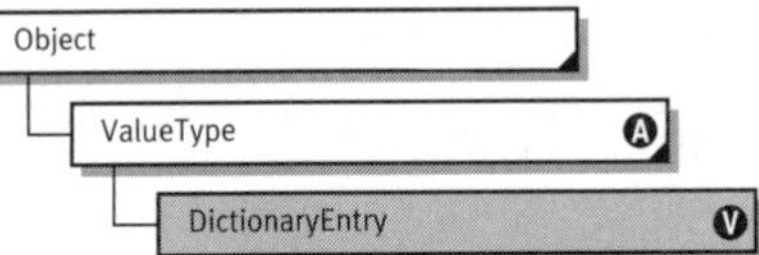


A B C D E F G H I J K L M N O P Q R S T U V W X Y Z

## Summary

Represents a dictionary entry consisting of a `System.Collections.DictionaryEntry.Key` and an associated `System.Collections.DictionaryEntry.Value`.

## Type Summary

```
public struct DictionaryEntry
{
  // Constructors
     public DictionaryEntry (object key, object value);

  // Properties
     public object Key { set; get; }
     public object Value { set; get; }
}
```

**AH** Note that we've used properties here when fields would have done. Using properties ensures that we can change the implementation later without breaking user code. In the design of the .NET Framework we preferred using properties over instance fields in almost every case.

**JR** When using the C# `foreach` statement with a `Hashtable`, each element through the loop is a `DictionaryEntry`. This is not obvious from the documentation and I know many programmers who have gotten stumped by this.

## Description

[*Note:* Some types that manage or access collections of objects, such as `System.Collections.Hashtable` and `System.Collections.IDictionaryEnumerator`, rely on the use of one or more pairs of a key object and an associated value object. `System.Collections.DictionaryEntry` provides this functionality. This structure supports the C# `foreach` semantics for `System.Collections.Hashtable`.]

## Example

```
using System;
using System.Collections;
namespace Samples
{
  public class DictionaryEntrySample
  {
    public static void Main()
    {
      Hashtable t = new Hashtable();
      t.Add("damien", "maire");
      t.Add("mark", "sacha");
      t.Add("brad", "tamara");
      foreach(DictionaryEntry d in t)
      {
        Console.WriteLine("Key: {0} Value: {1}",
                          d.Key, d.Value);
      }
    }
  }
}
```

The output is

```
Key: damien Value: maire
Key: mark Value: sacha
Key: brad Value: tamara
```

# System.IO Directory

BCL

## Summary

Provides information and performs operations on directories.

## Type Summary

```
public sealed class Directory
{
  // Methods
     MS public static DirectoryInfo CreateDirectory (string path);
        public static void Delete (string path);
        public static void Delete (string path,
                                   bool recursive);
        public static bool Exists (string path);
        public static DateTime GetCreationTime (string path);
MS CF 1.1 public static DateTime GetCreationTimeUtc (string path);
        public static string GetCurrentDirectory ();
        public static string[] GetDirectories (string path);
        public static string[] GetDirectories (string path,
                                               string searchPattern);
        public static string GetDirectoryRoot (string path);
        public static string[] GetFiles (string path);
        public static string[] GetFiles (string path,
                                         string searchPattern);
        public static string[] GetFileSystemEntries (string path);
        public static string[] GetFileSystemEntries (string path,
                                                     string searchPattern);
        public static DateTime GetLastAccessTime (string path);
MS CF 1.1 public static DateTime GetLastAccessTimeUtc (string path);
        public static DateTime GetLastWriteTime (string path);
MS CF 1.1 public static DateTime GetLastWriteTimeUtc (string path);
    MS CF public static string[] GetLogicalDrives ();
    MS CF public static DirectoryInfo GetParent (string path);
        public static void Move (string sourceDirName,
                                 string destDirName);
       CF public static void SetCreationTime (string path,
                                              DateTime creationTime);
MS CF 1.1 public static void SetCreationTimeUtc (string path,
                                                 DateTime creationTimeUtc);
        public static void SetCurrentDirectory (string path);
       CF public static void SetLastAccessTime (string path,
                                                DateTime lastAccessTime);
```

```
MS CF 1.1 public static void SetLastAccessTimeUtc (string path,
                                                  DateTime lastAccessTimeUtc);
       CF public static void SetLastWriteTime (string path,
                                               DateTime lastWriteTime);
MS CF 1.1 public static void SetLastWriteTimeUtc (string path,
                                                 DateTime lastWriteTimeUtc);
  }
```

**BA** During the standardization process we had some debate about the format of the file path. The question was whether we should allow a path format such as "C:\\foo\bar" or "\\foo\\bar" or "foo::bar"or all of these? In the end we decided it was acceptable to leave the path format up to each implementer. This does not have as large an effect on portability as you might guess, because most applications read this kind of path information in at runtime from the user, or from a configuration file native to the host system.

**BG** I came from a Unix background, and one of the first changes I made to our I/O package was to add support for using '/' as a directory separator. I believe implementers can vary `Path::DirectorySeparatorChar` and `AltDirectorySeparatorChar` as necessary for their platforms to support a common path separator character on all platforms, as well as handle their platform-specific characters. CLI implementations on Windows should use '\' and '/' respectively, whereas Unix implementations should use '/' and '\' and Mac implementations should probably use ':' and '\'.

## Description

Implementations are required to preserve the case of file and directory path strings, and to be case sensitive if and only if the current platform is case-sensitive.

[*Note:* In most `Directory` methods that accept *path* arguments, the path can refer to a file or a directory. ]

## Example

```
using System;
using System.IO;
namespace Samples
{
  public class DirectorySample
  {
    public static void Main()
    {
```

A B C D E F G H I J K L M N O P Q R S T U V W X Y Z

```
        string s = Directory.GetCurrentDirectory() +
                   @"\Test";
        Directory.CreateDirectory(s);
        DateTime d = Directory.GetLastWriteTime(s);
        Console.WriteLine("Last write time: {0}", d);
        d = d.AddYears(1);
        Directory.SetLastWriteTime(s, d);
        d = Directory.GetLastWriteTime(s);
        Console.WriteLine("Last write time: {0}", d);
      }
    }
  }
```

The output is

```
Last write time: 10/06/2003 2:29:42 PM
Last write time: 10/06/2004 2:29:42 PM
```

# DirectoryNotFoundException

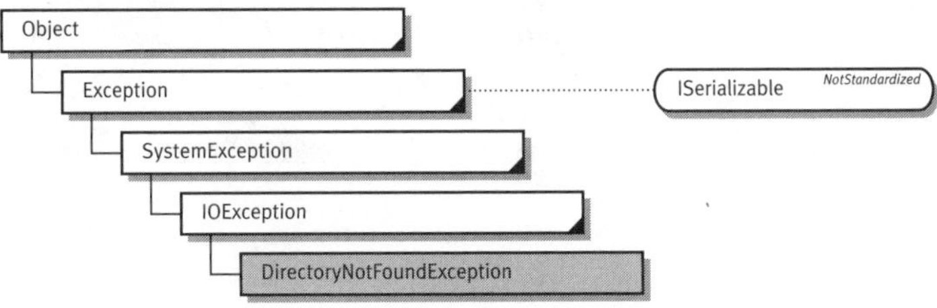


A B C D E F G H I J K L M N O P Q R S T U V W X Y Z

## Summary

Represents the error that occurs when part of a file or directory argument cannot be found.

## Type Summary

```
   public class DirectoryNotFoundException : IOException
   {
   // Constructors
      public DirectoryNotFoundException();
      public DirectoryNotFoundException(string message);
   CF public DirectoryNotFoundException(string message,Exception innerException);
MS CF protected DirectoryNotFoundException (SerializationInfo info,
                                             StreamingContext context);
   }
```

## Example

```
using System;
using System.IO;
namespace Samples
{
  public class DirectoryNotFoundExceptionSample
  {
    public static void Main()
    {
      try
      {
        string n = @"C:\foo\bar";
        string[] s = Directory.GetFiles(n);
      }
      catch(DirectoryNotFoundException e)
      {
        Console.WriteLine("Exception: {0}", e);
      }
    }
  }
}
```

The output is

```
Exception: System.IO.DirectoryNotFoundException: Could not find a part of the path
"C:\foo\bar".
   at System.IO.__Error.WinIOError(Int32 errorCode, String str)
   at System.IO.Directory.InternalGetFileDirectoryNames(String fullPath, Boolean
file)
   at System.IO.Directory.InternalGetFiles(String path, String searchPattern)
   at System.IO.Directory.GetFiles(String path, String searchPattern)
   at System.IO.Directory.GetFiles(String path)
   at Samples.DirectoryNotFoundExceptionSample.Main() in C:\Books\BCL\Samples\
System.IO\DirectoryNotFoundException\DirectoryNotFoundException.cs:line 13
```

# System DivideByZeroException

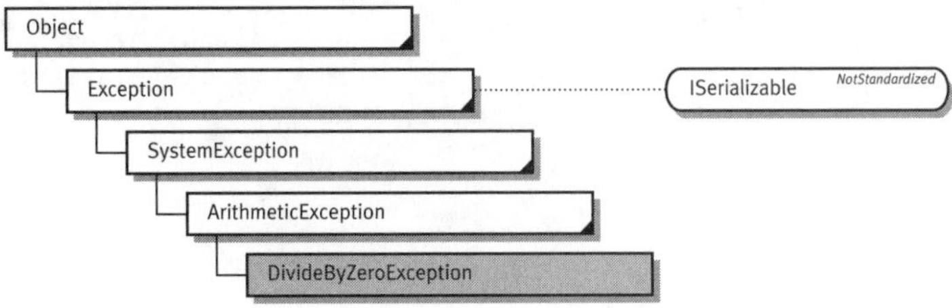


## Summary

Represents the error that is caused by an attempt to divide a number by zero.

## Type Summary

```
public class DivideByZeroException : ArithmeticException
{
  // Constructors
     public DivideByZeroException ();
     public DivideByZeroException (string message);
     public DivideByZeroException (string message,
                                   Exception innerException);
MS CF protected DivideByZeroException (SerializationInfo info,
                                   StreamingContext context);
}
```

## Example

```
using System;

namespace Samples
{
  public class DivideByZeroExceptionSample
  {
    public static void Main()
    {
      try
      {
        int i = 0;
        Console.WriteLine(42 / i);
      }
      catch(DivideByZeroException e)
      {
        Console.WriteLine("Exception: {0}", e);
      }
    }
  }
}
```

The output is

```
Exception: System.DivideByZeroException: Attempted to divide by zero.
   at Samples.DivideByZeroExceptionSample.Main() in C:\Books\BCL\Samples\System\
DivideByZeroException\DivideByZeroException.cs:line 12
```

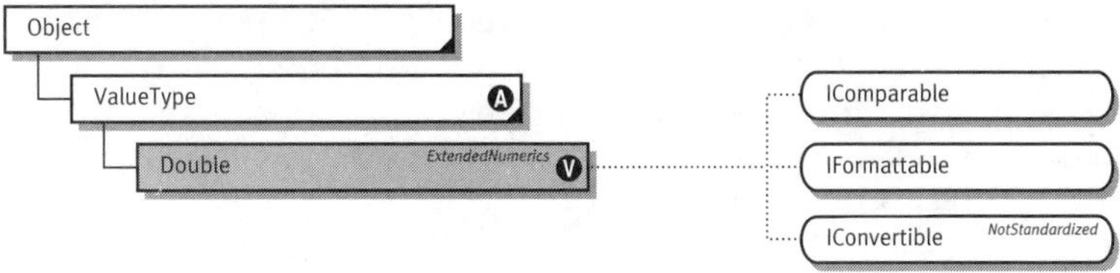


A B C D E F G H I J K L M N O P Q R S T U V W X Y Z

## Summary

Represents a 64-bit double-precision floating-point number.

## Type Summary

```
public struct Double : IComparable, IFormattable,
                       IConvertible
{
  // Fields
     public const double Epsilon = 4.9406564584124654E-324;
     public const double MaxValue = 1.7976931348623157E+308;
     public const double MinValue = -1.7976931348623157E+308;
     public const double NaN = (double)0.0 / (double)0.0;
     public const double NegativeInfinity = (double)-1.0 / (double)0.0;
     public const double PositiveInfinity = (double)1.0  / (double)0.0;

  // Methods
     public int CompareTo (object value);
     public override bool Equals (object obj);
     public override int GetHashCode ();
  MS public TypeCode GetTypeCode ();
     public static bool IsInfinity (double d);
     public static bool IsNaN (double d);
     public static bool IsNegativeInfinity (double d);
     public static bool IsPositiveInfinity (double d);
     public static double Parse (string s);
     public static double Parse (string s, NumberStyles style);
     public static double Parse (string s, NumberStyles style,
                                 IFormatProvider provider);
     public static double Parse (string s, IFormatProvider provider);
     public override string ToString ();
     public string ToString (string format);
     public string ToString (string format, IFormatProvider provider);
     public string ToString (IFormatProvider provider);
MS CF public static bool TryParse (string s, NumberStyles style,
                                  IFormatProvider provider,
                                  out double result);
```

Double Structure

```
    // Explicit Interface Members
    MS bool IConvertible.ToBoolean(IFormatProvider provider);
    MS byte IConvertible.ToByte(IFormatProvider provider);
    MS char IConvertible.ToChar(IFormatProvider provider);
    MS DateTime IConvertible.ToDateTime(IFormatProvider provider);
    MS decimal IConvertible.ToDecimal(IFormatProvider provider);
    MS double IConvertible.ToDouble(IFormatProvider provider);
    MS short IConvertible.ToInt16(IFormatProvider provider);
    MS int IConvertible.ToInt32(IFormatProvider provider);
    MS long IConvertible.ToInt64(IFormatProvider provider);
    MS sbyte IConvertible.ToSByte(IFormatProvider provider);
    MS float IConvertible.ToSingle(IFormatProvider provider);
    MS object IConvertible.ToType(Type type,IFormatProvider provider);
    MS ushort IConvertible.ToUInt16(IFormatProvider provider);
    MS uint IConvertible.ToUInt32(IFormatProvider provider);
    MS ulong IConvertible.ToUInt64(IFormatProvider provider);
}
```

**BA** Notice that we use the common casing of NaN for Not-A-Number. Strictly following the design guideline rules would have led us to `Double.Nan`. This is a case where we did the right thing in violating the guidelines. It reminds me of the line, "foolish consistency is the hobgoblin of little minds..." by Ralph Waldo Emerson.

**BG** You might wonder why this simple code would throw an OverflowException:

```
string s = Double.MaxValue.ToString();
double d = Convert.ToDouble(s);
```

The `Convert.ToDouble()` method throws an exception due to rounding errors. Note that the IEEE spec for doubles says that a double has about 15.7 decimal digits worth of precision, but to accurately represent that number you need to print out 17 digits to avoid rounding errors.

It is actually difficult to correctly generate those 17 digits on all hardware (at least in an efficient way). In the implementation of this class we happen to support it just fine on x86 due to some special case x86 assembly code. So on x86, you can use the "R" format (for round-trippable), but keep in mind that the "R" format may not work efficiently on all platforms. Here is an example of using the "R" format:

```
CultureInfo ci = CultureInfo.InvariantCulture;
Double d = Double.Parse(Double.MaxValue.ToString("R", ci), ci);
```

*CONTINUED*

As you may know, number formatting is culture sensitive. If you are writing code that needs to work identically on all machines, you should use the invariant culture. If you are writing a client application you can use the thread's current culture to get the appropriate decimal formatting for that culture.

**KG** The default formatting behavior for `Double` has caused some confusion. Simply stated, formatting a double by default selects the shortest available representation. For example:

```
Double d1 = 0.0004;
Double d2 = 0.00004;

Console.WriteLine(d1); //Prints 0.0004
Console.WriteLine(d2);  //Prints 4E-05
```

## Description

`System.Double` is a 64-bit double precision floating-point type that represents values ranging from approximately 5.0E–324 to 1.7E+308 and from approximately –5.0E–324 to –1.7E+308 with a precision of 15–16 decimal digits. The `System.Double` type conforms to standard IEC 60559:1989, Binary Floating-point Arithmetic for Microprocessor Systems.

A `System.Double` can represent the following values:

- The finite set of non-zero values of the form $s * m * 2^e$, where $s$ is 1 or –1, and $0 < m < 2^{53}$ and $-1075 <= e <= 970$.
- Positive infinity and negative infinity. Infinities are produced by operations that produce results with a magnitude greater than that which can be represented by a `System.Double`, such as dividing a non-zero number by zero. For example, using `System.Double` operands, `1.0 / 0.0` yields positive infinity, and `-1.0 / 0.0` yields negative infinity. Operations include passing parameters and returning values.
- The *Not-a-Number* value (NaN). NaN values are produced by invalid floating-point operations, such as dividing zero by zero.
- When performing binary operations, if one of the operands is a `System.Double`, then the other operand is required to be an integral type or a floating-point type (`System.Double` or `System.Single`). Prior to performing the operation, if the other operand is not a `System.Double`, it is converted to `System.Double`, and the operation is performed using at least `System.Double` range and precision. If the operation produces a numeric result, the type of the result is `System.Double`.

Double Structure

The floating-point operators, including the assignment operators, do not throw exceptions. Instead, in exceptional situations, the result of a floating-point operation is zero, infinity, or NaN, as described below:

- If the result of a floating-point operation is too small for the destination format, the result of the operation is zero.
- If the magnitude of the result of a floating-point operation is too large for the destination format, the result of the operation is positive infinity or negative infinity, as appropriate for the sign of the result.
- If a floating-point operation is invalid, the result of the operation is NaN.
- If one or both operands of a floating-point operation are NaN, the result of the operation is NaN.
- Conforming implementations of the CLI are permitted to perform floating-point operations using a precision that is higher than that required by the `System.Double` type. For example, hardware architectures that support an "extended" or "long double" floating-point type with greater range and precision than the `System.Double` type could implicitly perform all floating-point operations using this higher precision type. Expressions evaluated using a higher precision may cause a finite result to be produced instead of an infinity.

## Example

```
using System;

namespace Samples
{
  public class DoubleMaxValue
  {
    public static void Main()
    {
      Double max = Double.MaxValue,
             epsilon = Double.Epsilon,
             nan = Double.NaN,
             negativeInfinity = Double.NegativeInfinity,
             positiveInfinity = Double.PositiveInfinity,
             min = Double.MinValue;
      Console.WriteLine("MaxValue: {0}", max);
      Console.WriteLine("Epsilon: {0}", epsilon);
      Console.WriteLine("Nan: {0}", nan);
      Console.WriteLine("NegativeInfinity: {0}", negativeInfinity);
      Console.WriteLine("PositiveInfinity: {0}", positiveInfinity);
      Console.WriteLine("MinValue: {0}", min);
      string s = Double.MaxValue.ToString("R");
```

Double Structure

```
      Console.WriteLine("From String {0} yields {1}",
                        s, Double.Parse(s));
      string[] formats = {"C","E","e4","F","G","N","P","R"};
      foreach(string f in formats)
        Console.WriteLine("{0}.ToString(\"{1}\") yields {2}",
                        epsilon, f, epsilon.ToString(f));
    }
  }
}
```

The output is

```
MaxValue: 1.79769313486232E+308
Epsilon: 4.94065645841247E-324
Nan: NaN
NegativeInfinity: -Infinity
PositiveInfinity: Infinity
MinValue: -1.79769313486232E+308
From String 1.7976931348623157E+308 yields 1.79769313486232E+308
4.94065645841247E-324.ToString("C") yields $0.00
4.94065645841247E-324.ToString("E") yields 4.940656E-324
4.94065645841247E-324.ToString("e4") yields 4.9407e-324
4.94065645841247E-324.ToString("F") yields 0.00
4.94065645841247E-324.ToString("G") yields 4.94065645841247E-324
4.94065645841247E-324.ToString("N") yields 0.00
4.94065645841247E-324.ToString("P") yields 0.00 %
4.94065645841247E-324.ToString("R") yields 4.94065645841247E-324
```

# System DuplicateWaitObjectException



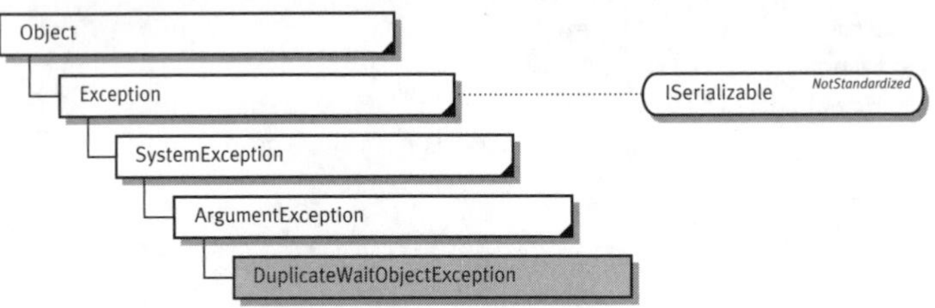


## Summary

Represents the error that occurs when an object appears more than once in an array of `System.Threading.WaitHandle` instances.

## Type Summary

```
   CF public class DuplicateWaitObjectException : ArgumentException
   {
     // Constructors
     CF public DuplicateWaitObjectException ();
     CF public DuplicateWaitObjectException (string parameterName);
     CF public DuplicateWaitObjectException (string parameterName,
                                             string message);
MS CF protected DuplicateWaitObjectException (SerializationInfo info,
                                              StreamingContext context);
   }
```

> **BA** See my comments on `ArgumentNullException`.

## Description

[*Note:* It is generally unnecessary for applications to throw `System.DuplicateWaitObjectException`. This exception is thrown by thread synchronization methods, such as `System.Threading.WaitHandle.WaitAll` and `System.Threading.WaitHandle.WaitAny`.]

## Example

```
using System;
using System.Threading;

namespace Samples
{
```

```
  public class DuplicateWaitObjectExceptionSample
  {
    public static AutoResetEvent[] autoResetEvents =
                                   new AutoResetEvent[2];
    public static void Main()
    {
      try
      {
        autoResetEvents[0] = new AutoResetEvent(false);
        autoResetEvents[1] = autoResetEvents[0];
        WaitHandle.WaitAll(autoResetEvents);
      }
      catch(DuplicateWaitObjectException e)
      {
        Console.WriteLine("Exception: {0}", e);
      }
    }
  }
}
```

The output is

```
Exception: System.DuplicateWaitObjectException: Duplicate objects in argument.
   at System.Threading.WaitHandle.WaitMultiple(WaitHandle[] waitHandles, Int32
millisecondsTimeout, Boolean exitContext, Boolean WaitAll)
   at System.Threading.WaitHandle.WaitAll(WaitHandle[] waitHandles, Int32
millisecondsTimeout, Boolean exitContext)
   at System.Threading.WaitHandle.WaitAll(WaitHandle[] waitHandles)
   at Samples.DuplicateWaitObjectExceptionSample.Main() in C:\Books\BCL\Samples\
System\DuplicateWaitObjectException\DuplicateWaitObjectException.cs:line 16
```

# System.Text Encoder

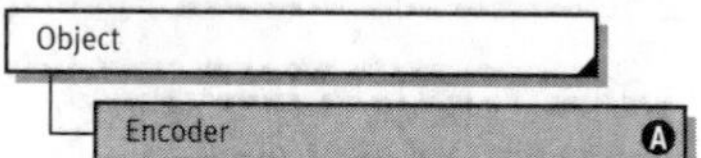




## Summary

Converts blocks of characters into blocks of bytes.

## Type Summary

```
public abstract class Encoder
{
  // Constructors
     protected Encoder ();

  // Methods
     public abstract int GetByteCount (char[] chars,
                                       int index,
                                       int count,
                                       bool flush);
     public abstract int GetBytes (char[] chars,
                                   int charIndex,
                                   int charCount,
                                   byte[] bytes,
                                   int byteIndex,
                                   bool flush);
}
```

## Description

[*Note:* Following instantiation of a `System.Text.Encoder`, sequential blocks of characters are converted into blocks of bytes through calls to the `System.Text.Encoder.GetBytes` method. The encoder maintains state between the conversions, allowing it to correctly encode character sequences that span adjacent blocks. An instance of a specific implementation of the `System.Text.Encoder` class is typically obtained through a call to the `System.Text.Encoding.GetEncoder`.]

# System.Text
# Encoding

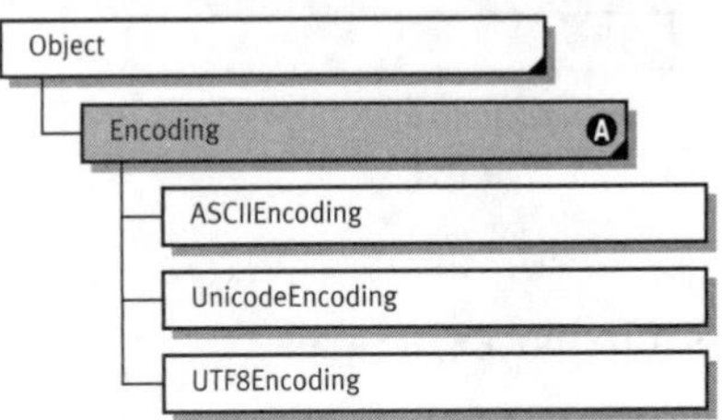


A B C D E F G H I J K L M N O P Q R S T U V W X Y Z

## Summary

Represents a character encoding.

## Type Summary

```
public abstract class Encoding : ICloneable
{
  // Constructors
     protected Encoding ();
  MS protected Encoding (int codePage);

  // Properties
     public static Encoding ASCII { get; }
     public static Encoding BigEndianUnicode { get; }
MS CF public virtual string BodyName { get; }
  MS public virtual int CodePage { get; }
     public static Encoding Default { get; }
MS CF public virtual string EncodingName { get; }
MS CF public virtual string HeaderName { get; }
MS CF public virtual bool IsBrowserDisplay { get; }
MS CF public virtual bool IsBrowserSave { get; }
MS CF public virtual bool IsMailNewsDisplay { get; }
MS CF public virtual bool IsMailNewsSave { get; }
     public static Encoding Unicode { get; }
  MS public static Encoding UTF7 { get; }
     public static Encoding UTF8 { get; }
  MS public virtual string WebName { get; }
MS CF public virtual int WindowsCodePage { get; }

  // Methods
     public static byte[] Convert (Encoding srcEncoding,
                                   Encoding dstEncoding,
                                   byte[] bytes);
     public static byte[] Convert (Encoding srcEncoding,
                                   Encoding dstEncoding,
                                   byte[] bytes,
                                   int index,
```

```
                                        int count);
      public override bool Equals (object value);
      public virtual int GetByteCount (char[] chars);
      public abstract int GetByteCount (char[] chars,
                                        int index,
                                        int count);
      public virtual int GetByteCount (string s);
      public virtual byte[] GetBytes (char[] chars);
      public virtual byte[] GetBytes (char[] chars,
                                      int index,
                                      int count);
      public abstract int GetBytes (char[] chars,
                                    int charIndex,
                                    int charCount,
                                    byte[] bytes,
                                    int byteIndex);
      public virtual byte[] GetBytes (string s);
      public virtual int GetBytes (string s, int charIndex,
                                   int charCount,
                                   byte[] bytes,
                                   int byteIndex);
      public virtual int GetCharCount (byte[] bytes);
      public abstract int GetCharCount (byte[] bytes,
                                        int index,
                                        int count);
      public virtual char[] GetChars (byte[] bytes);
      public virtual char[] GetChars (byte[] bytes,
                                      int index,
                                      int count);
      public abstract int GetChars (byte[] bytes,
                                    int byteIndex,
                                    int byteCount,
                                    char[] chars,
                                    int charIndex);
      public virtual Decoder GetDecoder ();
      public virtual Encoder GetEncoder ();
   MS public static Encoding GetEncoding (int codepage);
   MS public static Encoding GetEncoding (string name);
      public override int GetHashCode ();
      public abstract int GetMaxByteCount (int charCount);
      public abstract int GetMaxCharCount (int byteCount);
      public virtual byte[] GetPreamble ();
   CF public virtual string GetString (byte[] bytes);
      public virtual string GetString (byte[] bytes,
                                       int index,
                                       int count);
}
```

A B C D E F G H I J K L M N O P Q R S T U V W X Y Z

**YL** The CLR is totally based on the Unicode standard, and it uses UTF-16 internally as the encoding for the Unicode characters. When the CLR needs to interoperate with other encodings, `Encoding` class is used to handle the conversion from UTF-16 to other encodings. Traditionally, Win32 API provides `WideCharToMultiByte()` to convert UTF-16 characters to other codepages, and `MultiByteToWideChar()` to convert bytes in codepages to UTF-16 characters. The `Encoding.GetChars()` and `Encoding.GetBytes()` are designed to provide the same functionalities.

When `Encoding` was designed, one of the goals was to provide the encoding ability from both the Windows operating system and the `MLang`. `MLang` is a COM-based interfaced introduced in IE to provide more Internet-oriented globalization functionality. One of the important features that `MLang` provides is to support "buffered" operation in encoding. Because of the nature of the Internet, data is sent in packets. When codepage bytes are sent in packets, chances are that MBCS (Multi-Byte Character Set) bytes can be split in the middle. For example, a 3-byte UTF8 sequence can be split into one byte in the first packet and another two bytes in the second packet. `MLang` provides a function call to remember the state between two conversion calls, so that the final Unicode character can be assembled correctly. The `Encoding` class provides the same functionality by using the `Encoder` and `Decoder` class. `Encoder` supports the buffered operation for converting Unicode to bytes in other encodings. That is, if there is a surrogate split in two buffers, it will generate the bytes correctly by remembering the high-surrogate in the first buffer. Similarly, `Decoder` supports the buffered operation for *convert bytes* in other encoding back into Unicode characters. If a sequence of MBCS bytes is split, it will generate the Unicode characters by remembering the leading bytes in the first buffer.

The name of `Encoder` and `Decoder` can be confusing sometimes. The way to think about it is that `Encoder` *encodes* Unicode characters to bytes in other encodings, and `Decoder` *decodes* bytes in other encoding back into Unicode characters.

**BA** I really like what we did here by providing the common encodings right in the class. I find that takes it care of greater than 80% of the cases. And notice that, because we used properties, the encodings' creation can be delayed until they are first requested.

The ASCII and UTF8 properties are not cased correctly. They should be Utf8 and Ascii, respectively. We finalized the rules for casing properties too late to fix these issues.

*CONTINUED*

BG In retrospect I would have named the `Default` property more precisely. In the Microsoft CLI implementation, it returns an encoding representing the machine's current ANSI code page. ANSI code pages may have been a good idea in the early 90's before Unicode, and we still need to support reading text in various code pages; however they are no longer valuable in mainstream usage. So `Default` should either be a Unicode transformation format to represent all Unicode code points (such as UTF-8), or it should be named something like `DefaultCodePage`. In practice, any application that will run in more than one locale should probably never use this property.

JR Normally, there is no need for your application code to construct an `Encoding`-derived object (such as `ASCIIEncoding`). Instead, you normally obtain an `Encoding`-derived object by calling one of `Encoding` class's static, read-only properties. Here is an example:

```
ASCIIEncoding asciiEncoding = Encoding.ASCII;
```

This is more efficient because it returns a reference to a single `ASCIIEncoding` object rather than creating new `ASCIIEncoding` objects.

A B C D E F G H I J K L M N O P Q R S T U V W X Y Z

## Description

Characters are abstract entities that can be represented using many different character schemes or codepages. For example, Unicode UTF-16 encoding represents, or encodes, characters as sequences of 16-bit integers while Unicode UTF-8 represents the same characters as sequences of 8-bit bytes.

The BCL includes the following types derived from `System.Text.Encoding`:

- `System.Text.ASCIIEncoding`—encodes Unicode characters as 7-bit ASCII characters. This encoding only supports code points between U+0000 and U+007F inclusive.
- `System.Text.UnicodeEncoding`—encodes each Unicode character as two consecutive bytes. Both little-endian and big-endian byte orders are supported.
- `System.Text.UTF8Encoding`—encodes Unicode characters using the UTF-8 (UCS Transformation Format, 8-bit form) encoding. This encoding supports all Unicode character values.

An application can use the properties of this class such as `System.Text.Encoding.ASCII`, `System.Text.Encoding.Default`, `System.Text.Encoding.Unicode`, and `System.Text.Encoding.UTF8` to obtain encodings. Applications can initialize new instances of `System.Text.Encoding` objects through the `System.Text.ASCIIEncoding`, `System.Text.UnicodeEncoding`, and `System.Text.UTF8Encoding` classes.

Through an encoding, the `System.Text.Encoding.GetBytes` method is used to convert arrays of Unicode characters to arrays of bytes, and the `System.Text.Encoding.GetChars` method is used to convert arrays of bytes to arrays of Unicode characters. The `System.Text.Encoding.GetBytes` and `System.Text.Encoding.GetChars` methods maintain no state between conversions. When the data to be converted is only available in sequential blocks (such as data read from a stream) or when the amount of data is so large that it needs to be divided into smaller blocks, an application can choose to use a `System.Text.Decoder` or a `System.Text.Encoder` to perform the conversion. Decoders and encoders allow sequential blocks of data to be converted and they maintain the state required to support conversions of data that spans adjacent blocks. Decoders and encoders are obtained using the `System.Text.Encoding.GetDecoder` and `System.Text.Encoding.GetEncoder` methods.

The core `System.Text.Encoding.GetBytes` and `System.Text.Encoding.GetChars` methods require the caller to provide the destination buffer and ensure that the buffer is large enough to hold the entire result of the conversion. When using these methods, either directly on a `System.Text.Encoding` object or on an associated `System.Text.Decoder` or `System.Text.Encoder`, an application can use one of two methods to allocate destination buffers.

The `System.Text.Encoding.GetByteCount` and `System.Text.Encoding.GetCharCount` methods can be used to compute the exact size of the result of a particular conversion, and an appropriately sized buffer for that conversion can then be allocated.

The `System.Text.Encoding.GetMaxByteCount` and `System.Text.Encoding.GetMaxCharCount` methods can be used to compute the maximum possible size of a conversion of a given number of characters or bytes, regardless of the actual character or byte values, and a buffer of that size can then be reused for multiple conversions.

The first method generally uses less memory, whereas the second method generally executes faster.

## Example

```
using System;
using System.Text;
namespace Samples
{
  public class EncoderSample
  {
    public static void Main()
    {
      UTF8Encoding u = (UTF8Encoding) Encoding.UTF8;
      string s = "Pi is (\u03a0)";
      Byte[] bytes = u.GetBytes(s);
      foreach(Int16 i in bytes)
```

```
        Console.Write("{0}, ", i);
      Console.WriteLine();
      int count = u.GetCharCount(bytes, 0,
                           bytes.Length);
      char[] chars = new char[count];
      u.GetChars(bytes, 0, bytes.Length, chars, 0);
      foreach(Int16 i in chars)
        Console.Write("{0}, ", i);
      Console.WriteLine();
    }
  }
}
```

The output is

```
80, 105, 32, 105, 115, 32, 40, 206, 160, 41,
80, 105, 32, 105, 115, 32, 40, 928, 41,
```

# System.IO EndOfStreamException

BCL



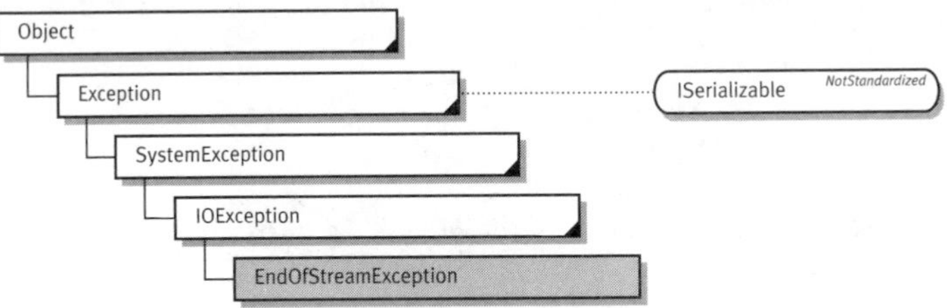


## Summary

Represents the error that occurs when an attempt is made to read past the end of a stream.

## Type Summary

```
public class EndOfStreamException : IOException
{
  // Constructors
     public EndOfStreamException ();
     public EndOfStreamException (string message);
     public EndOfStreamException (string message,
                                  Exception innerException);
MS CF protected EndOfStreamException (SerializationInfo info,
                                  StreamingContext context);
}
```

> **BA** Our general rule on the use of `Exceptions` is that they are to be used in *exceptional* situations only. By exceptional we mean situations that the client will very likely have to write special case error handling code. So, is reading to the end of a stream an exceptional situation? Not if you are reading byte-by-byte through the stream; in such a case you always read the end of the stream, so that is not an exceptional situation. However, if you are reading 32 bit values out of the stream and you find the end of the stream when you have read only 16 bits out then that *is* exceptional, and clearly an error case. The file format you are reading is likely corrupted. This latter case is where this exception should be used.

## Example

```
using System;
using System.IO;
using System.Text;
namespace Samples
{
  public class EndOfStreamExceptionSample
  {
    public static void Main()
    {
      string s = "filestream.txt";
      FileStream fs = new FileStream(s, FileMode.Open);
      BinaryReader br =
                  new BinaryReader(fs, Encoding.ASCII );
      try
      {
        while(true)
        {
          char c = br.ReadChar();
        }
      }
      catch(EndOfStreamException e )
      {
        Console.WriteLine("Exception: {0}", e);
      }
    }
  }
}
```

The output is

```
Exception: System.IO.EndOfStreamException: Unable to read beyond the end of the
stream.
   at System.IO.__Error.EndOfFile()
   at System.IO.BinaryReader.ReadChar()
   at Samples.EndOfStreamExceptionSample.Main() in C:\Books\BCL\Samples\System.IO\
EndOfStreamException\EndOfStreamException.cs:line 19
```

# System
# Enum

Object
ValueType (A)
Enum (A)
AttributeTargets (E)
DateTimeStyles (E)
NumberStyles (E)
UnicodeCategory (E)
FileAccess (E)
FileMode (E)
FileShare (E)
SeekOrigin (E)
EnvironmentPermissionAccess (E)
FileIOPermissionAccess (E)
PermissionState (E)
SecurityAction (E)
SecurityPermissionFlag (E)
ThreadPriority (E)
ThreadState (E)

IComparable
IFormattable
IConvertible NotStandardized



## Summary

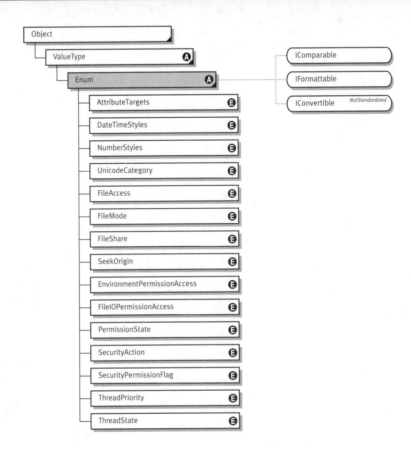

Provides support for all enumeration types. Serves as the base class for all enumeration types.

## Type Summary

```
public abstract class Enum : ValueType, IComparable,
                             IFormattable, IConvertible
{
  // Methods
  CF public int CompareTo (object target);
  CF public override bool Equals (object obj);
  CF public static string Format (Type enumType,
                                  object value,
                                  string format);
  CF public override int GetHashCode ();
```

```
CF public static string GetName (Type enumType,
                                 object value);
CF public static string[] GetNames (Type enumType);
MS public TypeCode GetTypeCode ();
   public static Type GetUnderlyingType (Type enumType);
CF public static Array GetValues (Type enumType);
   public static bool IsDefined (Type enumType,
                                 object value);
CF public static object Parse (Type enumType,
                               string value);
CF public static object Parse (Type enumType,
                               string value,
                               bool ignoreCase);
CF public static object ToObject (Type enumType,
                                  byte value);
CF public static object ToObject (Type enumType,
                                  int value);
CF public static object ToObject (Type enumType,
                                  long value);
   public static object ToObject (Type enumType,
                                  object value);
CF public static object ToObject (Type enumType,
                                  sbyte value);
CF public static object ToObject (Type enumType,
                                  short value);
CF public static object ToObject (Type enumType,
                                  uint value);
CF public static object ToObject (Type enumType,
                                  ulong value);
CF public static object ToObject (Type enumType,
                                  ushort value);
   public override string ToString ();
CF public string ToString (string format);
CF public string ToString (string format, IFormatProvider provider);
CF public string ToString (IFormatProvider provider);

// Explicit Interface Members
MS bool IConvertible.ToBoolean(IFormatProvider provider);
MS byte IConvertible.ToByte(IFormatProvider provider);
MS char IConvertible.ToChar(IFormatProvider provider);
MS DateTime IConvertible.ToDateTime(IFormatProvider provider);
MS decimal IConvertible.ToDecimal(IFormatProvider provider);
MS double IConvertible.ToDouble(IFormatProvider provider);
MS short IConvertible.ToInt16(IFormatProvider provider);
MS int IConvertible.ToInt32(IFormatProvider provider);
MS long IConvertible.ToInt64(IFormatProvider provider);
MS sbyte IConvertible.ToSByte(IFormatProvider provider);
MS float IConvertible.ToSingle(IFormatProvider provider);
```

```
    MS object IConvertible.ToType(Type type,IFormatProvider provider);
    MS ushort IConvertible.ToUInt16(IFormatProvider provider);
    MS uint IConvertible.ToUInt32(IFormatProvider provider);
    MS ulong IConvertible.ToUInt64(IFormatProvider provider);
}
```



**BA** Notice that `System.Enum` is the only reference type that extends `System.ValueType`. In general I discourage designs where there is one special class that does not follow the rules. In this case the rule is that all subclasses of `ValueType` are stack allocated values. However, in this case I believe it was warranted to be able to have all `Enums` to have a common base.

Notice that enums can have any integral underlying type. By default in C# it is `int`, but it could be `long` or `byte` etc. That is why we have all the overloads of `ToObject()`.

```
public enum FamilyMember : byte {
    Tamara = 0,
    Brad = 1,
    Boston = 2,
}
```

In practice, this feature is rarely used. Unless you need the additional space it is best to use the default type of `int`.

Notice that enum values in the CLR are not forced to be defined in the class at compile time. You can cast any value (of the same underlying type) to the enum type. That is why it is always a good idea to do a check to be sure your enum value is expected. This line of code is perfectly legal and verifiable.

```
FamilyMember fm = (FamilyMember) 42;
```

**BG** We really have two different concepts of enums. One is the straight, simple enumerated type containing distinct values such as the days of the week. The other is what we've called "bitfields," where we expect users to bitwise OR multiple fields together. While the CLR stores both of these as enums, I've always fancied that some language would distinguish between these cases, making bitwise operations on simple enums illegal. To make this distinction though, you must use the `FlagsAttribute` to indicate that an `enum` is a bitfield.

*CONTINUED*

JR Since enums have an integral underlying type, enums are considered primitive values by most compilers (including C#). Compiler primitive values are compiled directly into code. This causes an interesting problem: If an assembly defines a public enum type with a symbol, say `MaxEntriesInList`, set to 50 and then another assembly is built referring to `MaxEntriesInList`, the value 50 is extracted at compile time and embedded into the referencing assembly. At runtime, the assembly that defines the enum type may not be required at all. This sounds good at first; but, if the value of `MaxEntriesInList` is later changed from 50 to 100, the referencing assembly will not be aware of this change—it must be recompiled to pick up the new value, 100. If you want to have a runtime association of a value between assemblies, do not use enumerated types, use read-only fields instead.

A B C D E F G H I J K L M N O P Q R S T U V W X Y Z

## Description

A `System.Enum` is a distinct type with named constant members. Each enumeration type has a corresponding integral type called the *underlying type* of the enumeration type. This underlying type is required to be a system-supplied integer type that is large enough to represent all values defined in the enumeration; the field that holds the underlying type must be called `value__`. A `System.Enum` declaration is allowed to explicitly declare any integral type other than `System.Char` as an underlying type. This includes `System.Byte`, `System.SByte`, `System.Int16`, `System.Int32`, `System.Int64`, `System.UInt16`, `System.UInt32`, and `System.UInt64`. A `System.Enum` declaration that does not explicitly declare an underlying type has an underlying type of `System.Int32`.

`System.Enum` derives from `System.ValueType` but is not a value type. Programming languages typically provide syntax to declare sets of a specified enumeration type consisting of named constants and their values.

It is possible to treat instances of a `System.Enum` as bit fields containing multiple values. For more information, see `System.FlagsAttribute`.

[*Note:* `System.Enum` provides methods to compare instances of enumeration types, convert the value of an instance to its `System.String` representation, convert the `System.String` representation of a number to an instance of the enumeration type, and create an instance of a specified enumeration and value.]

## Example

The following example demonstrates the use of two types of enumerations, one with the `Flags` attribute applied and one without. It is fair to say, however, that use of the attribute is a little contrived in this sample.

## Enum Class

```
using System;
namespace Samples
{
  public class EnumToString
  {
    enum DayOfWeek {Sunday, Monday, Tuesday,
                    Wednesday, Thursday, Friday, Saturday};
    [Flags]
    enum MonthOfYear {January = 0x1, February = 0x2,
                      March = 0x4, April = 0x8, May = 0x10,
                      June = 0x20, July = 0x40, August = 0x80,
                      September = 0x100, Ocotber = 0x200,
                      November = 0x400, December = 0x800};
    public static void Main()
    {
      string[] f = {"D", "F", "X", "G"};
      DayOfWeek d = DayOfWeek.Saturday;
      foreach(string s in f)
        Console.WriteLine(
                  "Value {0} formatted with {1}: {2}",
                 d, s, d.ToString(s));
      ++d;
      foreach(string s in f)
        Console.WriteLine(
                  "Value {0} formatted with {1}: {2}",
                 d, s, d.ToString(s));
      MonthOfYear ThirtyDayMonths = MonthOfYear.September |
                                    MonthOfYear.April |
                                    MonthOfYear.June |
                                    MonthOfYear.November;
      Console.WriteLine("30 day months: {0}", ThirtyDayMonths);
    }
  }
}
```

The output is

```
Value Saturday formatted with D: 6
Value Saturday formatted with F: Saturday
Value Saturday formatted with X: 00000006
Value Saturday formatted with G: Saturday
Value 7 formatted with D: 7
Value 7 formatted with F: Monday, Saturday
Value 7 formatted with X: 00000007
Value 7 formatted with G: 7
30 day months: April, June, September, November
```

# System
# Environment

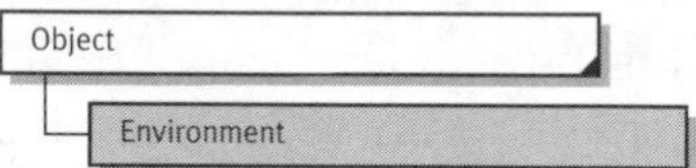


A B C D E F G H I J K L M N O P Q R S T U V W X Y Z

## Summary

Provides the current settings for, and information about, the execution environment.

## Type Summary

```
   public sealed class Environment
   {
     // Properties
     CF public static string CommandLine { get; }
  MS CF public static string CurrentDirectory { set; get; }
     CF public static int ExitCode { set; get; }
CF 1.1 public static bool HasShutdownStarted { get; }
  MS CF public static string MachineName { get; }
     CF public static string NewLine { get; }
     MS public static OperatingSystem OSVersion { get; }
     CF public static string StackTrace { get; }
  MS CF public static string SystemDirectory { get; }
        public static int TickCount { get; }
  MS CF public static string UserDomainName { get; }
  MS CF public static bool UserInteractive { get; }
  MS CF public static string UserName { get; }
        public static Version Version { get; }
  MS CF public static long WorkingSet { get; }

     // Methods
     CF public static void Exit (int exitCode);
  MS CF public static string ExpandEnvironmentVariables (string name);
     CF public static string[] GetCommandLineArgs ();
     CF public static string GetEnvironmentVariable (string variable);
     CF public static IDictionary GetEnvironmentVariables ();
  MS CF public static string GetFolderPath (Environment.SpecialFolder folder);
  MS CF public static string[] GetLogicalDrives ();
   }
```

BA One could argue that the `NewLine` member should have been a literal field rather than a property. The reason we did not use a literal field is because the value of `NewLine` changes from platform to platform. Literal values are burned into the call site so an application built for one platform would end up with the wrong value for `NewLine` when run on a different platform.

BG This class is a great example of what I would call a "static class," referring to a design pattern more than any language keyword. The class isn't instantiable (i.e., it has a private default constructor), is sealed, and all the members have to be static. `Console` is another example of a static class. However in the V1 implementation of the Microsoft CLI, I messed up and accidentally added a property to this class that wasn't static (`HasShutdownStarted`). Since it was an instance method on a class that could never be instantiated, no one could call it. We didn't discover the problem early enough in the product cycle to fix it before releasing V1.0.

If I were inventing a new language, I would explicitly add the concept of a static class into the language to help people avoid falling into this trap.

## Example

```
using System;
using System.Collections;
namespace Samples
{
  public class EnvironmentSample
  {
    public static void Main()
    {
      Console.WriteLine("Command line: {0}",
                        Environment.CommandLine);
      Console.WriteLine("CLR Version: {0}",
                        Environment.Version);
      string[] a = Environment.GetCommandLineArgs();
      foreach(string s in a)
        Console.WriteLine("Command Line Argument: {0}", s);
      IDictionary d = Environment.GetEnvironmentVariables();
      IDictionaryEnumerator e = d.GetEnumerator();
      while(e.MoveNext())
        Console.WriteLine("Key: {0} Value: {1}",
                          e.Key, e.Value);
    }
  }
}
```

The output is

```
Command line: Environment
CLR Version: 1.0.3705.288
Command Line Argument: Environment
Key: SystemDrive Value: C:
Key: USERPROFILE Value: C:\Documents and Settings\damien
Key: INCLUDE Value: C:\Program Files\Microsoft Visual Studio
.NET\VC7\ATLMFC\INCLUDE;C:\Program Files\Microsoft Visual Studio
.NET\VC7\INCLUDE;C:\Program Files\Microsoft Visual Studio
.NET\VC7\PlatformSDK\include\prerelease;C:\Program Files\Microsoft Visual Studio
.NET\VC7\PlatformSDK\include;C:\Program Files\Microsoft Visual Studio
.NET\FrameworkSDK\include;C:\Program Files\Microsoft Visual Studio
.NET\FrameworkSDK\include\
...
Key: HOMEPATH Value: \Documents and Settings\damien
Key: PROMPT Value: $P$G
Key: TEMP Value: C:\DOCUME~1\damien\LOCALS~1\Temp
Key: LIB Value: C:\Program Files\Microsoft Visual Studio
.NET\VC7\ATLMFC\LIB;C:\Program Files\Microsoft Visual Studio
.NET\VC7\LIB;C:\Program Files\Microsoft Visual Studio
.NET\VC7\PlatformSDK\lib\prerelease;C:\Program Files\Microsoft Visual Studio
.NET\VC7\PlatformSDK\lib;C:\Program Files\Microsoft Visual Studio
.NET\FrameworkSDK\lib;C:\Program Files\Microsoft Visual Studio
.NET\FrameworkSDK\Lib\
Key: PROCESSOR_REVISION Value: 080a
Key: SESSIONNAME Value: Console
```

# System.Security.Permissions EnvironmentPermission

BCL



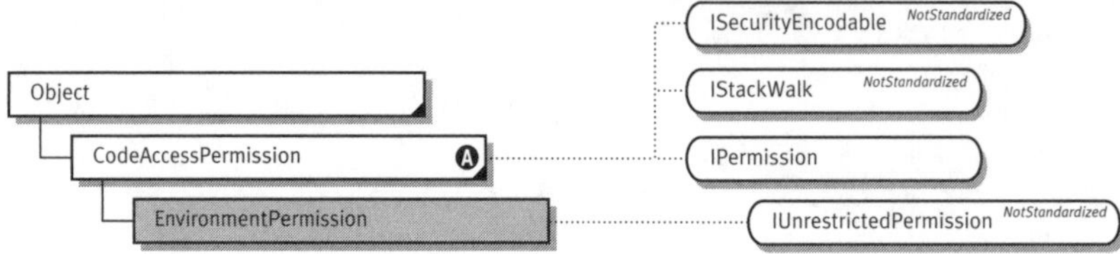


## Summary

Controls access to environment variables.

## Type Summary

```
   CF public sealed class EnvironmentPermission : CodeAccessPermission,
                                                  IUnrestrictedPermission
   {
     // Constructors
     CF public EnvironmentPermission(PermissionState state)
     CF public EnvironmentPermission(EnvironmentPermissionAccess flag,
                                     string pathList)

     // Methods
  MS CF public void AddPathList (EnvironmentPermissionAccess flag,
                                 string pathList);
     CF public override IPermission Copy ();
     CF public override void FromXml (SecurityElement esd);
  MS CF public string GetPathList (EnvironmentPermissionAccess flag);
     CF public override IPermission Intersect (IPermission target);
     CF public override bool IsSubsetOf (IPermission target);
  MS CF public bool IsUnrestricted ();
  MS CF public void SetPathList (EnvironmentPermissionAccess flag,
                                 string pathList);
     CF public override SecurityElement ToXml ();
     CF public override IPermission Union (IPermission other);
   }
```

## Description

[*Note:* `System.Security.Permissions.EnvironmentPermission` objects describe protected operations on environment variables. This permission distinguishes between the following types of access provided by `System.Security.Permissions.EnvironmentPermissionAccess`: These access levels are independent, meaning that rights to one do not imply rights to another. For example, `Write` permission does not imply permission to `Read`. `System.Security.Permissions.EnvironmentPermissionAccess` values can be combined using a bitwise OR operator. The `System.Environment` class is used to access environment variables, subject to the permissions defined by

`System.Security.Permissions.EnvironmentPermission`. Environment variables are case-insensitive.]

The XML encoding of a `System.Security.Permissions.EnvironmentPermission` instance is defined below in EBNF format. The following conventions are used:

- All non-literals in the grammar below are shown in normal type.
- All literals are in bold font.
- The following meta-language symbols are used:
  - '*' represents a meta-language symbol suffixing an expression that can appear zero or more times.
  - '?' represents a meta-language symbol suffixing an expression that can appear zero or one time.
  - '+' represents a meta-language symbol suffixing an expression that can appear one or more times.
  - '(',')' is used to group literals, non-literals, or a mixture of literals and non-literals.
  - '|' denotes an exclusive disjunction between two expressions.
  - '::=' denotes a production rule where a left-hand non-literal is replaced by a right-hand expression containing literals, non-literals, or both.
- BuildVersion refers to the build version of the shipping CLI. This is specified as a dotted build number such as '2412.0'.
- ECMAPubKeyToken ::= b77a5c561934e089
- EnvironmentVariable refers to the name of a single environment variable, such as 'PROMPT'.

The XML encoding of an `EnvironmentPermission` instance is as follows:

```
EnvironmentPermissionXML ::=
<IPermission
class="
System.Security.Permissions.EnvironmentPermission,
mscorlib,
Version=1.0.BuildVersion,
Culture=neutral,
PublicKeyToken=ECMAPubKeyToken"
version="1"
(
Unrestricted="true"
)
|
(
(Read=" EnvironmentVariable (; EnvironmentVariable)*" )?
(Write="EnvironmentVariable (; EnvironmentVariable)* " )?
)
/>
```

## Example

```
using System;
using System.Security;
using System.Security.Permissions;
namespace Samples
{
  public class EnvironmentPermissionSample
  {
    public static void Main()
    {
      string ev = "USERNAME";
      EnvironmentPermission p =
             new EnvironmentPermission(
                     EnvironmentPermissionAccess.Read,
                     ev);
      p.Assert();
      TestAccess(ev);
      CodeAccessPermission.RevertAssert();
      p.Deny();
      TestAccess(ev);
      CodeAccessPermission.RevertDeny();
      p.PermitOnly();
      TestAccess(ev);
      TestAccess("TEMP");
      CodeAccessPermission.RevertPermitOnly();
    }
    public static void TestAccess(string s)
    {
      try
      {
         Console.WriteLine("Variable {0} Value: {1}",
                 s,
                 Environment.GetEnvironmentVariable(s));
      }
      catch(Exception)
      {
        Console.WriteLine("Variable {0} cannot be read",
                          s);
      }
    }
  }
}
```

The output is

```
Variable USERNAME Value: damien
Variable USERNAME cannot be read
Variable USERNAME Value: damien
Variable TEMP cannot be read
```

# System.Security.Permissions EnvironmentPermissionAccess Enum

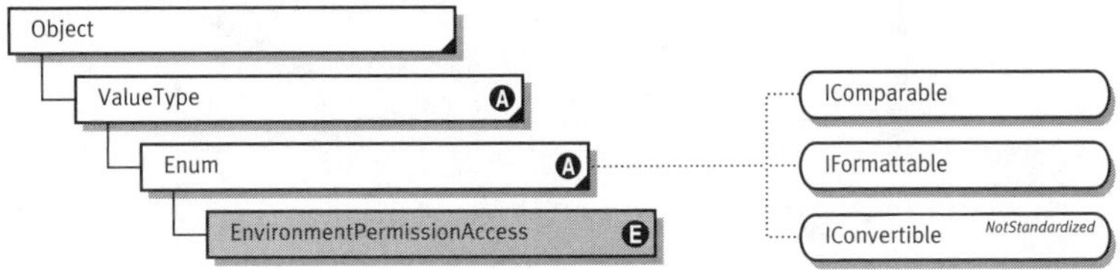




## Summary

Represents access to environment variables.

## Type Summary

```
CF public enum EnvironmentPermissionAccess  {
  CF AllAccess = Read|Write,
  CF NoAccess = 0x0,
  CF Read = 0x1,
  CF Write = 0x2,
}
```

## Description

[*Note:* This enumeration is used by the `System.Security.Permissions.EnvironmentPermission` class.]

## Example

```
using System;
using System.Security;
using System.Security.Permissions;
namespace Samples
{
  public class EnvironmentPermissionAccessSample
  {
    public static void Main()
    {
      try
      {
        string ev = "USERNAME";
        EnvironmentPermission p =
               new EnvironmentPermission(
                     EnvironmentPermissionAccess.Read,
                     ev);
        p.PermitOnly();
        Console.WriteLine("Variable {0} is {1}",
                     ev,
```

```
                        Environment.GetEnvironmentVariable(ev));
            CodeAccessPermission.RevertPermitOnly();
            p = new EnvironmentPermission(
                        EnvironmentPermissionAccess.NoAccess,
                        ev);
            p.PermitOnly();
            Console.WriteLine("Variable {0} is {1}",
                        ev,
                        Environment.GetEnvironmentVariable(ev));
          }
          catch(SecurityException e)
          {
            Console.WriteLine("Exception: {0}", e);
          }
        }
      }
    }
```

The output is

```
Variable USERNAME is damien
Exception: System.Security.SecurityException: Request for the permission of type
System.Security.Permissions.EnvironmentPermission, mscorlib, Version=1.0.3300.0,
Culture=neutral, PublicKeyToken=b77a5c561934e089 failed.
   at System.Security.SecurityRuntime.FrameDescHelper(FrameSecurityDescriptor
secDesc, IPermission demand, PermissionToken permToken)
   at System.Security.CodeAccessSecurityEngine.Check(PermissionToken permToken,
CodeAccessPermission demand, StackCrawlMark& stackMark, Int32 checkFrames, Int32
unrestrictedOverride)
   at System.Security.CodeAccessSecurityEngine.Check(CodeAccessPermission cap,
StackCrawlMark& stackMark)
   at System.Security.CodeAccessPermission.Demand()
   at System.Environment.GetEnvironmentVariable(String variable)
   at Samples.EnvironmentPermissionAccessSample.Main() in C:\Books\BCL\Samples\
System.Security\Permissions\EnvironmentPermissionAccess\
EnvironmentPermissionAccess.cs:line 27
```

# System.Security.Permissions EnvironmentPermissionAttribute

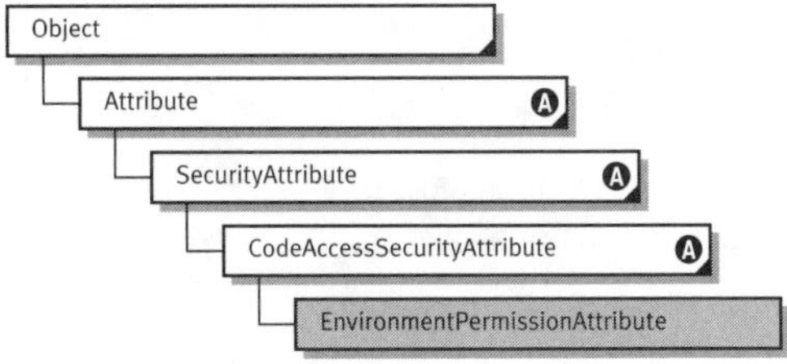




## Summary

Used to declaratively specify security actions to control access to environment variables.

## Type Summary

```
CF public sealed class EnvironmentPermissionAttribute :
                       CodeAccessSecurityAttribute
{
  // Constructors
  CF public EnvironmentPermissionAttribute(SecurityAction action);

  // Properties
  CF public string All { set;  }
  CF public string Read { set; get; }
  CF public string Write { set; get; }

  // Methods
  CF public override IPermission CreatePermission ();
}
```

## Description

Environment variable names are case-insensitive. Multiple environment variable names are specified by separating the names using the `System.IO.Path.PathSeparator` string.

[*Note:* The level of access to one or more environment variables is specified using the members of the current instance. For example, to specify read permissions for an environment variable, set the `System.Security.Permissions.EnvironmentPermissionAttribute.Read` property equal to the name of the environment variable. The security information declared by a security attribute is stored in the metadata of the attribute target, and is accessed by the system at runtime. Security attributes are used for declarative security only. For imperative security, use the corresponding permission class, `System.Security.Permissions.EnvironmentPermission`. The allowable `System.Security.Permissions.EnvironmentPermissionAttribute` targets are determined by the `System.Security.Permissions.SecurityAction` passed to the constructor.]

A
B
C
D
E
F
G
H
I
J
K
L
M
N
O
P
Q
R
S
T
U
V
W
X
Y
Z

## Example

```
using System;
using System.Security;
using System.Security.Permissions;
[assembly:EnvironmentPermissionAttribute(
              SecurityAction.RequestMinimum,
              Read="COMPUTERNAME;USERNAME")]
namespace Samples
{
  public class EnvironmentPermissionAttributeSample
  {
    public static void Main()
    {
      string[] v = {"USERNAME", "COMPUTERNAME"};
      foreach(string s in v)
        Console.WriteLine("Variable {0} Value: {1}",
                 s,
                 Environment.GetEnvironmentVariable(s));

    }
  }
}
```

The output is

```
Variable USERNAME Value: damien
Variable COMPUTERNAME Value: PROJECT42
```

# System
# EventArgs

## Summary

EventArgs is the base class for classes containing event data.

## Type Summary

```
public class EventArgs
{
  // Constructors
     public EventArgs ();

  // Fields
     public static readonly EventArgs Empty = new EventArgs();
}
```

**BA** Throughout the .NET Framework we encapsulate arguments to an event in subclasses of EventArgs. For example we prefer:

```
public delegate void AssemblyLoadEventHandler(object sender,
AssemblyLoadEventArgs args);
```

rather than

```
public delegate void AssemblyLoadEventHandler(object sender, Assembly
loadedAssembly);
```

If we want to add some new information in the event callback we can do it without breaking clients. For example, if we need to add information about the location an assembly was loaded from we would simply add a new property to the AssemblyLoadEventArgs class. If we did not have the EventArgs class we would have to create a whole new Delegate and a new event of that type with a different name. It would be really ugly. Encapsulating the event data in a subclass of EventArgs makes this scenario very smooth.

**JR** When raising an event, if you have no special event data to pass, you should pass EventArgs.Empty instead of null.

## Description

[*Note:* This class contains no event data; it is used by events that do not pass state information to an event handler when an event is raised. If the event handler requires state information, the application must create a subclass of this class to hold the data. For example, the `System.AssemblyLoadEventArgs` class is used to hold the data for assembly load events, and contains a `System.Reflection.Assembly` object that describes the loaded assembly. For details on events, see `System.EventHandler`.]

## Example

```
using System;
namespace Samples
{
  public class EventArgsSample
  {
    public delegate void MouseClickEventHandler(object sender,
                                   MouseClickEventArgs args);
    public class MouseClickEventArgs: EventArgs
    {
      private string s;
      public MouseClickEventArgs(string s)
      {
        this.s = s;
      }
      public string Label {get {return s;}}
    }
    public class MyButton
    {
      private string label;
      public MyButton(string label)
      {
        this.label = label;
      }
      public event MouseClickEventHandler MouseClick;
      public void SimulateButtonClicked()
      {
        if(MouseClick != null)
          MouseClick(this, new MouseClickEventArgs(label));
      }
    }
    public static void Main()
    {
      MyButton b =  new MyButton("Click me");
      b.MouseClick += new MouseClickEventHandler(ButtonClicked);
      b.SimulateButtonClicked();
    }
    public static void ButtonClicked(object sender,
                                MouseClickEventArgs args)
```

```
    {
      Console.WriteLine("Sender is {0}", sender);
      Console.WriteLine("Label is {0}", args.Label);
    }
  }
}
```

The output is

```
Sender is Samples.EventArgsSample+MyButton
Label is Click me
```

# System
# EventHandler Delegate

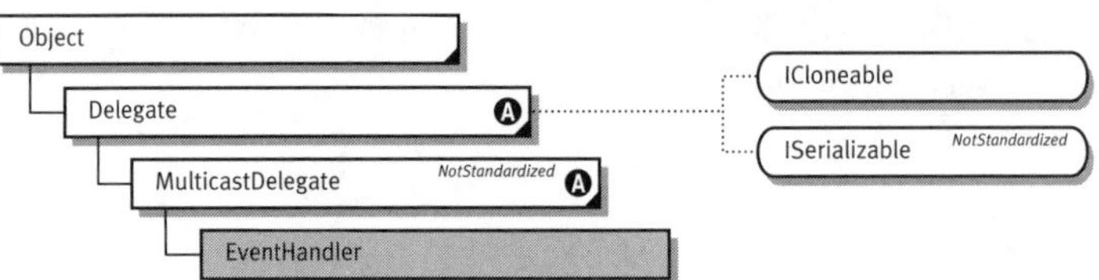


A B C D E F G H I J K L M N O P Q R S T U V W X Y Z

## Summary

Defines the shape of methods that are called in response to an event.

## Type Summary

```
public delegate void EventHandler (object sender,
                                   EventArgs e);
```

## Parameters

| Parameter | Description |
|---|---|
| sender | The object that raised the event. |
| e | A `System.EventArgs` instance that contains the event data. |

**BG** Note that we have to define delegates that are similar to `EventHandler` for every unique type of event, each consuming its own subclass of `EventArgs`. Here is a very common design pattern that could theoretically benefit from generics. Instead of defining a custom event handler for every type of event we could define this:

```
public delegate void EventHandler<T>(Object sender, T args) where T : EventArgs
```

Then events might use syntax similar to the following:

```
public event EventHandler<MouseEventArgs> MouseMoveEvent;
```

This would avoid a proliferation of classes in our documentation and in class listings such as Intellisense. This would also give us fewer classes to load, making our working set smaller and startup time faster.

EventHandler Delegate

## Description

[*Note:* A `System.EventHandler` instance is used to specify the methods that are invoked in response to an event. To associate an instance of `EventHandler` with an event, add the `EventHandler` instance to the event. The methods referenced by the `EventHandler` instance are invoked whenever the event is raised, until the `EventHandler` instance is removed from the event. If the event does not generate data, applications use the base class `System.EventArgs` for the event data object *e*. For more information, see `System.EventArgs`.] [*Note:* For additional information about events, see Partitions I and II of the CLI Specification.]

## Example

```
using System;
namespace Samples
{
  public class EventHandlerSample
  {
    public class MyButton
    {
      public event EventHandler MouseClick;
      public void SimulateButtonClicked()
      {
        if(MouseClick != null)
          MouseClick(this, EventArgs.Empty);
      }
    }
    public static void Main()
    {
      MyButton b =  new MyButton();
      b.MouseClick += new EventHandler(ButtonClicked);
      b.SimulateButtonClicked();
    }
    public static void ButtonClicked(object sender,
                                     EventArgs args)
    {
      Console.WriteLine("Sender is {0}", sender);
    }
  }
}
```

The output is

```
Sender is Samples.EventHandlerSample+MyButton
```

# System Exception

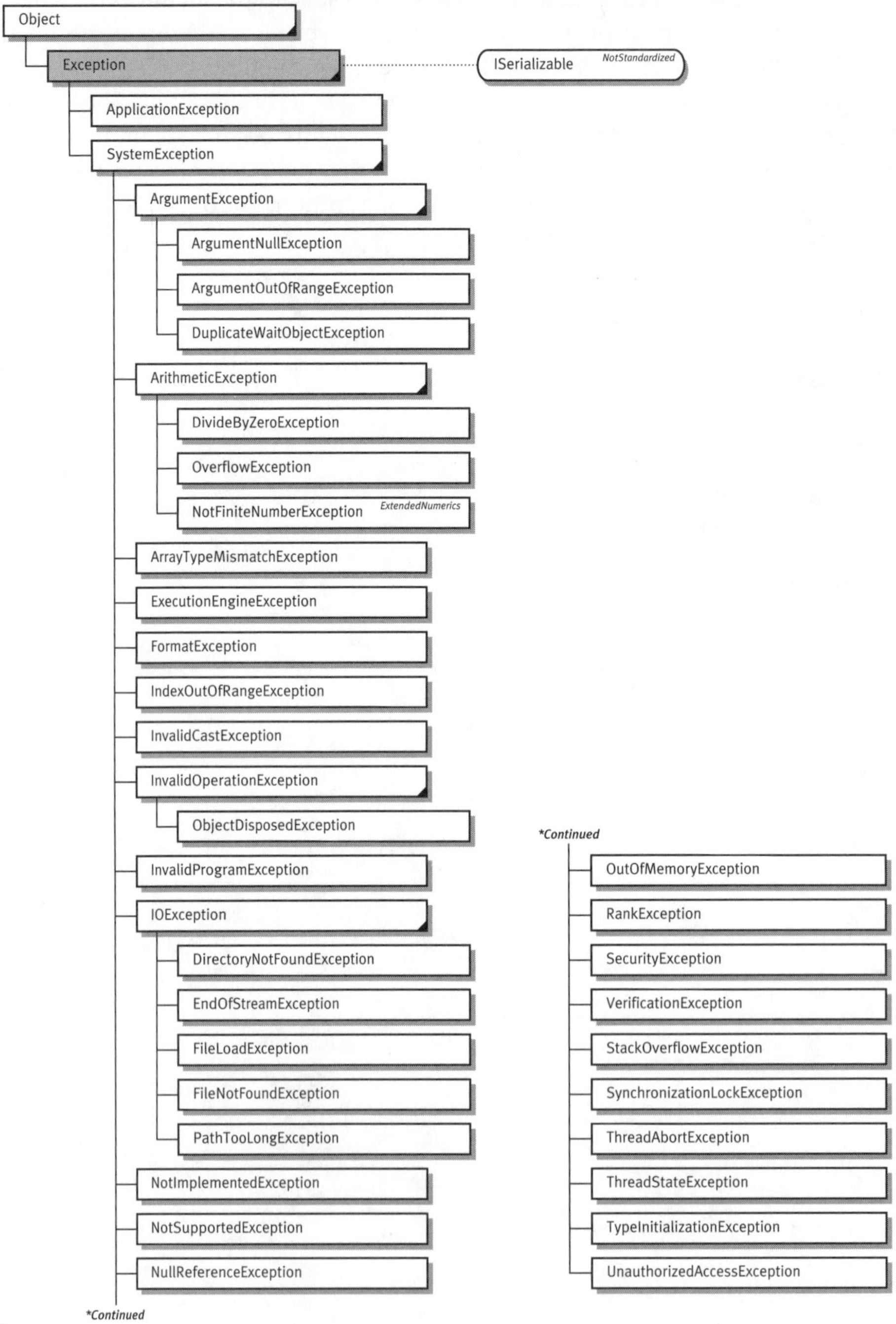

## Summary

Represents errors that occur during application execution.

## Type Summary

```
public class Exception : ISerializable
{
  // Constructors
     public Exception ();
     public Exception (string message);
     public Exception (string message, Exception innerException);
MS CF protected Exception (SerializationInfo info,
                           StreamingContext context);

  // Properties
MS CF public virtual string HelpLink { set; get; }
MS CF protected int HResult { set; get; }
     public Exception InnerException { get; }
     public virtual string Message { get; }
MS CF public virtual string Source { set; get; }
   CF public virtual string StackTrace { get; }
MS CF public MethodBase TargetSite { get; }

  // Methods
     public virtual Exception GetBaseException ();
MS CF public virtual void GetObjectData (SerializationInfo info,
                                        StreamingContext context);
     public override string ToString ();
}
```

**BA** In retrospect I would have made `Exception` abstract. One of the key benefits of exceptions over return codes is they immediately provide some information about what the problem is just by the name of the exception. But this benefit is undermined if the developers are lazy and simply write this code:

```
throw new Exception();
```

Making `Exception` abstract would have forced them to choose a more meaningful exception.

*CONTINUED*

A B C D E F G H I J K L M N O P Q R S T U V W X Y Z

**BG** I have been asked several times why we made `GetBaseException` a method instead of a property. To clarify, each exception can contain an inner exception, which is an exception that this exception is wrapping. In intuitive terms, the inner exception is the exception that caused this exception to be raised. However, since you could end up with a chain of exceptions wrapping other exceptions that is multiple levels deep, the `GetBaseException` method was added to tunnel through all the `InnerException` properties. Our thinking at the time told us operations that potentially take a long time should be methods, whereas properties should really be just like reading or writing to a public field with possibly one or two argument or state validation checks.

**JR** I agree with Brad, that `Exception` should have been defined as an abstract base class to prevent lazy developers from throwing `Exception` in their code. However, during development, the exact exception type name may not be known. To help with this, in my own projects, I define a `ToDoException` class that is marked with the `ObsoleteAttribute`. Then, when I feel lazy, I throw this exception, for example:

```
using System;
[Obsolete("Replace with a better exception someday.")]
sealed class ToDoException : Exception {
    public ToDoException() : base() {}
    public ToDoException(string message) : this(message, null) {}
    public ToDoException(string message, Exception innerException) :
base(message, innerException) {}
}
class App {
   static void Main() {
      throw new ToDoException("Something went wrong.");
   }
}
```

When I compile the above, I get a warning in Main: `x.cs(13,17): warning CS0618: 'ToDoException' is obsolete: 'Replace with a better exception someday.'` This is just a warning allowing me to continue to develop my application and always reminding me to replace `ToDoException` with another exception type when the exact name of the type is determined.

**JR** A properly designed exception class should also allow for serializability. Specifically, this means that the class should have the `System.SerializableAttribute` applied to it and the class should implement the `ISerializable` interface with its `GetObjectData` method and special constructor. These two methods should serialize/deserialize any fields in the class and should be sure to call the base class methods so that any fields in the base class are also serialized/deserialized. If the exception class is sealed, the constructor can be marked `private`; otherwise, mark the constructor as `protected`. Since `GetObjectData` is an interface method, mark it as `public`.

## Description

This class is the base class for all exceptions.

When an error occurs, either the system or the currently executing application reports it by throwing an exception containing information about the error. Once thrown, an exception is handled by the application or by the default exception handler.

[*Note:* For a description of the exception handling model, see Partition I of the CLI Specification.]

[*Note:* If an application handles exceptions that occur during the execution of a block of application code, the code is required to be placed within a `try` statement. Application code within a `try` statement is a *try block*. Application code that handles exceptions thrown by a try block is placed within a `catch` statement, and is called a *catch block*. Zero or more catch blocks are associated with a try block, and each catch block includes a type filter that determines the types of exceptions it handles. When an exception occurs in a try block, the system searches the associated catch blocks in the order they appear in application code, until it locates a catch block that handles the exception. A catch block handles an exception of type *T*, if the type filter of the catch block specifies *T* or any type that *T* derives from. The system stops searching after it finds the first catch block that handles the exception. For this reason, in application code, a catch block that handles a type must be specified before a catch block that handles its base types, as demonstrated in the example that follows this section. A catch block that handles `System.Exception` is specified last. If the catch blocks associated with the current try block do not handle the exception, and the current try block is nested within other try blocks in the current call, the catch blocks associated with the next enclosing try block are searched. If no catch block for the exception is found, the system searches previous nesting levels in the current call. If no catch block for the exception is found in the current call, the exception is passed up the call stack, and the previous stack frame is searched for a catch block that handles the exception. The search of the call stack continues until the exception is handled or there are no more frames in the call stack. If the top of the call stack is reached without finding a catch block that handles the exception, the default exception handler handles it and the application terminates.]

`System.Exception` types support the following features:

- Human-readable text that describes the error. [*Note:* See `System.Exception.Message` property.]
- The state of the call stack when the exception was thrown. [*Note:* See the `System.Exception.StackTrace` property.]

When there is a causal relationship between two or more exceptions, this information is maintained via the `System.Exception.InnerException` property.

The Base Class Library provides two types that inherit directly from `System.Exception`:

- `System.ApplicationException`
- `System.SystemException`

[*Note:* Most user-defined exceptions derive from `System.ApplicationException`. For more information, see `System.ApplicationException` and `System.SystemException`.]

## Example

```
using System;
namespace Samples
{
  public class ExceptionSample
  {
    public static void Main()
    {
      try
      {
        DivideBy(42, 0);
      }
      catch(Exception e)
      {
        Console.WriteLine("Exception caught:");
        Console.WriteLine("Message: {0}", e.Message);
        Console.WriteLine("Stack trace: {0}", e.StackTrace);
        Console.WriteLine("Inner exception (if any): {0}",
                          e.InnerException);
      }
    }
    public static int DivideBy(int i, int j)
    {
      try
      {
        return i / j;
      }
      catch(DivideByZeroException e)
      {
        throw new DivideByZeroException(
                    "Parameter j cannot be zero",
                    e);
      }
    }
  }
}
```

The output is

```
Exception caught:
Message: Parameter j cannot be zero
Stack trace:    at Samples.ExceptionSample.DivideBy(Int32 i, Int32 j) in
C:\Books\BCL\Samples\System\Exception\Exception.cs:line 30
   at Samples.ExceptionSample.Main() in C:\Books\BCL\Samples\System\Exception\
Exception.cs:line 11
Inner exception (if any): System.DivideByZeroException: Attempted to divide by zero.
   at Samples.ExceptionSample.DivideBy(Int32 i, Int32 j) in C:\Books\BCL\Samples\
System\Exception\Exception.cs:line 26
```

# System ExecutionEngineException

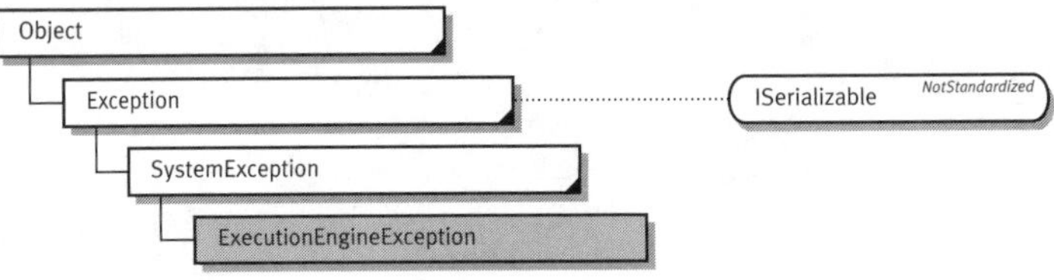


A B C D E F G H I J K L M N O P Q R S T U V W X Y Z

## Summary

Represents an internal error in the execution engine.

## Type Summary

```
CF public sealed class ExecutionEngineException : SystemException
{
  // Constructors
  CF public ExecutionEngineException ();
  CF public ExecutionEngineException (string message);
  CF public ExecutionEngineException (string message,
                                      Exception innerException);
}
```

**BA** Notice that even though this exception is not meant to be thrown by user code, we still include the pattern of exception constructors for consistency. During the standardization process we decided we would not attempt to justify following the exception constructor pattern, as we would inevitably get it wrong by missing some legitimate cases for throwing the exception. One concrete reason for needing these constructors is for testing code that wants to simulate an `ExecutionEngineException` being thrown.

**BG** Honestly, if you ever get an execution engine exception, you're almost guaranteed that you won't be able to recover from it. Common reasons for seeing this exception with the Microsoft CLI implementation include things like a corrupt unmanaged heap, meaning that the CLR's internal data structures are broken, or possibly a bug in the GC. You should only see these if you've hit a bug in the CLR, or possibly if you've corrupted native memory with unsafe code, COM Interop, or P/Invoke.

## Description

[*Note:* Execution engine errors are fatal errors that should never occur. Such errors occur mainly when the execution engine has been corrupted or data is missing. The system can throw this exception at any time. When possible, the system throws an exception that provides more information than the `System.ExecutionEngineException` exception. For information on conditions under which the CLI throws `System.ExecutionEngineException` exceptions, see Partition II of the CLI Specification. Applications should not throw `System.ExecutionEngineException`.]

A B C D E F G H I J K L M N O P Q R S T U V W X Y Z

## Summary

Provides information and performs operations on files.

## Type Summary

```
         public sealed class File
         {
            // Methods
               public static StreamWriter AppendText (string path);
               public static void Copy (string sourceFileName,
                                        string destFileName);
               public static void Copy (string sourceFileName,
                                        string destFileName,
                                        bool overwrite);
               public static FileStream Create (string path);
               public static FileStream Create (string path,
                                                int bufferSize);
               public static StreamWriter CreateText (string path);
               public static void Delete (string path);
               public static bool Exists (string path);
         MS CF public static FileAttributes GetAttributes (string path);
               public static DateTime GetCreationTime (string path);
     MS CF 1.1 public static DateTime GetCreationTimeUtc (string path);
               public static DateTime GetLastAccessTime (string path);
     MS CF 1.1 public static DateTime GetLastAccessTimeUtc (string path);
               public static DateTime GetLastWriteTime (string path);
     MS CF 1.1 public static DateTime GetLastWriteTimeUtc (string path);
               public static void Move (string sourceFileName,
                                        string destFileName);
               public static FileStream Open (string path,
                                              FileMode mode);
               public static FileStream Open (string path,
                                              FileMode mode,
                                              FileAccess access);
               public static FileStream Open (string path,
                                              FileMode mode,
                                              FileAccess access,
                                              FileShare share);
               public static FileStream OpenRead (string path);
               public static StreamReader OpenText (string path);
               public static FileStream OpenWrite (string path);
         MS CF public static void SetAttributes (string path,
                                                 FileAttributes fileAttributes);
```

```
        CF public static void SetCreationTime (string path,
                                               DateTime creationTime);
MS CF 1.1 public static void SetCreationTimeUtc (string path,
                                               DateTime creationTimeUtc);
        CF public static void SetLastAccessTime (string path,
                                               DateTime lastAccessTime);
MS CF 1.1 public static void SetLastAccessTimeUtc (string path,
                                               DateTime lastAccessTimeUtc);
        CF public static void SetLastWriteTime (string path,
                                               DateTime lastWriteTime);
MS CF 1.1 public static void SetLastWriteTimeUtc (string path,
                                               DateTime lastWriteTimeUtc);
  }
```

**BA** You will notice that the `File` class is not instantiable; it is merely a container for utility methods for working with a file on disk. During the design of the `IO` namespace we had much debate about providing a type whose instances represent a file on disk. Ultimately we decided against that design because it is very difficult to keep the state in the instance synchronized with the file system. For example, if a file gets renamed on disk we need to refresh the `Name` property which means we'd have to check everytime the `Name` property is accessed. And if the file gets deleted on disk, how would the object know that its data should be invalidated? This type of synchronization issue led us to believe that that it is a simpler model to have class with just static methods on it to perform operations on files.

## Description

Implementations of this class are required to preserve the case of path strings. Implementations are required to be case sensitive if and only if the platform is case-sensitive.

The following table describes the enumerations that are used to customize the behavior of various `System.IO.File` methods.

| Enumeration | Description |
|---|---|
| `System.IO.FileAccess` | Specifies read and write access to a file. |
| `System.IO.FileShare` | Specifies the level of access permitted for a file that is already in use. |
| `System.IO.FileMode` | Specifies whether the contents of an existing file are preserved or overwritten, and whether requests to create an existing file cause an exception. |

## Example

```
using System;
using System.IO;
namespace Samples
{
  public class FileSample
  {
    public static void Main()
    {
      string s = @"File.txt";
      if(File.Exists(s))
      {
        Console.WriteLine("File {0} already exists", s);
        File.Delete(s);
      }
      using(StreamWriter sw = File.CreateText(s))
      {
        Console.WriteLine("Can read: {0}",
                          sw.BaseStream.CanRead);
        Console.WriteLine("Can write: {0}",
                          sw.BaseStream.CanWrite);
        sw.WriteLine(DateTime.Now);
      }
    }
  }
}
```

The output is

```
File File.txt already exists
Can read: False
Can write: True
```

# System.IO
# FileAccess Enum

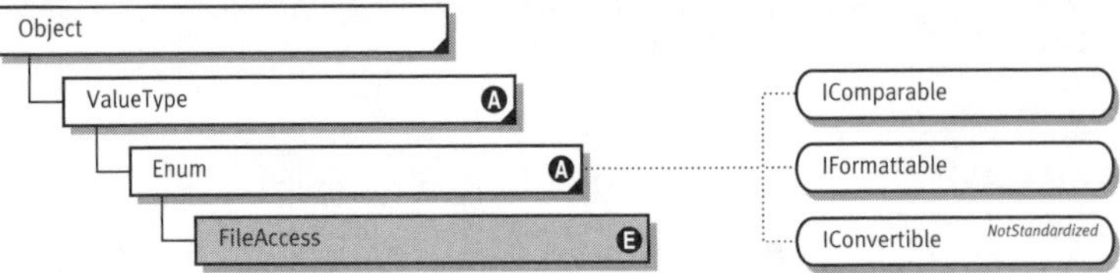




## Summary

Defines constants used to specify the level of file access being requested.

## Type Summary

```
public enum FileAccess  {
        Read = 0x1,
        ReadWrite = Read | Write,
        Write = 0x2,
}
```

> **BA** A large segment of our customers do not understand flag enums. Flag enums are enums whose values are meant to be combined using the bitwise OR operation. Many users would never think about using the bitwise OR operator (|) to combine values. That is why we always provide named values for the most common combinations. `ReadWrite` is an example of that. It is not strictly necessary, but it is much easier to discover than `FileAccess.Read | FileAccess.Write`.

## Example

```
using System;
using System.IO;
namespace Samples
{
  public class FileAccessSample
  {
    public static void Main()
    {
      string s = @"FileAccess.txt";
      FileAccess[] fa = {FileAccess.Read,
                         FileAccess.ReadWrite,
                         FileAccess.Write };
      foreach(FileAccess a in fa)
      {
```

FileAccess Enum

```
        using(FileStream fs = File.Open(s,
                                    FileMode.OpenOrCreate,
                                    a))
        {
          Display(fs, s, a);
          Console.WriteLine();
        }
      }
    }
    private static void Display(FileStream fs,
                                string s,
                                FileAccess a)
    {
      Console.WriteLine(
              "Can read from {0} when opened with {1}: {2}",
              s, a, fs.CanRead);
      Console.WriteLine(
              "Can write to {0} when opened with {1}: {2}",
              s, a, fs.CanWrite);
      Console.WriteLine(
              "Can seek in {0} when opened with {1}: {2}",
              s, a, fs.CanSeek);
      Console.WriteLine(
              "Async access to {0} when opened with {1}: {2}",
              s, a, fs.IsAsync);
    }
  }
}
```

The output is

```
Can read from FileAccess.txt when opened with Read: True
Can write to FileAccess.txt when opened with Read: False
Can seek in FileAccess.txt when opened with Read: True
Async access to FileAccess.txt when opened with Read: False
Can read from FileAccess.txt when opened with ReadWrite: True
Can write to FileAccess.txt when opened with ReadWrite: True
Can seek in FileAccess.txt when opened with ReadWrite: True
Async access to FileAccess.txt when opened with ReadWrite: False
Can read from FileAccess.txt when opened with Write: False
Can write to FileAccess.txt when opened with Write: True
Can seek in FileAccess.txt when opened with Write: True
Async access to FileAccess.txt when opened with Write: False
```

# System.Security.Permissions FileIOPermission

BCL

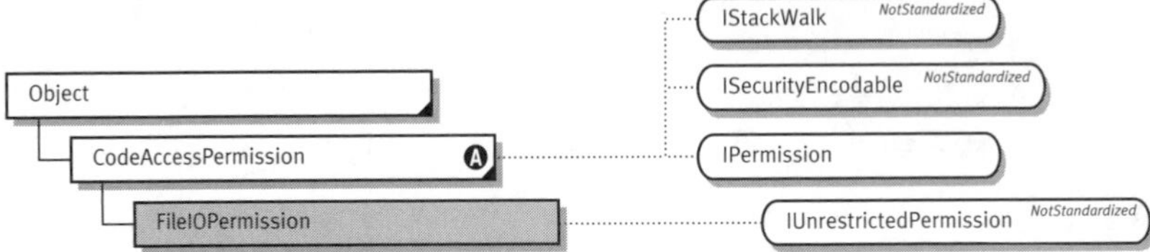


A B C D E F G H I J K L M N O P Q R S T U V W X Y Z

## Summary

Secures access to files and directories.

## Type Summary

```
   CF public sealed class FileIOPermission : CodeAccessPermission,
                                             IUnrestrictedPermission
   {
     // Constructors
     CF public FileIOPermission(PermissionState state)
     CF public FileIOPermission(FileIOPermissionAccess access, string path)
  MS CF public FileIOPermission(FileIOPermissionAccess access, string[] pathList)

     // Methods
  MS CF public void AddPathList (FileIOPermissionAccess access,
                                 string path);
  MS CF public void AddPathList (FileIOPermissionAccess access,
                                 string[] pathList);
     CF public override IPermission Copy ();
     CF public override void FromXml (SecurityElement esd);
  MS CF public string[] GetPathList (FileIOPermissionAccess access);
     CF public override IPermission Intersect (IPermission target);
     CF public override bool IsSubsetOf (IPermission target);
  MS CF public bool IsUnrestricted ();
  MS CF public void SetPathList (FileIOPermissionAccess access,
                                 string path);
  MS CF public void SetPathList (FileIOPermissionAccess access,
                                 string[] pathList);
     CF public override SecurityElement ToXml ();
     CF public override IPermission Union (IPermission other);
   }
```

**BG** `FileIOPermission` is a great idea. However, the implementation of this security check (and in our case, all the code that uses this security check) requires great care. This permission is based on string comparisons for determining whether a file is in or out of one of the sets of allowed or denied files. This has a couple of surprising properties:

*CONTINUED*

1. Since access is granted to a file based on its name and which directory it lives in, aliases for that file's data aren't covered by the security permission. Examples include cases like mapping a file as another drive (i.e., using the DOS subst command to make X: refer to a directory on C:) or more obscure features such as hard links, UNIX mount points, or NTFS reparse points.
2. Beyond aliases, some common file systems have some very loose rules for how to access files. For example, FAT and NTFS are case-insensitive, and allow you to add a period to the end of file names. Almost all file systems will allow you to go up a directory then back down to a different directory (i.e., "C:\foo\..\tmp\bar.txt" refers to the file "C:\tmp\bar.txt").
3. String comparison in the file system often works in a slightly surprising way.

We consider the first issue to be by design. If a user, such as the system administrator, has sufficient permissions to share out a portion of a drive and this can be used to circumvent permission checks, this may be intentional and useful. A great example is that you might want to deny code access to all of C:\; however, a particular directory on that drive has been shared out as a world-writable directory for logging, shared documents, or just a public drop folder. In this case, the administrator created the alias, possibly with the express purpose of creating a separate conceptual permission space.

The second issue is very tricky. It would ideally require that you obtain file names in a canonicalized form before doing the string comparisons. On Windows, getting a canonical name for a file (ignoring the aliasing issue above) requires that you open the file and get a handle to it. This can be expensive, especially for remote file systems. Instead, we are relying on path normalization to cover us. Any implementation of `Path.GetFullPathName` should be reviewed and tested against real file system behavior extremely closely.

The third issue is a bit more subtle. For a file system like NTFS, the file names can contain almost any Unicode character, and the file names are case-insensitive. However, the casing table used by a CLI implementation may differ from the casing table used by the file system. For example, NTFS writes the current OS's casing table to the file system when the file system is formatted, then all future OS's use that casing table for all case-insensitive comparisons. If an OS's casing table changes in a future release, to account for new Unicode characters or to correct mistakes, then it may be nearly impossible to do case-insensitive comparisons in exactly the same manner as the file system.

You might think this is a gaping security hole. In practice, changes to an OS's casing table are somewhat rare and generally limited to obscure Unicode characters that are not commonly in use. But a thorough CLI implementation should at least be aware of this problem and investigate whether it could cause problems for the file systems most commonly used with that CLI.

## Description

`System.Security.Permissions.FileIOPermission` objects describe protected operations on files and directories. Files and directories are specified using absolute paths. Case-sensitivity of files and directories is platform- and file system-dependent.

[*Note:* This permission distinguishes between the following types of file I/O access provided by `System.Security.Permissions.FileIOPermissionAccess`: These access levels are independent, meaning that rights to one do not imply rights to another. For example, `Write` permission does not imply permission to `Read` or `Append`. `System.Security.Permissions.FileIOPermissionAccess` values can be combined using a bitwise OR operator. For information on security considerations when accessing files, see `System.IO.FileStream`.]

The XML encoding of a `FileIOPermission` instance is defined below in EBNF format. The following conventions are used:

- All non-literals in the grammar below are shown in normal type.
- All literals are in bold font.
- The following meta-language symbols are used:
  - '*' represents a meta-language symbol suffixing an expression that can appear zero or more times.
  - '?' represents a meta-language symbol suffixing an expression that can appear zero or one time.
  - '+' represents a meta-language symbol suffixing an expression that can appear one or more times.
  - '(',')' is used to group literals, non-literals or a mixture of literals and non-literals.
  - ' | ' denotes an exclusive disjunction between two expressions.
  - '::= ' denotes a production rule where a left-hand non-literal is replaced by a right-hand expression containing literals, non-literals, or both.
- BuildVersion refers to the build version of the shipping CLI. This is specified as a dotted build number such as '2412.0'.
- ECMAPubKeyToken ::= b77a5c561934e089
- FileName refers to the full path and file name of a file, or to a path name, such as "C:\Temp\test.exe" or "C:\".

The XML encoding of a `FileIOPermission` instance is as follows:

```
FileIOPermissionXML ::=
<IPermissionclass="
System.Security.Permissions.FileIOPermission,
mscorlib,
Version=1.0.BuildVersion,
Culture=neutral,
PublicKeyToken=ECMAPubKeyToken"
version="1"
(
Unrestricted="true"
)
|
(
(Read="FileName (; FileName )*" ) ?
(Write="FileName (; FileName )*" ) ?
(Append="FileName (; FileName )*" ) ?
(PathDiscovery="FileName (; FileName )*" ) ?
)
/>
```

A B C D E F G H I J K L M N O P Q R S T U V W X Y Z

## Example

```
using System;
using System.IO;
using System.Security.Permissions;
using System.Security;
namespace Samples
{
  public class FileIOPermissionSample
  {
    public static void Main()
    {
      string s = Path.GetFullPath("FileIOPermission.txt");
      FileIOPermission p = new FileIOPermission(
                              FileIOPermissionAccess.Read |
                              FileIOPermissionAccess.Write |
                              FileIOPermissionAccess.Append,
                              s);
      p.Assert();
      TestAccess(s);
      CodeAccessPermission.RevertAssert();
      p.Deny();
      TestAccess(s);
      CodeAccessPermission.RevertDeny();
      p.PermitOnly();
      TestAccess(s);
```

```
        CodeAccessPermission.RevertPermitOnly();
      }
      static public void TestAccess(String s)
      {
         try
         {
           FileStream fs = new FileStream(
                               s, FileMode.OpenOrCreate);
           Console.WriteLine("File {0} opened or created",
                             s);
           fs.Close();
         }
         catch(Exception e)
         {
            Console.WriteLine(
                    "File {0} cannot be opened or created " +
                    Environment.NewLine +
                    "Reason was: {1}", s, e.Message);
         }
      }
   }
}
```

The output is

```
File C:\Books\BCL\Samples\System.Security\Permissions\
FileIOPermission\FileIOPermission.txt opened or created
File C:\Books\BCL\Samples\System.Security\Permissions\FileIOPermission\
FileIOPermission.txt cannot be opened or created
Reason was: Request for the permission of type
System.Security.Permissions.FileIOPermission, mscorlib, Version=1.0.3300.0,
Culture=neutral, PublicKeyToken=b77a5c561934e089 failed.
File C:\Books\BCL\Samples\System.Security\Permissions\FileIOPermission\
FileIOPermission.txt opened or created
```

BCL

# System.Security.Permissions FileIOPermissionAccess Enum

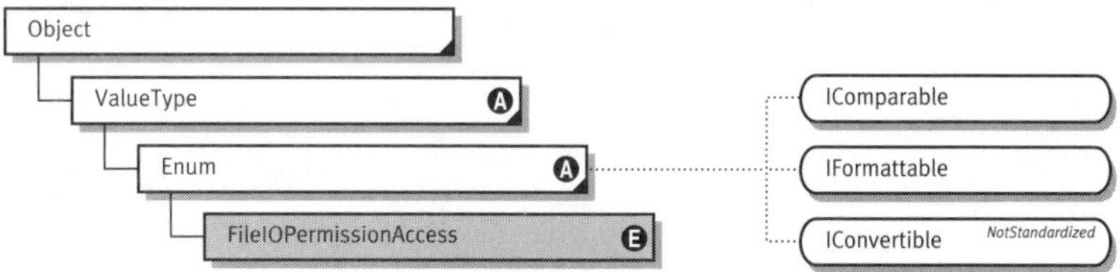


## Summary

Represents access to files and directories.

## Type Summary

```
CF public enum FileIOPermissionAccess  {
  CF AllAccess = Read | Write | Append | PathDiscovery,
  CF Append = 0x4,
  CF NoAccess = 0x0,
  CF PathDiscovery = 0x8,
  CF Read = 0x1,
  CF Write = 0x2,
}
```

## Description

[*Note:* This enumeration is used by the `System.Security.Permissions.FileIO-Permission` class. ]

## Example

```
using System;
using System.IO;
using System.Security.Permissions;
using System.Security;

namespace Samples
{
  public class FileIOPermissionAccessSample
  {
    public static void Main()
    {
      string s = Path.GetFullPath("FileIOPermission.txt");
      FileIOPermission p = new FileIOPermission(
                    FileIOPermissionAccess.Read |
                    FileIOPermissionAccess.Write |
                    FileIOPermissionAccess.Append |
                    FileIOPermissionAccess.PathDiscovery,
```

```
                          s);
        Console.WriteLine(p.ToXml());
      }
    }
  }
```

The output is

```
<IPermission class="System.Security.Permissions.FileIOPermission, mscorlib,
Version=1.0.3300.0, Culture=neutral, PublicKeyToken=b77a5c561934e089"
             version="1"
            Read="C:\Books\BCL\Samples\System.Security\Permissions\
FileIOPermissionAccess\FileIOPermission.txt"
             Write="C:\Books\BCL\Samples\System.Security\Permissions\
FileIOPermissionAccess\FileIOPermission.txt"
             Append="C:\Books\BCL\Samples\System.Security\Permissions\
FileIOPermissionAccess\FileIOPermission.txt"
             PathDiscovery="C:\Books\BCL\Samples\System.Security\Permissions\
FileIOPermissionAccess\FileIOPermission.txt"/>
```

# System.Security.Permissions FileIOPermissionAttribute

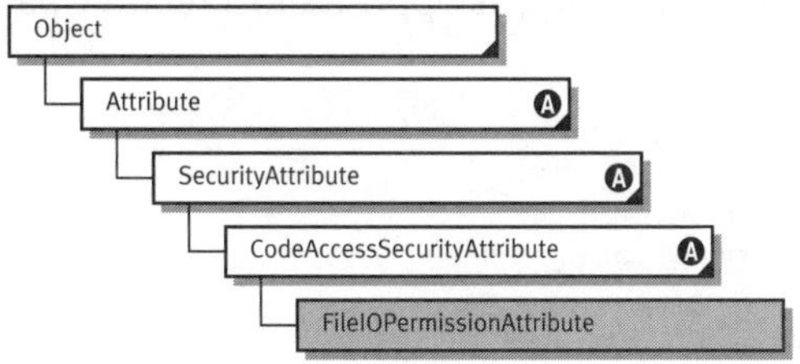


## Summary

Used to declaratively specify security actions to control access to files and directories.

## Type Summary

```
CF public sealed class FileIOPermissionAttribute : CodeAccessSecurityAttribute
{
  // Constructors
  CF public FileIOPermissionAttribute(SecurityAction action)

  // Properties
  CF public string All { get; set;  }
  CF public string Append { get; set;  }
  CF public string PathDiscovery { get; set;  }
  CF public string Read { get; set;  }
  CF public string Write { get; set;  }

  // Methods
  CF public override IPermission CreatePermission ();
}
```

## Description

[*Note:* The level of access to a file or directory is specified using the members of the current instance. For example, to specify read permissions for a file, set the `System.Security.Permissions.FileIOPermissionAttribute.Read` property equal to the name of the file. The security information declared by a security attribute is stored in the metadata of the attribute target, and is accessed by the system at runtime. Security attributes are used for declarative security only. For imperative security, use the corresponding permission class, `System.Security.Permissions.FileIOPermission`. The allowable `System.Security.Permissions.FileIOPermissionAttribute` targets are determined by the `System.Security.Permissions.SecurityAction` passed to the constructor.] Case-sensitivity of file and directory names is platform dependent. The set of characters that are valid for use in file and directory names is determined by the current file system.

## Example

Please note the use of an absolute path, as opposed to a relative path, in the following example.

```
using System;
using System.IO;
using System.Security;
using System.Security.Permissions;

[assembly:FileIOPermissionAttribute(
     SecurityAction.RequestMinimum,
     All=@"C:\Temp\BCL")]

namespace Samples
{
  public class FileIOPermissionAttributeSample
  {
    public static void Main()
    {
      using(FileStream output =
                         File.Create(@"c:\Temp\BCL\file.txt"))
      {
        Console.WriteLine("Name: {0}", output.Name);
      }
    }
  }
}
```

The output is

```
Name: c:\Temp\BCL\file.txt
```

BCL

# System.IO FileLoadException

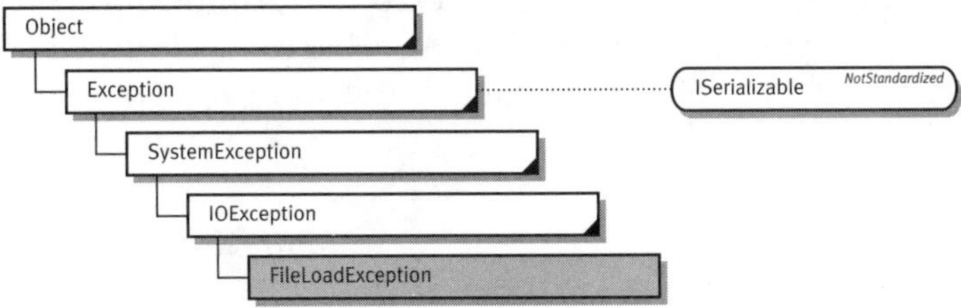


## Summary

Represents the error that occurs when a `System.Reflection.Assembly` file is found but cannot be loaded.

## Type Summary

```
 CF public class FileLoadException : IOException
 {
   // Constructors
   CF public FileLoadException()
MS CF protected FileLoadException (SerializationInfo info,
                                   StreamingContext context);
   CF public FileLoadException(string message)
   CF public FileLoadException(string message, Exception inner)
   CF public FileLoadException(string message, string fileName)
   CF public FileLoadException(string message, string fileName, Exception inner)

   // Properties
   CF public string FileName { get; }
MS CF public string FusionLog { get; }
   CF public override string Message { get; }

   // Methods
MS CF public override void GetObjectData (SerializationInfo info,
                                          StreamingContext context);
   CF public override string ToString ();
 }
```

**BA** See my comments on `FileNotFoundException`.

## Description

[*Note:* The `System.IO.FileLoadException` exception is thrown when the file fails to load because it cannot be located. If the file is located, but cannot be loaded due to insufficient permissions, a `System.Security.SecurityException` is thrown.]

## Example

```
using System;
using System.IO;
using System.Reflection;

namespace Samples
{
  public class FileLoadExceptionSample
  {
    public static void Main()
    {
      try
      {
        Assembly a = Assembly.LoadFrom(
                         "ModuleOnly.netmodule");
        Console.WriteLine(a.Location);
      }
      catch(FileLoadException e)
      {
        Console.WriteLine("Exception: {0}", e);
      }
    }
  }
}
```

The output is

```
Exception: System.IO.FileLoadException: The module 'ModuleOnly.netmodule' was
expected to contain an assembly manifest.
File name: "ModuleOnly.netmodule"
   at System.Reflection.Assembly.nLoad(AssemblyName fileName, String codeBase,
Boolean isStringized, Evidence assemblySecurity, Boolean throwOnFileNotFound,
Assembly locationHint, StackCrawlMark& stackMark)
   at System.Reflection.Assembly.InternalLoad(AssemblyName assemblyRef, Boolean
stringized, Evidence assemblySecurity, StackCrawlMark& stackMark)
   at System.Reflection.Assembly.LoadFrom(String assemblyFile, Evidence
securityEvidence)
   at System.Reflection.Assembly.LoadFrom(String assemblyFile)
   at Samples.FileLoadExceptionSample.Main() in C:\Books\BCL\Samples\System.IO\
FileLoadException\FileLoadException.cs:line 13
```

```
Fusion log follows:
=== Pre-bind state information ===
LOG: Where-ref bind. Location = C:\Books\BCL\Samples\System.IO\FileLoadException\
ModuleOnly.netmodule
LOG: Appbase = C:\Books\BCL\Samples\System.IO\FileLoadException\
LOG: Initial PrivatePath = NULL
Calling assembly : (Unknown).
===

LOG: Application configuration file does not exist.
LOG: Policy not being applied to reference at this time (private, custom, partial,
or location-based assembly bind).
LOG: Attempting download of new URL file:///C:/Books/BCL/Samples/System.IO/
FileLoadException/ModuleOnly.netmodule.
```

# System.IO
# FileMode Enum

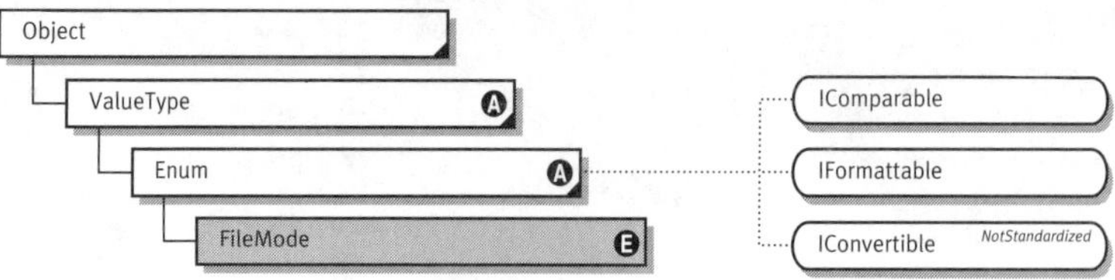




## Summary

Specifies how the operating system opens a file.

## Type Summary

```
public enum FileMode  {
     Append = 6,
     Create = 2,
     CreateNew = 1,
     Open = 3,
     OpenOrCreate = 4,
     Truncate = 5,
}
```

## Description

`System.IO.FileMode` values specify whether a file is created if one does not exist, and determine whether the contents of existing files are retained or overwritten.

## Example

```
using System;
using System.IO;

namespace Samples
{
  public class FileModeSample
  {
    public static void Main()
    {
      string s = @"FileMode.txt";
      FileMode[] filemodes = {FileMode.Append,
                              FileMode.Create,
                              FileMode.CreateNew,
                              FileMode.Open,
                              FileMode.OpenOrCreate,
                              FileMode.Truncate};
      foreach(FileMode fm in filemodes)
```

FileMode Enum

```
        {
          OpenFile(s, fm,FileAccess.Write);
        }
      }
      private static void OpenFile(string s,
                                   FileMode fm,
                                   FileAccess a)
      {
        try
        {
          using(FileStream fs = File.Open(s, fm, a))
          {
            Console.WriteLine(
                "Can seek in {0} when opened with {1} and {2}: {3}",
                   s, a, fm, fs.CanSeek);
          }
        }
        catch(Exception e)
        {
          Console.WriteLine(
              "Cannot open {0} with {1}, reason {2}",
              s, fm, e.Message);
        }
      }
    }
  }
```

The output is

```
Can seek in FileMode.txt when opened with Write and Append: True
Can seek in FileMode.txt when opened with Write and Create: True
Cannot open FileMode.txt with CreateNew, reason The file
"C:\Books\BCL\Samples\System.IO\FileMode\FileMode.txt" already exists.
Can seek in FileMode.txt when opened with Write and Open: True
Can seek in FileMode.txt when opened with Write and OpenOrCreate: True
Can seek in FileMode.txt when opened with Write and Truncate: True
```

# System.IO FileNotFoundException

BCL



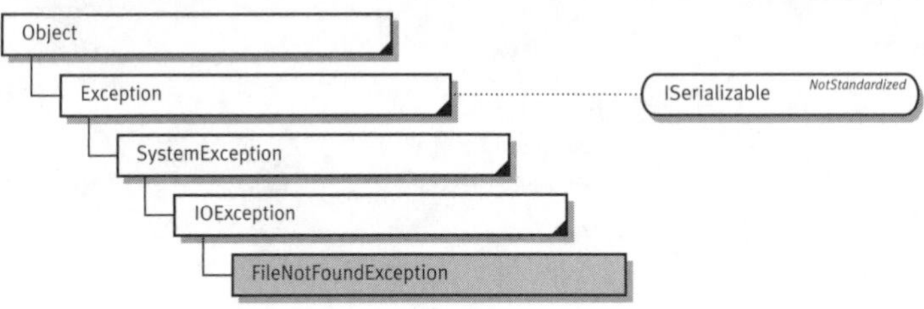


## Summary

Represents the error that occurs when a file path argument specifies a file that does not exist.

## Type Summary

```
   public class FileNotFoundException : IOException
   {
     // Constructors
        public FileNotFoundException()
 MS CF protected FileNotFoundException (SerializationInfo info,
                                        StreamingContext context);
        public FileNotFoundException(string message)
     CF public FileNotFoundException(string message, Exception innerException)
     CF public FileNotFoundException(string message, string fileName)
     CF public FileNotFoundException(string message, string fileName, Exception
innerException)

     // Properties
     CF public string FileName { get; }
 MS CF public string FusionLog { get; }
     CF public override string Message { get; }

     // Methods
 MS CF public override void GetObjectData (SerializationInfo info,
                                           StreamingContext context);
     CF public override string ToString ();
   }
```

**BA** You might think there are not any security issues associated with an exception. However, an exception such as this one can contain personally identifiable information in the file path (such as a user name). Exceptions by their nature pass information between layers of the call stack. Therefore if semi-trusted code calls a fully trusted library, the semi-trusted code can find out all the public information in the exception raised by the library. That is why it is always a good idea to carefully scrutinize any information visible via an exception. For example with the `FileNotFoundException` we are interested in protecting the discovery of a file path. Path discovery can be used by a hacker to tell the type and version of software installed on a machine and can often be used to locate user names and other personally identifiable information.

A B C D E F G H I J K L M N O P Q R S T U V W X Y Z

## Example

```
using System;
using System.IO;

namespace Samples
{
  public class FileNotFoundExceptionSample
  {
    public static void Main()
    {
      try
      {
        string s = "NotExists.txt";
        using(FileStream fs = File.Open(s, FileMode.Open))
        {
          Console.WriteLine("File opened: {0}", s);
        }
      }
      catch(FileNotFoundException e)
      {
        Console.WriteLine("Exception: {0}", e);
      }
    }
  }
}
```

The output is

```
Exception: System.IO.FileNotFoundException: Could not find file "C:\Books\BCL\
Samples\System.IO\FileNotFoundException\NotExists.txt".
File name: "C:\Books\BCL\Samples\System.IO\FileNotFoundException\NotExists.txt"
   at System.IO.__Error.WinIOError(Int32 errorCode, String str)
```

## FileNotFoundException Class

```
   at System.IO.FileStream..ctor(String path, FileMode mode, FileAccess access,
FileShare share, Int32 bufferSize, Boolean useAsync, String msgPath, Boolean
bFromProxy)
   at System.IO.FileStream..ctor(String path, FileMode mode, FileAccess access,
FileShare share)
   at System.IO.File.Open(String path, FileMode mode)
   at Samples.FileNotFoundExceptionSample.Main() in C:\Books\BCL\Samples\
System.IO\FileNotFoundException\FileNotFoundException.cs:line 13
```

# System.IO
# FileShare Enum

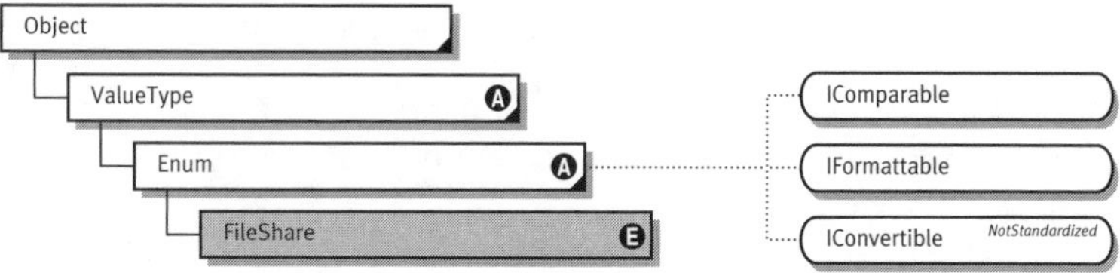




## Summary

Specifies the level of access permitted for a file that is already in use.

## Type Summary

```
  public enum FileShare  {
MS CF Inheritable = 0x10,
        None = 0x0,
        Read = 0x1,
        ReadWrite = Read | Write,
        Write = 0x2,
  }
```

## Description

This enumeration is used to specify the way in which multiple threads access the same file. The level of access is set by the first thread that requests access to the file. For example, if a thread opens a file and specifies `FileShare.Read`, other threads are permitted to open the file for reading but not for writing.

## Example

```
using System;
using System.IO;

namespace Samples
{
  public class FileShareSample
  {
    public static void Main()
    {
      string s = @"open.txt";
      FileShare[] fileShares = { FileShare.None,
                                 FileShare.Read,
                                 FileShare.ReadWrite,
                                 FileShare.Write};
      foreach(FileShare fs in fileShares)
      {
```

FileShare Enum

```
          using(FileStream a = File.Open(s,
                                         FileMode.OpenOrCreate,
                                         FileAccess.ReadWrite,
                                         fs))
          {
            Console.WriteLine("Opened with FileShare: {0}", fs);
            OpenAgain(s);
            Console.WriteLine();
          }
        }
      }
      public static void OpenAgain(string s)
      {
        try
        {
          using(FileStream a = File.Open(s,
                                         FileMode.Open,
                                         FileAccess.Read,
                                         FileShare.ReadWrite))
          {
            Console.WriteLine("Can open file again to read");
          }
        }
        catch(Exception)
        {
          Console.WriteLine("Can not open file again to read");
        }
      }
    }
  }
```

The output is

```
Opened with FileShare: None
Can not open file again to read

Opened with FileShare: Read
Can open file again to read

Opened with FileShare: ReadWrite
Can open file again to read

Opened with FileShare: Write
Can not open file again to read
```

# System.IO FileStream

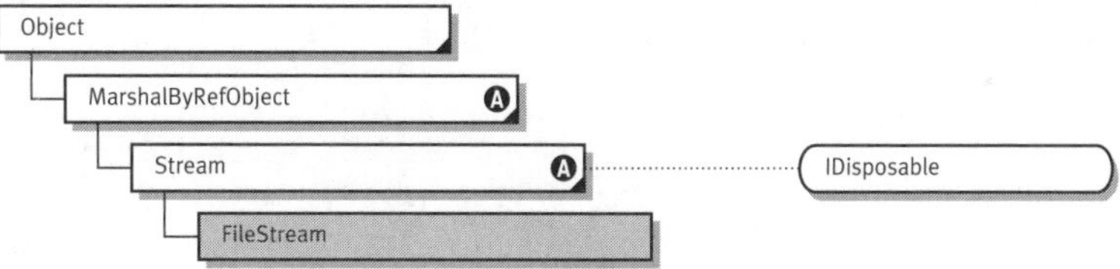




## Summary

Exposes a `System.IO.Stream` around a file, supporting both synchronous and asynchronous read and write operations.

## Type Summary

```
public class FileStream : Stream
{
  // Constructors
     public FileStream(string path, FileMode mode)
     public FileStream(string path, FileMode mode, FileAccess access)
     public FileStream(string path, FileMode mode, FileAccess access,
                                                  FileShare share)
     public FileStream(string path, FileMode mode, FileAccess access,
                                                FileShare share,
                                                int bufferSize)
     public FileStream(string path, FileMode mode, FileAccess access,
                                                 FileShare share,
                                                 int bufferSize,
                                                 bool useAsync)
MS CF public FileStream(IntPtr handle, FileAccess access)
MS CF public FileStream(IntPtr handle, FileAccess access, bool ownsHandle)
MS CF public FileStream(IntPtr handle, FileAccess access, bool ownsHandle,
                                                          int bufferSize)
MS CF public FileStream(IntPtr handle, FileAccess access, bool ownsHandle,
                                                          int bufferSize,
                                                          bool isAsync)

  // Properties
     public override bool CanRead { get; }
     public override bool CanSeek { get; }
     public override bool CanWrite { get; }
MS CF public virtual IntPtr Handle { get; }
     public virtual bool IsAsync { get; }
     public override long Length { get; }
  MS public string Name { get; }
     public override long Position { set; get; }
```

```
       // Methods
    CF public override IAsyncResult BeginRead (byte[] array,
                                               int offset,
                                               int numBytes,
                                               AsyncCallback userCallback,
                                               object stateObject);
    CF public override IAsyncResult BeginWrite (byte[] array,
                                                int offset,
                                                int numBytes,
                                                AsyncCallback userCallback,
                                                object stateObject);
       public override void Close ();
       protected virtual void Dispose (bool disposing);
    CF public override int EndRead (IAsyncResult asyncResult);
    CF public override void EndWrite (IAsyncResult asyncResult);
       ~FileStream () {}
       public override void Flush ();
 MS CF public virtual void Lock (long position,
                                 long length);
       public override int Read (byte[] array,
                                 int offset, int count);
       public override int ReadByte ();
       public override long Seek (long offset,
                                  SeekOrigin origin);
       public override void SetLength (long value);
 MS CF public virtual void Unlock (long position,
                                   long length);
       public override void Write (byte[] array,
                                   int offset,
                                   int count);
       public override void WriteByte (byte value);
  }
```

**BA** Notice that `FileStream` implements `IDisposable` in order to signal that there is a scarce resource (an OS file handle in this case) encapsulated in this type that the client code may need to explicitly free rather than waiting for the GC to free it eventually. This interface also enables C#'s `using(...)` statement.

When we introduced the `IDisposable` interface to the system the `FileStream` class had a single `Close()` method to close the OS file handle. We wanted the nice language support implementing `IDisposable` gave us but we did not want to have just a `Dispose()` method on this class as there are years of prior art teaching developers to expect to be able to "Close" a file. We also did not want there to be both a

*CONTINUED*

Close() and Dispose() method on the class that do exactly the same thing as that would undoubtedly confuse developers. That is why we decided to explicitly implement the Dispose method such that it does not show up as part of the public contract of FileStream, but is available only when the class is cast to the IDisposable interface. This design enables both the using() style support as well as an explicit Close() style.

```
//using style
using (FileStream f = new FileStream ("foo.txt", FileMode.Open)) {
   //read from f here…
}
//guaranteed f is closed here

//Close style
FileStream f = new FileStream ("foo.txt", FileMode.Open);
try {
   //read from f here…
}
finally {
   if (f != null) f.Close();
}
```

**BG** One of the nicer features of our Stream classes is that they all support one API for synchronous and asynchronous reads and writes. However, some OS's limit I/O operations on a given file handle to only synchronous or only asynchronous operations at one time. In Windows, you must open a file handle normally with CreateFile or in overlapped mode, via a somewhat obscure parameter to CreateFile. The useAsync parameter to the constructor exists to allow users to tell us which way they want the file opened.

However, CLI implementers still have the option (and I'd say the responsibility) to provide implementations of the synchronous read and write methods in terms of the async methods, and vice versa. Performance may be worse in these cases and async callbacks may be run synchronously, but the point is that the APIs must be usable at all times.

**KG** A great name for a great class. The problem is that this is not the class that should be in the most common scenario: reading and writing text in a file. For that usage people should be using StreamReader and StreamWriter. This class invariably leads people to rat-hole for a while before discovering the more appropriate, but less well-named alternates. It might have been better if StreamReader and StreamWriter were called FileReader and FileWriter.

*CONTINUED*

> **JR** As Brian points out, the asynchronous support of streams is a really nice feature. However, as Kit points out, `FileStreams` should typically be used with a `StreamReader`, `StreamWriter`, `BinaryReader`, or `BinaryWriter` class. Unfortunately, these classes do not expose the asynchronous support so you must perform synchronous I/O when using any of these "helper" classes.

A B C D E F G H I J K L M N O P Q R S T U V W X Y Z

## Description

`System.IO.FileStream` is used for reading and writing files on a file system, as well as other file-related operating system handles such as pipes, standard input, standard output. `System.IO.FileStream` buffers input and output for better performance.

The `System.IO.FileStream` class can open a file in one of two modes, either synchronously or asynchronously, with significant performance consequences for the synchronous methods (`System.IO.FileStream.Read` and `System.IO.FileStream.Write`) and the asynchronous methods (`System.IO.FileStream.BeginRead` and `System.IO.FileStream.BeginWrite`). Both sets of methods will work in either mode; however, the mode will affect the performance of these methods. `System.IO.FileStream` defaults to opening files synchronously, but provides a constructor to open files asynchronously.

When accessing files, a security check is performed when the file is created or opened. The security check is typically not done again unless the file is closed and reopened. [*Note:* Checking permissions when the file is first accessed minimizes the impact of the security check on application performance (since opening a file happens once, while reading and writing can happen multiple times).] Note that if an opened file is passed to an untrusted caller, the security system can, but is not required to, prevent the caller from accessing the file.

`System.IO.FileStream` objects support random access to files using the `System.IO.FileStream.Seek` method, and the `System.IO.Stream.CanSeek` properties of `System.IO.FileStream` instances encapsulating files are set to `true`. The `System.IO.FileStream.Seek` method allows the read/write position to be moved to any position within the file. This is done with byte offset reference point parameters. The byte offset is relative to the seek reference point, which can be the beginning, the current position, or the end of the underlying file, as represented by the three values of the `System.IO.SeekOrigin` enumeration.

If a `System.IO.FileStream` encapsulates a device that does not support seeking, its `System.IO.FileStream.CanSeek` property is `false`. [*Note:* For additional information, see `System.IO.Stream.CanSeek`.]

[*Note:* The `System.IO.File` class provides methods for the creation of `System.IO.FileStream` objects based on file paths. The `System.IO.MemoryStream` class creates a stream from a byte array and functions similarly to a `System.IO.FileStream`.]

## Example

```
using System;
using System.IO;
using System.Text;

namespace Samples
{
  public class FileStreamSample
  {
    public static void Main()
    {
      string s = "filestream.txt";
      using(FileStream fs = new FileStream(s,
                                FileMode.OpenOrCreate,
                                FileAccess.Write))
      {
        Console.WriteLine("FileStream opened on {0} ", fs.Name);
        DisplayInformationAboutStream(fs);
        string ds = String.Format("Written at: {0}\n",
                                   DateTime.Now.ToString());
        UTF8Encoding e = new UTF8Encoding();
        int count = e.GetByteCount(ds.ToCharArray(), 0, ds.Length);
        Byte[] bytes = new Byte[count];
        e.GetBytes(ds, 0, ds.Length, bytes, 0);
        fs.Seek(0, SeekOrigin.End);
        fs.Write(bytes, 0, bytes.Length);
      }
      using(FileStream fs = new FileStream(s, FileMode.Open,
                            FileAccess.Read))
      {
        Console.WriteLine("FileStream opened on {0}", fs.Name);
        DisplayInformationAboutStream(fs);
        const int limit = 80;
        Byte[] bytes = new byte[limit];
        Decoder d = Encoding.UTF8.GetDecoder();
        char[] chars = null;
        for(int i = fs.Read(bytes, 0, limit); i != 0;
            i = fs.Read(bytes, 0, limit))
        {
          int count = d.GetCharCount(bytes, 0, i);
          chars = new Char[count];
          count = d.GetChars(bytes, 0, i, chars, 0);
          Console.Write(new string(chars));
        }
      }
    }
    public static void DisplayInformationAboutStream(
                            FileStream fs)
    {
```

```
        Console.WriteLine("Can read from stream: {0}",
                          fs.CanRead);
        Console.WriteLine("Can write to stream: {0}",
                          fs.CanWrite);
        Console.WriteLine("Can seek in stream: {0}",
                          fs.CanSeek);
        Console.WriteLine("Async access to stream: {0}",
                          fs.IsAsync);
      }
    }
  }
```

The output is

```
FileStream opened on C:\Books\BCL\Samples\System.IO\FileStream\filestream.txt
Can read from stream: False
Can write to stream: True
Can seek in stream: True
Async access to stream: False
FileStream opened on C:\Books\BCL\Samples\System.IO\FileStream\filestream.txt
Can read from stream: True
Can write to stream: False
Can seek in stream: True
Async access to stream: False
Written at: 26/12/2002 10:53:22 AM
Written at: 26/12/2002 10:55:36 AM
Written at: 26/12/2002 10:55:39 AM
Written at: 26/12/2002 10:55:41 AM
Written at: 26/12/2002 10:55:43 AM
Written at: 9/03/2003 3:47:16 PM
Written at: 15/06/2003 10:52:58 AM
Written at: 15/06/2003 10:58:11 AM
Written at: 15/06/2003 10:58:20 AM
```

# System FlagsAttribute

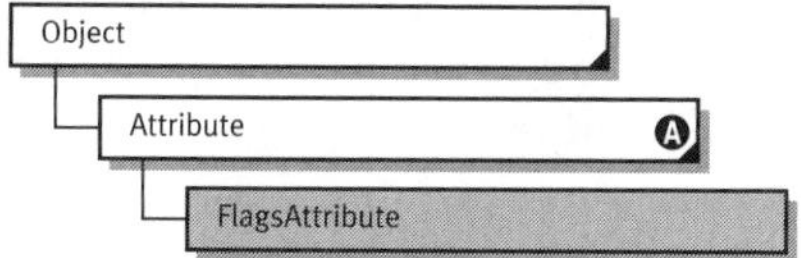


A B C D E F G H I J K L M N O P Q R S T U V W X Y Z

## Summary

Indicates that the `System.Enum` targeted by the current attribute is declared as a bit-field.

## Type Summary

```
public class FlagsAttribute : Attribute
{
  // Constructors
     public FlagsAttribute ();
}
```

**BA** Enums in the runtime are just like enums in the C++ programming language. That is, they are really just aliases for integral types. There is no enforcement in the runtime, languages, or verifier that ensures that a value stored in an enum has a valid name associated with it. For example, this is legal code:

```
FileMode f = (FileMode) 42;
```

The implication of this is that a robust library should always check to see if the value being passed in is legal. The `Flags` attribute indicates that the enum was designed such that not all the legal values have a name; some legal values are combinations of values with names. For example, in the `AttributeTargets` enum it is legal to combine values to specify that an attribute can be applied to a field or method:

```
AttributeTargets.Field | AttributeTargets.Method
```

**BA** One of our design guidelines is to name flag `enums` in the plural form to differentiate them at the call site from regular `enums`. For example, we have `AttributeTargets` rather than `AttributeTarget`.

**BG** See my comments on the `Enum` class.

FlagsAttribute Class

## Description

The `System.FlagsAttribute` class provides the consumer of a `System.Enum` with the information that the enumeration is to be used as a bit-field. Additionally, when formatting a `System.Enum`, using the `System.FlagsAttribute` causes a value that is a bitwise OR combination of multiple fields to print correctly.

[*Note:* Bit-fields are generally used for lists of elements that might occur in combination, whereas enumeration constants are generally used for lists of mutually exclusive elements. Therefore, bit-fields are designed to be combined with the bitwise OR operator to generate unnamed values, whereas enumerated constants are not. Languages vary in their usage of bit-fields compared to enumeration constants. This attribute can only be applied to enumerations.]

## Example

```
using System;

namespace Samples
{
  public class FlagsAttributeSample
  {
    [Flags]
    enum DayOfWeek {Sunday = 0x1, Monday = 0x2,
                    Tuesday = 0x4, Wednesday = 0x8,
                    Thursday = 0x10, Friday = 0x20,
                    Saturday = 0x40};
    public static void Main()
    {
      DayOfWeek weekDays = DayOfWeek.Monday |
                           DayOfWeek.Tuesday |
                           DayOfWeek.Wednesday |
                           DayOfWeek.Thursday |
                           DayOfWeek.Friday;
      Console.WriteLine("Week days: {0}", weekDays);
      DayOfWeek weekendDays = DayOfWeek.Sunday |
                              DayOfWeek.Saturday;
      Console.WriteLine("Weekend days: {0}", weekendDays);
    }
  }
}
```

The output is

```
Week days: Monday, Tuesday, Wednesday, Thursday, Friday
Weekend days: Sunday, Saturday
```

# System FormatException

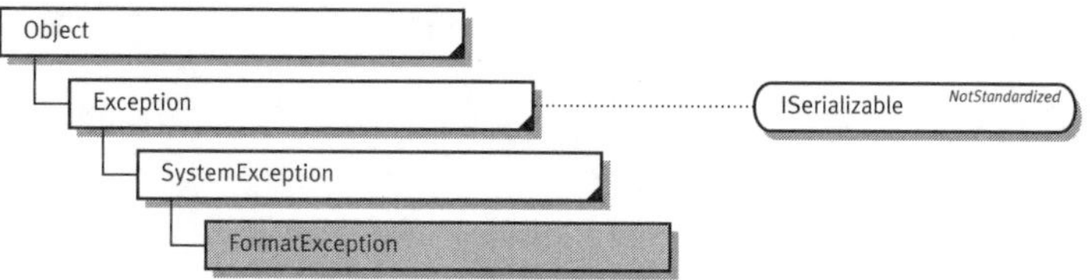


## Summary

Represents errors caused by passing incorrectly formatted arguments or invalid format specifiers to methods.

## Type Summary

```
   public class FormatException : SystemException
   {
     // Constructors
        public FormatException ();
MS CF   protected FormatException (SerializationInfo info,
                                  StreamingContext context);
        public FormatException (string message);
        public FormatException (string message,
                                Exception innerException);
   }
```

## Description

[*Note:* `System.FormatException` is thrown from `Parse` methods when a `System.String` being parsed contains characters that are not valid according to the specified style (passed via the *style* parameter) or default style. `System.FormatException` is thrown from `ToString` methods when a format specifier (passed via the *format* parameter) is not a valid format for the type of the current instance.]

## Example

```
using System;

namespace Samples
{
  public class FormatExceptionSample
  {
    public static void Main()
    {
      try
      {
        string s = "12.34";
```

```
        int i = Convert.ToInt32(s);
      }
      catch(FormatException e)
      {
        Console.WriteLine("Exception: {0}", e);
      }
    }
  }
}
```

The output is

```
Exception: System.FormatException: Input string was not in a correct format.
   at System.Number.ParseInt32(String s, NumberStyles style, NumberFormatInfo info)
   at System.Convert.ToInt32(String value)
   at Samples.FormatExceptionSample.Main() in C:\Books\BCL\Samples\System\
FormatException\FormatException.cs:line 12
```

## Summary

Provides a mechanism for programmatic control of the garbage collector.

## Type Summary

```
public sealed class GC
{
   // Properties
   MS public static int MaxGeneration { get; }

   // Methods
   MS public static void Collect ();
MS CF public static void Collect (int generation);
MS CF public static int GetGeneration (object obj);
MS CF public static int GetGeneration (WeakReference wo);
   MS public static long GetTotalMemory (bool forceFullCollection);
      public static void KeepAlive (object obj);
      public static void ReRegisterForFinalize (object obj);
      public static void SuppressFinalize (object obj);
      public static void WaitForPendingFinalizers ();
}
```

**JM** You will notice that there is neither a `Collect` method nor a `Generation` property in this class. They were there originally, but were removed, after much discussion and debate, because they offer an inadequate mechanism for specifying such behavior in a platform-independent way.

**JR** When I started consulting on the .NET Framework team in October of 1999, the `WaitForPendingFinalizers` method was called `RunFinalizers`. I didn't like this name because it implied that finalize methods were only executed when this was called. In reality, finalize methods are called when necessary and this method suspends the calling thread until all pending finalize methods have completed execution. I am responsible for the naming of the `WaitForPending-Finalizers` method.

## Description

[*Note:* The *garbage collector* is responsible for tracking and reclaiming objects allocated in managed memory. Periodically, the garbage collector performs a garbage collection to reclaim memory allocated to objects for which there are no valid references.

Garbage collections happen automatically when a request for memory cannot be satisfied using available free memory. A garbage collection consists of the following steps: During a collection, the garbage collector will not free an object if it finds one or more references to the object in managed code. However, the garbage collector does not recognize references to an object from unmanaged code, and may free objects that are being used exclusively in unmanaged code unless explicitly prevented from doing so.

The `System.GC.KeepAlive` method provides a mechanism that prevents the garbage collector from collecting objects that are still in use in unmanaged code. Implementations of the garbage collector should track the following information: Other than managed memory allocations, implementations of the garbage collector should not maintain information about resources held by an object, such as file handles or database connections.

When a type uses unmanaged resources that must be released before instances of the type are reclaimed, the type should implement a *finalizer*. In most cases, finalizers are implemented by overriding the `System.Object.Finalize` method; however, types written in C# or C++ implement destructors, which compilers turn into an override of `System.Object.Finalize`. In most cases, if an object has a finalizer, the garbage collector calls it prior to freeing the object. However, the garbage collector is not required to call finalizers in all situations.

Also, the garbage collector is not required to use a specific thread to finalize objects, or guarantee the order in which finalizers are called for objects that reference each other but are otherwise available for garbage collection. In scenarios where resources must be released at a specific time, classes should implement the `System.IDisposable` interface, which contains a single method (`System.IDisposable.Dispose`) that is used to perform resource management and cleanup tasks. Classes that implement `System.IDisposable.Dispose` must specify, as part of their class contract, if and when class consumers call the method to clean up the object.

The garbage collector does not, by default, call the `System.IDisposable.Dispose` method; however, implementations of the `System.IDisposable.Dispose` method can call methods in the `System.GC` class to customize the finalization behavior of the garbage collector.]

## Example

```
using System;

namespace Samples
{
  public class GCSample
  {
    private readonly string message;
    private int i;
    public GCSample(string s, int i)
    {
      message = s;
      this.i = i;
    }
    ~GCSample()
    {
      Console.WriteLine("In Finalize for \"{0}\"", message);
      if(--i > 0)
        GC.ReRegisterForFinalize(this);
    }
    public static void Main()
    {
      GCSample g1 = new GCSample("First", 5);
      GCSample g2 = new GCSample("Second", 5);
      GC.SuppressFinalize(g2);
      g1 = g2 = null;
      GC.WaitForPendingFinalizers();
    }
  }
}
```

The output is

```
In Finalize for "First"
```

BCL

# System.Collections Hashtable

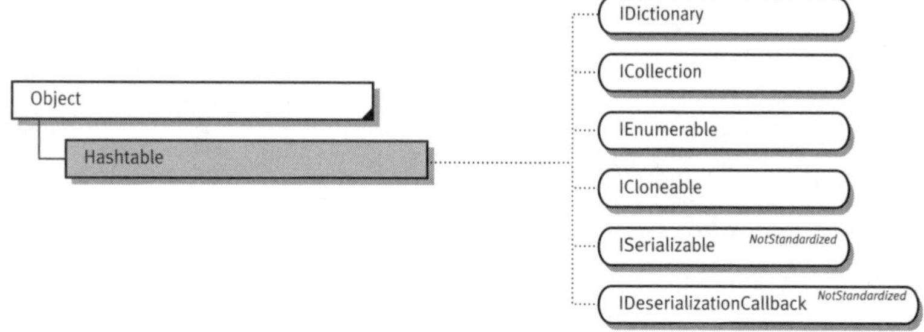


## Summary

Represents a hash table.

## Type Summary

```
public class Hashtable : IDictionary, ICollection,
                         IEnumerable, ISerializable,
                         IDeserializationCallback,
                         ICloneable
{
  // Constructors
     public Hashtable ();
     public Hashtable (int capacity);
  MS public Hashtable (int capacity, float loadFactor);
MS CF public Hashtable (int capacity, float loadFactor,
                        IHashCodeProvider hcp,
                        IComparer comparer);
     public Hashtable (int capacity, IHashCodeProvider hcp,
                        IComparer comparer);
     public Hashtable (IDictionary d);
MS CF public Hashtable (IDictionary d, float loadFactor);
MS CF public Hashtable (IDictionary d, float loadFactor,
                        IHashCodeProvider hcp,
                        IComparer comparer);
     public Hashtable (IDictionary d, IHashCodeProvider hcp,
                        IComparer comparer);
     public Hashtable (IHashCodeProvider hcp,
                        IComparer comparer);
MS CF protected Hashtable (SerializationInfo info,
                           StreamingContext context);

  // Properties
  MS protected IComparer comparer { set; get; }
     public virtual int Count { get; }
  MS protected IHashCodeProvider hcp { set; get; }
     public virtual bool IsFixedSize { get; }
     public virtual bool IsReadOnly { get; }
     public virtual bool IsSynchronized { get; }
```

```
        public virtual object this[object key] { set; get; }
        public virtual ICollection Keys { get; }
        public virtual object SyncRoot { get; }
        public virtual ICollection Values { get; }

     // Methods
        public virtual void Add (object key, object value);
        public virtual void Clear ();
        public virtual object Clone ();
        public virtual bool Contains (object key);
        public virtual bool ContainsKey (object key);
        public virtual bool ContainsValue (object value);
        public virtual void CopyTo (Array array,
                                    int arrayIndex);
        public virtual IDictionaryEnumerator GetEnumerator ();
        protected virtual int GetHash (object key);
  MS CF public virtual void GetObjectData (SerializationInfo info,
                                           StreamingContext context);
        protected virtual bool KeyEquals (object item,
                                          object key);
  MS CF public virtual void OnDeserialization (object sender);
        public virtual void Remove (object key);
        public static Hashtable Synchronized (Hashtable table);

     // Explicit Interface Members
        IEnumerator IEnumerable.GetEnumerator()
  }
```

**BA** In the early days of the BCL design we heavily debated the name of this class. Some felt it should be `HashTable` and others felt it should be `Hashtable` (lowercase t in table). There was ample prior art for both choices, so it really came down to what fit best in our library. The Pascal naming convention we adopted suggests that each word should begin with an initial uppercase character. So the debate boiled down to the question of what this class is. Is this class a table of hashes, that is, a Hash Table, or is it a single entity, a Hashtable? I think it is likely that the history of the data structure is as a special kind of table, but in the end we decided the data structure had entered the common lexicon as a single word—`Hashtable`.

**BG** `Hashtable` is currently subclassable, but we see little reason for users to subclass `Hashtable` themselves. All the interesting points of extensibility are already presented in other ways, by allowing users to pass in an `IHashCodeProvider` and `IComparer` for their keys. The only really good reason for subclassing `Hashtable` today is to add thread safety, to implement the `Synchronized` method. We did this by using an internal nested wrapper class that also subclasses `Hashtable`.

*CONTINUED*

However, it turns out this is not a great idea. It means a JIT will not be able to easily inline any of the method calls on `Hashtable` because they're all virtual. If we were starting over from scratch or designing a generic `Hashtable`-like class, we would probably make it sealed for performance reasons and sacrifice a little bit of usability. We could do this by making a thread-safe variant of `Hashtable`, or by recommending that all users of the type take a lock on the `Hashtable`'s `SyncRoot` object before editing it. For a collection like an `ArrayList`, `Stack`, or `Queue`, the latter solution is really most likely what people want because they often either have another piece of state that must be updated along with the collection or they require doing two operations on the collection (such as checking for the number of elements in a queue, then popping one if it's not empty). [See my comments in `ArrayList` for more details.]

**KC** `Hashtable`'s indexer returns `null` if the key is not found in the `Hashtable`. This is a design mistake. First, it's not possible to distinguish between a non-existent key and a `null` value at an existing key. Second, using `null` to represent an error condition is bad when moving to generic-based design; generic methods parameterized with a value type cannot return `null`.

## Description

A `System.Collections.Hashtable` represents a dictionary with a constant lookup time that contains entries of associated keys and values. The type of each entry in a `System.Collections.Hashtable` is `System.Collections.DictionaryEntry`. A statement that exposes each element in the collection is required to iterate over this type. [*Note:* See example.]

Objects used as keys in a `System.Collections.Hashtable` are required to either implement both `System.Object.GetHashCode` and `System.Object.Equals` or neither. Furthermore, for a particular key, these methods are required to produce the same results when called with the same parameters while that key exists in a particular `System.Collections.Hashtable`. Keys cannot be mutated while they are used in the table.

Every key in a `System.Collections.Hashtable` is required to be unique compared to every other key in the table. An object that implements `System.Collections.IComparer` can determine whether two keys are unequal. The default comparer for a key is the key's implementation of `System.Object.Equals`.

Each value in a `System.Collections.Hashtable` is required to provide its own hash function, which can be accessed by calling `System.Collections.Hashtable.GetHash`. Alternatively, if an object that implements `System.Collections.IHashCodeProvider` is passed to a `System.Collections.Hashtable` constructor, the custom hash function provided by that object is used for every value in the table.

[*Note:* The default capacity (i.e., the default number of entries that can be contained) of a `System.Collections.Hashtable` is zero. When an entry is added to the

System.Collections.Hashtable, the entry is placed into a bucket based on the hash code obtained from the System.Collections.IHashCodeProvider implementation of the table, or the System.Object.GetHashCode if no specific System.Collections.IHashCodeProvider was provided. Subsequent lookups of the key use the hash code of the key to search in only one particular bucket, substantially reducing the number of key comparisons required to find an entry. As entries are added to a System.Collections.Hashtable and the maximum capacity of the table is reached, the number of buckets in the table is automatically increased to the smallest prime number that is larger than twice the current number of buckets. A System.Collections.Hashtable can safely support one writer and multiple readers concurrently. To support multiple writers, all operations are required to be done through the wrapper returned by the System.Collections.Hashtable.Synchronized method.]

## Example

```
using System;
using System.Collections;

namespace Samples
{
  public class HashtableSample
  {
    public static void Main()
    {
      Hashtable ht = new Hashtable();
      ht.Add(1, "damien");
      ht.Add(4, "maire");
      ht.Add(2, "mark");
      ht.Add(5, "sacha");
      ht.Add(3, "brad");
      ht.Add(6, "tamara");
      DisplayHashtable(ht);
    }
    public static void DisplayHashtable(Hashtable ht)
    {
      Console.WriteLine("Count: {0}", ht.Count );
      IDictionaryEnumerator de = ht.GetEnumerator();
      while(de.MoveNext())
        Console.WriteLine("Key: {0} :    Value: {1}",
                          de.Key,
                          de.Value);
    }
  }
}
```

The output is

```
Count: 6
Key: 6 :    Value: tamara
Key: 5 :    Value: sacha
Key: 4 :    Value: maire
Key: 3 :    Value: brad
Key: 2 :    Value: mark
Key: 1 :    Value: damien
```

# System
# IAsyncResult Interface

IAsyncResult



## Summary

Supported by objects that represent the state of an asynchronous operation.

## Type Summary

```
public interface IAsyncResult
{
  // Properties
     object AsyncState { get; }
     WaitHandle AsyncWaitHandle { get; }
     bool CompletedSynchronously { get; }
     bool IsCompleted { get; }
}
```

**KC** `Cancel` is a very often-requested member. We decided not to add it as not all async operations can reliably support cancellations. It's bad to have interface members that cannot be implemented by a large percentage of types implementing the interface. Interface design is extremely difficult. It requires perfect balance between too few members (which makes the interface useless) and too many members, which makes the interface too hard or even impossible to implement in many cases.

**JR** I like the asynchronous programming model a lot and I recommend that everyone learn it and apply it where appropriate to improve the performance and scalability to their applications.

The object obtainable via the `AsyncWaitHandle` property is lazily constructed. That is, it isn't created unless you specifically query this property. You should avoid writing code to query this property since it is more efficient to use the asynchronous programming model with callback methods anyway. However, if you do query this property, you might want to explicitly close the underlying kernel object's handle by calling `WaitHandle`'s `Close` or `Dispose` method.

IAsyncResult Interface

## Description

An object that supports the System.IAsyncResult interface stores state information for an asynchronous operation, and provides a synchronization object to allow threads to be signaled when the operation completes.

System.IAsyncResult objects are returned by methods that begin asynchronous operations, such as System.IO.FileStream.BeginRead, and are passed to methods used to complete asynchronous operations, such as System.IO.FileStream.EndRead. System.IAsyncResult objects are also passed to methods invoked by System.AsyncCallback delegates when an asynchronous operation completes.

## Example

```
using System;
using System.Threading;

namespace Samples
{
  public class MyIAsyncResultSample
  {
    internal class MyIAsyncResult: IAsyncResult
    {
      internal Object stateObject;
      internal bool complete = false;
      internal AutoResetEvent jobDone;
      internal MyIAsyncResult(Object stateObject)
      {
        this.stateObject = stateObject;
        this.jobDone = new AutoResetEvent(false);
      }
      public virtual Object AsyncState {get { return stateObject; }}
      public bool IsCompleted { get {return complete; }}
      public WaitHandle AsyncWaitHandle {get {return jobDone; }}
      public bool CompletedSynchronously {get {return false; }}
    }
    internal class RandomNumberProvider
    {
      private static Random r = new Random();
      private void FillWithRandoms(object o)
      {
        MyIAsyncResult m = (MyIAsyncResult) o;
        int[] integers = (int[]) m.AsyncState;
        for(int i = 0; i < integers.Length; i++)
          integers[i] = r.Next();
        Thread.Sleep(1000);
        m.complete = true;
        m.jobDone.Set();
      }
```

IAsyncResult Interface

```
      public IAsyncResult BeginFillWithRandoms(int[] integers)
      {
        MyIAsyncResult m = new MyIAsyncResult(integers);
        ThreadPool.QueueUserWorkItem(
                     new WaitCallback(FillWithRandoms),
                     m);
        return m;
      }
    }
    public static void Main()
    {
       RandomNumberProvider r = new RandomNumberProvider();
       int[] integers = new int[5];
       IAsyncResult iar = r.BeginFillWithRandoms(integers);
       while(!iar.IsCompleted)
       {
          Console.WriteLine("Not complete yet");
          Thread.Sleep(500);
       }
       Console.WriteLine("Now complete");
       foreach(int i in integers)
          Console.WriteLine(i);
       iar = r.BeginFillWithRandoms(integers);
       Console.WriteLine("Will wait");
       iar.AsyncWaitHandle.WaitOne();
       foreach(int i in integers)
          Console.WriteLine(i);
    }
  }
}
```

The output is

```
Not complete yet
Not complete yet
Not complete yet
Now complete
1795940024
1936965058
337589761
1038014204
727149687
Will wait
847972885
1839223938
210272409
1187767220
1116260647
```

A B C D E F G H I J K L M N O P Q R S T U V W X Y Z

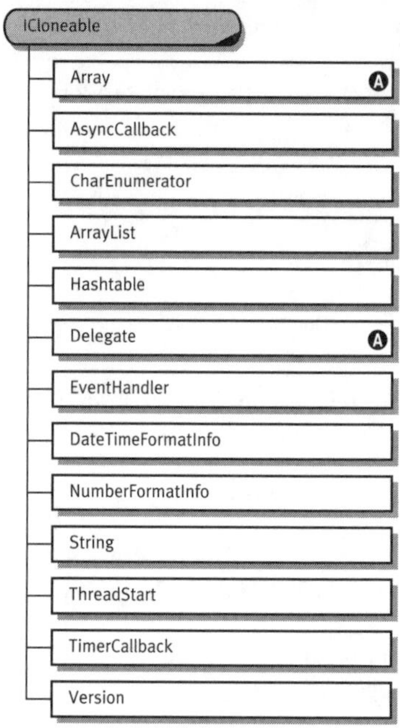


## Summary

Implemented by classes that require control over the way in which copies of instances are constructed.

## Type Summary

```
public interface ICloneable
{
  // Methods
     object Clone ();
}
```

**JR** The documentation for this interface states that `Clone` can make either a shallow or deep copy. This is ridiculous; the standard should have defined `Clone` as making a deep copy. Without a guarantee of the type of copy, you must be careful how you use a cloned object and have intimate knowledge of what `Clone` does for a type; this information is usually not documented, leading to problems.

*CONTINUED*

**KG** Echoing Jeffrey's comment, without a contract for `ICloneable`, which specifies whether it is deep or shallow, this interface is close to unusable. Defining a deep-copy version would have definitely been the most useful approach here.

Because of this loose contract, anyone utilizing the `ICloneable` aspect of a class really has no idea what he or she can then do with the class. Users can't assume that it's a tearaway version (the result of a deep copy), because if they manipulate the resulting "Clone" at all, then they may also be affecting the original. This may have unwanted side effects.

Unfortunately, the disparate implementations of this interface throughout the framework make it next to impossible to fix at this stage. You can just define a `Copy` method on classes in order to support your own deep-cloning; however, I do urge caution since this can be very difficult to guarantee. As soon as you have a reference to something which does not itself define a deep-clone mechanism, you cannot successfully define your own.

## Description

[*Note:* `System.ICloneable` contains the `System.ICloneable.Clone` method. The consumer of an object should call this method when a copy of the object is needed.]

## Example

```
using System;
using System.Collections;

namespace Samples
{
  public class ICloneableSample: ICloneable
  {
    private int i;
    private Hashtable h;
    public int AnInteger
    {
      get { return i;}
      set { i = value;}
    }
    public Hashtable AHashtable
    {
      get { return h;}
      set { h = value;}
    }
```

```
      public ICloneableSample()
      {
        i = 42;
        h = new Hashtable();
      }
      private ICloneableSample(int i, Hashtable ht)
      {
        this.i = i;
        h = (Hashtable) ht.Clone();
      }
      public object Clone()
      {
        return new ICloneableSample(i, h);
      }
      public static void Main()
      {
        ICloneableSample i1 = new ICloneableSample();
        i1.AHashtable.Add("one", "damien");
        ICloneableSample i2 = (ICloneableSample) i1.Clone();
        i2.AnInteger = 22;
        i2.AHashtable.Add("two", "brad");
        Console.WriteLine("i1.AnInteger {0} i1.AHashtable.Count {1}",
                          i1.AnInteger, i1.AHashtable.Count);
        Console.WriteLine("i2.AnInteger {0} i2.AHashtable.Count {1}",
                          i2.AnInteger, i2.AHashtable.Count);
      }
    }
  }
```

The output is

```
i1.AnInteger 42 i1.AHashtable.Count 1
i2.AnInteger 22 i2.AHashtable.Count 2
```

# System.Collections ICollection Interface



## Type Summary

```
public interface ICollection : IEnumerable
{
  // Properties
     int Count { get; }
     bool IsSynchronized { get; }
     object SyncRoot { get; }

  // Methods
     void CopyTo (Array array, int index);
}
```

## Summary

Serves as the base interface for implementing collection classes. Defines size, enumeration, and synchronization methods for all system collections.

**BG** In a future release of the Microsoft .NET Framework, we will be adding a new generic collections namespace that is similar to the existing one. We will not replace the current classes, but the new generic classes should provide most of the interesting functionality from what we did in V1. We have made a few changes to the generic collection interfaces, but they are small. The generic collections will implement our non-generic interfaces as well; as long as you are using our V1 interfaces in your public API's, you will be able to consume and return generic collections in the future if you want, albeit with some loss of efficiency.

Our eventual goal is to add generics into the CLS, which may enable us to do things such as writing new libraries that only use generics, as well as adding generic interfaces and/or methods to the base data types.

*CONTINUED*

**KC** This interface is causing some headaches. Not all collections can implement Count—for example, collections that get items on demand (pretty common). Also, IsSynchronized and SyncRoot members are rarely used (they should probably be on a separate interface). On the other hand, ICollection should probably have some methods to allow adding items to a collection.

**JR** The SyncRoot property is a bad idea. It exposes the object's lock object to the outside world where, in reality, the object should always be private to an object. In addition, the lock is expected to be manipulated via Monitor's methods or C#'s lock statement. This means that a collection cannot be made thread-safe using a read-write lock mechanism.

A B C D E F G H I J K L M N O P Q R S T U V W X Y Z

## Description

[*Note:* System.Collections.ICollection contains the System.Collections.ICollection.CopyTo method. The consumer of a collection object that implements this interface should call this method when copying the elements of that object to a System.Array.]

## Example

```
using System;
using System.Collections;

namespace Samples
{
  public class ICollectionSample
  {
    public static void Main()
    {
      ArrayList al = new ArrayList();
      al.Add("damien");
      al.Add("mark");
      al.Add("brad");
      Array a = Array.CreateInstance(typeof(string), al.Count);
      al.CopyTo(a, 0);
      Console.WriteLine("The contents of the array are:");
      for(int i = 0; i < a.Length; i++)
        Console.WriteLine("{0} ",a.GetValue(i));
    }
  }
}
```

The output is

```
The contents of the array are:
damien
mark
brad
```

# System
# IComparable Interface

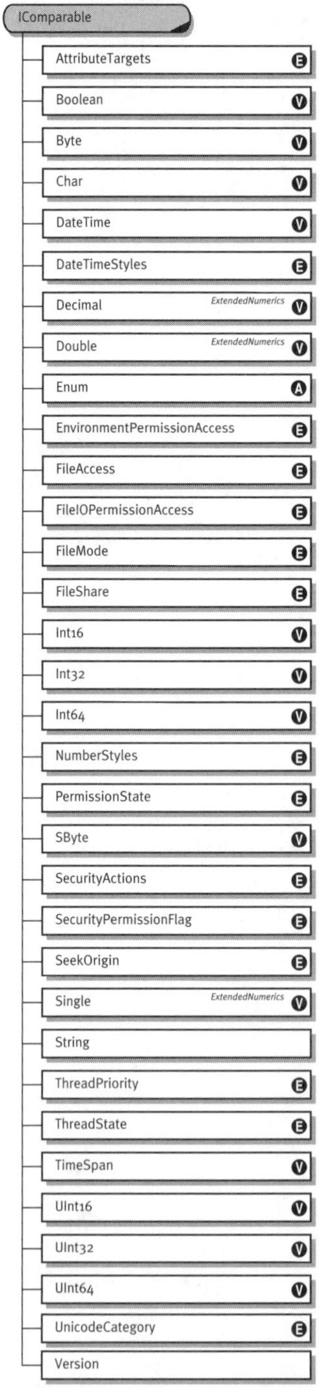

IComparable Interface

## Summary

Implemented by classes that support an ordering of instances of the class.

## Type Summary

```
public interface IComparable
{
  // Methods
     int CompareTo (object obj);
}
```

**BA** There is a natural tension between modeling a concept as an interface and as a base class. In this case it is clear that requiring developers to inherit from a `Comparable` base class to be comparable would have been too restrictive. However, this class does illustrate good design principles for any interface. It is simple; there are no complex contracts to be maintained between the members of the interface (because there is only one member). The concept is clearly an additive element of the class design rather than the center point of the design.

**JR** When defining a value type that implements `IComparable`, you should define a type-safe version of the method and you should apply C#'s explicit interface method implementation feature to the `CompareTo` method that takes `Object` as a parameter. This will reduce boxing (improving performance) and will give you more compile-time safety as well!

## Description

[*Note:* `System.IComparable` contains the `System.IComparable.CompareTo` method. The consumer of an object should call this method when sorting instances of a class.]

## Example

```
using System;

namespace Samples
{
  public class MyNameClass: IComparable
  {
    private string name;
    public MyNameClass(string name)
    {
      this.name = name;
```

```
    }
    public override string ToString()
    {
      return String.Format("Type: MyNameClass Value: {0}",
                           name);
    }
    public override bool Equals(object o)
    {
      if(null == o)
        return false;
      if(this.GetType() != o.GetType())
        return false;
      MyNameClass other = (MyNameClass) o;
      return name.Equals(other.name);
    }
    public override int GetHashCode()
    {
      return name.GetHashCode();
    }
    public int CompareTo(object o)
    {
      if(o is MyNameClass)
      {
        MyNameClass other = (MyNameClass) o;
        return name.CompareTo(other.name);
      }
      throw new ArgumentException("Different Types");
    }
  }
  public class IComparableSample
  {
    public static void Main()
    {
      MyNameClass[] names =
                    new MyNameClass[]{
                              new MyNameClass("damien"),
                              new MyNameClass("maire"),
                              new MyNameClass("mark"),
                              new MyNameClass("sacha"),
                              new MyNameClass("brad"),
                              new MyNameClass("sarah")};
      Array.Sort(names);
      foreach(MyNameClass m in names)
        Console.WriteLine(m);
    }
  }
}
```

The output is

```
Type: MyNameClass Value: brad
Type: MyNameClass Value: damien
Type: MyNameClass Value: maire
Type: MyNameClass Value: mark
Type: MyNameClass Value: sacha
Type: MyNameClass Value: sarah
```

# System.Collections
# IComparer Interface

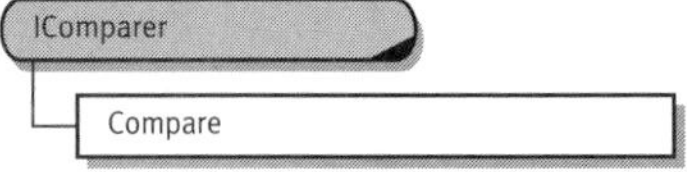


A B C D E F G H I J K L M N O P Q R S T U V W X Y Z

## Summary

Provides a mechanism to customize the sort ordering of a collection.

## Type Summary

```
public interface IComparer
{
  // Methods
     int Compare (object x, object y);
}
```

**BG** Note that the `IComparer` interface allows you to define your own ordering over types, when the original author may not have envisioned a need to sort the class. It's a great hook for comparison and sorting. Combined with `IHashCodeProvider`, you can use types as keys in a `Hashtable` even if the original class author neglected to override `Equals` and `GetHashCode` for their type.

## Description

The default implementation of this interface is `System.Collections.Comparer`.

[*Note:* `System.Collections.IComparer` contains the `System.Collections.IComparer.Compare` method. The consumer of an object should call this method when sorting members of a collection.]

## Example

```
using System;
using System.Collections;

namespace Samples
{
  public class IComparerSample
  {
    public class ToStringComparer: IComparer
    {
      public int Compare(Object a, Object b)
      {
        string s1 = a.ToString();
```

IComparer Interface

```
            string s2 = b.ToString();
            return s1.CompareTo(s2);
        }
    }
    public static void Main()
    {
        ArrayList a = new ArrayList();
        a.Add (0);
        a.Add("1");
        a.Add(2);
        a.Add(3);
        a.Add("4");
        a.Add(5);
        a.Add("6");
        SearchFor(a, "2");
        SearchFor(a, 1);
        SearchFor(a, 9);
    }
    public static void SearchFor(ArrayList a, object o)
    {
        int i = a.BinarySearch(o, new ToStringComparer());
        if(i > 0)
        {
            Console.WriteLine(
                "Object: {0}, was found at: {1}", o, i );
        }
        else if(~i == a.Count)
        {
            Console.WriteLine("Object: {0}, was not found", o);
            Console.WriteLine(
                "No object in the array had a greater value.");
        }
        else
        {
            Console.WriteLine("Object: {0}, was not found", o);
            Console.WriteLine(
                "The next larger object is at index: {0}.", ~i );
        }
    }
  }
}
```

The output is

```
Object: 2, was found at: 2
Object: 1, was found at: 1
Object: 9, was not found
No object in the array had a greater value.
```

# System.Collections IDictionary Interface

BCL

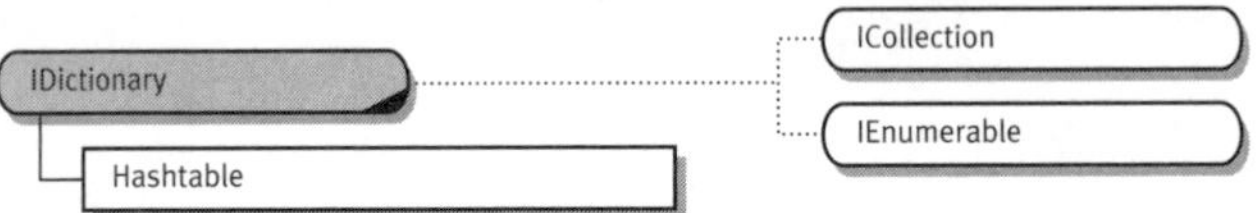


A B C D E F G H I J K L M N O P Q R S T U V W X Y Z

## Summary

Implemented by classes that support collections of associated keys and values (i.e., dictionaries).

## Type Summary

```
public interface IDictionary : ICollection, IEnumerable
{
  // Properties
     bool IsFixedSize { get; }
     bool IsReadOnly { get; }
     object this[object key] { set; get; }
     ICollection Keys { get; }
     ICollection Values { get; }

  // Methods
     void Add (object key, object value);
     void Clear ();
     bool Contains (object key);
     IDictionaryEnumerator GetEnumerator ();
     void Remove (object key);
}
```

## Description

[*Note:* Each key-value pair must have a unique non-`null` key, but the value of an association can be any object reference, including a `null` reference. The `System.Collections.IDictionary` interface allows the contained keys and values to be enumerated, but it does not imply any particular sort order. `System.Collections.IDictionary` implementations fall into three categories: read-only, fixed-size, and variable-size. A read-only implementation cannot be modified. A fixed-size implementation does not allow the addition or removal of elements, but it allows the modification of existing elements. A variable-size implementation allows the addition, removal, and modification of elements.]

## Example

```
using System;
using System.Collections;

namespace Samples
```

```
{
  public class IDictionarySample
  {
    public static void Main()
    {
      IDictionary id = new Hashtable();
      id.Add(1, "damien");
      id.Add(2, "mark");
      id.Add(3, "brad");
      DisplayDictionary(id);
      SortedList sl = new SortedList();
      sl.Add(1, "maire");
      sl.Add(2, "sacha");
      sl.Add(3, "tamara");
      DisplayDictionary(sl);
    }
    public static void DisplayDictionary(IDictionary id)
    {
      Console.WriteLine("Is fixed size: {0}", id.IsFixedSize);
      Console.WriteLine("Is read only: {0}", id.IsReadOnly);
      Console.WriteLine("Count: {0}", id.Count );
      Console.WriteLine("Number of keys: {0}", id.Keys.Count);
      foreach(DictionaryEntry de in id)
        Console.WriteLine("Key: {0} Value: {1}",
                          de.Key,
                          de.Value);
    }
  }
}
```

The output is

```
Is fixed size: False
Is read only: False
Count: 3
Number of keys: 3
Key: 3 Value: brad
Key: 2 Value: mark
Key: 1 Value: damien
Is fixed size: False
Is read only: False
Count: 3
Number of keys: 3
Key: 1 Value: maire
Key: 2 Value: sacha
Key: 3 Value: tamara
```

# System.Collections IDictionaryEnumerator Interface

BCL

A B C D E F G H I J K L M N O P Q R S T U V W X Y Z

## Summary

Implemented by classes that support the use of an enumerator over a dictionary (i.e., a collection of `System.Collections.DictionaryEntry` objects).

## Type Summary

```
public interface IDictionaryEnumerator : IEnumerator
{
  // Properties
     DictionaryEntry Entry { get; }
     object Key { get; }
     object Value { get; }
}
```

> **JR** `IDictionaryEnumerator`'s `Current` property returns an object of `DictionaryEntry` type. This is what you work with when using C#'s `foreach` statement with a type that implements the `IDictionary` interface.

## Description

[*Note:* `System.Collections.IDictionaryEnumerator` contains members that get the properties of `System.Collections.DictionaryEntry` objects. For detailed information regarding the use of an enumerator, see `System.Collections.IEnumerator`.]

## Example

```
using System;
using System.Collections;

namespace Samples
{
  public class IDictionarySample
  {
    public static void Main()
    {
      IDictionary id = new Hashtable();
      id.Add(1, "damien");
      id.Add(2, "mark");
      id.Add(3, "brad");
```

IDictionaryEnumerator Interface

```
      DisplayDictionary(id);
    }
    public static void DisplayDictionary(IDictionary id)
    {
      Console.WriteLine("Count: {0}", id.Count );
      IDictionaryEnumerator ide = id.GetEnumerator();
      while(ide.MoveNext())
      {
        DictionaryEntry de = ide.Entry;
        Console.WriteLine("Key: {0} Value: {1}",
                          de.Key,
                          de.Value);
      }
    }
  }
}
```

The output is

```
Count: 3
Key: 3 Value: brad
Key: 2 Value: mark
Key: 1 Value: damien
```

# System
# IDisposable Interface

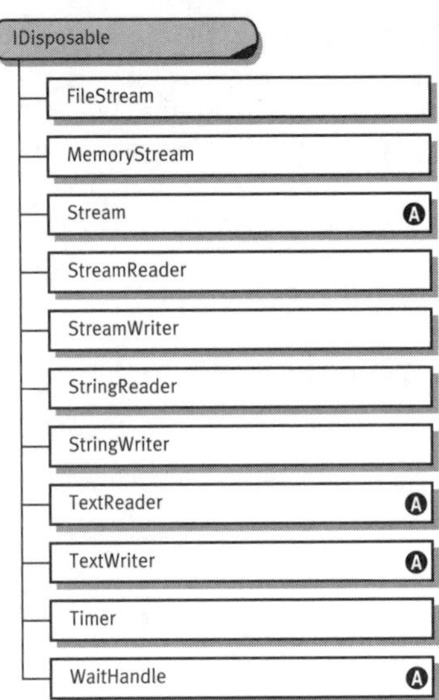




## Summary

Implemented by classes that require explicit control over resource cleanup.

## Type Summary

```
public interface IDisposable
{
  // Methods
     void Dispose ();
}
```

**BA** Credit for the `IDisposable` concept should go to the .NET Framework early beta testers for providing quite strong and vocal feedback on early pre-releases that such a concept was a requirement. Moving away from the deterministic finalization world of COM, VB, and Win32 development was always perceived as one of the biggest bets we made with the runtime. However, we rejected early attempts to add deterministic finalization to the CLR because of its performance and programming model implications.

*CONTINUED*

IDisposable Interface

The issues did not resurface in a serious way until shortly after our beta1 release. Customers gave us very clear feedback that some sort of mitigation of this problem was required. Through many hours of design meetings the IDisposable plan emerged as the winner. The combination of library support and language support (e.g., C#'s `using` statement), which didn't require us to change the guts of the runtime so late in the cycle, made it a winner. Clearly it is not a perfect solution, but it does address the 80% scenario quite nicely.

**JR** I was heavily involved in the creation of the `IDisposable` pattern and while it was not my first choice for a solution, it did meet a lot of the team's goals (which Brad pointed out). Note that any type that has an `IDisposable` type as a member should be `IDisposable` itself and, in its `Dispose` method, the member should be disposed. This makes the `IDisposable` pattern more difficult to work with than originally thought when it was first accepted.

## Description

Objects that need to free resources that cannot safely be reclaimed by the garbage collector implement the `System.IDisposable` interface.

It is a version-breaking change to add the `System.IDisposable` interface to an existing class, as it changes the semantics of the class.

[*Note:* `System.IDisposable` contains the `System.IDisposable.Dispose` method. The consumer of an object should call this method when the object is no longer needed. The `System.IDisposable` interface is generally provided for the release of unmanaged resources that need to be reclaimed in some order or time-dependent manner. It is important to note that the actual release of these resources happens at the first call to `System.IDisposable.Dispose` for any given object that supports this interface. Programmers should take care to pair the creation of objects that implement `IDisposable` with at most one invocation of the `Dispose` method. Though it is legal to invoke `Dispose` more than once, if this happens it may indicate the presence of a bug since such an object is usually rendered otherwise unusable after the first `Dispose` invocation.]

## Example

```
using System;

namespace Samples
{
  public class IDisposableSample: IDisposable
  {
    private bool disposed = false;
```

A B C D E F G H I J K L M N O P Q R S T U V W X Y Z

```
        public void Dispose()
        {
          lock(this)
          {
            if(disposed)
              return;
            GC.SuppressFinalize(this);
            Dispose(true);
            disposed = true;
          }
        }
        public void Close()
        {
          Dispose();
        }
        public void Dispose(bool b)
        {
          if(b)
          {
            Console.WriteLine("Dispose()/Close() called " +
                              "explicitly by user code");
            Console.WriteLine("Do cleanup necessary for " +
                              "this case");
          }
          Console.WriteLine("Do cleanup necessary for finalization");
        }
        ~IDisposableSample()
        {
          Dispose(false);
        }
        public static void Main()
        {
          IDisposableSample ids1 = new IDisposableSample();
          IDisposableSample ids2 = new IDisposableSample();
          IDisposableSample ids3 = new IDisposableSample();
          ids1.Close();
          ids2.Dispose();
          ids3 = null;
          GC.WaitForPendingFinalizers();
        }
      }
    }
```

The output is

```
Dispose()/Close() called explicitly by user code
Do cleanup necessary for this case
Do cleanup necessary for finalization
Dispose()/Close() called explicitly by user code
Do cleanup necessary for this case
Do cleanup necessary for finalization
Do cleanup necessary for finalization
```

# System.Collections IEnumerable Interface

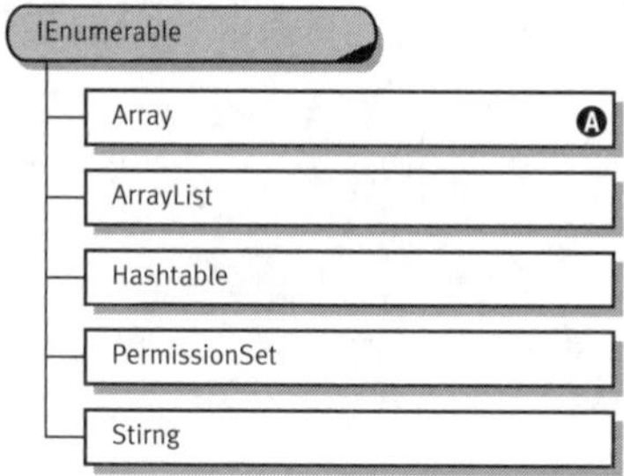


A B C D E F G H I J K L M N O P Q R S T U V W X Y Z

## Summary

Implemented by classes that support a simple iteration over instances of the collection.

## Type Summary

```
public interface IEnumerable
{
  // Methods
     IEnumerator GetEnumerator ();
}
```

**BA** It is interesting to look at how the C# `foreach` support works with types that implement `IEnumerable`.

For a C# program that looks like this:

```
foreach (int v in collection) { ... }
```

The C# compiler generates code that looks something like this:

```
IEnumerable ie = (IEnumerable) collection;
IEnumerator e = ie.GetEnumerator();
try {
  while (e.MoveNext()) {
     int v = (int) e.Current;
     ...
  }
}
finally {
  if (e is IDisposable) {
     ((IDisposable)e).Dispose();
  }
}
```

*CONTINUED*

IEnumerable Interface

A B C D E F G H I J K L M N O P Q R S T U V W X Y Z

In line 1, you see the first thing we do is cast the collection to the `IEnumerable` interface. Then in line 2 we get the `IEnumerator` and in line 4 we start iterating through the Enumerator. Line 6 is where the body of the `foreach` statement goes. Notice lines 9–12 is where the enumerator is disposed. We put this in a `finally` block so that it gets executed whether an exception gets thrown or not. This support for disposable enumerators was added relatively late in the design of the language when we discovered some specific cases where developers had to avoid using the `foreach` statement so they could explicity dispose of the enumerator.

In retrospect it would have been a good idea to have the `IEnumerator` implement the `IDisposable` interface to make lines 10–11 slightly more efficient and more importantly to make this aspect of the language's `foreach` support less of a special case and therefore more obvious to developers.

## Description

[*Note:* `System.Collections.IEnumerable` contains the `System.Collections.IEnumerable.GetEnumerator` method. The consumer of an object should call this method to obtain an enumerator for simple iteration over an instance of a collection. Implement this interface to support the `foreach` semantics of C#.]

## Example

```
using System;
using System.Collections;

namespace Samples
{
  public class IEnumerableSample
  {
    public static void Main()
    {
      IEnumerable s = "Hello world";
      IEnumerator ie = s.GetEnumerator();
      while(ie.MoveNext())
        Console.Write(ie.Current);
    }
  }
}
```

The output is

```
Hello world
```

# System.Collections IEnumerator Interface

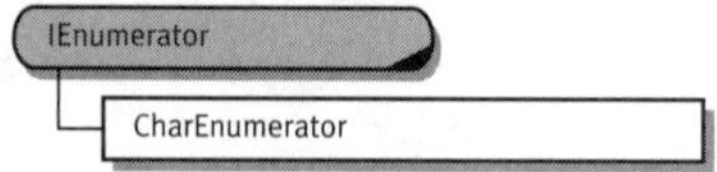




## Summary

Implemented by classes that support a simple iteration over a collection.

## Type Summary

```
public interface IEnumerator
{
  // Properties
     object Current { get; }

  // Methods
     bool MoveNext ();
     void Reset ();
}
```

> **BA** During the design of the BCL we debated long and hard about including the `Reset` method on this interface. On one side, we knew of several kinds of enumerators for which implementing `Reset` would be impractical. On the other side, we felt it was very important to provide some compatibility with COM's `IEnum` interface. So we compromised and included `Reset`, but took the unusual step of allowing implementers to throw a `NotSupportedException` if implementing `Reset` is not appropriate. Usually, having to throw a `NotSupportedException` from an interface implementation either means that the interface is not well designed, or that this class should not be implementing it.

## Description

[*Note:* `System.Collections.IEnumerator` contains the `System.Collections.IEnumerator.MoveNext` and `System.Collections.IEnumerator.Reset` methods and the `System.Collections.IEnumerator.Current` property. The consumer of an object should call these methods or use this property when iterating over or reading the elements of a collection. When an enumerator is instantiated or a call is made to `System.Collections.IEnumerator.Reset`, the enumerator is positioned immediately before the first element of the collection and a snapshot of the collection is taken. When the enumerator is in this position, a call to `System.Collections.IEnumera-`

tor.MoveNext is necessary before reading System.Collections.IEnumerator.Current from the collection. If changes are made to the collection (such as adding, modifying or deleting elements) the snapshot may get out of sync, causing the enumerator to throw a System.InvalidOperationException if the System.Collections.IEnumerator.MoveNext or System.Collections.IEnumerator.Reset are invoked. Two enumerators instantiated from the same collection at the same time can have different snapshots of the collection. Enumerators are intended to be used only to read data in the collection. An enumerator does not have exclusive access to the collection for which it was instantiated.]

## Example

```
using System;
using System.Collections;

namespace Samples
{
  public class IEnumeratorSample
  {
    public static void Main()
    {
      IEnumerable s = "Hello world";
      IEnumerator ie = s.GetEnumerator();
      while(ie.MoveNext())
        Console.Write(ie.Current);
      Console.WriteLine();
      ie.Reset();
      while(ie.MoveNext())
        Console.Write(ie.Current);
    }
  }
}
```

The output is

```
Hello world
Hello world
```

# System
# IFormatProvider Interface

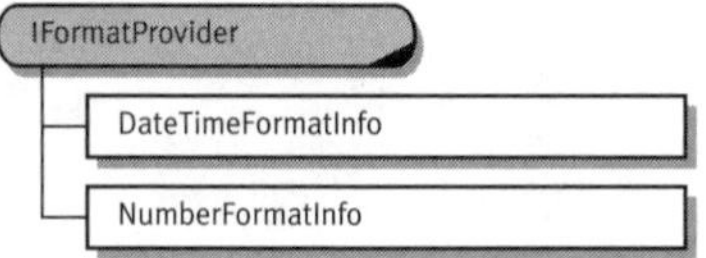


A B C D E F G H I J K L M N O P Q R S T U V W X Y Z

## Summary

Implemented by classes that supply objects that provide formatting services.

## Type Summary

```
public interface IFormatProvider
{
  // Methods
     object GetFormat (Type formatType);
}
```

## Description

[*Note:* When a *format specifier* includes symbols that vary by culture, such as the currency symbol included by the "C" and "c" formats, a *formatting object* supplies the actual characters used in a string representation of a numeric value. For example, a formatting object may supply "$" for the currency symbol. The formatting object for system-supplied numeric types is a `System.Globalization.NumberFormatInfo` instance. For `System.DateTime` instances, a `System.Globalization.DateTimeFormatInfo` is used. `System.IFormatProvider` contains the `System.IFormatProvider.GetFormat` method. The consumer of an object should call this method to obtain a formatting object.]

## Example

```
using System;
using System.Globalization;

namespace Samples
{
  public class MyFormatProviderSample: IFormatProvider,
                                       ICustomFormatter
  {
    public object GetFormat(Type t)
    {
      if(t == typeof(ICustomFormatter))
          return this;
      return null;
    }
    public string Format(string f, object o,
```

```
                                IFormatProvider p)
      {
        if(f == null)
          return String.Format("{0}", o);
        if(!f.StartsWith("-"))
        {
          if(o is IFormattable)
          {
            return ((IFormattable)o).ToString(f, p);
          }
          else if(o != null)
          {
            return o.ToString();
          }
        }
        return "Sample Formatted";
      }
      public static void Main()
      {
        MyFormatProviderSample m =
                              new MyFormatProviderSample();
        Console.WriteLine(String.Format(
                          m,
                          "First (no formatting): {0} \n" +
                          "Second (formatted '-'): {1:-}",
                          new object[] {m, m}));
      }
    }
  }
```

The output is

```
First (no formatting): Samples.MyFormatProviderSample
Second (formatted '-'): Sample Formatted
```

# System
# IFormattable Interface

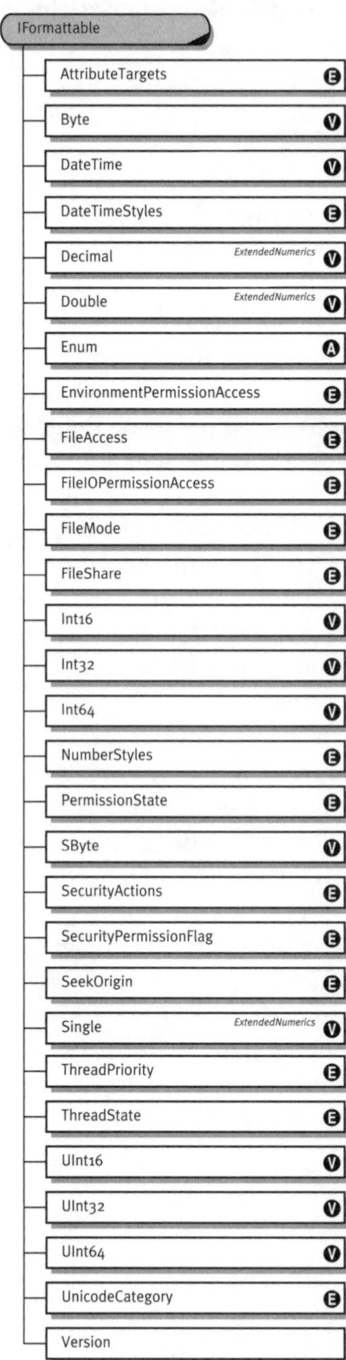

IFormattable Interface

## Summary

Implemented by classes that construct customizable string representations of objects.

## Type Summary

```
public interface IFormattable
{
  // Methods
     string ToString (string format, IFormatProvider formatProvider);
}
```

## Description

[*Note:* `System.IFormattable` contains the `System.IFormattable.ToString` method. The consumer of an object calls this method to obtain a formatted string representation of the value of the object.] A *format* is a string that describes the appearance of an object when it is converted to a string. Either standard or custom formats can be used. A standard format takes the form *Axx*, where *A* is a single alphabetic character called the *format specifier*, and *xx* is an integer between 0 and 99 inclusive, called the *precision specifier*. The format specifier controls the type of formatting applied to the value being represented as a string. The *precision specifier* controls the number of significant digits or decimal places in the string, if applicable. [*Note:* For the list of standard format specifiers, see the table below. Note that a given data type, such as `System.Int32`, might not support one or more of the standard format specifiers.]

[*Note:* When a format includes symbols that vary by culture, such as the currency symbol included by the "C" and "c" formats, a formatting object supplies the actual characters used in the string representation. A method may include a parameter to pass a `System.IFormatProvider` object that supplies a formatting object, or the method may use the default formatting object, which contains the symbol definitions for the current culture. The current culture typically uses the same set of symbols used system-wide by default. In the Base Class Library, the formatting object for system-supplied numeric types is a `System.Globalization.NumberFormatInfo` instance. For `System.DateTime` instances, a `System.Globalization.DateTimeFormatInfo` is used.]

The following table describes the standard format specifiers and associated formatting object members that are used with numeric data types in the Base Class Library.

IFormattable Interface

| Format Specifier | Description |
|---|---|
| C<br>c | Currency Format: Used for strings containing a monetary value. The System.Globalization.NumberFormatInfo.CurrencySymbol, System.Globalization.NumberFormatInfo.CurrencyGroupSizes, System.Globalization.NumberFormatInfo.CurrencyGroupSeparator, and System.Globalization.NumberFormatInfo.CurrencyDecimalSeparator members of a System.Globalization.NumberFormatInfo supply the currency symbol, size and separator for digit groupings, and decimal separator, respectively.<br>System.Globalization.NumberFormatInfo.CurrencyNegativePattern and System.Globalization.NumberFormatInfo.CurrencyPositivePattern determine the symbols used to represent negative and positive values. For example, a negative value may be prefixed with a minus sign, or enclosed in parentheses.<br>If the precision specifier is omitted, System.Globalization.NumberFormatInfo.CurrencyDecimalDigits determines the number of decimal places in the string. Results are rounded to the nearest representable value when necessary. |
| D<br>d | Decimal Format: (This format is valid only when specified with integral data types.) Used for strings containing integer values. Negative numbers are prefixed with the negative number symbol specified by the System.Globalization.NumberFormatInfo.NegativeSign property.<br>The precision specifier determines the minimum number of digits that appear in the string. If the specified precision requires more digits than the value contains, the string is left-padded with zeros. If the precision specifier specifies fewer digits than are in the value, the precision specifier is ignored. |
| E<br>e | Scientific (Engineering) Format: Used for strings in one of the following forms:<br>[–]*m.ddddddE+xxx*<br>[–]*m.ddddddE-xxx*<br>[–]*m.dddddde+xxx*<br>[–]*m.dddddde-xxx*<br>The negative number symbol ('–') appears only if the value is negative, and is supplied by the System.Globalization.NumberFormatInfo.NegativeSign property.<br>Exactly one non-zero decimal digit (*m*) precedes the decimal separator ('.'), which is supplied by the System.Globalization.NumberFormatInfo.NumberDecimalSeparator property.<br>The precision specifier determines the number of decimal places (*dddddd*) in the string. If the precision specifier is omitted, six decimal places are included in the string.<br>The exponent (*+/–xxx*) consists of either a positive or negative number symbol followed by a minimum of three digits (*xxx*). The exponent is left-padded with zeros, if necessary. The case of the format specifier ('E' or 'e') determines the case used for the exponent prefix (E or e) in the string. Results are rounded to the nearest representable value when necessary. The positive number symbol is supplied by the System.Globalization.NumberFormatInfo.PositiveSign property. |

IFormattable Interface



| Format Specifier | Description |
|---|---|
| `F`<br>`f` | `Fixed-Point Format`: Used for strings in the following form:<br>"[–]*m.dd...d*"<br>At least one non-zero decimal digit (*m*) precedes the decimal separator ('.'), which is supplied by the `System.Globalization.NumberFormatInfo.NumberDecimalSeparator` property.<br>A negative number symbol sign ('–') precedes *m* only if the value is negative. This symbol is supplied by the `System.Globalization.NumberFormatInfo.NegativeSign` property.<br>The precision specifier determines the number of decimal places (*dd...d*) in the string. If the precision specifier is omitted, `System.Globalization.NumberFormatInfo.NumberDecimalDigits` determines the number of decimal places in the string. Results are rounded to the nearest representable value when necessary. |
| `G`<br>`g` | `General Format`: The string is formatted in either fixed-point format ('F' or 'f') or scientific format ('E' or 'e').<br>For integral types:<br>Values are formatted using fixed-point format if *exponent* < precision specifier, where *exponent* is the exponent of the value in scientific format. For all other values, scientific format is used.<br>If the precision specifier is omitted, a default precision equal to the field width required to display the maximum value for the data type is used, which results in the value being formatted in fixed-point format. The default precisions for integral types are as follows:<br>`System.Int16`, `System.UInt16` - 5<br>`System.Int32`, `System.UInt32` - 10<br>`System.Int64`, `System.UInt64` - 19<br>For Single, Decimal, and Double types:<br>Values are formatted using fixed-point format if *exponent* >= –4 and *exponent* < precision specifier, where *exponent* is the exponent of the value in scientific format. For all other values, scientific format is used. Results are rounded to the nearest representable value when necessary.<br>If the precision specifier is omitted, the following default precisions are used:<br>`System.Single`: 7<br>`System.Double`: 15<br>`System.Decimal`: 29<br>For all types:<br>- The number of digits that appear in the result (not including the exponent) will not exceed the value of the precision specifier; values are rounded as necessary.<br>- The decimal point and any trailing zeros after the decimal point are removed whenever possible.<br>- The case of the format specifier ('G' or 'g') determines whether 'E' or 'e' prefixes the scientific format exponent. |

IFormattable Interface

| Format Specifier | Description |
|---|---|
| N<br>n | Number Format: Used for strings in the following form:<br>[–]*d,ddd,ddd.dd...d*<br>The representation of negative values is determined by the System.Globalization.NumberFormatInfo.NumberNegativePattern property. If the pattern includes a negative number symbol ('–'), this symbol is supplied by the System.Globalization.NumberFormatInfo.NegativeSign property.<br>At least one non-zero decimal digit (*d*) precedes the decimal separator ('.'), which is supplied by the System.Globalization.NumberFormatInfo.NumberDecimalSeparator property. Digits between the decimal point and the most significant digit in the value are grouped using the group size specified by the System.Globalization.NumberFormatInfo.NumberGroupSizes property. The group separator (',') is inserted between each digit group, and is supplied by the System.Globalization.NumberFormatInfo.NumberGroupSeparator property.<br>The precision specifier determines the number of decimal places (*dd...d*). If the precision specifier is omitted, System.Globalization.NumberFormatInfo.NumberDecimalDigits determines the number of decimal places in the string. Results are rounded to the nearest representable value when necessary. |
| P<br>p | Percent Format: Used for strings containing a percentage. The System.Globalization.NumberFormatInfo.PercentSymbol, System.Globalization.NumberFormatInfo.PercentGroupSizes, System.Globalization.NumberFormatInfo.PercentGroupSeparator, and System.Globalization.NumberFormatInfo.PercentDecimalSeparator members of a System.Globalization.NumberFormatInfo supply the percent symbol, size and separator for digit groupings, and decimal separator, respectively.<br>System.Globalization.NumberFormatInfo.PercentNegativePattern and System.Globalization.NumberFormatInfo.PercentPositivePattern determine the symbols used to represent negative and positive values. For example, a negative value may be prefixed with a minus sign, or enclosed in parentheses.<br>If no precision is specified, the number of decimal places in the result is determined by System.Globalization.NumberFormatInfo.PercentDecimalDigits. Results are rounded to the nearest representable value when necessary.<br>The result is scaled by 100 (.99 becomes 99%). |

IFormattable Interface

| Format Specifier | Description |
|---|---|
| R<br>r | `Round trip Format`: (This format is valid only when specified with `System.Double` or `System.Single`.) Used to ensure that the precision of the string representation of a floating-point value is such that parsing the string does not result in a loss of precision when compared to the original value. If the maximum precision of the data type (7 for `System.Single` and 15 for `System.Double`) would result in a loss of precision, the precision is increased by two decimal places. If a precision specifier is supplied with this format specifier, it is ignored. This format is otherwise identical to the fixed-point format. |
| X<br>x | `Hexadecimal Format`: (This format is valid only when specified with integral data types.) Used for string representations of numbers in Base 16. The precision determines the minimum number of digits in the string. If the precision specifies more digits than the number contains, the number is left-padded with zeros. The case of the format specifier ('X' or 'x') determines whether uppercase or lowercase letters are used in the hexadecimal representation. |

If the numerical value is a `System.Single` or `System.Double` with a value of `NaN`, `PositiveInfinity`, or `NegativeInfinity`, the format specifier is ignored, and one of the following is returned: `System.Globalization.NumberFormatInfo.NaNSymbol`, `System.Globalization.NumberFormatInfo.PositiveInfinitySymbol`, or `System.Globalization.NumberFormatInfo.NegativeInfinitySymbol`.

A custom format is any string specified as a format that is not in the form of a standard format string (Axx) described above. The following table describes the characters that are used in constructing custom formats.

IFormattable Interface

| Format Specifier | Description |
|---|---|
| 0 (zero) | `Zero placeholder`: If the value being formatted has a digit in the position where a '0' appears in the custom format, then that digit is copied to the output string; otherwise a zero is stored in that position in the output string. The position of the leftmost '0' before the decimal separator and the rightmost '0' after the decimal separator determines the range of digits that are always present in the output string.<br>The number of zero and/or digit placeholders after the decimal separator determines the number of digits that appear after the decimal separator. Values are rounded as necessary. |
| # | `Digit placeholder`: If the value being formatted has a digit in the position where a '#' appears in the custom format, then that digit is copied to the output string; otherwise, nothing is stored in that position in the output string. Note that this specifier never stores the '0' character if it is not a significant digit, even if '0' is the only digit in the string. (It does display the '0' character in the output string if it is a significant digit.)<br>The number of zero and/or digit placeholders after the decimal separator determines the number of digits that appear after the decimal separator. Values are rounded as necessary. |
| . (period) | `Decimal separator`: The leftmost '.' character in the format string determines the location of the decimal separator in the formatted value; any additional '.' characters are ignored. The `System.Globalization.NumberFormatInfo.NumberDecimalSeparator` property determines the symbol used as the decimal separator. |
| , (comma) | `Group separator and number scaling`: The ',' character serves two purposes. First, if the custom format contains this character between two zero or digit placeholders (0 or #) and to the left of the decimal separator if one is present, then the output will have group separators inserted between each group of digits to the left of the decimal separator. The `System.Globalization.NumberFormatInfo.NumberGroupSeparator` and `System.Globalization.NumberFormatInfo.NumberGroupSizes` properties determine the symbol used as the group separator and the number of digits in each group, respectively.<br>If the format string contains one or more ',' characters immediately to the left of the decimal separator, then the number will be scaled. The scale factor is determined by the number of group separator characters immediately to the left of the decimal separator. If there are x characters, then the value is divided by $1000^X$ before it is formatted. For example, the format string '0,,' will divide a value by one million. Note that the presence of the ',' character to indicate scaling does not insert group separators in the output string. Thus, to scale a number by 1 million and insert group separators, use a custom format similar to "#,##0,,". |
| % (percent) | `Percentage placeholder`: The presence of a '%' character in a custom format causes a number to be multiplied by 100 before it is formatted. The percent symbol is inserted in the output string at the location where the '%' appears in the format string. The `System.Globalization.NumberFormatInfo.PercentSymbol` property determines the percent symbol. |

IFormattable Interface

| Format Specifier | Description |
|---|---|
| E0<br>E+0<br>E–0<br>e0<br>e+0<br>e–0 | `Engineering format`: If any of the strings 'E', 'E+', 'E–', 'e', 'e+', or 'e–' is present in a custom format and is followed immediately by at least one '0' character, then the value is formatted using scientific notation. The number of '0' characters following the exponent prefix (E or e) determines the minimum number of digits in the exponent. The 'E+' and 'e+' formats indicate that a positive or negative number symbol always precedes the exponent. The 'E', 'E–', 'e', or 'e–' formats indicate that a negative number symbol precedes negative exponents; no symbol precedes positive exponents. The positive number symbol is supplied by the `System.Globalization.NumberFormatInfo.PositiveSign` property. The negative number symbol is supplied by the `System.Globalization.NumberFormatInfo.NegativeSign` property. |
| \ (backslash) | `Escape character`: In some languages, such as C#, the backslash character causes the next character in the custom format to be interpreted as an escape sequence. It is used with C language formatting sequences, such as "\n" (newline). In some languages, the escape character itself is required to be preceded by an escape character when used as a literal. Otherwise, the compiler interprets the character as an escape sequence. This escape character is not required to be supported in all programming languages. |
| 'ABC'<br>"ABC" | `Literal string`: Characters enclosed in single or double quotes are copied to the output string literally, and do not affect formatting. |
| ; (semicolon) | `Section separator`: The ';' character is used to separate sections for positive, negative, and zero numbers in the format string. (This feature is described in detail below.) |
| Other | `All other characters`: All other characters are stored in the output string as literals in the position in which they appear. |

Note that for fixed-point format strings (strings not containing an 'E0', 'E+0', 'E–0', 'e0', 'e+0', or 'e–0'), numbers are rounded to as many decimal places as there are zero or digit placeholders to the right of the decimal separator. If the custom format does not contain a decimal separator, the number is rounded to the nearest integer. If the number has more digits than there are zero or digit placeholders to the left of the decimal separator, the extra digits are copied to the output string immediately before the first zero or digit placeholder.

A custom format can contain up to three sections separated by section separator characters to specify different formatting for positive, negative, and zero values. The sections are interpreted as follows:

- **One section:** The custom format applies to all values (positive, negative, and zero). Negative values include a negative sign.

- **Two sections:** The first section applies to positive values and zeros, and the second section applies to negative values. If the value to be formatted is negative but becomes zero after rounding according to the format in the second section, then the resulting zero is formatted according to the first section. Negative values do not include a negative sign to allow full control over representations of negative values. For example, a negative can be represented in parentheses using a custom format similar to "####.####;(####.####)".
- **Three sections:** The first section applies to positive values, the second section applies to negative values, and the third section applies to zeros. The second section can be empty (nothing appears between the semicolons), in which case the first section applies to all nonzero values, and negative values include a negative sign. If the number to be formatted is nonzero but becomes zero after rounding according to the format in the first or second section, then the resulting zero is formatted according to the third section.

The `System.Enum` and `System.DateTime` types also support using format specifiers to format string representations of values. The meaning of a specific format specifier varies according to the kind of data (numeric, date/time, enumeration) being formatted. See `System.Enum` and `System.Globalization.DateTimeFormatInfo` for a comprehensive list of the format specifiers supported by each type.

## Example

```
using System;

namespace Samples
{
  public class IFormattableSample
  {
    public static void Main()
    {
      double d = 123.12345678901234;
      string[] strings = {"C","E","e","F","G","N","P","R"};
      foreach(string s in strings)
        Console.WriteLine("{0:R} as {1}: {2}",
                          d, s, d.ToString(s,null));
      strings = new string[]{"D","x","X"};
      int i = 255;
      foreach(string s in strings)
        Console.WriteLine("{0} as {1}: {2}",
                          i, s, i.ToString(s,null));
    }
  }
}
```

The output is

```
123.12345678901234 as C: $123.12
123.12345678901234 as c: $123.12
123.12345678901234 as E: 1.231235E+002
123.12345678901234 as e: 1.231235e+002
123.12345678901234 as F: 123.12
123.12345678901234 as G: 123.123456789012
123.12345678901234 as g: 123.123456789012
123.12345678901234 as N: 123.12
123.12345678901234 as n: 123.12
123.12345678901234 as P: 12,312.35 %
123.12345678901234 as p: 12,312.35 %
123.12345678901234 as R: 123.12345678901234
123.12345678901234 as r: 123.12345678901234
2147483647 as D: 2147483647
2147483647 as d: 2147483647
2147483647 as x: 7fffffff
2147483647 as X: 7FFFFFFF
2147483647 as D42: 000000000000000000000000000000002147483647
2147483647 as d42: 000000000000000000000000000000002147483647
2147483647 as x42: 00000000000000000000000000000000007fffffff
2147483647 as X42: 00000000000000000000000000000000007FFFFFFF
2147483647 as "C": $2,147,483,647.00
2147483647 as "C": R$ 2.147.483.647,00
2147483647 as "C": 2ÿ147ÿ483ÿ647,00 Sk
2147483647 as "C": HK$2,147,483,647.00
```

# System.Collections IHashCodeProvider Interface

IHashCodeProvider

## Summary

Implemented by classes that support custom hash functions for instances of the class.

## Type Summary

```
public interface IHashCodeProvider
{
  // Methods
     int GetHashCode (object obj);
}
```

**BG** Note that the `IHashCodeProvider` interface allows you to define your own hash function for a given object. This allows users to either override it for special comparisons such as case-insensitive string lookup, or to replace a poorly written hash function on a third party data type. Combined with `IComparer`, you can use types as keys in a `Hashtable` even if the original author neglected to override `Equals` and `GetHashCode` on their type.

One note on `IHashCodeProvider`—many of our users either don't get the type or don't understand when they need to do it. We've found instances where people want to use a case-insensitive `Hashtable`, yet they remember to specify the `IComparer` but not the `IHashCodeProvider`, giving them incorrect results.

We are considering replacing `IHashCodeProvider` and unifying it with `IComparer` in a new `IKeyComparer` interface that would define `CompareTo`, `Equals`, and `GetHashCode` methods. It turns out that `Hashtable` only needs to compare whether two keys are equal, not establish an ordering over two particular keys. For certain data types, doing an equality check can be done more quickly than a comparison. Strings in the Microsoft CLR implementation fall into this bucket, since we internally store the length of the String. `Equals` on strings is defined as a bit-wise equality check (which isn't linguistically correct, of course).

## Description

[*Note:* `System.Collections.IHashCodeProvider` contains the `System.Collections.IHashCodeProvider.GetHashCode` method. The consumer of an object should call this method to obtain a hash code for the object using a custom hash function.]

## Example

```
using System;
using System.Collections;

namespace Samples
{
  public class IHashCodeProviderSample
  {
    public class MyComparer: IComparer
    {
      public int Compare(Object a, Object b)
      {
        return ((IComparable)a).CompareTo(b);
      }
    }
    public class MyHashCodeProvider: IHashCodeProvider
    {
      public int GetHashCode(Object o)
      {
        return o.GetHashCode();
      }
    }

    public static void Main()
    {
      Hashtable ht1 = new Hashtable(
                     CaseInsensitiveHashCodeProvider.Default,
                     new MyComparer());
      Hashtable ht2 = new Hashtable(new MyHashCodeProvider(),
                                     new MyComparer());
      AddEntires(ht1);
      AddEntires(ht2);
      DisplayEntires(ht1);
      DisplayEntires(ht2);
    }
    public static void AddEntires(Hashtable ht)
    {
      ht.Add("One","damien");
      ht.Add("two", "brad");
      ht.Add("Three", "mark");
      ht.Add("four", "Maire");
```

IHashCodeProvider Interface

```
      ht.Add("Five", "sacha");
      ht.Add("six", "Sarah");
    }
    public static void DisplayEntires(Hashtable ht)
    {
      Console.WriteLine("Count: {0}", ht.Count );
      IDictionaryEnumerator de = ht.GetEnumerator();
      while(de.MoveNext())
        Console.WriteLine("Key: {0}   \tValue: {1}",
                          de.Key,
                          de.Value);
    }
  }
}
```

The output is

```
Count: 6
Key: One   Value: damien
Key: Three   Value: mark
Key: four   Value: Maire
Key: Five   Value: sacha
Key: two   Value: brad
Key: six   Value: Sarah
Count: 6
Key: six   Value: Sarah
Key: One   Value: damien
Key: four   Value: Maire
Key: two   Value: brad
Key: Three   Value: mark
Key: Five   Value: sacha
```

# System.Collections
# IList Interface

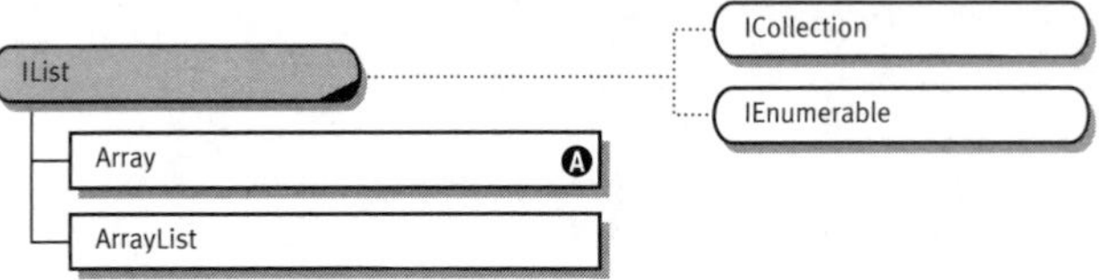




## Summary

Implemented by classes that support a collection of objects that can be individually indexed.

## Type Summary

```
public interface IList : ICollection, IEnumerable
{
  // Properties
     bool IsFixedSize { get; }
     bool IsReadOnly { get; }
     object this[int index] { set; get; }

  // Methods
     int Add (object value);
     void Clear ();
     bool Contains (object value);
     int IndexOf (object value);
     void Insert (int index, object value);
     void Remove (object value);
     void RemoveAt (int index);
}
```

**BA** `IList` and `IDictionary` are examples of interfaces that are slightly more complex and central to the design than I would have liked. Ordinarily I would have liked to make these abstract base classes in order to share some implementation and to version more easily. One of the compelling reasons that made us decide to make this an interface is to support strongly typed collections. We use strongly typed collections heavily in Windows Forms and ASP.NET to enable an easier programming model. Tools and compilers can help developers catch errors at design time rather than runtime.

*CONTINUED*

IList Interface

To define a collection of `MenuItems` you would want the indexer to be strongly typed to return `MenuItems` as:

```
public MenuItems this [int index] {get; set;}
```

In most cases we also wanted this collection of `MenuItems` to be an `IList` as well such that we could build services that work against all lists (such as databinding). In such a case you would want the indexer to be typed loosely so that it can handle any kind of elements:

```
public object this [int index] {get; set;}
```

You will notice that a class cannot have both of these methods as they differ only in return type (`MenuItem` vs. `Object`). However, if we define the loosely typed methods to be part of an interface we are able to use explicit member implementation to get around this limitation.

```
public MenuItems this [int index] {get; set;}
public object IList.this [int index] {get; set;}
```

Now when the `MenuItemColleciton` is used directly the indexer returns a menu item, and when it is cast to `IList` the indexer returns `Object`.

## Description

[*Note:* `System.Collections.IList` implementations fall into three categories: read-only, fixed-size, and variable-size. A read-only list cannot be modified. A fixed-size list allows the modification of existing elements, but does not allow the addition or removal of elements. A variable-size list allows the modification, addition, and removal of elements.]

## Example

```
using System;
using System.Collections;

namespace Samples
{
  public class MySimpleList: IList
  {
    private object[] objects;
    private int counter = 0;
    private int modifications = 0;
    public MySimpleList(int i)
    {
```

IList Interface

```
    if(i <= 0)
      throw new ArgumentOutOfRangeException();
    objects = new object[i];
  }
  public IEnumerator GetEnumerator()
    {return new Enumerator(this);}
  public int Count {get {return counter - 1;}}
  public bool IsSynchronized {get {return false;}}
  public object SyncRoot {get {return this;}}
  public void CopyTo(System.Array array, int index)
  {
    objects.CopyTo(array, index);
  }
  public bool IsFixedSize {get {return false;}}
  public bool IsReadOnly {get {return false;}}
  public Object this[int index]
  {
    get
    {
      if(index < 0 || index >= counter)
        throw new ArgumentOutOfRangeException();
      return objects[index];
    }
    set
    {
      if(index < 0 || index >= counter)
        throw new ArgumentOutOfRangeException();
      objects[index] = value;
      modifications++;
    }
  }
  public int Add(Object item)
  {
    if(counter == objects.Length)
      Resize();
    objects[counter++] = item;
    modifications++;
    return counter - 1;
  }
  public void Clear()
  {
    if(counter > 0)
    {
      Array.Clear(objects, 0, counter);
      counter = 0;
    }
    modifications++;
  }
```

IList Interface

```
public bool Contains(Object value)
{
  return IndexOf(value) >= 0;
}
public int IndexOf(Object value)
{
  return ((IList)objects).IndexOf(value);
}
public void Insert(int index, Object value)
{
  if(index < 0 || index > counter)
    throw new ArgumentOutOfRangeException();
  if(counter == objects.Length)
    Resize();
  if(index < counter)
    Array.Copy(objects, index, objects, index + 1, counter - index);
  objects[index] = value;
  counter++;
  modifications++;
}
public void Remove(Object item)
{
  int index = IndexOf(item);
  if(index >= 0)
    RemoveAt(index);
  modifications++;
}
public void RemoveAt(int index)
{
  if(index < 0 || index >= counter)
    throw new ArgumentOutOfRangeException();
  counter--;
  if(index < counter)
  {
    Array.Copy(objects, index + 1,
               objects, index, counter - index);
  }
  objects[counter] = null;
  modifications++;
}
private void Resize()
{
  if(objects.Length == counter)
  {
    object[] tmp = new object[counter * 2];
    objects.CopyTo(tmp, 0);
    objects = tmp;
  }
}
public struct Enumerator: IEnumerator
```

```
      {
        private MySimpleList list;
        private object[] objects;
        private int maxIndex;
        private int counter;
        private int modifications;
        internal Enumerator(MySimpleList list)
        {
          this.list = list;
          objects = list.objects;
          counter = -1;
          maxIndex = list.counter;
          modifications = list.modifications;
        }
        public Object Current {get {return objects[counter];}}
        public bool MoveNext()
        {
          Valid();
          if(counter == maxIndex)
            return false;
          counter++;
          return true;
        }
        void IEnumerator.Reset()
        {
          Valid();
          counter = -1;
        }
        private void Valid()
        {
          if(modifications != list.modifications)
            throw new InvalidOperationException();
        }
      }
    }
    public class IListSample
    {
      public static void Main()
      {
        IList il = new MySimpleList(1);
        Console.WriteLine("Is fixed size: {0}", il.IsFixedSize);
        Console.WriteLine("Is read only: {0}", il.IsReadOnly);
        string name = "TAMARA";
        string[] strings = {"damien", "mark", "brad",
                            "maire", "sacha", name};
        foreach(string s in strings)
          il.Add(s);
        DisplayList(il);
```

```
      il.Insert(il.IndexOf(name), name.ToLower());
      il.Remove(name.ToUpper());
      DisplayList(il);
      foreach(string s in strings)
        il.Add(s.ToUpper());
      DisplayList(il);
      il.RemoveAt(il.Count);
      DisplayList(il);
      il.Clear();
      DisplayList(il);
    }
    public static void DisplayList(IList il)
    {
      Console.WriteLine("The values in the list are:");
      foreach(object o in il)
        Console.Write("{0} ", o);
      Console.WriteLine();
    }
  }
}
```

The output is

```
Is fixed size: False
Is read only: False
The values in the list are:
damien mark brad maire sacha TAMARA
The values in the list are:
damien mark brad maire sacha tamara
The values in the list are:
damien mark brad maire sacha tamara DAMIEN MARK BRAD MAIRE SACHA TAMARA
The values in the list are:
damien mark brad maire sacha tamara DAMIEN MARK BRAD MAIRE SACHA
The values in the list are:
```

# System IndexOutOfRangeException

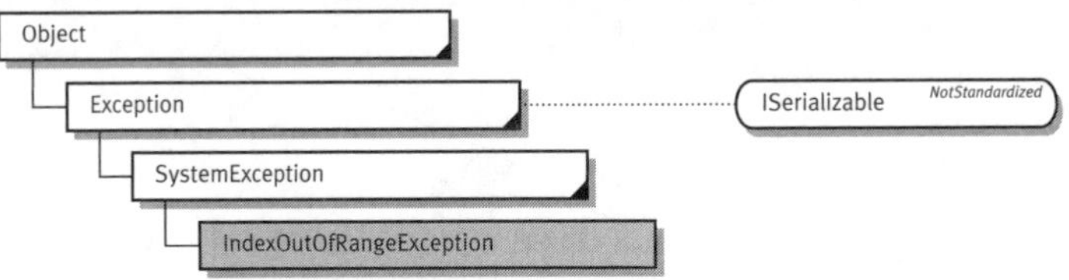


A B C D E F G H I J K L M N O P Q R S T U V W X Y Z

## Summary

Represents the error that occurs when an attempt is made to access an element of an array with an index that is outside the bounds of the array.

## Type Summary

```
public sealed class IndexOutOfRangeException : SystemException
{
  // Constructors
     public IndexOutOfRangeException ();
     public IndexOutOfRangeException (string message);
     public IndexOutOfRangeException (string message,
                                      Exception innerException);
}
```

## Example

```
using System;

namespace Samples
{
  public class IndexOutOfRangeExceptionSample
  {
    public static void Main()
    {
      try
      {
        string[] strings = {"zero", "one", "two"};
        strings[3] = "three";
      }
      catch(Exception e)
      {
        Console.WriteLine("Exception: {0}", e);
      }
    }
  }
}
```

The output is

```
Exception: System.IndexOutOfRangeException: Index was outside the bounds of the
array.
   at Samples.IndexOutOfRangeExceptionSample.Main() in C:\Books\BCL\Samples\
System\IndexOutOfRangeException\IndexOutOfRangeException.cs:line 12
```

# System
# Int16 Structure

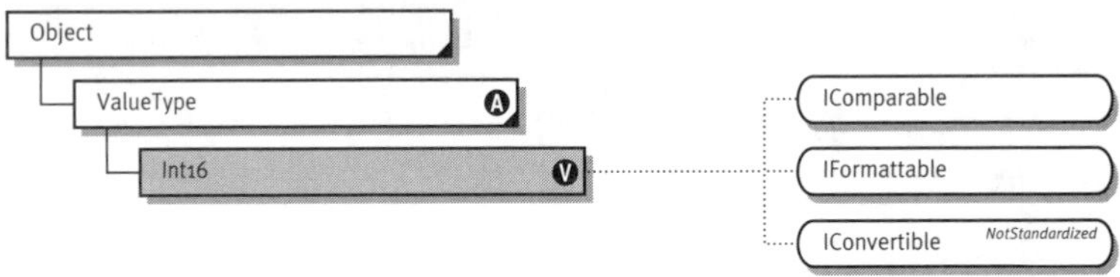




## Summary

Represents a 16-bit signed integer.

## Type Summary

```
public struct Int16 : IComparable, IFormattable,
                      IConvertible
{
  // Fields
     public const short MaxValue = 32767;
     public const short MinValue = -32768;

  // Methods
     public int CompareTo (object value);
     public override bool Equals (object obj);
     public override int GetHashCode ();
  MS public TypeCode GetTypeCode ();
     public static short Parse (string s);
     public static short Parse (string s, NumberStyles style);
     public static short Parse (string s, NumberStyles style,
                                IFormatProvider provider);
  CF public static short Parse (string s, IFormatProvider provider);
     public override string ToString ();
     public string ToString (string format);
     public string ToString (string format, IFormatProvider provider);
     public string ToString (IFormatProvider provider);

  // Explicit Interface Members
  MS bool IConvertible.ToBoolean(IFormatProvider provider);
  MS byte IConvertible.ToByte(IFormatProvider provider);
  MS char IConvertible.ToChar(IFormatProvider provider);
  MS DateTime IConvertible.ToDateTime(IFormatProvider provider);
  MS decimal IConvertible.ToDecimal(IFormatProvider provider);
  MS double IConvertible.ToDouble(IFormatProvider provider);
  MS short IConvertible.ToInt16(IFormatProvider provider);
  MS int IConvertible.ToInt32(IFormatProvider provider);
  MS long IConvertible.ToInt64(IFormatProvider provider);
  MS sbyte IConvertible.ToSByte(IFormatProvider provider);
```

Int16 Structure

```
    MS float IConvertible.ToSingle(IFormatProvider provider);
    MS object IConvertible.ToType(Type type,IFormatProvider provider);
    MS ushort IConvertible.ToUInt16(IFormatProvider provider);
    MS uint IConvertible.ToUInt32(IFormatProvider provider);
    MS ulong IConvertible.ToUInt64(IFormatProvider provider);
  }
```

## Description

The `System.Int16` data type represents integer values ranging from negative 32,768 to positive 32,767; that is, hexadecimal: 0x8000 to 0x7FFF.

## Example

```
using System;

namespace Samples
{
  public class Int16Sample
  {
    public static void Main()
    {
      short max = short.MaxValue,
            min = short.MinValue;
      Console.WriteLine("MaxValue: {0}", max);
      Console.WriteLine("MinValue: {0}", min);
      Console.WriteLine("Is {0} equal to {1}: {2}",
                        max, max, max.Equals(max));
      Console.WriteLine("Is {0} equal to {1}: {2}",
                        max, min, max.Equals(min));
      Console.WriteLine("{0} has hashcode of: {1}",
                        max, max.GetHashCode());
      Console.WriteLine("{0} has hashcode of: {1}",
                        min, min.GetHashCode());
      string s = max.ToString();
      Console.WriteLine("\"{0}\" parsed from string yields: {1}",
                        s, Int16.Parse(s));
      s = min.ToString();
      Console.WriteLine("\"{0}\" parsed from string yields: {1}",
                        s, Int16.Parse(s));
      string[] formats = {"c", "d", "e", "f",
                          "g", "n", "p", "x" };
      foreach(string f in formats)
        Console.WriteLine("{0}: {1}", max, max.ToString(f));
    }
  }
}
```

Int16 Structure

The output is

```
MaxValue: 32767
MinValue: -32768
Is 32767 equal to 32767: True
Is 32767 equal to -32768: False
32767 has hashcode of: 2147450879
-32768 has hashcode of: -2147450880
"32767" parsed from string yields: 32767
"-32768" parsed from string yields: -32768
32767: $32,767.00
32767: 32767
32767: 3.276700e+004
32767: 32767.00
32767: 32767
32767: 32,767.00
32767: 3,276,700.00 %
32767: 7fff
```

# System
# Int32 Structure

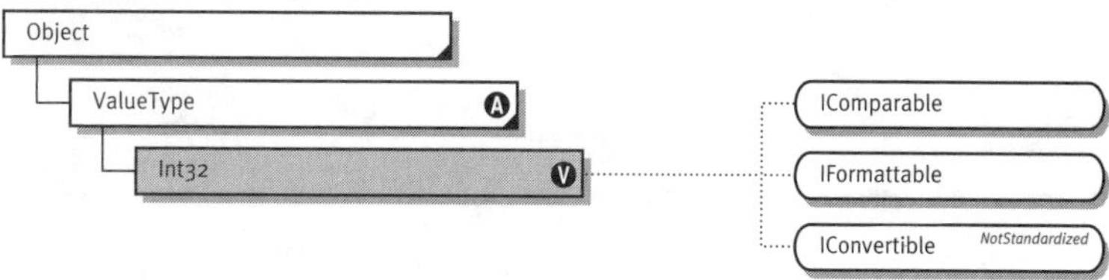




## Summary

Represents a 32-bit signed integer.

## Type Summary

```
public struct Int32 : IComparable, IFormattable,
                      IConvertible
{
  // Fields
     public const int MaxValue = 2147483647;
     public const int MinValue = -2147483648;

  // Methods
     public int CompareTo (object value);
     public override bool Equals (object obj);
     public override int GetHashCode ();
  MS public TypeCode GetTypeCode ();
     public static int Parse (string s);
     public static int Parse (string s, NumberStyles style);
     public static int Parse (string s, NumberStyles style,
                              IFormatProvider provider);
     public static int Parse (string s, IFormatProvider provider);
     public override string ToString ();
     public string ToString (string format);
     public string ToString (string format, IFormatProvider provider);
     public string ToString (IFormatProvider provider);

  // Explicit Interface Members
  MS bool IConvertible.ToBoolean(IFormatProvider provider);
  MS byte IConvertible.ToByte(IFormatProvider provider);
  MS char IConvertible.ToChar(IFormatProvider provider);
  MS DateTime IConvertible.ToDateTime(IFormatProvider provider);
  MS decimal IConvertible.ToDecimal(IFormatProvider provider);
  MS double IConvertible.ToDouble(IFormatProvider provider);
  MS short IConvertible.ToInt16(IFormatProvider provider);
  MS int IConvertible.ToInt32(IFormatProvider provider);
  MS long IConvertible.ToInt64(IFormatProvider provider);
  MS sbyte IConvertible.ToSByte(IFormatProvider provider);
  MS float IConvertible.ToSingle(IFormatProvider provider);
  MS object IConvertible.ToType(Type type,IFormatProvider provider);
  MS ushort IConvertible.ToUInt16(IFormatProvider provider);
```

Int32 Structure

```
    MS uint IConvertible.ToUInt32(IFormatProvider provider);
    MS ulong IConvertible.ToUInt64(IFormatProvider provider);
}
```



**BA** We had lots of debate about the naming of the base types. Because of the multiple programming language aspects of the platform many of the obvious names were ruled out as the languages differ in their meaning for names such as Integer (for example, 16 bits in VB, 32 bits in Java). So we decided to use names that are technically accurate and encourage language vendors to alias the names to their language's types. For example, in C#, the keyword `int` is simply an alias for `System.Int32`. If you spend much time looking at raw IL you will recognize that the IL language designers decided to use byte count rather than bit count to represent the same values. So in IL the `Int32` value is encoded as `I4`. This is an example of different parts of the system optimizing for their own customers. Luckily few folks using the library are forced to understand the IL representation, and vice versa.

One of our guidelines for value types (`structs`) is that they be immutable so that they behave more like the built-in primitive types (`Int32`, `Double`, etc.). An object is immutable if it has no methods or properties that change the state of the object. Although it may be counterintuitive, integers are immutable. For example, consider an instance of the `Int32` structure with the value five. That instance is always five and can not be changed. You can add one to it and you get a new instance, namely six, but the five-ness of the five remains. A given location in memory can be assigned one instance or another, but the value of those instances can never change.

**BG** Note that the `Parse` method throws a `FormatException` when parsing a string that is not a number. There is no predicate to determine whether a string can be parsed. In this particular case, checking to see whether a string can be parsed is a somewhat common operation and particularly expensive. Since there isn't a significant additional cost to parsing a data type vs. telling whether a string iscan be parsed, and since most often when checking whether a data type can be parsed, you then want to parse the data type, we opted to *not* add a method like `IsParsible(String)`. We added a `TryParse` method to `Double` for this purpose in the Microsoft CLR implementation and we intend to add `TryParse` to all the base data types in a future version.

**JR** I have run into some developers who like the fact that on some C systems, `int` is a 32-bit value and on some other systems, `int` may be represented by a different number of bits. Personally, I don't like this, and I think that this makes programming much

CONTINUED

Int32 Structure

more difficult. Recompiling some C code for a different platform could give wildly different results. I applaud the BCL for giving the numeric types names indicating their bit width. There is no doubt that an `Int32` will be a 32-bit integer on any and all CLI-compliant systems, giving me the confidence to know that my existing code should perform just fine when recompiled or re-JIT compiled.

## Description

The `System.Int32` data type represents integer values ranging from negative 2,147,483,648 to positive 2,147,483,647; that is, hexadecimal 0x80000000 to 0x7FFFFFFF.

## Example

```
using System;

namespace Samples
{
  public class Int32Sample
  {
    public static void Main()
    {
      int max = int.MaxValue,
          min = int.MinValue;
      Console.WriteLine("MaxValue: {0}", max);
      Console.WriteLine("MinValue: {0}", min);
      Console.WriteLine("Is {0} equal to {1}: {2}",
                        max, max, max.Equals(max));
      Console.WriteLine("Is {0} equal to {1}: {2}",
                        max, min, max.Equals(min));
      Console.WriteLine("{0} has hashcode of: {1}",
                        max, max.GetHashCode());
      Console.WriteLine("{0} has hashcode of: {1}",
                        min, min.GetHashCode());
      string s = max.ToString();
      Console.WriteLine("\"{0}\" parsed from string yields: {1}",
                        s, Int32.Parse(s));
      s = min.ToString();
      Console.WriteLine("\"{0}\" parsed from string yields: {1}",
                        s, Int32.Parse(s));
      string[] formats = {"c", "d", "e", "f",
                          "g", "n", "p", "x" };
      foreach(string f in formats)
        Console.WriteLine("{0}: {1}", max, max.ToString(f));
    }
  }
}
```

Int32 Structure

The output is

```
MaxValue: 2147483647
MinValue: -2147483648
Is 2147483647 equal to 2147483647: True
Is 2147483647 equal to -2147483648: False
2147483647 has hashcode of: 2147483647
-2147483648 has hashcode of: -2147483648
"2147483647" parsed from string yields: 2147483647
"-2147483648" parsed from string yields: -2147483648
2147483647: $2,147,483,647.00
2147483647: 2147483647
2147483647: 2.147484e+009
2147483647: 2147483647.00
2147483647: 2147483647
2147483647: 2,147,483,647.00
2147483647: 214,748,364,700.00 %
2147483647: 7fffffff
```

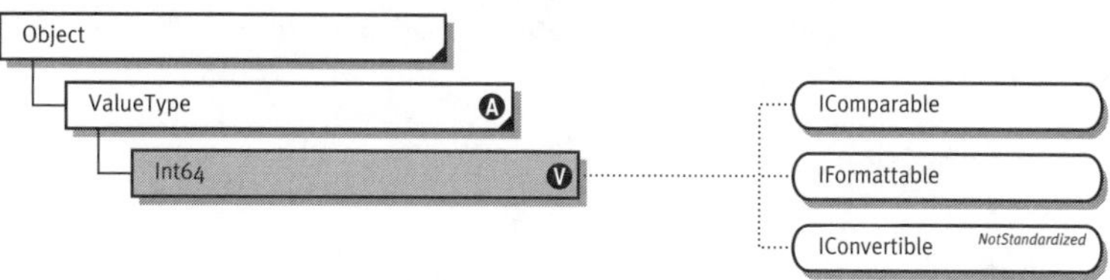


## Summary

Represents a 64-bit signed integer.

## Type Summary

```
public struct Int64 : IComparable, IFormattable,
                      IConvertible
{
  // Fields
     public const long MaxValue = 9223372036854775807;
     public const long MinValue = -9223372036854775808;

  // Methods
     public int CompareTo (object value);
     public override bool Equals (object obj);
     public override int GetHashCode ();
  MS public TypeCode GetTypeCode ();
     public static long Parse (string s);
     public static long Parse (string s, NumberStyles style);
     public static long Parse (string s, NumberStyles style,
                               IFormatProvider provider);
  CF public static long Parse (string s, IFormatProvider provider);
     public override string ToString ();
     public string ToString (string format);
     public string ToString (string format, IFormatProvider provider);
     public string ToString (IFormatProvider provider);

  // Explicit Interface Members
  MS bool IConvertible.ToBoolean(IFormatProvider provider);
  MS byte IConvertible.ToByte(IFormatProvider provider);
  MS char IConvertible.ToChar(IFormatProvider provider);
  MS DateTime IConvertible.ToDateTime(IFormatProvider provider);
  MS decimal IConvertible.ToDecimal(IFormatProvider provider);
  MS double IConvertible.ToDouble(IFormatProvider provider);
  MS short IConvertible.ToInt16(IFormatProvider provider);
  MS int IConvertible.ToInt32(IFormatProvider provider);
  MS long IConvertible.ToInt64(IFormatProvider provider);
  MS sbyte IConvertible.ToSByte(IFormatProvider provider);
  MS float IConvertible.ToSingle(IFormatProvider provider);
```

Int64 Structure

```
    MS object IConvertible.ToType(Type type,IFormatProvider provider);
    MS ushort IConvertible.ToUInt16(IFormatProvider provider);
    MS uint IConvertible.ToUInt32(IFormatProvider provider);
    MS ulong IConvertible.ToUInt64(IFormatProvider provider);
  }
```

## Description

The `System.Int64` data type represents integer values ranging from negative 9,223,372,036,854,775,808 to positive 9,223,372,036,854,775,807; that is, hexadecimal 0x8000000000000000 to 0x7FFFFFFFFFFFFFFF.

## Example

```
using System;

namespace Samples
{
  public class Int64Sample
  {
    public static void Main()
    {
      long max = long.MaxValue,
           min = long.MinValue;
      Console.WriteLine("MaxValue: {0}", max);
      Console.WriteLine("MinValue: {0}", min);
      Console.WriteLine("Is {0} equal to {1}: {2}",
                        max, max, max.Equals(max));
      Console.WriteLine("Is {0} equal to {1}: {2}",
                        max, min, max.Equals(min));
      Console.WriteLine("{0} has hashcode of: {1}",
                        max, max.GetHashCode());
      Console.WriteLine("{0} has hashcode of: {1}",
                        min, min.GetHashCode());
      string s = max.ToString();
      Console.WriteLine("\"{0}\" parsed from string yields: {1}",
                        s, Int64.Parse(s));
      s = min.ToString();
      Console.WriteLine("\"{0}\" parsed from string yields: {1}",
                        s, Int64.Parse(s));
      string[] formats = {"c", "d", "e", "f",
                          "g", "n", "p", "x" };
      foreach(string f in formats)
        Console.WriteLine("{0}: {1}", max, max.ToString(f));
    }
  }
}
```

Int64 Structure

The output is

```
MaxValue: 9223372036854775807
MinValue: -9223372036854775808
Is 9223372036854775807 equal to 9223372036854775807: True
Is 9223372036854775807 equal to -9223372036854775808: False
9223372036854775807 has hashcode of: -2147483648
-9223372036854775808 has hashcode of: -2147483648
"9223372036854775807" parsed from string yields: 9223372036854775807
"-9223372036854775808" parsed from string yields: -9223372036854775808
9223372036854775807: $9,223,372,036,854,775,807.00
9223372036854775807: 9223372036854775807
9223372036854775807: 9.223372e+018
9223372036854775807: 9223372036854775807.00
9223372036854775807: 9223372036854775807
9223372036854775807: 9,223,372,036,854,775,807.00
9223372036854775807: 922,337,203,685,477,580,700.00 %
9223372036854775807: 7fffffffffffffff
```

# Interlocked

## Summary

The `System.Threading.Interlocked` class provides atomic operations for variables that are shared by multiple threads.

## Type Summary

```
public sealed class Interlocked
{
  // Methods
  CF public static float CompareExchange (ref float location1,
                                          float value,
                                          float comparand);
     public static int CompareExchange (ref int location1,
                                        int value,
                                        int comparand);
     public static object CompareExchange (ref object location1,
                                           object value,
                                           object comparand);
     public static int Decrement (ref int location);
  CF public static long Decrement (ref long location);
  CF public static float Exchange (ref float location1,
                                   float value);
     public static int Exchange (ref int location1,
                                 int value);
     public static object Exchange (ref object location1,
                                    object value);
     public static int Increment (ref int location);
  CF public static long Increment (ref long location);
}
```

**BA** This is one of the very few examples of places in the library where usage of *by-reference* parameters is warranted, and it is this exact example that pushed us to include them in the CLS. In *general by reference* parameters make the APIs much harder to use and should be avoided in good library design.

**JR** Methods that take an `Object` by reference are not that useful, because the only thing you can pass is a reference to a `System.Object` object; it is not legal to pass a reference to an object whose type is derived from `Object`.

## Description

The System.Threading.Interlocked methods protect against errors that can occur when the scheduler switches contexts while a thread is updating a variable that can be accessed by other threads. The members of this class do not throw exceptions.

[*Note:* The System.Threading.Interlocked.Increment method and its counterpart, System.Threading.Interlocked.Decrement, increment or decrement a variable and store the resulting value as an atomic operation. The System.Threading.Interlocked.Exchange method atomically exchanges the values of the specified variables. The System.Threading.Interlocked.CompareExchange method provides an atomic operation that compares two values and stores a third value in one of the variables, based on the outcome of the comparison.]

## Example

```
using System;
using System.Threading;
using System.Collections;

namespace Samples
{
  public class InterlockedSample
  {
    private static Hashtable ht = new Hashtable();
    public static void Add(object key, object value)
    {
      Monitor.Enter(ht);
      ht.Add(key, value);
      Thread.Sleep(1000);
      Monitor.Exit(ht);
    }
    public static void Display()
    {
      Monitor.Enter(ht);
      IDictionaryEnumerator ide = ht.GetEnumerator();
      while(ide.MoveNext())
        Console.WriteLine("Key: {0}, Value: {1}",
                          ide.Key,
                          ide.Value);
      Monitor.Exit(ht);
    }
    public static void StartHere(Object o)
    {
      Add(Interlocked.Increment(ref number), o);
      if(Interlocked.Decrement(ref threads) == 0)
         threadsDone.Set();
    }
```

A B C D E F G H I J K L M N O P Q R S T U V W X Y Z

```
        static int number = 0;
        static int threads = 5;
        static AutoResetEvent threadsDone =
                 new AutoResetEvent(false);
        public static void Main()
        {
          for(int i = 0; i < threads; i++)
          {
            ThreadPool.QueueUserWorkItem(
                        new WaitCallback(StartHere),
                        "Add");
          }
          threadsDone.WaitOne();
          Display();
        }
    }
}
```

The output is

```
Key: 5, Value: Add
Key: 4, Value: Add
Key: 3, Value: Add
Key: 2, Value: Add
Key: 1, Value: Add
```

A B C D E F G H I J K L M N O P Q R S T U V W X Y Z

# System
# InvalidCastException

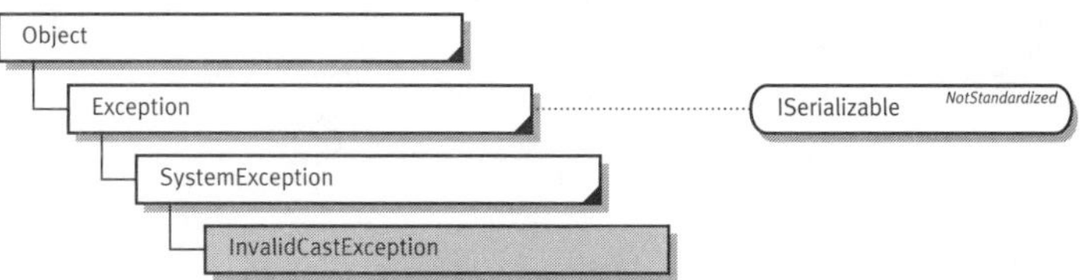




## Summary

Represents the error that occurs when an explicit conversion (casting operation) fails because the source type cannot be converted to the destination type.

## Type Summary

```
public class InvalidCastException : SystemException
{
  // Constructors
     public InvalidCastException ();
     public InvalidCastException (string message);
     public InvalidCastException (string message,
                                 Exception innerException);
MS CF protected InvalidCastException (SerializationInfo info,
                                   StreamingContext context);
}
```

## Description

[*Note:* For information on conversions supported by the system, see the `System.Convert` class. For errors that occur when the destination type can store source type values, but is not large enough to store a specific source value, see `System.OverflowException` exception.]

## Example

```
using System;

namespace s
{
  public class InvalidCastExceptionSample
  {
    public static void Main()
    {
      try
      {
        Object o = new Object();
        string s = (string) o;
```

```
        }
        catch(InvalidCastException e)
        {
          Console.WriteLine("Exception: {0}", e);
        }
      }
    }
  }
```

The output is

```
Exception: System.InvalidCastException: Specified cast is not valid.
   at s.InvalidCastExceptionSample.Main() in C:\Books\BCL\Samples\System\
InvalidCastException\InvalidCastException.cs:line 12
```

# System
# InvalidOperationException

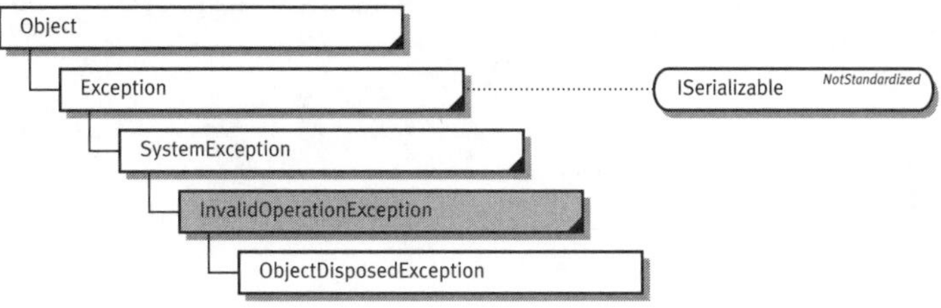




## Summary

Represents the error that occurs when an operation cannot be performed.

## Type Summary

```
  public class InvalidOperationException : SystemException
  {
    // Constructors
       public InvalidOperationException ();
       public InvalidOperationException (string message);
       public InvalidOperationException (string message,
                                          Exception innerException);
MS CF protected InvalidOperationException (SerializationInfo info,
                                          StreamingContext context);
  }
```

## Description

[*Note:* `System.InvalidOperationException` is typically thrown when the state of one or more objects determines whether an operation can be performed. For example, when initially enumerating over a set of objects, if the enumerator has not been positioned over the first element via a call to `System.Collections.IEnumerator.MoveNext`, the system throws a `System.InvalidOperationException` exception when `System.Collections.IEnumerator.Current` is accessed. The `System.InvalidOperationException` exception should not be thrown for errors caused by invalid arguments. For invalid argument errors, throw `System.ArgumentException` or one of its derived types, such as `System.ArgumentNullException` or `System.ArgumentOutOfRangeException`. The ldflda IL instruction throws `System.InvalidOperationException`.]

## Example

```
using System;
using System.Collections;

namespace Samples
{
  public class InvalidOperationExceptionSample
  {
    public static void Main()
    {
      try
      {
        string[] strings = {"zero", "one", "two"};
        IEnumerator ie = strings.GetEnumerator();
        Console.Write("{0}", ie.Current);
      }
      catch(InvalidOperationException e)
      {
        Console.WriteLine("Exception: {0}", e);
      }
    }
  }
}
```

The output is

```
Exception: System.InvalidOperationException: Enumeration has not started. Call
MoveNext.
   at System.SZArrayEnumerator.get_Current()
   at Samples.InvalidOperationExceptionSample.Main() in C:\Books\BCL\Samples\
System\InvalidOperationException\InvalidOperationException.cs:line 14
```

# System InvalidProgramException

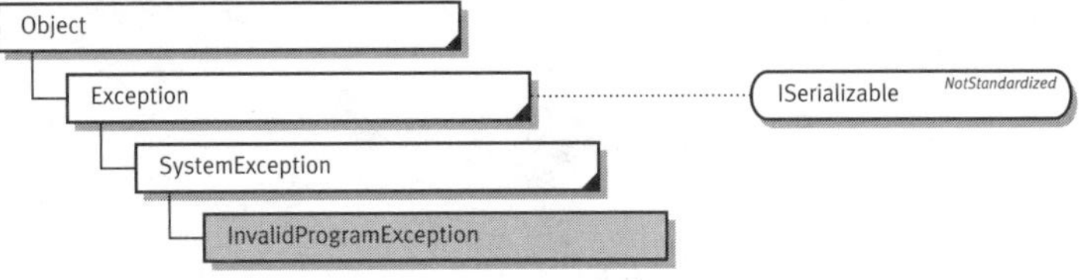


## Summary

Represents the error that occurs when a program contains invalid IL instructions or metadata.

## Type Summary

```
public sealed class InvalidProgramException : SystemException
{
  // Constructors
     public InvalidProgramException ();
     public InvalidProgramException (string message);
     public InvalidProgramException (string message,
                                     Exception inner);
}
```

> **KG** This class contains one of those silly mistakes that pop their heads up too often. The `innerException` parameter in 95% of the framework is called `innerException`; here it is just called `inner`. Another learning exercise is to get checking and consistency tools in place sooner rather than later.

## Description

[*Note:* This exception is thrown by the system when a compiler emits incorrect IL or metadata.]

# System.IO IOException

BCL

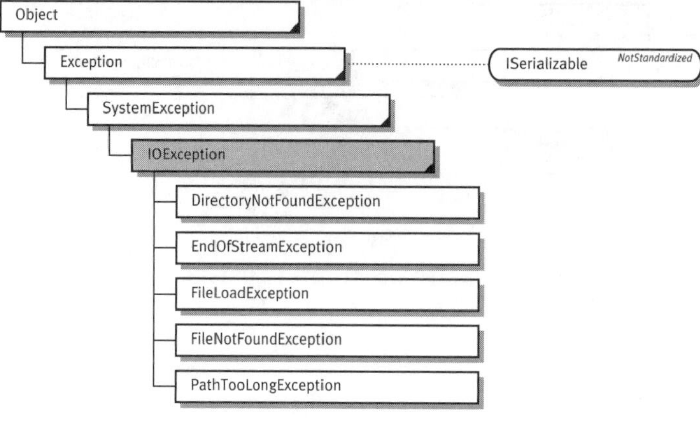


A B C D E F G H I J K L M N O P Q R S T U V W X Y Z

## Summary

Represents the error that occurs when an I/O operation fails.

## Type Summary

```
   public class IOException : SystemException
   {
     // Constructors
        public IOException ();
        public IOException (string message);
MS CF   public IOException (string message, int hresult);
        public IOException (string message, Exception innerException);
MS CF   protected IOException (SerializationInfo info,
                               StreamingContext context);
   }
```

## Description

`System.IO.IOException` is the base class for exceptions thrown while accessing information using streams, files, and directories.

[*Note:* The Base Class Library includes the following types, each of which is derived from `System.IO.IOException`: Where appropriate, use these types instead of `System.IO.IOException`.]

## Example

```
using System;
using System.IO;

namespace Samples
{
  public class IOExceptionSample
  {
    public static void Main()
    {
      try
      {
        string n = @"C:\foo\bar";
        string[] s = Directory.GetFiles(n);
      }
      catch(IOException e)
      {
        Console.WriteLine("Exception: {0}", e);
      }
    }
  }
}
```

The output is

```
Exception: System.IO.DirectoryNotFoundException: Could not find a part of the path
"C:\foo\bar".
   at System.IO.__Error.WinIOError(Int32 errorCode, String str)
   at System.IO.Directory.InternalGetFileDirectoryNames(String fullPath, Boolean
file)
   at System.IO.Directory.InternalGetFiles(String path, String searchPattern)
   at System.IO.Directory.GetFiles(String path, String searchPattern)
   at System.IO.Directory.GetFiles(String path)
   at Samples.IOExceptionSample.Main() in C:\Books\BCL\Samples\System.IO\
IOException\IOException.cs:line 13
```

# System.Security IPermission Interface

BCL

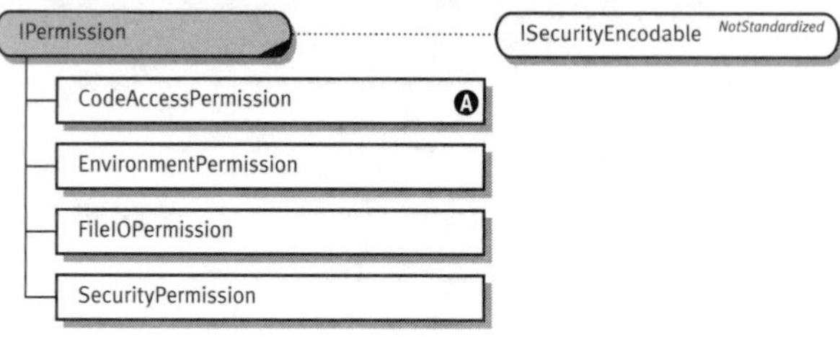




## Summary

Defines methods implemented by permission types.

## Type Summary

```
CF public interface IPermission : ISecurityEncodable
{
  // Methods
  CF IPermission Copy ();
  CF void Demand ();
  CF IPermission Intersect (IPermission target);
  CF bool IsSubsetOf (IPermission target);
  CF IPermission Union (IPermission target);
}
```

## Description

[*Note:* Permission types describe a level of access to secured operations or resources, such as files or environment variables. Permission instances do not confer the right to access a resource or perform an operation; the security system determines whether or not requested permissions are granted. Permissions are used by both application code and the security system in the following ways.]

## Example

```
using System;
using System.Security;
using System.Security.Permissions;

namespace Samples
{
  public class IPermissionSample
  {
    public static void Main()
    {
      EnvironmentPermission ep1 =
```

IPermission Interface

```
            new EnvironmentPermission(
                EnvironmentPermissionAccess.Read,
                "COMPUTERNAME");
        IPermission ip1 = ep1;
        IPermission ip2 = ep1.Copy();
        ep1.AddPathList(EnvironmentPermissionAccess.Read,
                   "USERNAME");
        Console.WriteLine("ip1 is: {0}", ip1);
        Console.WriteLine("ip2 is: {0}", ip2);
        Console.WriteLine("Is ip2 a subset of ip1: {0}",
                          ip2.IsSubsetOf(ip1));
        Console.WriteLine("Is ip1 a subset of ip2: {0}",
                          ip1.IsSubsetOf(ip2));
        Console.WriteLine("Is ip1 a subset of ip1: {0}",
                          ip1.IsSubsetOf(ip1));
        Console.WriteLine("ip1.Intersect(ip2): {0}",
                          ip1.Intersect(ip2));
        Console.WriteLine("ip1.Union(ip2): {0}",
                          ip1.Union(ip2));
    }
  }
}
```

The output is

```
ip1 is: <IPermission class="System.Security.Permissions.EnvironmentPermission,
mscorlib, Version=1.0.3300.0, Culture=neutral, PublicKeyToken=b77a5c561934e089"
             version="1"
             Read="COMPUTERNAME;USERNAME"/>

ip2 is: <IPermission class="System.Security.Permissions.EnvironmentPermission,
mscorlib, Version=1.0.3300.0, Culture=neutral, PublicKeyToken=b77a5c561934e089"
             version="1"
             Read="COMPUTERNAME"/>

Is ip2 a subset of ip1: True
Is ip1 a subset of ip2: False
Is ip1 a subset of ip1: True
ip1.Intersect(ip2): <IPermission
class="System.Security.Permissions.EnvironmentPermission, mscorlib,
Version=1.0.3300.0, Culture=neutral, PublicKeyToken=b77a5c561934e089"
             version="1"
             Read="COMPUTERNAME"/>

ip1.Union(ip2): <IPermission class="System.Security.Permissions.
EnvironmentPermission, mscorlib, Version=1.0.3300.0, Culture=neutral,
PublicKeyToken=b77a5c561934e089"
             version="1"
             Read="USERNAME;COMPUTERNAME"/>
```

# System MarshalByRefObject

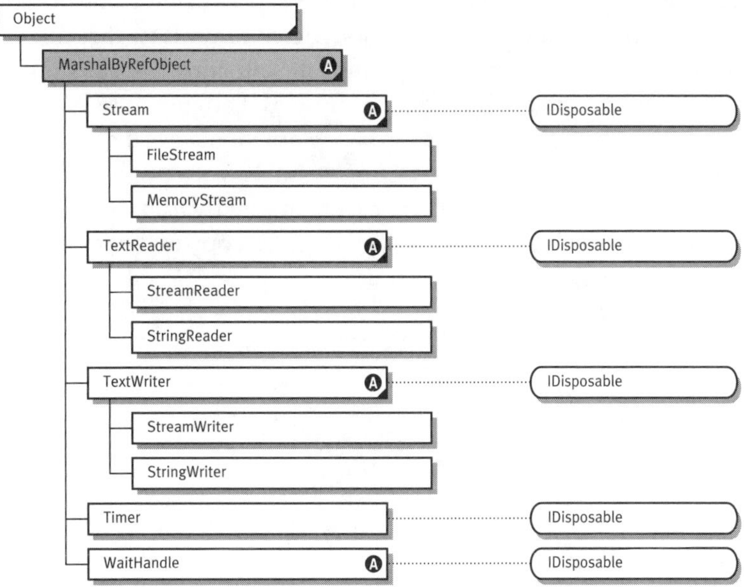




## Summary

Enables access to objects across application domain boundaries in implementations that support remoting.

## Type Summary

```
   public abstract class MarshalByRefObject
   {
      // Constructors
MS    protected MarshalByRefObject ();

      // Methods
MS CF public virtual ObjRef CreateObjRef (Type requestedType);
MS CF public object GetLifetimeService ();
MS CF public virtual object InitializeLifetimeService ();
   }
```

**BA** The meaning of this class is only interesting when you consider cross-process or cross-machine remoting. That functionality was not included as part of the CLI standard. However, we needed to keep this placeholder type in the standard, as many of the types in the standard extend from it.

## Description

[*Note:* An application domain is a partition in an OS process where one or more applications reside. Objects in the same application domain communicate directly. Objects that reside in different application domains communicate either by transporting copies of objects across application domain boundaries, or by exchanging messages via proxy.]

`System.MarshalByRefObject` is the base class for objects that communicate across application domain boundaries by exchanging messages via a proxy. Objects that do not inherit from `System.MarshalByRefObject` are implicitly *marshal by value*. When a remote application references a *marshal by value* object, a copy of the object is passed across application domain boundaries.

A B C D E F G H I J K L M N O P Q R S T U V W X Y Z

## Summary

Provides constants and static methods for trigonometric, logarithmic, and other common mathematical functions.

## Type Summary

```
   public sealed class Math
   {
     // Fields
        public const double E = 2.7182818284590452354;
        public const double PI = 3.14159265358979323846;

     // Methods
        public static decimal Abs (decimal value);
        public static double Abs (double a);
        public static float Abs (float a);
        public static int Abs (int value);
        public static long Abs (long value);
        public static sbyte Abs (sbyte value);
        public static short Abs (short value);
        public static double Acos (double d);
        public static double Asin (double d);
        public static double Atan (double d);
        public static double Atan2(double y, double x);
CF 1.1 public static long BigMul (int a, int b);
        public static double Ceiling (double a);
        public static double Cos (double d);
        public static double Cosh (double value);
CF 1.1 public static int DivRem (int a, int b,
                                   out int result);
CF 1.1 public static long DivRem (long a, long b,
                                    out long result);
        public static double Exp (double a);
        public static double Floor (double a);
        public static double IEEERemainder (double x,
                                            double y);
        public static double Log (double a);
     CF public static double Log (double a, double newBase);
        public static double Log10(double a);
        public static byte Max (byte val1, byte val2);
        public static decimal Max (decimal val1,
                                    decimal val2);
```

```
        public static double Max (double val1, double val2);
        public static float Max (float val1, float val2);
        public static int Max (int val1, int val2);
        public static long Max (long val1, long val2);
        public static sbyte Max (sbyte val1, sbyte val2);
        public static short Max (short val1, short val2);
        public static uint Max (uint val1, uint val2);
        public static ulong Max (ulong val1, ulong val2);
        public static ushort Max (ushort val1, ushort val2);
        public static byte Min (byte val1, byte val2);
        public static decimal Min (decimal val1,
                                   decimal val2);
        public static double Min (double val1, double val2);
        public static float Min (float val1, float val2);
        public static int Min (int val1, int val2);
        public static long Min (long val1, long val2);
        public static sbyte Min (sbyte val1, sbyte val2);
        public static short Min (short val1, short val2);
        public static uint Min (uint val1, uint val2);
        public static ulong Min (ulong val1, ulong val2);
        public static ushort Min (ushort val1, ushort val2);
        public static double Pow (double x, double y);
        public static decimal Round (decimal d);
     MS public static decimal Round (decimal d,
                                     int decimals);
        public static double Round (double a);
        public static double Round (double value,
                                    int digits);
        public static int Sign (decimal value);
        public static int Sign (double value);
        public static int Sign (float value);
        public static int Sign (int value);
        public static int Sign (long value);
        public static int Sign (sbyte value);
        public static int Sign (short value);
        public static double Sin (double a);
        public static double Sinh (double value);
        public static double Sqrt (double a);
        public static double Tan (double a);
        public static double Tanh (double value);
    }
```

**BA** The decision to include `Decimal` in many of the overloads in this class was not obvious in the original design because the `Decimal` class does not have native support in the runtime. That is, none of the IL instructions operate directly on `Decimals` in the same way they do on `doubles`, `ints`, etc.

# System.IO MemoryStream

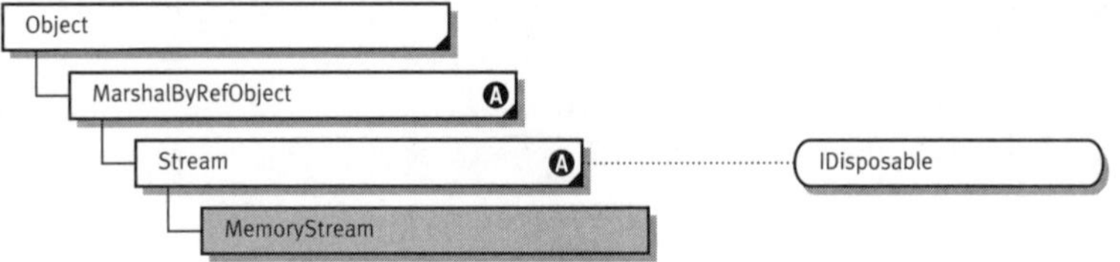


## Summary

Provides support for creating and using a stream whose backing store is memory.

## Type Summary

```
public class MemoryStream : Stream
{
  // Constructors
     public MemoryStream ();
     public MemoryStream (byte[] buffer);
     public MemoryStream (byte[] buffer, bool writable);
     public MemoryStream (byte[] buffer, int index,
                          int count);
     public MemoryStream (byte[] buffer, int index,
                          int count, bool writable);
     public MemoryStream (byte[] buffer, int index,
                          int count, bool writable,
                          bool publiclyVisible);
     public MemoryStream (int capacity);

  // Properties
     public override bool CanRead { get; }
     public override bool CanSeek { get; }
     public override bool CanWrite { get; }
     public virtual int Capacity { set; get; }
     public override long Length { get; }
     public override long Position { set; get; }

  // Methods
     public override void Close ();
     public override void Flush ();
     public virtual byte[] GetBuffer ();
     public override int Read (byte[] buffer,
                               int offset, int count);
     public override int ReadByte ();
     public override long Seek (long offset,
                                SeekOrigin loc);
     public override void SetLength (long value);
```

```
        public virtual byte[] ToArray ();
        public override void Write (byte[] buffer,
                                    int offset,
                                    int count);
        public override void WriteByte (byte value);
        public virtual void WriteTo (Stream stream);
    }
```

A B C D E F G H I J K L M N O P Q R S T U V W X Y Z

## Description

The `System.IO.MemoryStream` class creates streams that have memory as a backing store instead of a disk or a network connection. `System.IO.MemoryStream` encapsulates data stored as an unsigned byte array. The encapsulated data is directly accessible in memory. Memory streams can reduce the need for temporary buffers and files in an application.

The *current position* of a stream is the position at which the next read or write operation takes place. The current position can be retrieved or set through the `System.IO.MemoryStream.Seek` method. When a new instance of `System.IO.MemoryStream` is created, the current position is set to zero.

[*Note:* Memory streams created with an unsigned byte array provide a non-resizable stream view of the data. When using a byte array, you can neither append to nor shrink the stream, although you might be able to modify the existing contents depending on the parameters passed into the constructor.]

## Example

```
using System;
using System.IO;

namespace Samples
{
  public class MemoryStreamSample
  {
    public static void Main()
    {
      byte[] bytes = {0, 1, 2, 3, 4, 5, 6, 7, 8, 9};
      using(MemoryStream ms = new MemoryStream(bytes,
                                               0,
                                               bytes.Length))
      {
        DisplayInformationAboutStream(ms);
        bytes = new Byte[5];
        ms.Read(bytes, 0, bytes.Length);
        foreach(Byte b in bytes)
          Console.WriteLine(b);
      }
      using(MemoryStream ms = new MemoryStream(256))
```

```
        {
          ms.SetLength(10);
          DisplayInformationAboutStream(ms);
          byte[] bytes1 = ms.GetBuffer();
          ms.SetLength(1024);
          DisplayInformationAboutStream(ms);
          Byte[] bytes2 = ms.GetBuffer();
          Console.WriteLine("Are the buffers the same: {0}",
                            Object.ReferenceEquals(bytes1, bytes2));
        }
      }
      public static void DisplayInformationAboutStream(
                            MemoryStream ms)
      {
        Console.WriteLine("Can read from stream: {0}",
                          ms.CanRead);
        Console.WriteLine("Can write to stream: {0}",
                          ms.CanWrite);
        Console.WriteLine("Can seek in stream: {0}",
                          ms.CanSeek);
        Console.WriteLine("Capacity of stream: {0}",
                          ms.Capacity);
        Console.WriteLine("Length of stream: {0}",
                          ms.Length);
        Console.WriteLine("Position in stream: {0}",
                          ms.Position);
      }
    }
}
```

The output is

```
Can read from stream: True
Can write to stream: True
Can seek in stream: True
Capacity of stream: 10
Length of stream: 10
Position in stream: 0
0
1
2
3
4
Can read from stream: True
Can write to stream: True
Can seek in stream: True
Capacity of stream: 256
Length of stream: 10
```

```
Position in stream: 0
Can read from stream: True
Can write to stream: True
Can seek in stream: True
Capacity of stream: 1024
Length of stream: 1024
Position in stream: 0
Are the buffers the same: False
```

# System.Threading Monitor

## Summary

Provides a mechanism that synchronizes access to objects.

## Type Summary

```
public sealed class Monitor
{
  // Methods
        public static void Enter (object obj);
        public static void Exit (object obj);
     CF public static void Pulse (object obj);
     CF public static void PulseAll (object obj);
     CF public static bool TryEnter (object obj);
     CF public static bool TryEnter (object obj,
                                     int millisecondsTimeout);
     CF public static bool TryEnter (object obj,
                                     TimeSpan timeout);
     CF public static bool Wait (object obj);
     CF public static bool Wait (object obj, int millisecondsTimeout);
  MS CF public static bool Wait (object obj, int millisecondsTimeout,
                                 bool exitContext);
     CF public static bool Wait (object obj, TimeSpan timeout);
  MS CF public static bool Wait (object obj, TimeSpan timeout,
                                 bool exitContext);
}
```

**BG** I believe the vast majority of managed code developers don't need to know this class exists. In just about all cases where I've needed synchronization, I use the C# `lock` keyword (which of course uses `Monitor.Enter` and `Exit`), subclasses of `WaitHandle` like `ManualResetEvent`, then interlocked operations, in that order of frequency. While the `Monitor` class probably is useful in some contexts, it's a little obscure to most users.

**JR** For Microsoft's implementation of the CLI, thread synchronization using `Monitor` methods is not guaranteed to be fair. In other words, threads are not always synchronized in first-in/first-out order. For most applications, this is not a huge problem. It is more likely a problem for embedded applications or applications that control hardware. For these kinds of applications, managed code is a questionable direction to go anyway.

## Description

The `System.Threading.Monitor` class controls access to objects by granting a single thread a lock for an object. Object locks provide the ability to restrict access to a block of code, commonly called a critical section. While a thread owns the lock for an object no other thread can acquire the lock for the object. Additionally, the `System.Threading.Monitor` class can be used to ensure that no other thread may access a section of application code being executed by the lock owner, unless the other thread is executing the code using a different locked object.

The following information is maintained for each synchronized object:

- A reference to the thread that currently holds the lock.
- A reference to a "ready queue," which contains the threads that are ready to obtain the lock.
- A reference to a "waiting queue," which contains the threads that are waiting for notification of a change in the state of the locked object.

The following table describes the actions taken by threads that access synchronized objects:

| Action | Description |
|---|---|
| enter | Acquires a lock for an object. Also marks the beginning of a critical section. No other thread can enter the critical section unless they are executing the instructions in the critical section using a different locked object. [*Note:* See the `System.Threading.Monitor.Enter` and `System.Threading.Monitor.TryEnter` methods.] |
| wait | Releases the lock on an object in order to permit other threads to lock and access the object. The calling thread waits while another thread accesses the object. Pulse signals (see below) are used to notify waiting threads about changes to an object's state. [*Note:* See `System.Threading.Monitor.Wait`.] |
| pulse (signal) | Sends a signal to one or more waiting threads. The signal notifies a waiting thread that the state of the locked object has changed, and the owner of the lock is ready to release the lock. The waiting thread is placed in the object's ready queue so that it may eventually receive the lock for the object. Once the thread has the lock, it can check the new state of the object to see if the required state has been reached. [*Note:* See `System.Threading.Monitor.Pulse` and `System.Threading.Monitor.PulseAll`.] |
| exit | Releases the lock on an object. Also marks the end of a critical section protected by the locked object. [*Note:* See `System.Threading.Monitor.Exit`.] |

The System.Threading.Monitor.Enter and System.Threading.Monitor.Exit methods are used to mark the beginning and end of a critical section. If the critical section is a set of contiguous instructions, then the lock acquired by the System.Threading.Monitor.Enter method guarantees that only a single thread can execute the enclosed code with the locked object. This facility is typically used to synchronize access to a static or instance method of a class. If an instance method requires synchronized thread access, the instance method invokes the System.Threading.Monitor.Enter and corresponding System.Threading.Monitor.Exit methods using itself (the current instance) as the object to lock. Since only one thread can hold the lock on the current instance, the method can only be executed by one thread at a time. Static methods are protected in a similar fashion using the System.Type object of the current instance as the locked object.

[*Note:* The functionality provided by the System.Threading.Monitor.Enter and System.Threading.Monitor.Exit methods is identical to that provided by the C# lock statement. If a critical section spans an entire method, the locking facility described above can be achieved by placing the System.Runtime.CompilerServices.MethodImplAttribute on the method, and specifying the System.Runtime.CompilerServices.MethodImplOptions.Synchronized option. Using this attribute, the System.Threading.Monitor.Enter and System.Threading.Monitor.Exit statements are not needed. Note that the attribute causes the current thread to hold the lock until the method returns; if the lock can be released sooner, use the System.Threading.Monitor class (or C# lock statement) instead of the attribute. While it is possible for the System.Threading.Monitor.Enter and System.Threading.Monitor.Exit statements that lock and release a given object to cross member and/or class boundaries, this practice is strongly discouraged.]

## Example

```
using System;
using System.Threading;
using System.Collections;

namespace Samples
{
  public class MonitorSample
  {
    private static Hashtable ht = new Hashtable();
    public static void Add(object key, object value)
    {
      Monitor.Enter(ht);
      ht.Add(key, value);
      Thread.Sleep(1000);
      Monitor.Exit(ht);
    }
    public static bool AddNoWait(object key, object value)
```

```
    {
      if(Monitor.TryEnter(ht))
      {
        ht.Add(key, value);
        Thread.Sleep(1000);
        Monitor.Exit(ht);
        return true;
      }
      return false;
    }
    public static bool AddWithWaitTime(object key,
                                       object value,
                                       int waitTime)
    {
      if(Monitor.TryEnter(ht, waitTime))
      {
        ht.Add(key, value);
        Thread.Sleep(1000);
        Monitor.Exit(ht);
        return true;
      }
      return true;
    }
    public static void Display()
    {
      Monitor.Enter(ht);
      IDictionaryEnumerator ide = ht.GetEnumerator();
      while(ide.MoveNext())
        Console.WriteLine("Key: {0}, Value: {1}",
                          ide.Key,
                          ide.Value);
      Monitor.Exit(ht);
    }
    public static void StartHere(Object o)
    {
      int i = (int) o;
      Add(i, "Add");
      i += 10;
      Console.WriteLine(
             "AddNoWait for thread {0} succeeded: {1}",
             o, AddNoWait(i, "AddNoWait"));
      i += 10;
      Console.WriteLine(
               "AddNoWait for thread {0} succeeded: {1}",
               o, AddNoWait(i, "AddNoWait"));
      i += 10;
      Console.WriteLine(
             "AddWithWaitTime for thread {0} succeeded: {1}",
             o, AddWithWaitTime(i, "AddWithWaitTime", 100));
      if(Interlocked.Decrement(ref threads) == 0)
```

```
        {
          Monitor.Enter(ht);
          Monitor.Pulse(ht);
          Monitor.Exit(ht);
        }
      }
      static int threads = 5;
      public static void Main()
      {
        Monitor.Enter(ht);
        for(int i = 0; i < threads; i++)
        {
          ThreadPool.QueueUserWorkItem(
                     new WaitCallback(StartHere),
                     i);
        }
        Monitor.Wait(ht);
        Monitor.Exit(ht);
        Display();
      }
  }
}
```

The output is

```
AddNoWait for thread 0 succeeded: False
AddNoWait for thread 0 succeeded: False
AddWithWaitTime for thread 0 succeeded: True
AddNoWait for thread 1 succeeded: False
AddNoWait for thread 1 succeeded: False
AddWithWaitTime for thread 1 succeeded: True
AddNoWait for thread 2 succeeded: False
AddNoWait for thread 2 succeeded: False
AddWithWaitTime for thread 2 succeeded: True
AddNoWait for thread 3 succeeded: False
AddNoWait for thread 3 succeeded: False
AddWithWaitTime for thread 3 succeeded: True
AddNoWait for thread 4 succeeded: True
AddNoWait for thread 4 succeeded: True
AddWithWaitTime for thread 4 succeeded: True
Key: 14, Value: AddNoWait
Key: 34, Value: AddWithWaitTime
Key: 33, Value: AddWithWaitTime
Key: 32, Value: AddWithWaitTime
Key: 31, Value: AddWithWaitTime
Key: 24, Value: AddNoWait
Key: 4, Value: Add
Key: 3, Value: Add
Key: 2, Value: Add
Key: 1, Value: Add
Key: 0, Value: Add
```

# System NotFiniteNumberException

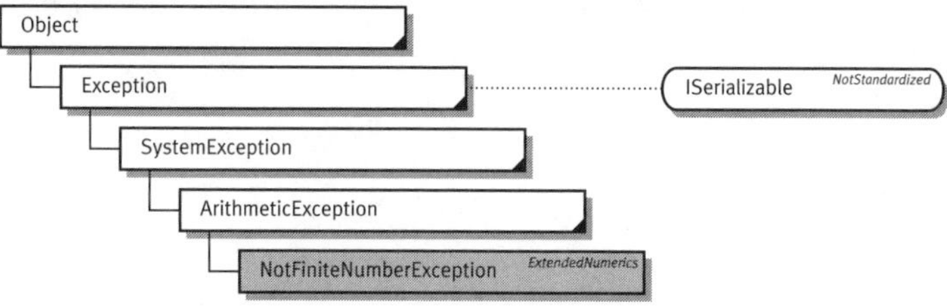




## Summary

Represents the error that occurs when an arithmetic operation cannot be performed on a floating-point value that is not a finite number.

## Type Summary

```
   public class NotFiniteNumberException : ArithmeticException
   {
     // Constructors
        public NotFiniteNumberException ();
     CF public NotFiniteNumberException (double offendingNumber);
        public NotFiniteNumberException (string message);
     CF public NotFiniteNumberException (string message,
                                         double offendingNumber);
     CF public NotFiniteNumberException (string message,
                                         double offendingNumber,
                                         Exception innerException);
  MS CF protected NotFiniteNumberException (SerializationInfo info,
                                            StreamingContext context);

     // Properties
     CF public double OffendingNumber { get; }

     // Methods
  MS CF public override void GetObjectData (SerializationInfo info,
                                            StreamingContext context);
   }
```

NotFiniteNumberException Class

## Description

This exception is thrown when an operand of an arithmetic operation is, and is not permitted to be, one of the following:

Positive infinity
Negative infinity
NaN (Not-a-Number)

[*Note:* Operations involving `System.Double` or `System.Single` operations throw this exception.]

# System
# NotImplementedException

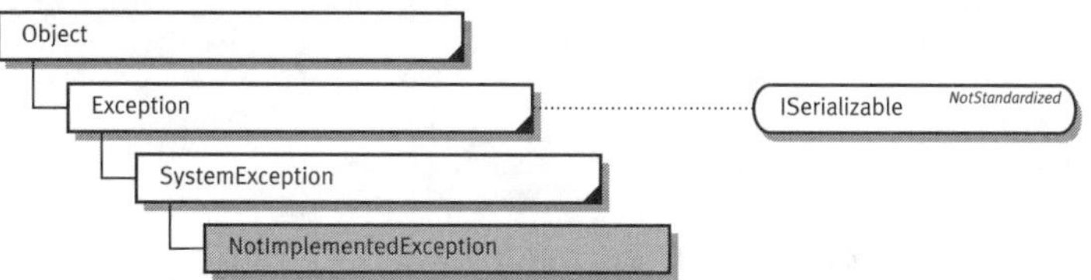


A B C D E F G H I J K L M N O P Q R S T U V W X Y Z

## Summary

Represents the error that occurs when a requested operation is not implemented for a given type.

## Type Summary

```
  CF public class NotImplementedException : SystemException
  {
    // Constructors
    CF public NotImplementedException ();
    CF public NotImplementedException (string message);
    CF public NotImplementedException (string message,
                                       Exception innerException);
MS  CF protected NotImplementedException (SerializationInfo info,
                                          StreamingContext context);
  }
```

## Description

[*Note:* A number of the types and constructs, specified elsewhere in this Standard, are not required of CLI implementations that conform only to the Kernel Profile. For example, the floating-point feature set consists of the floating-point data types `System.Single` and `System.Double`. If support for these is omitted from an implementation, any attempt to reference a signature that includes the floating-point data types results in an exception of type `System.NotImplementedException`.]

## Example

```
using System;

namespace Samples
{
  public class NotImplementedExceptionSample
  {
    public static void NotImplementedMethod(float f)
    {
      throw new NotImplementedException();
```

```
        }
        public static void Main()
        {
          try
          {
            NotImplementedMethod(0);
          }
          catch(NotImplementedException e)
          {
            Console.WriteLine("Exception: {0}", e);
          }
        }
      }
    }
```

The output is

```
Exception: System.NotImplementedException: The method or operation is not implemented.
   at Samples.NotImplementedExceptionSample.NotImplementedMethod(Single f) in
C:\Books\BCL\Samples\System\NotImplementedException\NotImplementedException.cs:line 9
   at Samples.NotImplementedExceptionSample.Main() in C:\Books\BCL\Samples\System\
NotImplementedException\NotImplementedException.cs:line 15
```

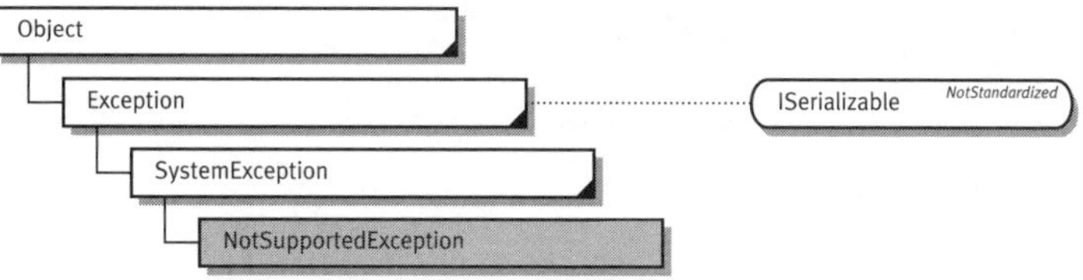




## Summary

Represents the error that occurs when an object cannot perform an operation.

## Type Summary

```
public class NotSupportedException : SystemException
{
  // Constructors
    public NotSupportedException ();
    public NotSupportedException (string message);
    public NotSupportedException (string message,
                                  Exception innerException);
MS CF protected NotSupportedException (SerializationInfo info,
                                       StreamingContext context);
}
```

## Description

[*Note:* `System.NotSupportedException` is thrown when it is never possible for the object to perform the requested operation. A typical scenario is when a base class declares a method that derived classes are required to implement, and the method is invoked on the base class. When a method throws `System.NotSupportedException` this usually indicates that the derived classes must provide an implementation of the method, and callers must invoke the method on the derived class. For scenarios where it is sometimes possible for the object to perform the requested operation, and the object state determines whether the operation can be performed, see `System.InvalidOperationException`.]

## Example

```
using System;
using System.IO;

namespace Samples
{
  public class NotSupprotedExceptionSample
  {
    public static void Main()
```

```
      {
        Byte[] bytes = {0, 1, 2, 3, 4, 5, 6, 7, 8, 9};
        MemoryStream ms = new MemoryStream(
                                bytes,0, bytes.Length,
                                false, false);
        try
        {
          ms.WriteByte((Byte)0);
        }
        catch(NotSupportedException e)
        {
          Console.WriteLine("Exception: {0}", e);
        }
        finally
        {
          ms.Close();
        }
      }
    }
  }
```

The output is

```
Exception: System.NotSupportedException: Stream does not support writing.
   at System.IO.__Error.WriteNotSupported()
   at System.IO.MemoryStream.WriteByte(Byte value)
   at Samples.NotSupprotedExceptionSample.Main() in C:\Books\BCL\Samples\System\
NotSupportedException\NotSupportedException.cs:line 16
```

# System NullReferenceException

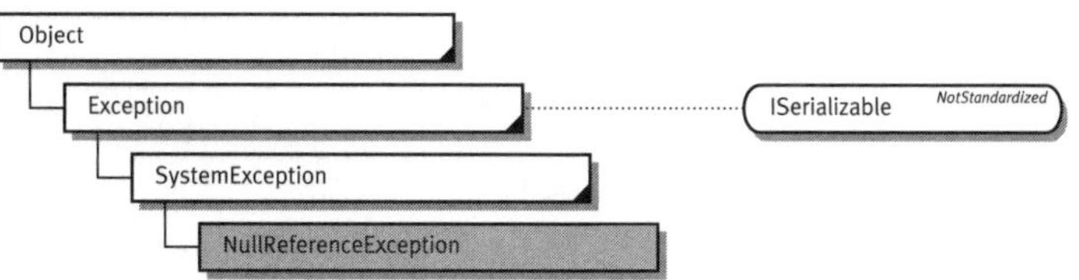


## Summary

Represents the error that occurs when there is an attempt to dereference a `null` object reference.

## Type Summary

```
   public class NullReferenceException : SystemException
   {
     // Constructors
        public NullReferenceException ();
        public NullReferenceException (string message);
        public NullReferenceException (string message,
                                       Exception innerException);
MS CF protected NullReferenceException (SerializationInfo info,
                                       StreamingContext context);
   }
```

**BA** As hard as we tried in the BCL design to be language-neutral, sometimes it was just impossible. The name of this exception seems obvious to most C# or C++ developers but not to a VB developer. The VB language uses the keyword "`Nothing`" to represent this concept. So getting a `NullReferenceException` frequently does not help the VB user determine what the problem is.

## Description

[*Note:* Applications throw the `System.ArgumentNullException` rather than `System.NullReferenceException`.]

## Example

```
using System;

namespace Samples
{
  public class NullReferenceExceptionSample
  {
    public static void Main()
    {
      string s = null;
      try
      {
        Console.WriteLine(s.ToUpper());
      }
      catch(NullReferenceException e)
      {
        Console.WriteLine("Exception: {0}", e);
      }
    }
  }
}
```

The output is

```
Exception: System.NullReferenceException: Object reference not set to an instance
of an object.
   at Samples.NullReferenceExceptionSample.Main() in C:\Books\BCL\Samples\System\
NullReferenceException\NullReferenceException.cs:line 12
```

# System.Globalization NumberFormatInfo

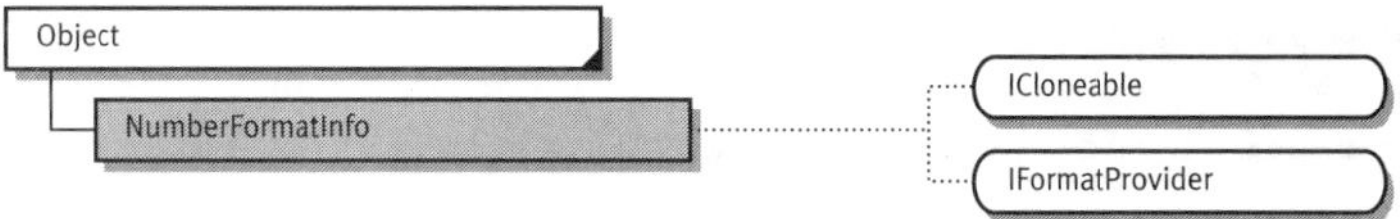




## Summary

Supplies culture-specific formatting information for string representations of numeric values.

## Type Summary

```
public sealed class NumberFormatInfo : ICloneable,
                                       IFormatProvider
{
  // Constructors
     public NumberFormatInfo ();

  // Properties
     public int CurrencyDecimalDigits { set; get; }
     public string CurrencyDecimalSeparator { set; get; }
     public string CurrencyGroupSeparator { set; get; }
     public int[] CurrencyGroupSizes { set; get; }
     public int CurrencyNegativePattern { set; get; }
     public int CurrencyPositivePattern { set; get; }
     public string CurrencySymbol { set; get; }
     public static NumberFormatInfo CurrentInfo { get; }
     public static NumberFormatInfo InvariantInfo { get; }
     public bool IsReadOnly { get; }
     public string NaNSymbol { set; get; }
     public string NegativeInfinitySymbol { set; get; }
     public string NegativeSign { set; get; }
     public int NumberDecimalDigits { set; get; }
     public string NumberDecimalSeparator { set; get; }
     public string NumberGroupSeparator { set; get; }
     public int[] NumberGroupSizes { set; get; }
     public int NumberNegativePattern { set; get; }
     public int PercentDecimalDigits { set; get; }
     public string PercentDecimalSeparator { set; get; }
     public string PercentGroupSeparator { set; get; }
     public int[] PercentGroupSizes { set; get; }
     public int PercentNegativePattern { set; get; }
     public int PercentPositivePattern { set; get; }
     public string PercentSymbol { set; get; }
     public string PerMilleSymbol { set; get; }
     public string PositiveInfinitySymbol { set; get; }
     public string PositiveSign { set; get; }
```

```
   // Methods
      public object Clone ();
      public object GetFormat (Type formatType);
   MS public static NumberFormatInfo GetInstance (IFormatProvider formatProvider);
      public static NumberFormatInfo ReadOnly (NumberFormatInfo nfi);
  }
```

## Description

`System.Globalization.NumberFormatInfo` supplies symbols such as currency symbols and decimal separators.

[*Note:* A `System.Globalization.NumberFormatInfo` instance typically contains the set of symbols for a specific language and culture. Instances of `System.Globalization.NumberFormatInfo` may be created to provide customized formatting information.]

## Example

```
using System;
using System.Globalization;

namespace Samples
{
  public class NumberFormatInfoSample
  {
    public static void Main()
    {
      CultureInfo c = new CultureInfo("en-NZ");
      NumberFormatInfo n = c.NumberFormat;
      Console.WriteLine("CurrencyDecimalDigits: {0}",
                        n.CurrencyDecimalDigits);
      Console.WriteLine("CurrencyDecimalSeparator: {0}",
                        n.CurrencyDecimalSeparator);
      Console.WriteLine("CurrencyGroupSeparator: {0}",
                        n.CurrencyGroupSeparator);
      Console.Write("CurrencyGroupSizes: ");
      int[] integers = n.CurrencyGroupSizes;
      foreach(int i in integers)
        Console.Write(i);
      Console.WriteLine();
      Console.WriteLine("CurrencyNegativePattern: {0}",
                        n.CurrencyNegativePattern);
      Console.WriteLine("CurrencyPositivePattern: {0}",
                        n.CurrencyPositivePattern);
      Console.WriteLine("CurrencySymbol: {0}",
                        n.CurrencySymbol);
      Console.WriteLine("IsReadOnly: {0}",
                        n.IsReadOnly);
      Console.WriteLine("NaNSymbol: {0}",
```

```
                        n.NaNSymbol);
      Console.WriteLine("NegativeInfinitySymbol: {0}",
                        n.NegativeInfinitySymbol);
      Console.WriteLine("NegativeSign: {0}",
                        n.NegativeSign);
      Console.WriteLine("NumberDecimalDigits: {0}",
                        n.NumberDecimalDigits);
      Console.WriteLine("NumberDecimalSeparator: {0}",
                        n.NumberDecimalSeparator);
      Console.WriteLine("NumberGroupSeparator: {0}",
                        n.NumberGroupSeparator);
      Console.Write("NumberGroupSizes: ",
                        n.NumberGroupSizes);
      integers = n.NumberGroupSizes;
      foreach(int i in integers)
        Console.Write(i);
      Console.WriteLine();
      Console.WriteLine("NumberNegativePattern: {0}",
                        n.NumberNegativePattern);
      Console.WriteLine("PercentDecimalDigits: {0}",
                        n.PercentDecimalDigits);
      Console.WriteLine("PercentDecimalSeparator: {0}",
                        n.PercentDecimalSeparator);
      Console.WriteLine("PercentGroupSeparator: {0}",
                        n.PercentGroupSeparator);
      Console.Write("PercentGroupSizes: ");
      integers = n.PercentGroupSizes;
      foreach(int i in integers)
        Console.Write(i);
      Console.WriteLine();
      Console.WriteLine("PercentNegativePattern: {0}",
                        n.PercentNegativePattern);
      Console.WriteLine("PercentPositivePattern: {0}",
                        n.PercentPositivePattern);
      Console.WriteLine("PercentSymbol: {0}",
                        n.PercentSymbol);
      Console.WriteLine("PerMilleSymbol: {0}",
                        n.PerMilleSymbol);
      Console.WriteLine("PositiveInfinitySymbol: {0}",
                        n.PositiveInfinitySymbol);
      Console.WriteLine("PositiveSign: {0}",
                        n.PositiveSign);
    }
  }
}
```

The output is

```
CurrencyDecimalDigits: 2
CurrencyDecimalSeparator: .
CurrencyGroupSeparator: ,
CurrencyGroupSizes: 3
CurrencyNegativePattern: 1
CurrencyPositivePattern: 0
CurrencySymbol: $
IsReadOnly: False
NaNSymbol: NaN
NegativeInfinitySymbol: -Infinity
NegativeSign: -
NumberDecimalDigits: 2
NumberDecimalSeparator: .
NumberGroupSeparator: ,
NumberGroupSizes: 3
NumberNegativePattern: 1
PercentDecimalDigits: 2
PercentDecimalSeparator: .
PercentGroupSeparator: ,
PercentGroupSizes: 3
PercentNegativePattern: 0
PercentPositivePattern: 0
PercentSymbol: %
PerMilleSymbol: %
PositiveInfinitySymbol: Infinity
PositiveSign: +
```

# System.Globalization NumberStyles Enum

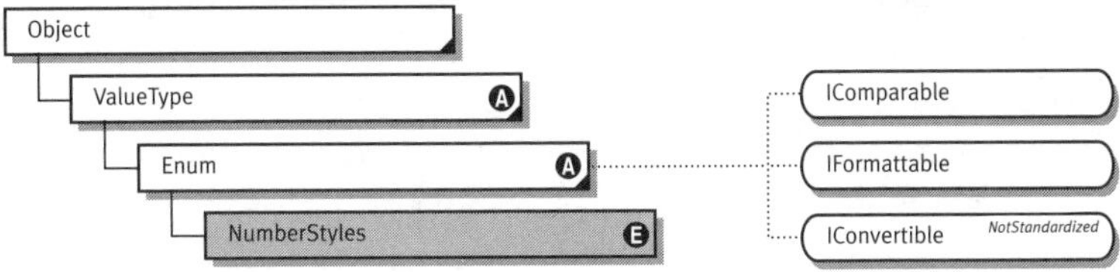




## Summary

Specifies styles for `System.String` representations of numeric values.

## Type Summary

```
public enum NumberStyles  {
      AllowCurrencySymbol = 0x100,
      AllowDecimalPoint = 0x20,
      AllowExponent = 0x80,
      AllowHexSpecifier = 0x200,
      AllowLeadingSign = 0x4,
      AllowLeadingWhite = 0x1,
      AllowParentheses = 0x10,
      AllowThousands = 0x40,
      AllowTrailingSign = 0x8,
      AllowTrailingWhite = 0x2,
      Any = AllowLeadingWhite | AllowTrailingWhite | AllowLeadingSign |
            AllowTrailingSign | AllowParentheses | AllowDecimalPoint |
            AllowThousands | AllowExponent | AllowCurrencySymbol,
      Currency = AllowLeadingWhite | AllowTrailingWhite | AllowLeadingSign |
                 AllowTrailingSign | AllowParentheses | AllowDecimalPoint |
                 AllowThousands | AllowCurrencySymbol,
      Float = AllowLeadingWhite | AllowTrailingWhite | AllowLeadingSign |
              AllowDecimalPoint | AllowExponent,
      HexNumber = AllowLeadingWhite | AllowTrailingWhite | AllowHexSpecifier,
      Integer = AllowLeadingWhite | AllowTrailingWhite | AllowLeadingSign,
      None = 0x0,
      Number = AllowLeadingWhite | AllowTrailingWhite | AllowLeadingSign |
               AllowTrailingSign | AllowDecimalPoint | AllowThousands,
 }
```

> **BA** This class is great example of defining the common combination of flags so that most users will not have to figure out how to put bitwise OR values together.

## Description

System.Globalization.NumberStyles define the presence and/or location of various elements in a System.String representation of a numeric value. [*Note:* For example, the System.Globalization.NumberStyles.AllowParentheses style describes strings where the numeric value is enclosed in parentheses, such as "(432.00)".]

[*Note:* Where symbols such as a currency symbol are allowed in a System.Globalization.NumberStyles pattern, a System.Globalization.NumberFormatInfo instance defines the System.String representations of the symbols. System.Globalization.NumberStyles values are passed to methods that convert between System.String and numeric data types, such as the Parse methods implemented by numeric base types. To specify multiple System.Globalization.NumberStyles values, use the bitwise OR operator. For a list of the valid white space characters, see the System.String class.]

## Example

```
using System;
using System.Globalization;

namespace Samples
{
  public class NumberStylesSample
  {
    public static void Main()
    {
      string s = "$42";
      Console.WriteLine("Convert from String {0} yields {1}",
                        s, Int32.Parse(s,
                          NumberStyles.AllowCurrencySymbol));
      s = "42.0";
      Console.WriteLine("Convert from String {0} yields {1}",
                        s, Int32.Parse(s,
                          NumberStyles.AllowDecimalPoint));
      s = "3.40282347E+38";
      Console.WriteLine("Convert from String {0} yields {1}",
                        s, Single.Parse(s,
                          NumberStyles.AllowExponent |
                          NumberStyles.AllowDecimalPoint));
      s = "2A";
      Console.WriteLine("Convert from String {0} yields {1}",
                        s, Int32.Parse(s,
                          NumberStyles.AllowHexSpecifier));
      s = "+42";
      Console.WriteLine("Convert from String {0} yields {1}",
                        s, Int32.Parse(s,
                          NumberStyles.AllowLeadingSign));
```

```
      s = "\n\t 42";
      Console.WriteLine("Convert from String {0} yields {1}",
                        s, Int32.Parse(s,
                          NumberStyles.AllowLeadingWhite));
      s = "(42)";
      Console.WriteLine("Convert from String {0} yields {1}",
                        s, Int32.Parse(s,
                          NumberStyles.AllowParentheses));
      s = "4,242";
      Console.WriteLine("Convert from String {0} yields {1}",
                        s, Int32.Parse(s,
                          NumberStyles.AllowThousands));
      s = "42-";
      Console.WriteLine("Convert from String {0} yields {1}",
                        s, Int32.Parse(s,
                          NumberStyles.AllowTrailingSign));
      s = "42\n\t  ";
      Console.WriteLine("Convert from String {0} yields {1}",
                        s, Int32.Parse(s,
                          NumberStyles.AllowTrailingWhite));
      s = "\n\t  (42.0)    ";
      Console.WriteLine("Convert from String {0} yields {1}",
                        s, Int32.Parse(s,
                          NumberStyles.Any));
      s = "\t $4242.0    ";
      Console.WriteLine("Convert from String {0} yields {1}",
                        s, Int32.Parse(s,
                          NumberStyles.Currency));
      s = "\t +3.40282347E+38  ";
      Console.WriteLine("Convert from String {0} yields {1}",
                        s, Single.Parse(s,
                          NumberStyles.Float));
      s = "  2A  ";
      Console.WriteLine("Convert from String {0} yields {1}",
                        s, Int32.Parse(s,
                          NumberStyles.HexNumber));
      s = "  +42  ";
      Console.WriteLine("Convert from String {0} yields {1}",
                        s, Int32.Parse(s,
                          NumberStyles.Integer));
      s = "42";
      Console.WriteLine("Convert from String {0} yields {1}",
                        s, Int32.Parse(s,
                          NumberStyles.None));
    }
  }
}
```

NumberStyles Enum

The output is

```
Convert from String $42 yields 42
Convert from String 42.0 yields 42
Convert from String 3.40282347E+38 yields 3.402823E+38
Convert from String 2A yields 42
Convert from String +42 yields 42
Convert from String
 42 yields 42
Convert from String (42) yields -42
Convert from String 4,242 yields 4242
Convert from String 42- yields -42
Convert from String 42
   yields 42
Convert from String
  (42.0) yields -42
Convert from String  $4242.0     yields 4242
Convert from String  +3.40282347E+38   yields 3.402823E+38
Convert from String   2A   yields 42
Convert from String   +42   yields 42
Convert from String 42 yields 42
```

# System Object

## Summary

Provides support for classes. This class is the root of the object hierarchy.



## Type Summary

```
public class Object
{
  // Constructors
     public Object ();

  // Methods
     public virtual bool Equals (object obj);
  CF public static bool Equals (object objA,
                                object objB);
     ~object () ;
     public virtual int GetHashCode ();
     public Type GetType ();
     protected object MemberwiseClone ();
  CF public static bool ReferenceEquals (object objA,
                                         object objB);
     public virtual string ToString ();
 }
```

**BA** The static `Equals` method on `Object` was a relatively late addition to the class. We added it only after seeing a large number of utility versions of the same code. The common problem nearly everyone had with the instance version of `Equals` is that you had to make sure the value was not `null` before calling the `Equals` method. So to check to see if instances a and b were equal you had to write the error-prone code:

```
if (a != null && a.Equals(b) ) //they are equal
```

To make matters worse, in many cases if A and B are both `null`, they should be treated as equal. So that made the code completely untenable:

```
if ((a == null && b == null) || (a != null && a.Equals(b)) //they are equal
```

After recognizing this pattern we decided to canonicalize it in the static `Equals` method of `Object`.

*CONTINUED*

**JM** As with any group of travelers, the ECMA standard committee had to come up with ways to amuse each other. Early on in the standardization effort, I fell victim to a classic standardization amusement. Each month the committee would go out to a local restaurant for dinner where someone would mention to the waitstaff that it was my birthday. This happened every month for almost a year and half. This class was discussed at my third "birthday" party.

**JR** I think it's unfortunate that `Object` offers `Equals` and `GetHashCode` methods since these concepts are meaningless for most types. And, `IComparable` exists which is a superset of `Equals`. The whole equality thing got kind of messed up. The semantic of `Object`'s `Equals` method is to offer value equality. However, `Object`'s `Equals` method is really identity: do the two object references refer to the same, exact object? On the other hand, `ValueType`'s `Equals` method is truly value equality, not identity. C#'s == operator does identity for reference types and value equality for value types. But a type can overload the == operator for reference types making it value equality. But a programmer can obtain identity for reference types by casting both sides of the == operator to `Object` ensuring that the overloaded == operator method doesn't get called. In my *Applied Microsoft .NET Framework Programming* book, it took me about 10 pages to explain all the ins and outs of equality and identity.

## Description

[*Note:* Classes derived from `System.Object` may override the following methods of the `System.Object` class:]

## Example

```
using System;

namespace Samples
{
  public class ObjectSample
  {
    public static void Main()
    {
      Object o = new Object();
      Console.WriteLine("Are they equal: {0}",
                        o.Equals(new Object()));
      Console.WriteLine("Are they equal: {0}",
                        o.Equals(o));
      Console.WriteLine("GetHashcode yields {0}",
                        o.GetHashCode());
```

```
            Console.WriteLine("GetHashcode yields {0}",
                              new Object().GetHashCode());
            Console.WriteLine("o.ToString(): {0}", o.ToString());
        }
    }
}
```

The output is

```
Are they equal: False
Are they equal: True
GetHashcode yields 3
GetHashcode yields 5
o.ToString(): System.Object
```

# System ObjectDisposedException

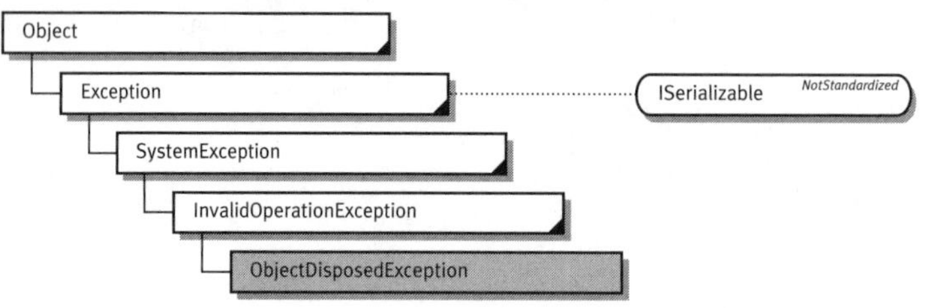




## Summary

Represents the error that occurs when an operation is performed on a disposed object.

## Type Summary

```
   public class ObjectDisposedException : InvalidOperationException
   {
     // Constructors
        public ObjectDisposedException (string objectName);
        public ObjectDisposedException (string objectName,
                                        string message);
MS CF protected ObjectDisposedException (SerializationInfo info,
                                          StreamingContext context);

     // Properties
     CF public override string Message { get; }
        public string ObjectName { get; }

     // Methods
MS CF public override void GetObjectData (SerializationInfo info,
                                          StreamingContext context);
   }
```

## Description

[*Note:* For additional information about disposing objects, see the `System.IDisposable` interface.]

## Example

```
using System;
using System.IO;

namespace Samples
{
  public class ObjectDisposedExceptionSample
  {
```

```
    public static void Main()
    {
      MemoryStream ms = new MemoryStream(16);
      ms.Close();
      try
      {
        ms.ReadByte();
      }
      catch(ObjectDisposedException e)
      {
        Console.WriteLine("Exception: {0}", e);
      }
    }
  }
}
```

The output is

```
Exception: System.ObjectDisposedException: Cannot access a closed Stream.
   at System.IO.__Error.StreamIsClosed()
   at System.IO.MemoryStream.ReadByte()
   at Samples.ObjectDisposedExceptionSample.Main() in C:\Books\BCL\Samples\System\
ObjectDisposedException\ObjectDisposedException.cs:line 14
```

# System
# ObsoleteAttribute

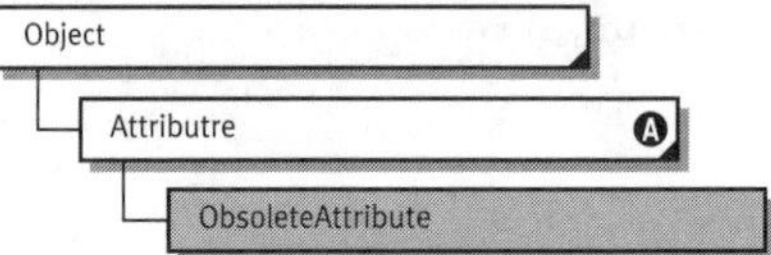


A B C D E F G H I J K L M N O P Q R S T U V W X Y Z

## Summary

Indicates that the target of the current attribute will be removed in future versions of the assembly in which the target is contained.

## Type Summary

```
public sealed class ObsoleteAttribute : Attribute
{
  // Constructors
     public ObsoleteAttribute ();
     public ObsoleteAttribute (string message);
     public ObsoleteAttribute (string message,
                               bool error);

  // Properties
     public bool IsError { get; }
     public string Message { get; }
}
```

**BA** You'll notice that this attribute is sealed. In general I am not a huge fan of sealing classes by default, but for custom attributes that you expect to be looked up at runtime it is a good idea to seal them, because then reflection can use a slightly faster code path to look them up.

## Description

[*Note:* Marking an item as obsolete provides consumers of that item the information that the item will be not be available in future versions of the assembly in which it is contained. A `System.ObsoleteAttribute` has a `System.ObsoleteAttribute.Message` property that can be used to suggest alternative ways of obtaining the functionality provided by the item, i.e., a workaround. This class also has a `System.ObsoleteAttribute.IsError` property that designates whether a compiler will treat usage of the obsolete item as an error. If this property is `false`, the compiler will issue a warning if the obsolete item is used and the compiler supports the generation of such warnings. This attribute can be applied to any valid attribute target except assemblies, parameters, and return values. For a complete list of valid attribute targets, see `System.AttributeTargets`.]

## Example

```
using System;

namespace Samples
{
  public class ObsoleteAttributeSample
  {
    [ObsoleteAttribute("Use NewMethod")]
    public static void OldMethod()
    {
      Console.WriteLine("Hi world!");
    }
    public static void NewMethod()
    {
      Console.WriteLine("Hello world!");
    }
    public static void Main()
    {
      OldMethod();
    }
  }
}
```

An example compile-time result is

```
Microsoft (R) Program Maintenance Utility Version 7.00.9466
Copyright (C) Microsoft Corporation.  All rights reserved.

        csc /debug ObsoleteAttribute.cs
Microsoft (R) Visual C# .NET Compiler version 7.00.9466
for Microsoft (R) .NET Framework version 1.0.3705
Copyright (C) Microsoft Corporation 2001. All rights reserved.

ObsoleteAttribute.cs(18,7): warning CS0618:
        'Samples.ObsoleteAttributeSample.OldMethod()' is obsolete: 'Use
        NewMethod'
```

# System
# OutOfMemoryException

BCL

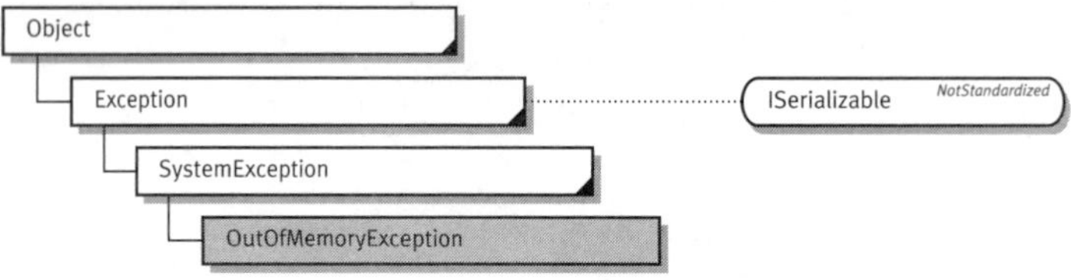


A B C D E F G H I J K L M N O P Q R S T U V W X Y Z

## Summary

Represents the error that occurs when insufficient memory prevents the current memory allocation from succeeding.

## Type Summary

```
   public class OutOfMemoryException : SystemException
   {
     // Constructors
        public OutOfMemoryException ();
        public OutOfMemoryException (string message);
        public OutOfMemoryException (string message,
                                     Exception innerException);
  MS CF protected OutOfMemoryException (SerializationInfo info,
                                        StreamingContext context);
   }
```

## Example

```
using System;
using System.Drawing;

namespace Samples
{
  public class OutOfMemoryExceptionSample
  {
    public static void Main()
    {
      try
      {
        Image i = Image.FromFile("BookCover.pdf");
      }
      catch(OutOfMemoryException e)
      {
        Console.WriteLine("Exception: {0}" , e);
      }
    }
  }
}
```

The output is

```
Exception: System.OutOfMemoryException: Out of memory.
   at System.Drawing.Image.FromFile(String filename, Boolean
useEmbeddedColorManagement)
   at System.Drawing.Image.FromFile(String filename)
   at Samples.OutOfMemoryExceptionSample.Main() in C:\Books\BCL\Samples\System\
OutOfMemoryException\OutOfMemoryException.cs:line 12
```

# System OverflowException

BCL

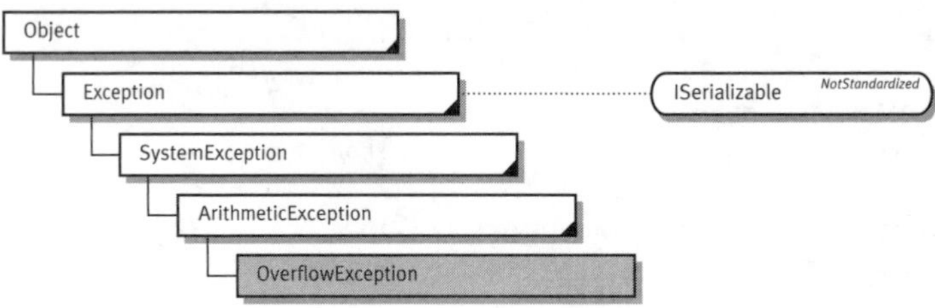




## Summary

Represents the error that occurs when the result of an arithmetic operation is too large to be represented by the destination type.

## Type Summary

```
public class OverflowException : ArithmeticException
{
  // Constructors
     public OverflowException ();
     public OverflowException (string message);
     public OverflowException (string message,
                              Exception innerException);
MS CF protected OverflowException (SerializationInfo info,
                                   StreamingContext context);
}
```

## Description

In languages that detect overflow, this is the exception that gets thrown. For example, in C#, the `checked` keyword is used to detect overflow conditions. A `System.OverflowException` exception occurs only in a `checked` context.

## Example

```
using System;

namespace Samples
{
  public class OverflowExceptionSample
  {
    public static void Main()
    {
      try
      {
        string s = Int64.MaxValue.ToString();
```

```
        int i = Int32.Parse(s);
      }
      catch(OverflowException e)
      {
        Console.WriteLine("Exception: {0}" , e);
      }
    }
  }
}
```

The output is

```
Exception: System.OverflowException: Value was either too large or too small for an
Int32.
   at System.Number.ParseInt32(String s, NumberStyles style, NumberFormatInfo info)
   at System.Int32.Parse(String s)
   at Samples.OverflowExceptionSample.Main() in C:\Books\BCL\Samples\System\
OverflowException\OverflowException.cs:line 12
```

# System.IO Path

## Summary

Performs operations on `System.String` instances that contain file or directory path information.

## Type Summary

```
public sealed class Path
{
  // Fields
     public static readonly char AltDirectorySeparatorChar = '/';
     public static readonly char DirectorySeparatorChar = '\\';
  MS public static readonly char[] InvalidPathChars = {'\"', '<', '>', '|',
                                                     '\0', '\b', (Char)16,
                                                     (Char)17, (Char)18,
                                                     (Char)20, (Char)21,
                                                     (Char)22, (Char)23,
                                                     (Char)24, (Char)25 };
     public static readonly char PathSeparator = ';';
  MS public static readonly char VolumeSeparatorChar = ':';

  // Methods
     public static string ChangeExtension (string path,
                                           string extension);
     public static string Combine (string path1,
                                   string path2);
     public static string GetDirectoryName (string path);
     public static string GetExtension (string path);
     public static string GetFileName (string path);
     public static string GetFileNameWithoutExtension (string path);
     public static string GetFullPath (string path);
     public static string GetPathRoot (string path);
     public static string GetTempFileName ();
     public static string GetTempPath ();
     public static bool HasExtension (string path);
     public static bool IsPathRooted (string path);
}
```

> **JM** The `Combine` method had an interesting ride in the standardization process. It was originally part of the `Path` class, then removed because it was thought to be too platform-specific, then added back because it was decided it was not any more platform-specific than any of the other methods in this class.
>
> **KG** Users often expect that the `Path` class actually interacts with the `FileSystem`, but in truth, it only performs string manipulations. This provides a great mechanism for interacting with other I/O classes, but can seem obscure. Be wary when using this class. A common assumption is that members such as `GetFullPath()` will only return a valid value if the path exists. However, all the API does is check the string to see if it is rooted, and if not, then provides a root for it (based on the current directory) and concatenates this with the string to provide a result. `Path` itself never checks against the file system for its operations since it can't guess your intent. You would simply need to create the file.

## Description

A path is a string that provides the location of a file or directory. A path does not necessarily point to a location on disk; for example, a path may map to a location in memory or on a device. Paths are composed of the components described below. Component names are shown in *italics* and the following table describes the symbols used in component definitions:

| Symbol | Description |
| --- | --- |
| <> | Indicates a path component. |
| {} | Indicates a grouping; either all components in a grouping are present, or none is permitted to be present. |
| * | Indicates that the component or grouping that immediately precedes this symbol can appear zero, one, or multiple times. |
| ? | Indicates that the component or grouping that immediately precedes this symbol can appear zero or one times. |
| + | Indicates string concatenation. |

The components that define a path are as follows:

- *Directory Name:* A string that specifies one or more directory levels in a file system. If a directory name contains multiple levels, a *directory separator character* separates the levels; however, a directory name does not begin or end with a directory separator character. In the example path C:/foo/bar/bat.txt, the directory name is "foo/bar". `System.IO.Path.GetDirectoryName` returns the directory name component of a path. Note that this method does include a beginning separator character if one is included in the specified path.
- *Directory Separator Character:* An implementation-defined constant string containing a single printable non-alphanumeric character used to separate levels in a file system. In the example path C:/foo/bar/bat.txt, the directory separator character is "/". The `System.IO.Path.DirectorySeparatorChar` and `System.IO.Path.AltDirectorySeparatorChar` store implementation-defined directory separator characters.
- *Extension:* A string that consists of the characters at the end of a file name, from and including the last *extension separator character.* The minimum and maximum lengths of extension components are platform-specific. In the example path C:/foo/bar/bat.txt, the extension is ".txt". The `System.IO.Path.GetExtension` method returns the extension component of a path.
- *Extension Separator Character:* An implementation-defined constant string composed of a single character that appears after the last character in the *file base* component indicating the beginning of the *extension* component. If the extension separator character is the first character in a *file name,* it is not interpreted as an extension separator character. If more than one extension separator character appears in a file name, only the last occurrence is the extension separator character; all other occurrences are part of the file base component. In the example path C:/foo/bar/bat.txt, the extension separator character is ".".
- *File Base:* A string containing the *filename* with the *extension* component removed. In the example path C:/foo/bar/bat.txt, the file base is "bat". The `System.IO.Path.GetFileNameWithoutExtension` method returns the file base component of a path.
- *File Name:* A string containing all information required to uniquely identify a file within a directory. This component is defined as follows:

  ```
  <file base>{+<extension>}?
  ```

  The file name component is commonly referred to as a relative file name. In the example path C:/foo/bar/bat.txt, the file name is "bat.txt". The `System.IO.Path.GetFileName` method returns the file name component of a path.
- *Full Directory Name:* A string containing all information required to uniquely identify a directory within a file system. This component is defined as follows:

  ```
  <path root>+<directory name>
  ```

The full directory name component is commonly referred to as the absolute directory name. In the example path C:/foo/bar/bat.txt, the full directory name is "C:/foo/bar ".

- *Full Path:* A string containing all information required to uniquely identify a file within a file system. This component is defined as follows:

```
<full directory name>+<directory separator character>+<file name>
```

  The full path component is commonly referred to as the absolute file name. In the example path C:/foo/bar/bat.txt, the full path is "C:/foo/bar/bat.txt". The `System.IO.Path.GetFullPath` method returns the full path component.

- *Path Root:* A string containing all information required to uniquely identify the highest level in a file system. The component is defined as follows:

```
{<volume identifier>+<volume separator character>}?+<directory separator
character>
```

  In the example path C:/foo/bar/bat.txt, the path root is "C:/". The `System.IO.Path.GetPathRoot` method returns the path root component.

- *Volume Identifier:* A string composed of a single alphabetic character that uniquely defines a drive or volume in a file system. This component is optional; on systems that do not support volume identifiers, this component is required to be a zero length string. In the example path C:/foo/bar/bat.txt, the path root is "C:". In the example path, \\myserver\myshare\foo\bar\baz.txt the path root is "\\myserver\myshare".
- *Volume Separator Character:* A string composed of a single alphabetic character used to separate the *volume identifier* from other components in a path. This component can appear in a path only if a volume identifier is present. This component is optional; on systems that do not support the volume identifier component, the volume separator character component is required to be a zero length string.

The exact format of a path is determined by the current platform. For example, on Windows systems a path can start with a volume identifier, while this element is not present in Unix system paths. On some systems, paths containing file names can contain extensions. The format of an extension is platform-dependent; for example, some systems limit extensions to three characters, while others do not. The current platform and possibly the current file system determine the set of characters used to separate the elements of a path, and the set of characters that cannot be used when specifying paths. Because of these differences, the fields of the `System.IO.Path` class as well as the exact behavior of some members of the `System.IO.Path` class are determined by the current platform and/or file system.

A path contains either absolute or relative location information. Absolute paths fully specify a location: the file or directory can be uniquely identified regardless of the current location. A full path or full directory name component is present in an absolute path. Relative paths specify a partial location: the current working directory

A B C D E F G H I J K L M N O P Q R S T U V W X Y Z

is used as the starting point when locating a file specified with a relative path. [*Note:* To determine the current working directory, call `System.IO.Directory.GetCurrentDirectory`.]

Most members of the `Path` class do not interact with the file system and do not verify the existence of the file or directory specified by a path string. `System.IO.Path` members that modify a path string, such as `System.IO.Path.ChangeExtension`, have no effect on files and directories in the file system. `System.IO.Path` members do, however, validate the contents of a specified path string, and throw `System.ArgumentException` if the string contains characters that are not valid in path strings, as defined by the current platform and file system. Implementations are required to preserve the case of file and directory path strings, and to be case-sensitive if and only if the current platform is case-sensitive.



## Example

```
using System;
using System.IO;

namespace Samples
{
  public class PathSamples
  {
    public static void Main()
    {
      Console.WriteLine(
                "Path.AltDirectorySeparatorChar: {0}",
                Path.AltDirectorySeparatorChar);
      Console.WriteLine(
                "Path.DirectorySeparatorChar: {0}",
                Path.DirectorySeparatorChar);
      Console.Write("Path.InvalidPathChars: ");
      foreach(char c in Path.InvalidPathChars)
        Console.Write(c);
      Console.WriteLine();
      Console.WriteLine(
                "Path.PathSeparator={0}",
                Path.PathSeparator);
      Console.WriteLine(
                "Path.VolumeSeparatorChar={0}",
                Path.VolumeSeparatorChar);
      string s = Path.GetFullPath("s.text");
      Console.WriteLine("ChangeExtension: {0}",
                Path.ChangeExtension(s, "txt"));
      Console.WriteLine("Combine: {0}",
                        Path.Combine(
                          Path.GetDirectoryName(s),
```

```
                        "Path.cs"));
        Console.WriteLine("GetExtension: {0}",
                          Path.GetExtension(s));
        Console.WriteLine("GetFileName: {0}",
                          Path.GetFileName(s));
        Console.WriteLine(
                "GetFileNameWithoutExtension: {0}",
                Path.GetFileNameWithoutExtension(s));
        Console.WriteLine("GetFullPath: {0}",
                        Path.GetFullPath("Path.cs"));
        Console.WriteLine("GetPathRoot: {0}",
                        Path.GetPathRoot(s));
        s = Path.GetTempFileName();
        Console.WriteLine("GetTempFileName: {0}", s);
        File.Delete(s);
        Console.WriteLine("GetTempPath: {0}",
                        Path.GetTempPath());
        Console.WriteLine("HasExtension {0}: {1}",
                        s ,Path.HasExtension(s));
        s = Path.GetFileNameWithoutExtension(s);
        Console.WriteLine("HasExtension {0}: {1}",
                        s ,Path.HasExtension(s));
        Console.WriteLine("IsPathRooted {0}: {1}",
                        s ,Path.IsPathRooted(s));
      }
    }
  }
```

The output is

```
Path.AltDirectorySeparatorChar: /
Path.DirectorySeparatorChar: \
Path.InvalidPathChars: "<>|▶◀↕¶§▬↨↑↓
Path.PathSeparator=;
Path.VolumeSeparatorChar=:
ChangeExtension: C:\Books\BCL\Samples\System.IO\Path\s.txt
Combine: C:\Books\BCL\Samples\System.IO\Path\Path.cs
GetExtension: .text
GetFileName: s.text
GetFileNameWithoutExtension: s
GetFullPath: C:\Books\BCL\Samples\System.IO\Path\Path.cs
GetPathRoot: C:\
GetTempFileName: C:\DOCUME~1\damien\LOCALS~1\Temp\tmp73.tmp
GetTempPath: C:\DOCUME~1\damien\LOCALS~1\Temp\
HasExtension C:\DOCUME~1\damien\LOCALS~1\Temp\tmp73.tmp: True
HasExtension tmp73: False
IsPathRooted tmp73: False
```

# System.IO PathTooLongException

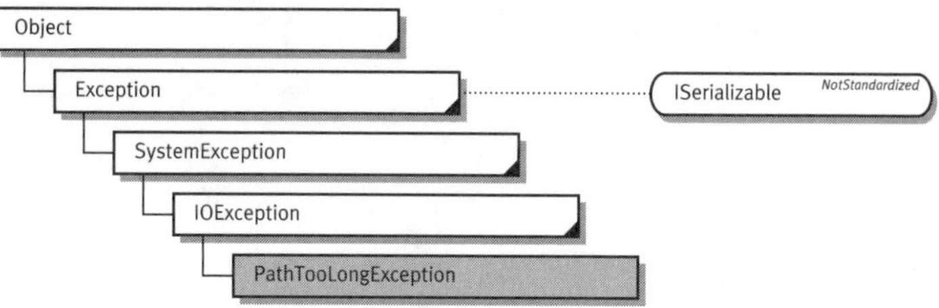


## Summary

Represents the error that occurs when a directory or file name is longer than the system-defined maximum length.

## Type Summary

```
public class PathTooLongException : IOException
{
  // Constructors
     public PathTooLongException();
     public PathTooLongException(string message);
     public PathTooLongException(string message, Exception innerException);
MS CF protected PathTooLongException (SerializationInfo info,
                                       StreamingContext context);
}
```

## Example

```
using System;
using System.IO;

namespace Samples
{
  public class PathTooLongExceptionSample
  {
    public static void Main()
    {
      try
      {
        string p = @"This\Is\A\Very\Long\Path\" +
                   @"But\It\Is\Only\An\Example\";
        string s = @"C:\" + p + p + p + p + p + p +
                   "filename.txt";
        FileStream fs = File.Create(s);
      }
```

```
      catch(PathTooLongException e)
      {
        Console.WriteLine("Exception: {0}", e);
      }
    }
  }
}
```

The output is

```
Exception: System.IO.PathTooLongException: The path is too long after being fully
qualified.  Make sure path is less than 260 characters.
   at System.IO.Path.nGetFullPathHelper(String path, Char[] invalidPathChars,
Char[] whitespaceChars, Char directorySeparator, Char altDirectorySeparator,
Boolean fullCheck, String& newPath)
   at System.IO.Path.GetFullPathInternal(String path)
   at System.IO.FileStream..ctor(String path, FileMode mode, FileAccess access,
FileShare share, Int32 bufferSize, Boolean useAsync, String msgPath, Boolean
bFromProxy)
   at System.IO.FileStream..ctor(String path, FileMode mode, FileAccess access,
FileShare share, Int32 bufferSize)
   at System.IO.File.Create(String path)
   at Samples.PathTooLongExceptionSample.Main() in C:\Books\BCL\Samples\System.IO\
PathTooLongException\PathTooLongException.cs:line 16
```

# System.Security PermissionSet

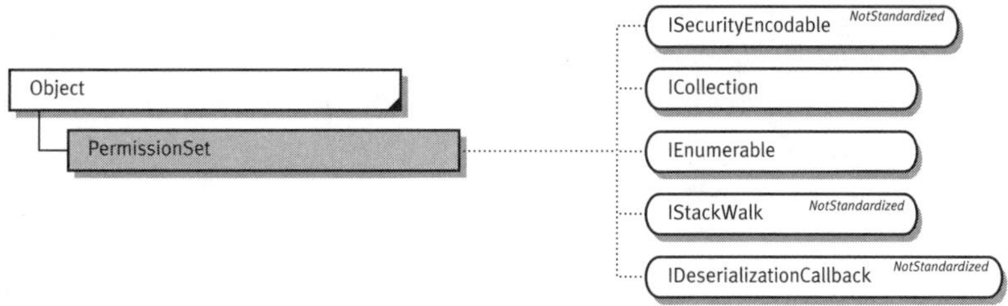


## Summary

Represents a collection that can contain different kinds of permissions and perform security operations.

## Type Summary

```
   CF public class PermissionSet : ISecurityEncodable,
                                   ICollection, IEnumerable,
                                   IStackWalk, IDeserializationCallback
   {
   // Constructors
   CF public PermissionSet (PermissionSet permSet);
   CF public PermissionSet (PermissionState state);

   // Properties
MS CF public virtual int Count { get; }
MS CF public virtual bool IsReadOnly { get; }
MS CF public virtual bool IsSynchronized { get; }
MS CF public virtual object SyncRoot { get; }

   // Methods
   CF public virtual IPermission AddPermission(IPermission perm);
   CF public virtual void Assert();
MS CF public bool ContainsNonCodeAccessPermissions ();
MS CF public static byte[] ConvertPermissionSet (string inFormat,
                                                  byte[] inData,
                                                  string outFormat);
   CF public virtual PermissionSet Copy ();
   CF public virtual void CopyTo (Array array,
                                  int index);
   CF public virtual void Demand();
   CF public virtual void Deny();
   CF public virtual void FromXml (SecurityElement et);
   CF public virtual IEnumerator GetEnumerator();
   CF public virtual bool IsSubsetOf(PermissionSet target);
   CF public virtual void PermitOnly();
   CF public override string ToString ();
```

```
   CF public virtual SecurityElement ToXml ();
   CF public virtual PermissionSet Union(PermissionSet other);

   // Explicit Interface Members
MS CF void IDeserializationCallback.OnDeserialization (object sender);
   }
```

## Description

[*Note:* Use `System.Security.PermissionSet` to perform operations on different permission types as a group.]

The XML encoding of a `System.Security.PermissionSet` instance is defined below in EBNF format. The following conventions are used:

- All non-literals in the grammar below are shown in normal type.
- All literals are in bold font.
- The following meta-language symbols are used:
- '*' represents a meta-language symbol suffixing an expression that can appear zero or more times.
- '?' represents a meta-language symbol suffixing an expression that can appear zero or one time.
- '+' represents a meta-language symbol suffixing an expression that can appear one or more times.
- '(',')' is used to group literals, non-literals, or a mixture of literals and non-literals.
- ' | ' denotes an exclusive disjunction between two expressions.
- '::= ' denotes a production rule where a left hand non-literal is replaced by a right hand expression containing literals, non-literals, or both.

The XML encoding of a `System.Security.PermissionSet` instance is as follows:

```
PermissionSet::=
(
<PermissionSet
class="System.Security.PermissionSet"
version="1" Unrestricted="true"/>
)
|
(
<PermissionSet
class="System.Security.PermissionSet"
version="1">
DnsPermissionXML ?
SocketPermissionXML ?
```

```
WebPermissionXML ?
EnvironmentPermissionXML ?
FileIOPermissionXML ?
ReflectionPermissionXML ?
SecurityPermissionXML ?
CustomPermissionXML *
</PermissionSet>
)
```

`CustomPermissionXML` represents any custom permission. The XML encoding for custom permissions makes use of the following symbols:

- `ClassName` is the name of the class implementing the permission. `AssemblyName` is the name of the assembly that contains the class implementing the permission.
- `Version` is the version number indicating the version of the assembly implementing the permission.
- `StrongNamePublicKeyToken` is the strong name public key token constituting the strong name of the assembly that implements the permission.
- `version` is version information for the custom permission. Format and content are defined by the author of the custom permission.
- `PermissionAttributes` is any attribute and attribute value on the `System.Security.IPermission` element used by the permission to represent a particular permission state, for example, unrestricted= `"true"`. Format and content are defined by the author of the custom permission.
- `PermissionXML` is any valid XML used by the permission to represent permission state. Format and content are defined by the author of the custom permission.

The XML encoding of a custom permission instance is as follows:

```
CustomPermissionXML ::=
<IPermission class="
ClassName,
AssemblyName,
Version=Version,
Culture=neutral,
PublicKeyToken=StrongNamePublicKeyToken"
version="version"
(PermissionAttributes)*
>
(PermissionXML)?
</IPermission>
```

## Example

```
using System;
using System.Security;
using System.Security.Permissions;
using System.IO;

namespace Samples
{
  public class PermissionSetSample
  {
    private const string
                    environmentVariable = "USERNAME";
    private const string
                    filename = "FileIOPermission.txt";
    public static void Main()
    {
      PermissionSet ps1 =
              new PermissionSet(PermissionState.None);
      EnvironmentPermission ep =
              new EnvironmentPermission(
                      EnvironmentPermissionAccess.Read,
                      environmentVariable);
      ps1.AddPermission(ep);
      PermissionSet ps2 =
              new PermissionSet(PermissionState.None);
      string s = Path.GetFullPath(filename);
      FileIOPermission fp =
              new FileIOPermission(
                    FileIOPermissionAccess.Read |
                    FileIOPermissionAccess.Write |
                    FileIOPermissionAccess.Append,
                    s);
      ps2.AddPermission(fp);
      PermissionSet ps = ps1.Union(ps2);
      Console.WriteLine("Count: {0}",
                        ps.Count);
      Console.WriteLine("Is read only: {0}",
                        ps.IsReadOnly);
      Console.WriteLine(
                 "Contains Non-CodeAccessPermissions: {0}",
                 ps.ContainsNonCodeAccessPermissions());
      Console.WriteLine(
                 "ps1.IsSubsetOf(ps): {0}",
                 ps1.IsSubsetOf(ps));
      Console.WriteLine(
                 "ps.IsUnrestricted(): {0}",
                 ps.IsUnrestricted());
      Console.WriteLine(ps);
```

```
      ps.Assert();
      TestAccess();
      CodeAccessPermission.RevertAssert();
      ps.Deny();
      TestAccess();
      CodeAccessPermission.RevertDeny();
      ps.PermitOnly();
      TestAccess();
      CodeAccessPermission.RevertPermitOnly();
    }
    public static void TestAccess()
    {
      try
      {
         Console.WriteLine("Variable {0} Value: {1}",
                   environmentVariable,
                   Environment.GetEnvironmentVariable(
                              environmentVariable));
      }
      catch(Exception)
      {
        Console.WriteLine("Variable {0} cannot be read",
                          environmentVariable);
      }
      try
      {
        FileStream fs = new FileStream(
                             filename,
                             FileMode.OpenOrCreate);
        Console.WriteLine("File {0} can be accessed",
                          filename);
        fs.Close();
      }
      catch (Exception)
      {
        Console.WriteLine("File {0} cannot be accessed",
                          filename);
      }
    }
  }
}
```

The output is

```
Count: 2
Is read only: False
Contains Non-CodeAccessPermissions: False
ps1.IsSubsetOf(ps): True
```

## PermissionSet Class

```
ps.IsUnrestricted(): False
<PermissionSet class="System.Security.PermissionSet"
               version="1">
   <IPermission class="System.Security.Permissions.EnvironmentPermission,
mscorlib, Version=1.0.3300.0, Culture=neutral, PublicKeyToken=b77a5c561934e089"
                version="1"
                Read="USERNAME"/>
   <IPermission class="System.Security.Permissions.FileIOPermission, mscorlib,
Version=1.0.3300.0, Culture=neutral, PublicKeyToken=b77a5c561934e089"
                version="1"
                Read="C:\Books\BCL\Samples\System.Security\PermissionSet\
FileIOPermission.txt"
                Write="C:\Books\BCL\Samples\System.Security\PermissionSet\
FileIOPermission.txt"
                Append="C:\Books\BCL\Samples\System.Security\PermissionSet\
FileIOPermission.txt"/>
</PermissionSet>

Variable USERNAME Value: damien
File FileIOPermission.txt can be accessed
Variable USERNAME cannot be read
File FileIOPermission.txt cannot be accessed
Variable USERNAME Value: damien
File FileIOPermission.txt can be accessed
```

# System.Security.Permissions PermissionState Enum

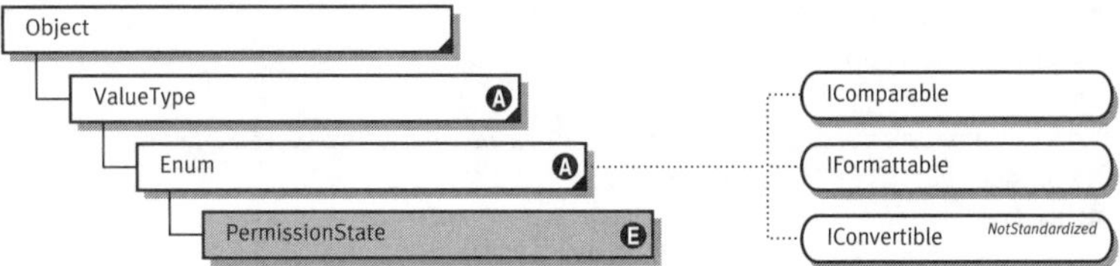


## Summary

Represents a value specifying whether an entity, at creation, should have full or no access to resources.

## Type Summary

```
CF public enum PermissionState {
  CF None = 0,
  CF Unrestricted = 1,
}
```

## Description

[*Note:* Code access permission objects supply a constructor that takes a `System.Security.Permissions.PermissionState` value specifying that the new instance is either fully restricted (`System.Security.Permissions.PermissionState.None`) or unrestricted (`System.Security.Permissions.PermissionState.Unrestricted`). A fully restricted permission object disallows access to a resource; an unrestricted permission object allows full access to a resource. For example, a fully restricted `System.Security.Permissions.FileIOPermission` object disallows access to files and directories, while an unrestricted object of the same type allows full access to all files and directories in the file system.]

## Example

```
using System;
using System.Security;
using System.Security.Permissions;

namespace Samples
{
  public class PermissionStateSample
  {
    public static void Main()
    {
      PermissionSet ps1 =
       new PermissionSet(PermissionState.None);
      EnvironmentPermission ep =
```

```
                new EnvironmentPermission(
                        EnvironmentPermissionAccess.Read,
                        "USERNAME");
         ps1.AddPermission(ep);
         PermissionSet ps2 =
                new PermissionSet(PermissionState.Unrestricted);
         PermissionSet ps = ps1.Union(ps2);
         Console.WriteLine(
                   "ps1.IsUnrestricted(): {0}",
                   ps1.IsUnrestricted());
         Console.WriteLine(
                   "ps2.IsUnrestricted(): {0}",
                   ps2.IsUnrestricted());
         Console.WriteLine(
                   "ps.IsUnrestricted(): {0}",
                   ps.IsUnrestricted());
       }
    }
}
```

The output is

```
ps1.IsUnrestricted(): False
ps2.IsUnrestricted(): True
ps.IsUnrestricted(): True
```

## Summary

Generates pseudo-random numbers.

## Type Summary

```
public class Random
{
  // Constructors
     public Random ();
     public Random (int Seed);

  // Methods
     public virtual int Next ();
     public virtual int Next (int maxValue);
     public virtual int Next (int minValue, int maxValue);
     public virtual void NextBytes (byte[] buffer);
     public virtual double NextDouble ();
  MS protected virtual double Sample ();
}
```

> **KG** The Random class provides a great mechanism for generating "pseudo"-random numbers. Don't use it for mission-critical random generations, however, since it can't be considered reliable enough for truly random generation.

## Description

Instances of this class are initialized using a "seed," or starting value. The series of numbers generated by instances of the class are repeatable: given the same seed value, all instances of this class generate the same series of numbers.

[*Note:* The numbers generated by this class are chosen with equal probability from a finite set of numbers. The numbers are generated by a definite mathematical algorithm and are therefore not truly random, but are sufficiently random for practical purposes. For this reason, the numbers are considered to be pseudo-random.]

## Example

```
using System;

namespace Samples
{
  public class RandomSample
  {
    public static void Main()
    {
      Random r = new Random();
      DisplayNumbers(r, 4);
      r = new Random();
      DisplayNumbers(r, 4);
      r = new Random(unchecked(
                       (int)DateTime.Now.Ticks));
      DisplayNumbers(r, 4);
      Byte[] bytes = new Byte[4];
      r.NextBytes(bytes);
      Console.WriteLine("Bytes");
      foreach(Byte b in bytes)
        Console.Write("{0} ", b);
      Console.WriteLine();
    }
    public static void DisplayNumbers(Random r, int number)
    {
      Console.WriteLine("Integers");
      for(int i = 0; i < number; i++)
        Console.Write("{0} ", r.Next());
      Console.WriteLine();
      Console.WriteLine("Doubles");
      for(int i = 0; i < number; i++)
        Console.Write("{0} ", r.NextDouble());
      Console.WriteLine();
    }
  }
}
```

The output is

```
Integers
610101060 182710372 541839654 1122923352
Doubles
0.0368340453304509 0.107627541342577 0.0506987171483686 0.135695314563669
Integers
1091681015 41376261 520106915 1411608088
Doubles
0.551691442984944 0.84660560816834 0.531265693032772 0.152539342712862
```

```
Integers
620796866 1169353365 91436196 2009606433
Doubles
0.948118089208434 0.42210969953896 0.893776561084099 0.835302507428128
Bytes
220 87 84 101
```

# System
# RankException

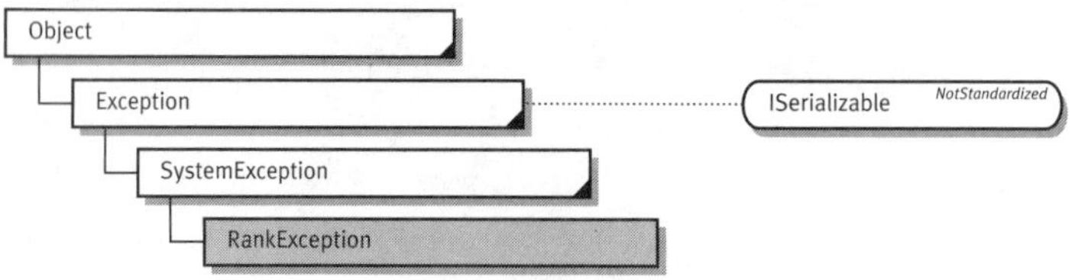


## Summary

Represents the error that occurs when an array with an incorrect number of dimensions is passed to a method.

## Type Summary

```
public class RankException : SystemException
{
  // Constructors
     public RankException ();
     public RankException (string message);
     public RankException (string message, Exception innerException);
MS CF protected RankException (SerializationInfo info,
                                 StreamingContext context);
}
```

## Example

```
using System;

namespace Samples
{
  public class RankExceptionSample
  {
    public static void Main()
    {
      try
      {
        Array a = Array.CreateInstance(
                        typeof(int), 5);
        Array b = Array.CreateInstance(
                        typeof(int), 5, 5);
        Array.Copy(a, b, 5);
      }
      catch(RankException e)
      {
        Console.WriteLine("Exception: {0}" , e);
      }
    }
  }
}
```

The output is

```
Exception: System.RankException: The specified arrays must have the same number of
dimensions.
   at System.Array.Copy(Array sourceArray, Int32 sourceIndex, Array
destinationArray, Int32 destinationIndex, Int32 length)
   at System.Array.Copy(Array sourceArray, Array destinationArray, Int32 length)
   at Samples.RankExceptionSample.Main() in C:\Books\BCL\Samples\System\
RankException\RankException.cs:line 15
```

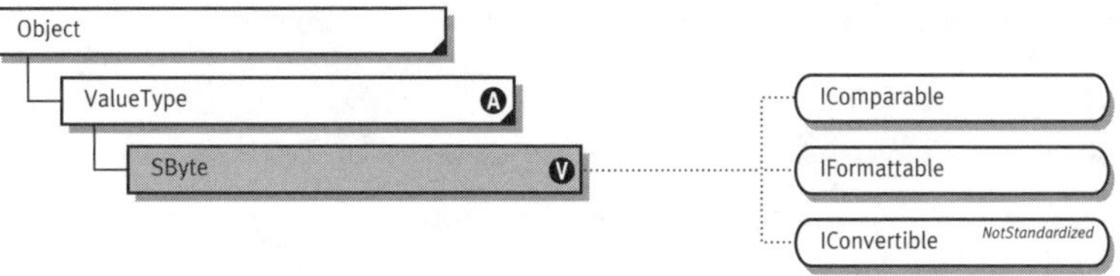


## Summary

Represents an 8-bit signed integer. This type is not CLS-compliant.

## Type Summary

```
public struct SByte : IComparable, IFormattable,
                      IConvertible
{
   // Fields
      public const sbyte MaxValue = 127;
      public const sbyte MinValue = -128;

   // Methods
      public int CompareTo (object obj);
      public override bool Equals (object obj);
      public override int GetHashCode ();
MS CF public TypeCode GetTypeCode ();
      public static sbyte Parse (string s);
      public static sbyte Parse (string s, NumberStyles style);
      public static sbyte Parse (string s, NumberStyles style,
                                 IFormatProvider provider);
   CF public static sbyte Parse (string s, IFormatProvider provider);
      public override string ToString ();
      public string ToString (string format);
      public string ToString (string format, IFormatProvider provider);
      public string ToString (IFormatProvider provider);

   // Explicit Interface Members
   MS bool IConvertible.ToBoolean(IFormatProvider provider);
   MS byte IConvertible.ToByte(IFormatProvider provider);
   MS char IConvertible.ToChar(IFormatProvider provider);
   MS DateTime IConvertible.ToDateTime(IFormatProvider provider);
   MS decimal IConvertible.ToDecimal(IFormatProvider provider);
   MS double IConvertible.ToDouble(IFormatProvider provider);
   MS short IConvertible.ToInt16(IFormatProvider provider);
   MS int IConvertible.ToInt32(IFormatProvider provider);
   MS long IConvertible.ToInt64(IFormatProvider provider);
   MS sbyte IConvertible.ToSByte(IFormatProvider provider);
   MS float IConvertible.ToSingle(IFormatProvider provider);
   MS object IConvertible.ToType(Type type,IFormatProvider provider);
```

```
    MS ushort IConvertible.ToUInt16(IFormatProvider provider);
    MS uint IConvertible.ToUInt32(IFormatProvider provider);
    MS ulong IConvertible.ToUInt64(IFormatProvider provider);
  }
```

**BA** See `System.Byte` for my thoughts on the naming of this class.

## Description

The `System.SByte` data type represents integer values ranging from negative 128 to positive 127; that is, hexadecimal 0x80 to 0x7F.

## Example

```
using System;

namespace Samples
{
  public class SByteSample
  {
    public static void Main()
    {
      sbyte max = sbyte.MaxValue,
            min = sbyte.MinValue;
      Console.WriteLine("MaxValue: {0}", max);
      Console.WriteLine("MinValue: {0}", min);
      Console.WriteLine("Is {0} equal to {1}: {2}",
                        max, max, max.Equals(max));
      Console.WriteLine("Is {0} equal to {1}: {2}",
                        max, min, max.Equals(min));
      Console.WriteLine("{0} has hashcode of: {1}",
                        max, max.GetHashCode());
      Console.WriteLine("{0} has hashcode of: {1}",
                        min, min.GetHashCode());
      string s = max.ToString();
      Console.WriteLine("\"{0}\" parsed from string yields: {1}",
                       s, SByte.Parse(s));
      s = min.ToString();
      Console.WriteLine("\"{0}\" parsed from string yields: {1}",
                        s, SByte.Parse(s));
      string[] formats = {"c", "d", "e", "f",
                          "g", "n", "p", "x" };
      foreach(string f in formats)
        Console.WriteLine("{0}: {1}", max, max.ToString(f));
    }
  }
}
```

SByte Structure

The output is

```
MaxValue: 127
MinValue: -128
Is 127 equal to 127: True
Is 127 equal to -128: False
127 has hashcode of: 32639
-128 has hashcode of: 32640
"127" parsed from string yields: 127
"-128" parsed from string yields: -128
127: $127.00
127: 127
127: 1.270000e+002
127: 127.00
127: 127
127: 127.00
127: 12,700.00 %
127: 7f
```

# System.Security.Permissions SecurityAction Enum

BCL

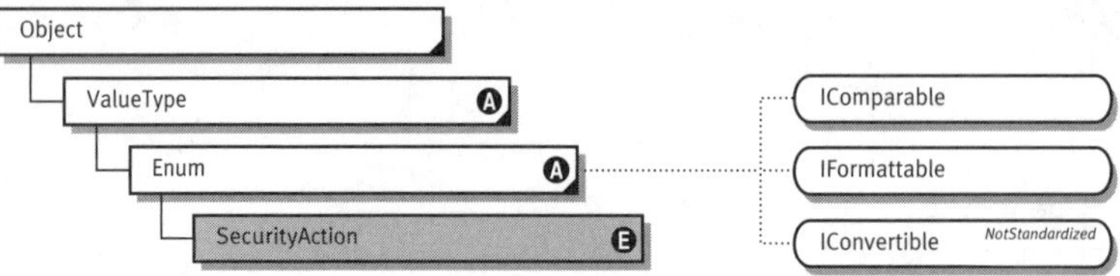


## Summary

Specifies security actions that can be performed using declarative security.

## Type Summary

```
CF public enum SecurityAction  {
  CF Assert = 3,
  CF Demand = 2,
  CF Deny = 4,
  CF InheritanceDemand= 7,
  CF LinkDemand = 6,
  CF PermitOnly = 5,
  CF RequestMinimum = 8,
  CF RequestOptional = 9,
  CF RequestRefuse = 10,
}
```

## Description

[*Note*: For information about using declarative security and security actions, see Partition II of the CLI Specification.]

[*Note:* Declarative security is specified using types derived from `System.Security.Permissions.SecurityAttribute`. The following table describes the attribute targets supported by each of the security actions. For additional information on attribute targets, see `System.Attribute`.]

## Example

```
using System;
using System.Security;
using System.Security.Permissions;

[assembly:EnvironmentPermissionAttribute(
                SecurityAction.RequestMinimum,
                Read="COMPUTERNAME;USERNAME")]
```

SecurityAction Enum

```
namespace Samples
{
  public class SecurityActionSample
  {
    public static void Main()
    {
      string[] v = {"USERNAME", "COMPUTERNAME"};
      foreach(string s in v)
        Console.WriteLine("Variable {0} Value: {1}",
                  s,
                  Environment.GetEnvironmentVariable(s));

    }
  }
}
```

The output is

```
Variable USERNAME Value: damien
Variable COMPUTERNAME Value: PROJECT42
```

# System.Security.Permissions SecurityAttribute



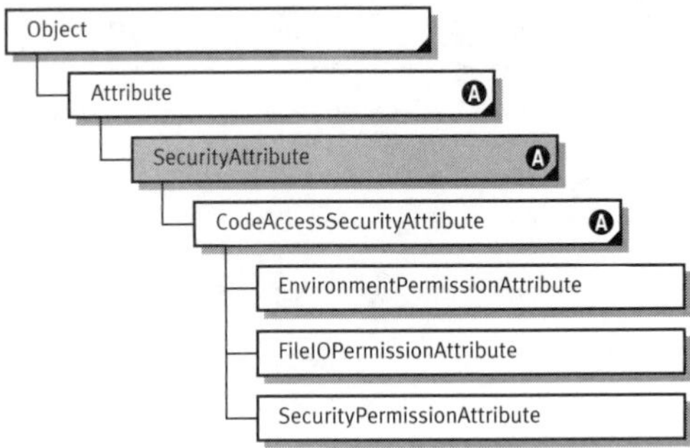




## Summary

This is the base class for attributes used by the security system.

## Type Summary

```
  CF public abstract class SecurityAttribute : Attribute
  {
    // Constructors
    CF public SecurityAttribute (SecurityAction action);

    // Properties
 MS CF public SecurityAction Action { set; get; }
    CF public bool Unrestricted { set; get; }

    // Methods
    CF public abstract IPermission CreatePermission ();
  }
```

## Example

```
using System;
using System.Security;
using System.Security.Permissions;

[assembly:EnvironmentPermissionAttribute(
                SecurityAction.RequestMinimum,
                Read="COMPUTERNAME;USERNAME")]

namespace Samples
{
  public class SecurityAttribute
  {
    public static void Main()
```

```
    {
      string[] v = {"USERNAME", "COMPUTERNAME"};
      foreach(string s in v)
        Console.WriteLine("Variable {0} Value: {1}",
                  s,
                  Environment.GetEnvironmentVariable(s));
    }
  }
}
```

The output is:

```
Variable USERNAME Value: damien
Variable COMPUTERNAME Value: PROJECT42
```

# System.Security SecurityElement

BCL

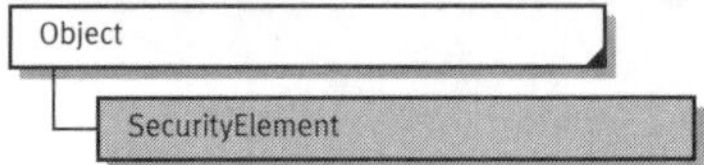


## Summary

Represents the XML object model for encoding security objects.

## Type Summary

```
   CF public sealed class SecurityElement
   {
      // Properties
MS CF public Hashtable Attributes { set; get; }
MS CF public ArrayList Children { set; get; }
MS CF public string Tag { set; get; }
MS CF public string Text { set; get; }

      // Methods
MS CF public void AddAttribute (string name, string value);
MS CF public void AddChild (SecurityElement child);
MS CF public string Attribute (string name);
MS CF public bool Equal (SecurityElement other);
MS CF public static string Escape (string str);
MS CF public static bool IsValidAttributeName (string name);
MS CF public static bool IsValidAttributeValue (string value);
MS CF public static bool IsValidTag (string tag);
MS CF public static bool IsValidText (string text);
MS CF public string SearchForTextOfTag (string tag);
   CF public override string ToString ();
   }
```

## Description

The simple XML object model for an element consists of the following parts:

- The tag is the element name.
- The attributes are zero or more name/value attribute pairs on the element.
- The children are zero or more elements nested within `<tag>` and `</tag>`.
- An attribute name must be at least one character, and cannot be `null`. If element-based value representation is used, elements with a text string that is `null` are represented in the `<tag/>` form; otherwise, text is delimited by the `<tag>` and `</tag>` tokens. Both forms can be combined with attributes, which are shown if present.

- The tags, attributes, and text are case-sensitive. The XML form contains quotation marks and escape sequences where necessary. String values that include characters invalid for use in XML result in a `System.ArgumentException`. These rules apply to all properties and methods.

[*Note:* This class is intended to be a lightweight implementation of a simple XML object model for use within the security system, and not for use as a general XML object model. It is strongly suggested that properties of a security element are expressed as attributes, and property values are expressed as attribute values. Specifically, avoid nesting text within tags. For any `<tag>text</tag>` representation a representation of type `<tag value="text"/>` is usually available. Using attribute-based XML representations aids in readability. For performance reasons, character validity is checked only when the element is encoded into XML form, and not on every set of a property or method call. Static methods allow explicit checking where needed. This class is used only by the system; applications cannot create instances of the `System.Security.SecurityElement` type.]

## Example

```
using System;
using System.Security;
using System.Security.Permissions;

namespace Samples
{
  public class SecurityElementSample
  {
    public static void Main()
    {
      EnvironmentPermission p1 =
                new EnvironmentPermission(
                    EnvironmentPermissionAccess.Read,
                    "COMPUTERNAME");
      SecurityElement s = p1.ToXml();
      Console.WriteLine(s.ToString());
    }
  }
}
```

The output is:

```
<IPermission class="System.Security.Permissions.EnvironmentPermission, mscorlib,
Version=1.0.3300.0, Culture=neutral, PublicKeyToken=b77a5c561934e089"
             version="1"
             Read="COMPUTERNAME"/>
```

# System.Security SecurityException

BCL

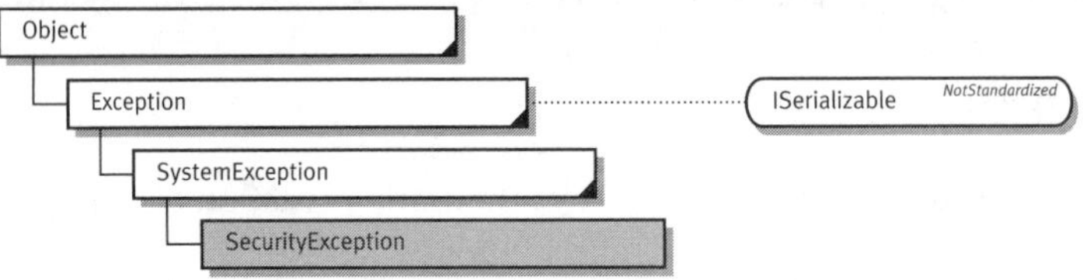


## Summary

Represents the error that occurs when an application does not have the permissions required to access a resource or perform a secured operation.

## Type Summary

```
   public class SecurityException : SystemException
   {
       // Constructors
          public SecurityException ();
          public SecurityException (string message);
          public SecurityException (string message,
                                    Exception inner);
    MS CF public SecurityException (string message,
                                    Type type);
    MS CF public SecurityException (string message,
                                    Type type, string state);
    MS CF protected SecurityException (SerializationInfo info,
                                       StreamingContext context);

       // Properties
MS CF 1.1 public string GrantedSet { get; }
    MS CF public string PermissionState { get; }
    MS CF public Type PermissionType { get; }
MS CF 1.1 public string RefusedSet { get; }

       // Methods
    MS CF public override void GetObjectData (SerializationInfo info,
                                              StreamingContext context);
    MS CF public override string ToString ();
   }
```

## Description

[*Note*: For more information about permissions and security, see Partition V of the CLI specification. The following IL instructions throw `System.Security.SecurityException`:]

## Example

```
using System;
using System.Security;
using System.Security.Permissions;

namespace Samples
{

  public class SecurityExceptionSample
  {
    [EnvironmentPermissionAttribute(
                SecurityAction.PermitOnly,
                Read="USERNAME")]
    static void Main(string[] args)
    {
      string s = "COMPUTERNAME";
      try
      {
        Console.WriteLine("Variable {0} Value: {1}", s,
                Environment.GetEnvironmentVariable(s));
      }
      catch(SecurityException e)
      {
        Console.WriteLine("Exception {0}", e);
      }
    }
  }
}
```

The output is:

```
Exception System.Security.SecurityException: Request for the permission of type
System.Security.Permissions.EnvironmentPermission, mscorlib, Version=1.0.3300.0,
Culture=neutral, PublicKeyToken=b77a5c561934e089 failed.
   at System.Security.SecurityRuntime.FrameDescHelper(FrameSecurityDescriptor
secDesc, IPermission demand, PermissionToken permToken)
   at System.Security.CodeAccessSecurityEngine.Check(PermissionToken permToken,
CodeAccessPermission demand, StackCrawlMark& stackMark, Int32 checkFrames, Int32
unrestrictedOverride)
   at System.Security.CodeAccessSecurityEngine.Check(CodeAccessPermission cap,
StackCrawlMark& stackMark)
   at System.Security.CodeAccessPermission.Demand()
   at System.Environment.GetEnvironmentVariable(String variable)
   at Samples.SecurityExceptionSample.Main(String[] args) in C:\Books\BCL\Samples\
System.Security\SecurityException\SecurityException.cs:line 18
```

# System.Security.Permissions SecurityPermission

BCL

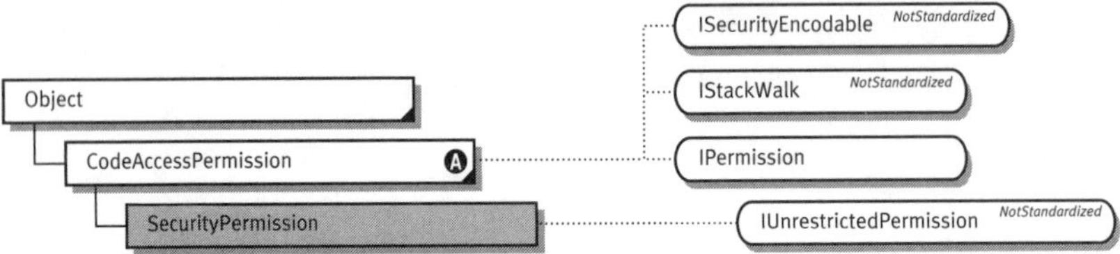




## Type Summary

```
CF public sealed class SecurityPermission : CodeAccessPermission,
                                             IUnrestrictedPermission
   {
     // Constructors
     CF public SecurityPermission (PermissionState state);
     CF public SecurityPermission (SecurityPermissionFlag flag);

     // Properties
  MS CF public SecurityPermissionFlag Flags { set; get; }

     // Methods
     CF public override IPermission Copy ();
     CF public override void FromXml (SecurityElement esd);
     CF public override IPermission Intersect (IPermission target);
     CF public override bool IsSubsetOf (IPermission target);
  MS CF public bool IsUnrestricted ();
     CF public override SecurityElement ToXml ();
     CF public override IPermission Union (IPermission target);
   }
```

## Summary

Describes a set of security permissions applied to code.

## Description

The `System.Security.Permissions.SecurityPermissionFlag` enumeration defines the permissions secured by this class.

The XML encoding of a `System.Security.Permissions.SecurityPermission` instance is defined below in EBNF format. The following conventions are used:

- All non-literals in the grammar below are shown in normal type.
- All literals are in bold font.
- The following meta-language symbols are used:
  - Constructs and initializes a new instance of the `System.Collections.Hashtable` class with the specified initial capacity.

- '*' represents a meta-language symbol suffixing an expression that can appear zero or more times. '?' represents a meta-language symbol suffixing an expression that can appear zero or one time.
- '+' represents a meta-language symbol suffixing an expression that can appear one or more times.
- '(',')' is used to group literals, non-literals, or a mixture of literals and non-literals.
- ' | ' denotes an exclusive disjunction between two expressions.
- '::= ' denotes a production rule where a left-hand non-literal is replaced by a right-hand expression containing literals, non-literals, or both.
- BuildVersion refers to the build version of the shipping CLI. This is a dotted build number such as '2412.0'.
- ECMAPubKeyToken ::= b77a5c561934e089
- SecurityPermissionFlag = Assertion | ControlThread | Execution | SkipVerification | UnmanagedCode

Each SecurityPermissionFlag literal can appear in the XML no more than once. For example, `Flags=Assertion,Assertion` is illegal.

```
SecurityPermission ::=
<IPermission
class="
System.Security.Permissions.SecurityPermission,
mscorlib,
Version=1.0.BuildVersion,
Culture=neutral,
PublicKeyToken=ECMAPubKeyToken"
version="1"
(
Unrestricted="true"
)
|
(
Flags="SecurityPermissionFlag (, SecurityPermissionFlag)* ")
| ()
/>
```

## Example

```
using System;
using System.Security;
using System.Security.Permissions;

namespace Samples
{
  public class SecurityPermissionSample
```

A B C D E F G H I J K L M N O P Q R S T U V W X Y Z

```
{
  public static void Main()
  {
    try
    {
      SecurityPermission sp =
        new SecurityPermission(
          SecurityPermissionFlag.Assertion);
      DoAssert();
      sp.Deny();
      DoAssert();
    }
    catch(Exception e)
    {
      Console.WriteLine("Exception: {0}", e);
    }
  }
  [SecurityPermissionAttribute(
    SecurityAction.Demand, Assertion=true)]
  public static void DoAssert()
  {
    EnvironmentPermission p =
           new EnvironmentPermission(
                   EnvironmentPermissionAccess.Read,
                   "USERNAME");
    p.Assert();
    Console.WriteLine("Assert succeeded");
  }
 }
}
```

The output is:

```
Assert succeeded
Exception: System.Security.SecurityException: Request failed.
   at System.Security.SecurityRuntime.FrameDescSetHelper(FrameSecurityDescriptor
secDesc, PermissionSet demandSet, PermissionSet& alteredDemandSet)
   at Samples.SecurityPermissionSample.DoAssert() in C:\Books\BCL\Samples\
System.Security\Permissions\SecurityPermission\SecurityPermission.cs:line 29
   at Samples.SecurityPermissionSample.Main() in C:\Books\BCL\Samples\
System.Security\Permissions\SecurityPermission\SecurityPermission.cs:line 18
```

# System.Security.Permissions SecurityPermissionAttribute

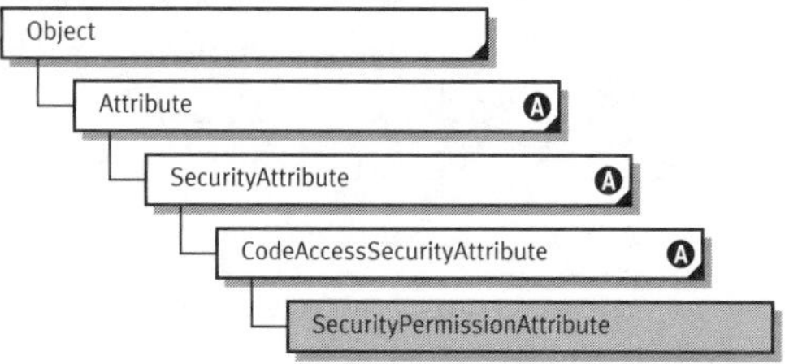


## Summary

Used to apply a security action and a set of security permissions to program code.

## Type Summary

```
CF public sealed class SecurityPermissionAttribute : CodeAccessSecurityAttribute
  {
     // Constructors
     CF public SecurityPermissionAttribute(SecurityAction action);

     // Properties
  MS CF public bool Assertion { set; get; }
  MS CF public bool ControlAppDomain { set; get; }
  MS CF public bool ControlDomainPolicy { set; get; }
  MS CF public bool ControlEvidence { set; get; }
  MS CF public bool ControlPolicy { set; get; }
  MS CF public bool ControlPrincipal { set; get; }
  MS CF public bool ControlThread { set; get; }
  MS CF public bool Execution { set; get; }
     CF public SecurityPermissionFlag Flags { set; get; }
  MS CF public bool Infrastructure { set; get; }
  MS CF public bool RemotingConfiguration { set; get; }
  MS CF public bool SerializationFormatter { set; get; }
  MS CF public bool SkipVerification { set; get; }
  MS CF public bool UnmanagedCode { set; get; }

     // Methods
     CF public override IPermission CreatePermission();
  }
```

## Description

[*Note:* The security permissions are defined in the `System.Security.Permissions.SecurityPermissionFlag` enumeration and are specified using the `System.Security.Permissions.SecurityPermissionAttribute.Flags` property. The security information declared by a security attribute is stored in the metadata of

A B C D E F G H I J K L M N O P Q R S T U V W X Y Z

the attribute target, and is accessed by the system at runtime. Security attributes are used for declarative security only. For imperative security, use the corresponding permission class, `System.Security.Permissions.SecurityPermission`. The allowable `System.Security.Permissions.SecurityPermissionAttribute` targets are determined by the `System.Security.Permissions.SecurityAction` passed to the constructor.]

A B C D E F G H I J K L M N O P Q R S T U V W X Y Z

## Example

```
using System;
using System.Security;
using System.Security.Permissions;

namespace Samples
{
  public class SecurityPermissionAttributeSample
  {
    public static void Main()
    {
      try
      {
        SecurityPermission sp =
          new SecurityPermission(
            SecurityPermissionFlag.Assertion);
        DoAssert();
        sp.Deny();
        DoAssert();
      }
      catch(Exception e)
      {
        Console.WriteLine("Exception: {0}", e);
      }
    }
    [SecurityPermissionAttribute(
      SecurityAction.Demand, Assertion=true)]
    public static void DoAssert()
    {
      Console.WriteLine("In method: DoAssert()");
      EnvironmentPermission p =
             new EnvironmentPermission(
                     EnvironmentPermissionAccess.Read,
                     "USERNAME");
      p.Assert();
      Console.WriteLine("Assert succeeded");
    }
  }
}
```

The output is:

```
In method: DoAssert()
Assert succeeded
Exception: System.Security.SecurityException: Request failed.
   at System.Security.SecurityRuntime.FrameDescSetHelper(FrameSecurityDescriptor
secDesc, PermissionSet demandSet, PermissionSet& alteredDemandSet)
   at Samples.SecurityPermissionAttributeSample.DoAssert() in C:\Books\BCL\
Samples\System.Security\Permissions\SecurityPermissionAttribute\SecurityPermission
Attribute.cs:line 29
   at Samples.SecurityPermissionAttributeSample.Main() in C:\Books\BCL\Samples\
System.Security\Permissions\SecurityPermissionAttribute\SecurityPermissionAttribut
e.cs:line 18
```

# System.Security.Permissions SecurityPermissionFlag Enum

BCL

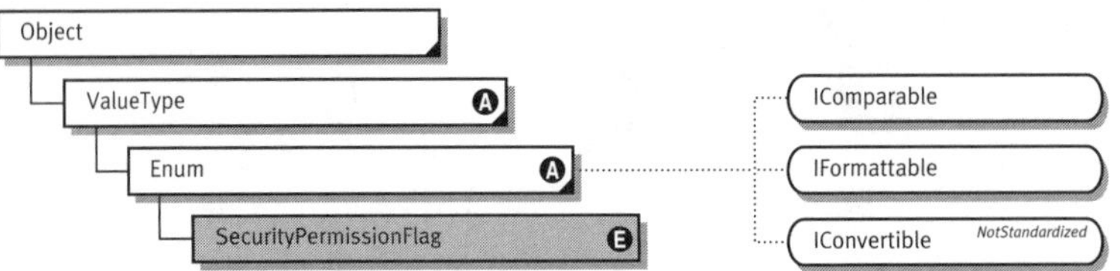


## Summary

Specifies a set of security permissions applied to a `System.Security.Permissions.SecurityPermission` instance.

## Type Summary

```
   CF public enum SecurityPermissionFlag  {
MS CF AllFlags = Assertion | UnmanagedCode | SkipVerification | Execution |
                 ControlThread | ControlEvidence | ControlPolicy |
                 SerializationFormatter | ControlDomainPolicy |
                 ControlPrincipal | ControlAppDomain |
                 RemotingConfiguration | Infrastructure | BindingRedirects,
   CF Assertion = 0x1,
MS CF BindingRedirects = 0x2000,
MS CF ControlAppDomain = 0x400,
MS CF ControlDomainPolicy = 0x100,
MS CF ControlEvidence = 0x20,
MS CF ControlPolicy = 0x40,
MS CF ControlPrincipal = 0x200,
   CF ControlThread = 0x10,
   CF Execution = 0x8,
MS CF Infrastructure = 0x1000,
   CF NoFlags = 0x0,
MS CF RemotingConfiguration = 0x800,
MS CF SerializationFormatter = 0x80,
   CF SkipVerification = 0x4,
   CF UnmanagedCode= 0x2,
 }
```

## Description

This enumeration is used by `System.Security.Permissions.SecurityPermission`.

`System.Security.Permissions.SecurityPermissionFlag` is a bit-field; specify multiple values using the bitwise OR operator.

For information on security, see Partition II of the CLI Specification.

[*Note:* Many of these flags are powerful and should only be granted to highly trusted code.]

## Example

```
using System.Security;
using System.Security.Permissions;

namespace Samples
{
  public class SecurityPermissionFlagSample
  {
    public static void Main()
    {
      SecurityPermission sp1 =
        new SecurityPermission(
          SecurityPermissionFlag.Assertion);
      SecurityPermission sp2 =
        new SecurityPermission(
          SecurityPermissionFlag.ControlEvidence);
      SecurityPermission sp3 =
        new SecurityPermission(
          SecurityPermissionFlag.Execution);
      SecurityPermission sp4 =
        new SecurityPermission(
          SecurityPermissionFlag.SkipVerification);
      IPermission ip = sp1.Union(sp2);
      ip = ip.Union(sp3);
      ip = ip.Union(sp4);
      Console.WriteLine(ip);
    }
  }
}
```

The output is:

```
<IPermission class="System.Security.Permissions.SecurityPermission, mscorlib,
Version=1.0.3300.0, Culture=neutral, PublicKeyToken=b77a5c561934e089"
             version="1"
             Flags="Assertion, SkipVerification, Execution, ControlEvidence"/>
```

# System.IO
# SeekOrigin Enum

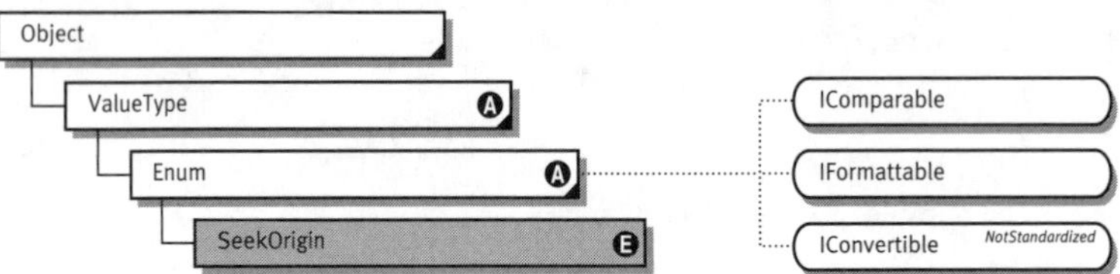




## Summary

Defines the seek reference positions.

## Type Summary

```
public enum SeekOrigin  {
      Begin = 0,
      Current = 1,
      End = 2,
}
```

## Description

The `System.IO.SeekOrigin` enumeration is used by the overrides of the `System.IO.Stream.Seek` method to set the seek reference point in a stream, which allows you to specify an offset from the reference point.

## Example

```
using System;
using System.IO;
using System.Text;

namespace Samples
{
  public class SeekOriginSample
  {
    public static void Main()
    {
      string s = "filestream.txt";
      FileStream fs = new FileStream(s,
                                     FileMode.OpenOrCreate,
                                     FileAccess.Write);
      fs.Seek(0, SeekOrigin.Begin);
      Console.WriteLine("Position: {0}",
                        fs.Position);
      fs.Seek(1, SeekOrigin.Current);
      Console.WriteLine("Position: {0}",
```

SeekOrigin Enum

```
                         fs.Position);
      fs.Seek(0, SeekOrigin.End);
      Console.WriteLine("Position: {0}",
                         fs.Position);
      fs.Seek(-1, SeekOrigin.End);
      Console.WriteLine("Position: {0}",
                         fs.Position);
      fs.Close();
    }
  }
}
```

The output is:

```
Position: 0
Position: 1
Position: 35
Position: 34
```

# System
# Single Structure

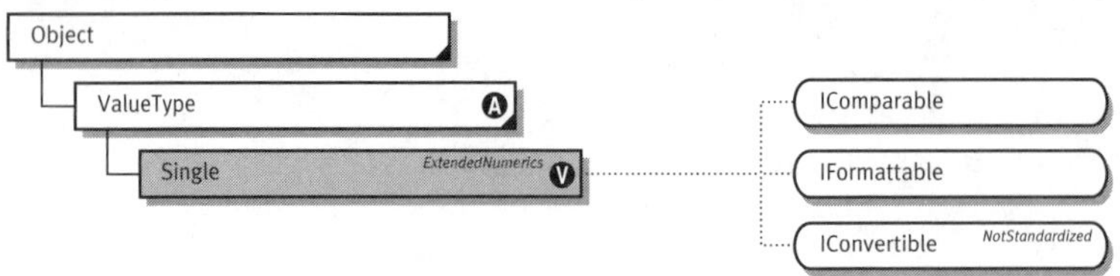


A B C D E F G H I J K L M N O P Q R S T U V W X Y Z

## Summary

Represents a 32-bit single-precision floating-point number.

## Type Summary

```
public struct Single : IComparable, IFormattable,
                       IConvertible
{
  // Fields
     public const float Epsilon = (float)1.4e-45;
     public const float MaxValue = (float)3.40282346638528859e+38;
     public const float MinValue = (float)-3.40282346638528859e+38;
     public const float NaN = (float)0.0 / (float)0.0;
     public const float NegativeInfinity = (float)-1.0 / (float)0.0;
     public const float PositiveInfinity = (float)1.0  / (float)0.0;

  // Methods
     public int CompareTo (object value);
     public override bool Equals (object obj);
     public override int GetHashCode ();
  MS public TypeCode GetTypeCode ();
     public static bool IsInfinity (float f);
     public static bool IsNaN (float f);
     public static bool IsNegativeInfinity (float f);
     public static bool IsPositiveInfinity (float f);
     public static float Parse (string s);
     public static float Parse (string s, NumberStyles style);
     public static float Parse (string s, NumberStyles style,
                                IFormatProvider provider);
     public static float Parse (string s, IFormatProvider provider);
     public override string ToString ();
     public string ToString (string format);
     public string ToString (string format, IFormatProvider provider);
     public string ToString (IFormatProvider provider);
```

Single Structure

```
    // Explicit Interface Members
    MS bool IConvertible.ToBoolean(IFormatProvider provider);
    MS byte IConvertible.ToByte(IFormatProvider provider);
    MS char IConvertible.ToChar(IFormatProvider provider);
    MS DateTime IConvertible.ToDateTime(IFormatProvider provider);
    MS decimal IConvertible.ToDecimal(IFormatProvider provider);
    MS double IConvertible.ToDouble(IFormatProvider provider);
    MS short IConvertible.ToInt16(IFormatProvider provider);
    MS int IConvertible.ToInt32(IFormatProvider provider);
    MS long IConvertible.ToInt64(IFormatProvider provider);
    MS sbyte IConvertible.ToSByte(IFormatProvider provider);
    MS float IConvertible.ToSingle(IFormatProvider provider);
    MS object IConvertible.ToType(Type type,IFormatProvider provider);
    MS ushort IConvertible.ToUInt16(IFormatProvider provider);
    MS uint IConvertible.ToUInt32(IFormatProvider provider);
    MS ulong IConvertible.ToUInt64(IFormatProvider provider);
}
```

> **BG** See my comments for `Double`.

## Description

`System.Single` is a 32-bit single precision floating-point type that represents values ranging from approximately 1.5E–45 to 3.4E+38 and from approximately –1.5E–45 to –3.4E+38 with a precision of 7 decimal digits. The `System.Single` type conforms to standard IEC 60559:1989, Binary Floating-Point Arithmetic for Microprocessor Systems.

A `System.Single` can represent the following values:

- The finite set of non-zero values of the form $s * m * 2^e$, where $s$ is 1 or –1, and $0 < m < 2^{24}$ and $-149 <= e <= 104$.
- Positive infinity and negative infinity. Infinities are produced by operations that produce results with a magnitude greater than that which can be represented by a `System.Single`, such as dividing a non-zero number by zero. For example, using `System.Single` operands, 1.0 / 0.0 yields positive infinity, and –1.0 / 0.0 yields negative infinity. Operations include passing parameters and returning values.
- The *Not-a-Number* value (NaN). NaN values are produced by invalid floating-point operations, such as dividing zero by zero.

When performing binary operations, if one of the operands is a floating-point type (`System.Double` or `System.Single`), then the other operand is required to be an integral type or a floating-point type and the operation is evaluated as follows:

- If one of the operands is of an integral type, then that operand is converted to the floating-point type of the other operand.
- Then, if either of the operands is of type `System.Double`, the other operand is converted to `System.Double`, and the operation is performed using at least the range and precision of the `System.Double` type. For numeric operations, the type of the result is `System.Double`.
- Otherwise, the operation is performed using at least the range and precision of the `System.Single` type and, for numeric operations, the type of the result is `System.Single`.

The floating-point operators, including the assignment operators, do not throw exceptions. Instead, in exceptional situations, the result of a floating-point operation is zero, infinity, or NaN, as described below:

- If the result of a floating-point operation is too small for the destination format, the result of the operation is zero.
- If the magnitude of the result of a floating-point operation is too large for the destination format, the result of the operation is positive infinity or negative infinity.
- If a floating-point operation is invalid, the result of the operation is NaN.
- If one or both operands of a floating-point operation are NaN, the result of the operation is NaN.

Conforming implementations of the CLI are permitted to perform floating-point operations using a precision that is higher than that required by the `System.Single` type. For example, hardware architectures that support an "extended" or "long double" floating-point type with greater range and precision than the `System.Single` type could implicitly perform all floating-point operations using this higher precision type. Expressions evaluated using a higher precision may cause a finite result to be produced instead of an infinity.

## Example

```
using System;

namespace Samples
{
  public class SingleSample
  {
    public static void Main()
```

Single Structure

```
    {
      Single max = Single.MaxValue,
             epsilon = Single.Epsilon,
             nan = Single.NaN,
             negativeInfinity = Single.NegativeInfinity,
             positiveInfinity = Single.PositiveInfinity,
             min = Single.MinValue;
      Console.WriteLine("MaxValue: {0}", max);
      Console.WriteLine("Epsilon: {0}", epsilon);
      Console.WriteLine("Nan: {0}", nan);
      Console.WriteLine("NegativeInfinity: {0}", negativeInfinity);
      Console.WriteLine("PositiveInfinity: {0}", positiveInfinity);
      Console.WriteLine("MinValue: {0}", min);
      string s = Single.MaxValue.ToString("R");
      Console.WriteLine("From String {0} yields {1}",
                        s, Single.Parse(s));
      string[] formats = {"C","E","e4","F","G","N","P","R"};
      foreach(string f in formats)
        Console.WriteLine("{0}.ToString(\"{1}\") yields {2}",
                          epsilon, f, epsilon.ToString(f));
    }
  }
}
```

The output is

```
MaxValue: 1.79769313486232E+308
Epsilon: 4.94065645841247E-324
Nan: NaN
NegativeInfinity: -Infinity
PositiveInfinity: Infinity
MinValue: -1.79769313486232E+308
From String 1.7976931348623157E+308 yields 1.79769313486232E+308
4.94065645841247E-324.ToString("C") yields $0.00
4.94065645841247E-324.ToString("E") yields 4.940656E-324
4.94065645841247E-324.ToString("e4") yields 4.9407e-324
4.94065645841247E-324.ToString("F") yields 0.00
4.94065645841247E-324.ToString("G") yields 4.94065645841247E-324
4.94065645841247E-324.ToString("N") yields 0.00
4.94065645841247E-324.ToString("P") yields 0.00 %
4.94065645841247E-324.ToString("R") yields 4.94065645841247E-324
```

# System StackOverflowException

BCL

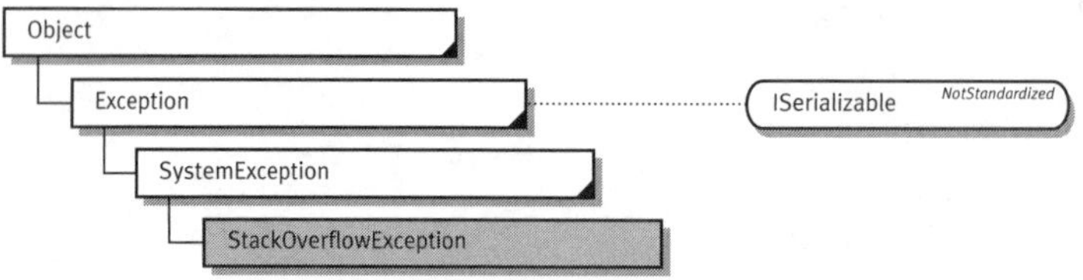




## Summary

Represents the error that occurs when the execution stack overflows due to too many method calls.

## Type Summary

```
public sealed class StackOverflowException : SystemException
{
  // Constructors
     public StackOverflowException ();
     public StackOverflowException (string message);
     public StackOverflowException (string message,
                                   Exception innerException);
}
```

## Description

[*Note:* `System.StackOverflowException` is thrown for execution stack overflow errors, typically in the case of a very deep or unbounded recursion. The localloc IL instruction throws `System.StackOverflowException`.]

## Example

```
using System;

namespace Samples
{
  public class StackOverflowSample
  {
    public static void recurse()
    {
      recurse();
    }
    public static void Main()
```

```
    {
      try
      {
        recurse();
      }
      catch(StackOverflowException e)
      {
        Console.WriteLine("Exception: {0}", e);
      }
    }
  }
}
```

The output is

```
Exception: System.StackOverflowException: Exception of type
System.StackOverflowException was thrown.
```

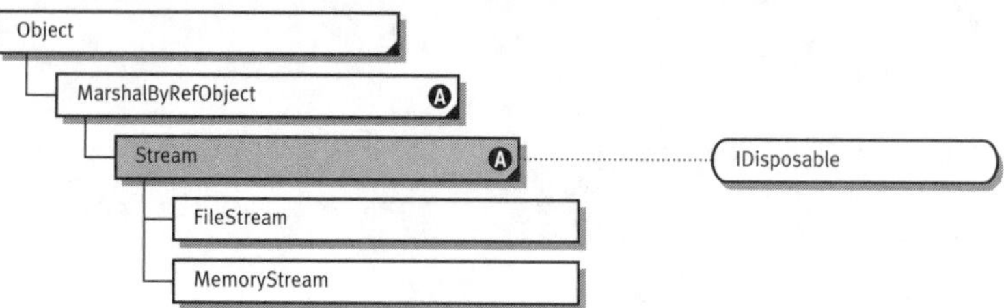




## Summary

Abstract base class for all stream implementations.

## Type Summary

```
public abstract class Stream : MarshalByRefObject,
                               IDisposable
{
  // Constructors
     protected Stream ();

  // Fields
     public static readonly Stream Null;

  // Properties
     public abstract bool CanRead { get; }
     public abstract bool CanSeek { get; }
     public abstract bool CanWrite { get; }
     public abstract long Length { get; }
     public abstract long Position { set; get; }

  // Methods
     public virtual IAsyncResult BeginRead (byte[] buffer,
                                            int offset,
                                            int count,
                                            AsyncCallback callback,
                                            object state);
     public virtual IAsyncResult BeginWrite (byte[] buffer,
                                             int offset,
                                             int count,
                                             AsyncCallback callback,
                                             object state);
     public virtual void Close ();
     protected virtual WaitHandle CreateWaitHandle ();
     public virtual int EndRead (IAsyncResult asyncResult);
     public virtual void EndWrite (IAsyncResult asyncResult);
     public abstract void Flush ();
     public abstract int Read (byte[] buffer,
                               int offset, int count);
```

```
        public virtual int ReadByte ();
        public abstract long Seek (long offset,
                                   SeekOrigin origin);
        public abstract void SetLength (long value);
        public abstract void Write (byte[] buffer,
                                    int offset,
                                    int count);
        public virtual void WriteByte (byte value);

    // Explicit Interface Members
        void IDisposable.Dispose ();
}
```

**BA** We designed this class to be the base type for all kinds of streams in the system, many of which have different capabilities. Some streams do not support random access (such as `NetworkStream`) and others only support reading rather than writing. We could have factored these flavors of streams into different interfaces, `IStream` with very little common functionality, `IReadableStream` with the read functionality, `IWriteableStream` with the writing functionality, and `ISeekableStream` with the seeking functionality. We opted not to go this route for a couple of reasons.

First, this option has too many interfaces to deal with and understand. Scanning through the reference pages of a book such as this one, it would be cumbersome to understand the relationships. Second, the scenarios where we needed to enforce a contract (such as "only writable streams can be passed to a method") were narrow.

Therefore we decided to model `Read`, `Write`, and `Seek` in this class and allow subclasses to throw a `NotSupportedException` where required. As is our practice, we provided predicates (`CanRead`, `CanWrite`, `CanSeek`) to allow clients to avoid causing an exception to be raised.

**KG** `Stream` is a clear situation where a class makes perfect sense for some users, and not for others. A typical VB user has never been exposed to the concept of streams and it can seem very forbidding. In general that is OK, because those types of users should not be using this class directly. However, the unfortunate outcome is that the naming standard affected more critical classes such as `StreamReader`, which we do expect anyone to be able to use.

**KC** `Stream` is an awesome base class that is a workhorse of the library. Stream-based I/O takes full advantage of the object-oriented nature of the CLR and helps in decoupling large parts of the library: xml, file io, networking, etc.

A B C D E F G H I J K L M N O P Q R S T U V W X Y Z

## Description

Streams involve three fundamental operations:

- You can read from streams. Reading is the transfer of data from a stream into a data structure, such as an array of bytes.
- You can write to streams. Writing is the transfer of data from a data structure into a stream.
- Streams can support seeking. Seeking is the querying and modifying of the current position within a stream. Seek capability depends on the kind of backing store a stream has. For example, network streams have no unified concept of a current position, and therefore typically do not support seeking.

All classes that represent streams inherit from the `System.IO.Stream` class. The `System.IO.Stream` class and its subclasses provide a generic view of data sources and repositories, isolating the programmer from the specific details of the operating system and underlying devices.

Subclasses are required to provide implementations only for the synchronous read and write methods. The asynchronous read and write methods are implemented via the synchronous ones. [*Note:* The `System.IO.Stream` synchronous read and write methods are `System.IO.Stream.Read` and `System.IO.Stream.Write`. The asynchronous read and write methods are `System.IO.Stream.BeginRead`, `System.IO.Stream.EndRead`, `System.IO.Stream.BeginWrite`, and `System.IO.Stream.EndWrite`.]

Depending on the underlying data source or repository, streams might support only some of these capabilities. An application can query a stream for its capabilities by using the `System.IO.Stream.CanRead`, `System.IO.Stream.CanWrite`, and `System.IO.Stream.CanSeek` properties.

The `System.IO.Stream.Read` and `System.IO.Stream.Write` methods read and write data in a variety of formats. For streams that support seeking, the `System.IO.Stream.Seek` and `System.IO.Stream.SetLength` methods and the `System.IO.Stream.Position` and `System.IO.Stream.Length` properties can be used to query and modify the current position and length of a stream.

Some stream implementations perform local buffering of the underlying data to improve performance. For such streams, the `System.IO.Stream.Flush` method can be used to clear any internal buffers and ensure that all data has been written to the underlying data source or repository.

Calling `System.IO.Stream.Close` on a `System.IO.Stream` flushes any buffered data, essentially calling `System.IO.Stream.Flush` for you. `System.IO.Stream.Close` also releases operating system resources such as file handles, network connections, or memory used for any internal buffering.

If you need a `System.IO.Stream` with no backing store (i.e., a bit bucket), use `System.IO.Stream.Null`.

## Example

```
using System;
using System.IO;
using System.Text;
using System.Threading;

namespace Samples
{
  public class MyEncodedStream: Stream
  {
    private Stream s;
    public MyEncodedStream(Stream s)
    {
      this.s = s;
    }
    public override bool CanRead {get {return s.CanRead;}}
    public override bool CanSeek {get {return s.CanSeek;}}
    public override bool CanWrite {get {return s.CanWrite;}}
    public override void Close() {s.Close();}
    public override void Flush() {s.Flush();}
    public override long Length {get {return s.Length;}}
    public override long Position
    {
      get {return s.Position;}
      set {s.Position = value;}
    }
    public override int Read(byte[] buffer,
                             int offset,
                             int count)
    {
      int bytesRead = s.Read(buffer, offset, count);
      for(int i = 0; i < bytesRead; i++)
        if(buffer[i] == byte.MaxValue)
          buffer[i] = byte.MinValue;
        else
          buffer[i] = ++buffer[i];
      return bytesRead;
    }
    public override long Seek(long offset, SeekOrigin origin)
    {
      return s.Seek(offset, origin);
    }
    public override void SetLength(long value)
    {
```

```
      s.SetLength(value);
    }
    public override  void Write(byte[] buffer, int offset,
                                  int count)
    {
      for(int i = 0; i < buffer.Length; i++)
        if(buffer[i] == byte.MinValue)
          buffer[i] = byte.MaxValue;
        else
          buffer[i] = --buffer[i];
      s.Write(buffer, offset, count);
    }
  }
  public class StreamSample
  {
    public class StateHolder
    {
      public byte[] bytes;
      public Stream s;
    }
    public static void Main()
    {
      MemoryStream ms = new MemoryStream();
      using(Stream s = new MyEncodedStream(ms))
      {
        DisplayInformationAboutStream(s);
        byte[] bytes = new byte[]{73, 66, 77, 87, 78, 84};
        s.Write(bytes, 0, bytes.Length);
        s.Seek(0, SeekOrigin.Begin);
        bytes = new Byte[6];
        ms.Read(bytes, 0, bytes.Length);
        foreach(byte b in bytes)
          Console.Write("{0}, ", b);
        Console.WriteLine();
        ms.Seek(0, SeekOrigin.Begin);
        s.Read(bytes, 0, bytes.Length);
        foreach(byte b in bytes)
          Console.Write("{0}, ", b);
        Console.WriteLine();
        Console.WriteLine("Position: {0}", s.Position);
        s.Seek(0, SeekOrigin.Begin);
        StateHolder sh = new StateHolder();
        sh.bytes = new byte[1000];
        sh.s = s;
        AsyncCallback ac = new AsyncCallback(CallMe);
        s.BeginRead(sh.bytes, 0, sh.bytes.Length, ac, sh);
        Thread.Sleep(1000);
      }
```

```
    }
    public static void CallMe(IAsyncResult asyncResult)
    {
      StateHolder sh = (StateHolder) asyncResult.AsyncState;
      int count = sh.s.EndRead(asyncResult);
      Console.WriteLine("Bytes read: {0} ", count);
      if(count != 0)
      {
        for(int i = 0; i < count; i++)
          Console.Write("{0}, ", sh.bytes[i]);
        Console.WriteLine();
      }
    }
    public static void DisplayInformationAboutStream(Stream s)
    {
      Console.WriteLine("Can read from stream: {0}", s.CanRead);
      Console.WriteLine("Can write to stream: {0}", s.CanWrite);
      Console.WriteLine("Can seek in stream: {0}", s.CanSeek);
    }
  }
}
```

The output is

```
Can read from stream: True
Can write to stream: True
Can seek in stream: True
72, 65, 76, 86, 77, 83,
73, 66, 77, 87, 78, 84,
Position: 6
Bytes read: 6
73, 66, 77, 87, 78, 84,
```

# System.IO StreamReader

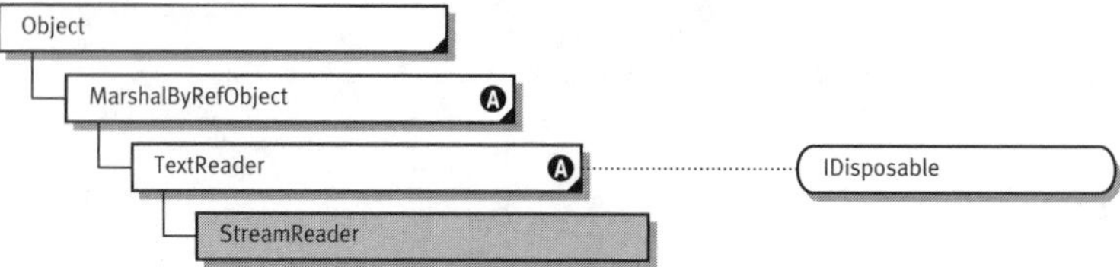


## Summary

Implements a `System.IO.Stream` that reads characters from a byte stream in a particular encoding.

## Type Summary

```
public class StreamReader : TextReader
{
  // Constructors
     public StreamReader (string path);
     public StreamReader (string path, bool detectEncodingFromByteOrderMarks);
     public StreamReader (string path, Encoding encoding);
     public StreamReader (string path, Encoding encoding,
                          bool detectEncodingFromByteOrderMarks);
     public StreamReader (string path, Encoding encoding,
                          bool detectEncodingFromByteOrderMarks,
                          int bufferSize);
     public StreamReader (Stream stream);
     public StreamReader (Stream stream, bool
                          detectEncodingFromByteOrderMarks);
     public StreamReader (Stream stream, Encoding encoding);
     public StreamReader (Stream stream, Encoding encoding,
                          bool detectEncodingFromByteOrderMarks);
     public StreamReader (Stream stream, Encoding encoding,
                          bool detectEncodingFromByteOrderMarks,
                          int bufferSize);

  // Fields
  MS public static readonly StreamReader Null;

  // Properties
     public virtual Stream BaseStream { get; }
     public virtual Encoding CurrentEncoding { get; }

  // Methods
     public override void Close ();
     public void DiscardBufferedData ();
     protected override void Dispose (bool disposing);
```

```
        public override int Peek ();
        public override int Read ();
        public override int Read (char[] buffer,
                                  int index, int count);
        public override string ReadLine ();
        public override string ReadToEnd ();
    }
```

> **KG** One of the most useful I/O classes, with one of the most confusing names. `FileReader` would have helped users find this class a lot more easily.

## Description

The `System.IO.StreamReader` class is designed for character input in a particular `System.Text.Encoding`, whereas subclasses of `System.IO.Stream` are designed for byte input and output.

[*Note:* `System.IO.StreamReader` defaults to UTF-8 encoding unless specified otherwise, instead of defaulting to the ANSI code page for the current system. UTF-8 handles Unicode characters correctly and provides consistent results on localized versions of the operating system. When reading from a `System.IO.Stream`, it is more efficient to use a buffer that is the same size as the internal buffer of the stream. By default, a `System.IO.StreamReader` is not thread safe. For a thread-safe wrapper, see `System.IO.TextReader.Synchronized`.]

## Example

```
using System;
using System.IO;
using System.Text;

namespace Samples
{
  public class StreamReaderSample
  {
    public static void Main()
    {
      string s = "streamreader.txt";
      using(StreamReader sr = new StreamReader(s))
      {
        DisplayInformationAboutStream(sr);
        Console.WriteLine(sr.ReadLine());
        Console.WriteLine((Char)sr.Peek());
        Console.WriteLine(sr.ReadLine());
      }
```

```
        Byte[] bytes = {72, 101, 108, 108, 111, (byte) '\n',
                        87, 111, 114, 108, 100};
        MemoryStream ms = new MemoryStream(bytes,
                                          0,
                                          bytes.Length);
        using(StreamReader sr = new StreamReader(ms))
        {
          DisplayInformationAboutStream(sr);
          Console.WriteLine(sr.ReadLine());
          Console.WriteLine((Char)sr.Peek());
          Console.WriteLine(sr.ReadLine());
        }
      }
      public static void DisplayInformationAboutStream(
                           StreamReader sr)
      {
        Console.WriteLine("CurrentEncoding: {0}",
                          sr.CurrentEncoding);
        Console.WriteLine("Can read from stream: {0}",
                          sr.BaseStream.CanRead);
        Console.WriteLine("Can write to stream: {0}",
                          sr.BaseStream.CanWrite);
        Console.WriteLine("Can seek in stream: {0}",
                          sr.BaseStream.CanSeek);
      }
    }
  }
```

The output is

```
CurrentEncoding: System.Text.UTF8Encoding
Can read from stream: True
Can write to stream: False
Can seek in stream: True
Hello world!
G
Goodbye world!
CurrentEncoding: System.Text.UTF8Encoding
Can read from stream: True
Can write to stream: True
Can seek in stream: True
Hello
W
World
```

# System.IO StreamWriter

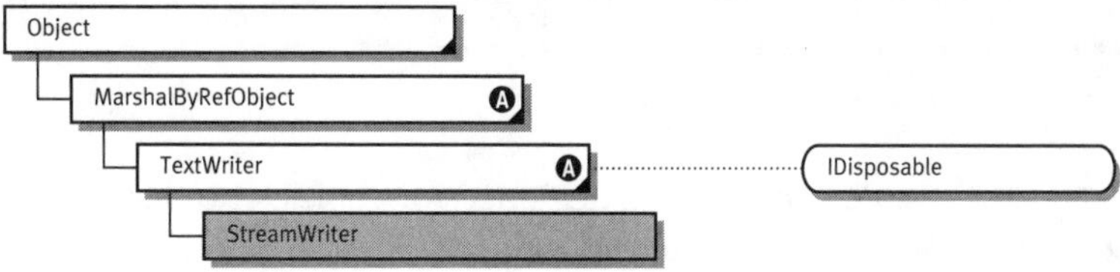


## Summary

Implements a `System.IO.Stream` wrapper that writes characters to a stream in a particular encoding.

## Type Summary

```
public class StreamWriter : TextWriter
{
  // Constructors
     public StreamWriter (string path);
     public StreamWriter (string path, bool append);
     public StreamWriter (string path, bool append,
                          Encoding encoding);
     public StreamWriter (string path, bool append,
                          Encoding encoding,
                          int bufferSize);
     public StreamWriter (Stream stream);
     public StreamWriter (Stream stream, Encoding encoding);
     public StreamWriter (Stream stream, Encoding encoding,
                          int bufferSize);

  // Fields
  MS public static readonly StreamWriter Null;

  // Properties
     public virtual bool AutoFlush { set; get; }
     public virtual Stream BaseStream { get; }
     public override Encoding Encoding { get; }

  // Methods
     public override void Close ();
     protected override void Dispose (bool disposing);
  CF ~StreamWriter () {}
     public override void Flush ();
     public override void Write (char value);
     public override void Write (char[] buffer);
     public override void Write (char[] buffer,
                                 int index, int count);
     public override void Write (string value);
}
```

**KG** See my comments on the `StreamReader` class.



## Description

The `System.IO.StreamWriter` class is designed for character output in a particular `System.Text.Encoding`, whereas subclasses of `System.IO.Stream` are designed for byte input and output.

`System.IO.StreamWriter` defaults to using an instance of `System.Text.UTF8-Encoding` unless specified otherwise. This instance of `System.Text.UTF8Encoding` is constructed such that the `System.Text.Encoding.GetPreamble` method returns the Unicode byte order mark written in UTF-8. The preamble of the encoding is added to a stream when you are not appending to an existing stream. This means any text file you create with `System.IO.StreamWriter` has three byte order marks at its beginning. UTF-8 handles all Unicode characters correctly and gives consistent results on localized versions of the operating system.

[*Note:* By default, `System.IO.StreamWriter` is not thread safe. For a thread-safe wrapper, see `System.IO.TextWriter.Synchronized`.]

## Example

```
using System;
using System.IO;
using System.Text;

namespace Samples
{
  public class StreamWriterSample
  {
    public static void Main()
    {
      string s = "streamwriter.txt";
      using(StreamWriter sw = new StreamWriter(s))
      {
        DisplayInformationAboutStream(sw);
        sw.WriteLine(DateTime.Now.ToString());
      }
      MemoryStream ms = new MemoryStream();
      using(StreamWriter sw = new StreamWriter(ms))
      {
        DisplayInformationAboutStream(sw);
        sw.WriteLine(DateTime.Now.ToString());
        Byte[] bytes = ((MemoryStream)sw.BaseStream).ToArray();
        foreach(Byte b in bytes)
          Console.Write((char)b);
```

```
      }
    }
    public static void DisplayInformationAboutStream(
                          StreamWriter sw)
    {
      Console.WriteLine("Encoding: {0}",
                        sw.Encoding);
      Console.WriteLine("Can read from stream: {0}",
                        sw.BaseStream.CanRead);
      Console.WriteLine("Can write to stream: {0}",
                        sw.BaseStream.CanWrite);
      Console.WriteLine("Can seek in stream: {0}",
                        sw.BaseStream.CanSeek);
    }
  }
}
```

The output is

```
Encoding: System.Text.UTF8Encoding
Can read from stream: False
Can write to stream: True
Can seek in stream: True
Encoding: System.Text.UTF8Encoding
Can read from stream: True
Can write to stream: True
Can seek in stream: True
```

# System
# String

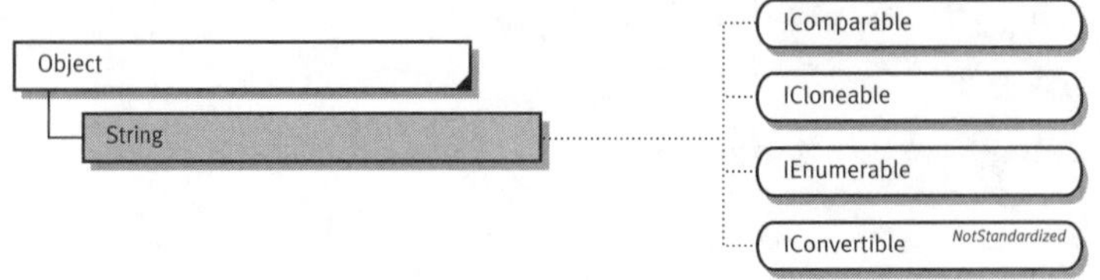


A B C D E F G H I J K L M N O P Q R S T U V W X Y Z

## Summary

Represents an immutable series of characters.

## Type Summary

```
public sealed class String : IComparable, ICloneable,
                             IConvertible, IEnumerable
{
  // Constructors
     unsafe public String (char* value);
     unsafe public String (char* value, int startIndex,
                           int length);
     public String (char c, int count);
     public String (char[] value);
     public String (char[] value, int startIndex,
                    int length);
  MS unsafe public String (sbyte* value);
MS CF unsafe public String (sbyte* value, int startIndex,
                           int length);
  CF unsafe public String (sbyte* value, int startIndex,
                           int length, Encoding enc);

  // Fields
     public static readonly string Empty = "";

  // Properties
     public char this[int index] { get; }
     public int Length { get; }

  // Methods
     public object Clone ();
     public static int Compare (string strA,
                                int indexA, string strB,
                                int indexB, int length);
     public static int Compare (string strA,
                                int indexA, string strB,
                                int indexB, int length,
                                bool ignoreCase);
  MS public static int Compare (string strA,
                                int indexA, string strB,
```

```
                                int indexB, int length,
                                bool ignoreCase,
                                CultureInfo culture);
   public static int Compare (string strA,
                              string strB);
   public static int Compare (string strA,
                              string strB,
                              bool ignoreCase);
MS public static int Compare (string strA,
                              string strB,
                              bool ignoreCase,
                              CultureInfo culture);
   public static int CompareOrdinal (string strA,
                                     int indexA,
                                     string strB,
                                     int indexB,
                                     int length);
   public static int CompareOrdinal (string strA,
                                     string strB);
   public int CompareTo (object value);
MS public int CompareTo (string strB);
MS public static string Concat (object arg0);
   public static string Concat (object arg0,
                                object arg1);
   public static string Concat (object arg0,
                                object arg1,
                                object arg2);
MS CF public static string Concat (object arg0,
                                object arg1,
                                object arg2,
                                object arg3);
   public static string Concat (params object[] args);
   public static string Concat (string str0,
                                string str1);
   public static string Concat (string str0,
                                string str1,
                                string str2);
MS public static string Concat (string str0,
                                string str1,
                                string str2,
                                string str3);
   public static string Concat (params string[] values);
   public static string Copy (string str);
   public void CopyTo (int sourceIndex, char[] destination,
                       int destinationIndex,
                       int count);
   public bool EndsWith (string value);
   public override bool Equals (object obj);
MS public bool Equals (string value);
```

```
   public static bool Equals (string a, string b);
   public static string Format (string format,
                                object arg0);
   public static string Format (string format,
                                object arg0,
                                object arg1);
   public static string Format (string format,
                                object arg0,
                                object arg1,
                                object arg2);
   public static string Format (string format,
                                params object[] args);
   public static string Format (IFormatProvider provider,
                                string format,
                                params object[] args);
CF public CharEnumerator GetEnumerator();
   public override int GetHashCode ();
MS public TypeCode GetTypeCode ();
   public int IndexOf (char value);
   public int IndexOf (char value, int startIndex);
   public int IndexOf (char value, int startIndex,
                       int count);
   public int IndexOf (string value);
   public int IndexOf (string value, int startIndex);
   public int IndexOf (string value, int startIndex,
                       int count);
   public int IndexOfAny (char[] anyOf);
   public int IndexOfAny (char[] anyOf, int startIndex);
   public int IndexOfAny (char[] anyOf, int startIndex,
                          int count);
   public string Insert (int startIndex, string value);
   public static string Intern (string str);
   public static string IsInterned (string str);
   public static string Join (string separator,
                              string[] value);
   public static string Join (string separator,
                              string[] value,
                              int startIndex,
                              int count);
   public int LastIndexOf (char value);
   public int LastIndexOf (char value, int startIndex);
   public int LastIndexOf (char value, int startIndex,
                           int count);
   public int LastIndexOf (string value);
   public int LastIndexOf (string value, int startIndex);
   public int LastIndexOf (string value, int startIndex,
                           int count);
   public int LastIndexOfAny (char[] anyOf);
   public int LastIndexOfAny (char[] anyOf,
```

```
                                  int startIndex);
      public int LastIndexOfAny (char[] value,
                                  int startIndex,
                                  int count);
      public static bool operator ==(string a,
                                     string b);
      public static bool operator !=(string a,
                                     string b);
      public string PadLeft (int totalWidth);
      public string PadLeft (int totalWidth, char paddingChar);
      public string PadRight (int totalWidth);
      public string PadRight (int totalWidth,
                               char paddingChar);
      public string Remove (int startIndex, int count);
      public string Replace (char oldChar, char newChar);
      public string Replace (string oldValue,
                              string newValue);
      public string[] Split (params char[] separator);
   CF public string[] Split (char[] separator,
                              int count);
      public bool StartsWith (string value);
      public string Substring (int startIndex);
      public string Substring (int startIndex,
                                int length);
      public char[] ToCharArray ();
   CF public char[] ToCharArray (int startIndex,
                                  int length);
      public string ToLower ();
   MS public string ToLower (CultureInfo culture);
      public override string ToString ();
      public string ToString (IFormatProvider provider);
      public string ToUpper ();
   MS public string ToUpper (CultureInfo culture);
      public string Trim ();
      public string Trim (params char[] trimChars);
      public string TrimEnd (params char[] trimChars);
      public string TrimStart (params char[] trimChars);

   // Explicit Interface Members
   CF IEnumerator IEnumerable.GetEnumerator();
   MS bool IConvertible.ToBoolean(IFormatProvider provider);
   MS byte IConvertible.ToByte(IFormatProvider provider);
   MS char IConvertible.ToChar(IFormatProvider provider);
   MS DateTime IConvertible.ToDateTime(IFormatProvider provider);
   MS decimal IConvertible.ToDecimal(IFormatProvider provider);
   MS double IConvertible.ToDouble(IFormatProvider provider);
   MS short IConvertible.ToInt16(IFormatProvider provider);
   MS int IConvertible.ToInt32(IFormatProvider provider);
   MS long IConvertible.ToInt64(IFormatProvider provider);
```

```
    MS sbyte IConvertible.ToSByte(IFormatProvider provider);
    MS float IConvertible.ToSingle(IFormatProvider provider);
    MS object IConvertible.ToType(Type type,IFormatProvider provider);
    MS ushort IConvertible.ToUInt16(IFormatProvider provider);
    MS uint IConvertible.ToUInt32(IFormatProvider provider);
    MS ulong IConvertible.ToUInt64(IFormatProvider provider);
}
```

**AH** While it may seem obvious, one of the big advantages of .NET is that it defines a single representation for strings. During its evolution, the Windows platform has accrued quite a collection of string representations: ANSI strings, Unicode strings, `null` terminated strings, length prefixed strings, etc. Unifying all of those has made .NET a much simpler and safer place to program.

**BA** Why did we seal the `String` class? This is one of the most common questions about the BCL. In general I am not a big fan of sealing classes arbitrarily. As a general rule we designed classes in the BCL with extensibility in mind. However, from a pragmatic standpoint that is not always possible. Because a fully extensible design is not always practical, we use non-virtual members by default and only use virtual members where they have been designed for extensibility. This limits the number of places in the implementation of the class that may be calling into user code. However, in the case of `String` it was necessary to seal it because the JIT needs to understand the exact physical layout of the string to perform optimizations.

`String` being immutable is a very nice thing for the type system. It means you do not have to worry about ownership issues. You can pass a reference to a string in your internal implementation to clients without a worry that they will modify your data. However, when building up a string this immutability frequently means lots of copies of the string are being made. For example, in the following code snippet each line creates a new copy of the string:

```
string s = "As ";
s+=" You ";
s = s.Append ("wish    ");
s = s.ToUpper();
s = s.Trim();
```

In general this is not a problem. The GC is tuned to take care of small short-lived allocations like this. But in performance-sensitive parts of your application (such as a tight loop) it could be an issue. In such cases, we recommend using `StringBuilder`.

*CONTINUED*

**BG** `String` has three different ways to test for equality. The first is the `Compare` family of methods, which are generally case-sensitive and use the current thread's culture for the comparison rules, but the comparison is always linguistically correct. By this, I mean we handle somewhat obscure Unicode concepts like combining characters and diacritics in the manner required by the Unicode specification. The second is `CompareOrdinal` and `Equals`, which do bitwise comparisons in memory, similar to C's `memcmp` or `strcmp` methods. A memory comparison such as this works consistently on all machines, independent of their culture. The third way to do string comparison with the .NET Framework is by using the `CompareInfo` class, which can be culture-sensitive or not, can be case-insensitive, and can special-case certain language aspects, such as kana handling in Japanese or specifying string sorting instead of word sorting.

**KG** We get more requests to add functionality to the `String` class than any other. You can see that it already has a plethora of operations: we therefore consider all new functionality carefully before adding it. `String` is one of the hardest classes to modify since even the smallest and most innocuous change will have effects that we do not even consider. Expect `String` to grow over time and for any APIs to be long-lived.

**JR** Note that a `String` is really a set of UTF-16 code points, which will be a character unless the code point represents a high or low surrogate value. To properly traverse the characters of a string, you should use the `System.Globalization.StringInfo` class's methods.

## Description

An *index* is the position of a character within a string. The first character in the string is at index 0. The length of a string is the number of characters it is made up of. The last accessible *index* of a string instance is `System.String.Length-1`.

Strings are immutable; once created, the contents of a `System.String` do not change. Combining operations, such as `System.String.Replace`, cannot alter existing strings. Instead, such operations return a new string that contains the results of the operation, an unchanged string, or the null value. To perform modifications to a `System.String` use the `System.Text.StringBuilder`.

Implementations of `System.String` are required to contain a variable-length character buffer positioned a fixed number of bytes after the beginning of the String object. [*Note:* The `System.Runtime.CompilerServices.RuntimeHelpers.OffsetToStringData` method returns the number of bytes between the start of the String object and the character buffer. This information is intended primarily for use by compilers, not application programmers. For additional information, see `System.Runtime.CompilerServices.RuntimeHelpers.OffsetToStringData`.]

[*Note:* Comparisons and searches are case-sensitive by default and unless otherwise specified, use the culture defined for the current thread to determine the order of the alphabet used by the strings. This information is then used to compare the two strings on a character-by-character basis. Uppercase letters evaluate greater than their lower case equivalents. The following characters are considered white space when present in a `System.String` instance: 0x9, 0xA, 0xB, 0xC, 0xD, 0x20, 0xA0, 0x2000, 0x2001, 0x2002, 0x2003, 0x2004, 0x2005, 0x2006, 0x2007, 0x2008, 0x2009, 0x200A, 0x200B, 0x3000, and 0xFEFF. The null character is defined as hexadecimal 0x00. The `System.String(System.String)` constructor is omitted for performance reasons. If you need a copy of a `System.String`, consider using `System.String.Copy` or the `System.Text.StringBuilder` class. To insert a formatted string representation of an object into a string use the `System.String.Format` methods. These methods take one or more arguments to be formatted and a format string. The format string contains literals and zero or more format specifications in the form { *N* [, *M*][:*formatSpecifier*]}, where: If an object referenced in the format string implements `System.IFormattable`, then the `System.IFormattable.ToString` method of the object provides the formatting. If the argument does not implement `System.IFormattable`, then the `System.Object.ToString` method of the object provides default formatting, and *formatSpecifier*, if present, is ignored. For an example that demonstrates this, see Example 2. To include a curly bracket in a formatted string, specify the bracket twice; for example, specify "{{" to include "{" in the formatted string. See Example 1. The `System.Console` class exposes the same functionality as the `System.String.Format` methods via `System.Console.Write` and `System.Console.WriteLine`. The primary difference is that the `System.String.Format` methods return the formatted string, while the `System.Console` methods write the formatted string to a stream.]

## Examples

### *Example 1*

```
using System;

namespace Samples
{
  public class StringSample
  {
    public static void Main()
    {
      string s = "Hello World!";
      Console.WriteLine("\"{0}\".Length: {1}",
                        s, s.Length);
```

```
        Console.WriteLine("\"{0}\".ToUpper(): {1}",
                          s, s.ToUpper());
        Console.WriteLine("\"{0}\".ToLower(): {1}",
                          s, s.ToLower());
        char c = 'l';
        Console.WriteLine("\"{0}\".IndexOf({1}): {2}",
                          s, c, s.IndexOf(c));
        int i = 5;
        Console.WriteLine("\"{0}\".IndexOf({1}, {2}): {3}",
                          s, c, i, s.IndexOf(c,i));
        Console.WriteLine("\"{0}\".LastIndexOf({1}): {2}",
                          s, c, s.LastIndexOf(c));
      }
    }
}
```

The output is

```
"Hello World!".Length: 12
"Hello World!".ToUpper(): HELLO WORLD!
"Hello World!".ToLower(): hello world!
"Hello World!".IndexOf(l): 2
"Hello World!".IndexOf(l, 5): 9
"Hello World!".LastIndexOf(l): 9
```

### *Example 2*

```
using System;

namespace Samples
{
  public class StringFormatSample
  {
    public class FortyTwoNotFormattable
    {
      public override string ToString()
      {
        return "*42";
      }
    }
    public class FortyTwoFormattable: IFormattable
    {
      public override string ToString()
      {
            return "#42";
      }
      public string ToString(string format,
                             IFormatProvider formatProvider)
```

```
        {
              return 42.ToString(format, formatProvider);
        }
      }
      public static void Main()
      {
        FortyTwoNotFormattable noFormatting =
                                 new FortyTwoNotFormattable();
        FortyTwoFormattable formatting = new FortyTwoFormattable();
        Console.WriteLine("object");
        Console.WriteLine(noFormatting);
        Console.WriteLine(formatting);
        Console.WriteLine("object.ToString()");
        Console.WriteLine(noFormatting.ToString());
        Console.WriteLine(formatting.ToString());
        Console.WriteLine("String.Format(\"{0}\", object)");
        Console.WriteLine(String.Format("{0}", noFormatting));
        Console.WriteLine(String.Format("{0}", formatting));
        Console.WriteLine("String.Format(\"{0,15:P}\", object)");
        Console.WriteLine(String.Format("{0,15:P}", noFormatting));
        Console.WriteLine(String.Format("{0,15:P}", formatting));
      }
    }
  }
```

The output is

```
object
*42
42
object.ToString()
*42
#42
String.Format("{0}", object)
*42
42
String.Format("{0,15:P}", object)
             *42
     4,200.00 %
```

# System.Text StringBuilder

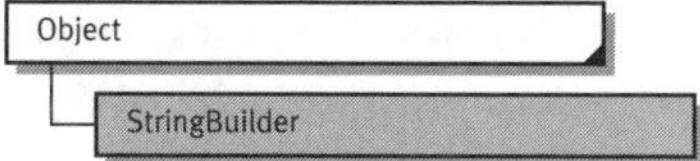




## Summary

Represents a mutable string of characters.

## Type Summary

```
public sealed class StringBuilder
{
  // Constructors
     public StringBuilder ();
     public StringBuilder (int capacity);
  MS public StringBuilder (int capacity, int maxCapacity);
     public StringBuilder (string value);
  MS public StringBuilder (string value, int capacity);
  MS public StringBuilder (string value, int startIndex,
                           int length, int capacity);

  // Properties
     public int Capacity { set; get; }
     public char this[int index] { set; get; }
     public int Length { set; get; }
  MS public int MaxCapacity { get; }

  // Methods
     public StringBuilder Append (bool value);
     public StringBuilder Append (byte value);
     public StringBuilder Append (char value);
     public StringBuilder Append (char value, int repeatCount);
     public StringBuilder Append (char[] value);
     public StringBuilder Append (char[] value, int startIndex, int charCount);
  CF public StringBuilder Append (decimal value);
     public StringBuilder Append (double value);
     public StringBuilder Append (float value);
     public StringBuilder Append (int value);
     public StringBuilder Append (long value);
     public StringBuilder Append (object value);
     public StringBuilder Append (sbyte value);
     public StringBuilder Append (short value);
     public StringBuilder Append (string value);
     public StringBuilder Append (string value, int startIndex, int count);
     public StringBuilder Append (uint value);
     public StringBuilder Append (ulong value);
```

```
    public StringBuilder Append (ushort value);
 CF public StringBuilder AppendFormat (string format, object arg0);
 CF public StringBuilder AppendFormat (string format, object arg0,
                                       object arg1);
 CF public StringBuilder AppendFormat (string format, object arg0,
                                       object arg1, object arg2);
 CF public StringBuilder AppendFormat (string format, object[] args);
    public StringBuilder AppendFormat (params IFormatProvider provider,
                                       string format, params object[] args);
 CF public int EnsureCapacity (int capacity);
 CF public bool Equals (StringBuilder sb);
 CF public StringBuilder Insert (int index, bool value);
 CF public StringBuilder Insert (int index, byte value);
 CF public StringBuilder Insert (int index, char value);
    public StringBuilder Insert (int index, char[] value);
    public StringBuilder Insert (int index, char[] value,
                                 int startIndex, int charCount);
 CF public StringBuilder Insert (int index, decimal value);
 CF public StringBuilder Insert (int index, double value);
 CF public StringBuilder Insert (int index, float value);
 CF public StringBuilder Insert (int index, int value);
 CF public StringBuilder Insert (int index, long value);
 CF public StringBuilder Insert (int index, object value);
 CF public StringBuilder Insert (int index, sbyte value);
 CF public StringBuilder Insert (int index, short value);
    public StringBuilder Insert (int index, string value);
    public StringBuilder Insert (int index, string value, int count);
 CF public StringBuilder Insert (int index, uint value);
 CF public StringBuilder Insert (int index, ulong value);
 CF public StringBuilder Insert (int index, ushort value);
    public StringBuilder Remove (int startIndex, int length);
    public StringBuilder Replace (char oldChar, char newChar);
    public StringBuilder Replace (char oldChar, char newChar,
                                  int startIndex, int count);
    public StringBuilder Replace (string oldValue, string newValue);
    public StringBuilder Replace (string oldValue, string newValue,
                                  int startIndex, int count);
    public override string ToString ();
    public string ToString (int startIndex,
                            int length);
}
```

**BA** Notice we overload several of the methods with all the base types (`Insert`, `Append`, etc). As a general rule this is not necessary. Because `System.Object` is the root of the inheritance hierarchy for all types in the system just having a single method that takes `System.Object` will work. One issue with doing that is casting a base type (or any value type for that matter) to an `Object` in order to call this method is a boxing operation that creates temporary memory on the GC heap. In general this is not a problem because the GC is tuned to handle small short-lived instances such as these. However, in a tight loop it could be an issue. Therefore, we provide these special cases that avoid the box.

**KG** In retrospect, putting the `StringBuilder` class in the `System.Text` namespace was a mistake. People cannot find it, even though they know what it is for. It should have been in the `System` namespace.

**KC** `StringBuilder` should be in the root `System` namespace. Any real-life application has need for it and it's more related to `String` than to other types in `System.Text` in which it resides. `Namespace` factoring is another tricky part of designing large reusable libraries. Too many types in one namespace make the namespace diffcult to understand. Too few types in a namespace make the namespace difficult to use. Namespaces should help in avoiding and resolving naming conflicts and to organize types in a logical hierarchy. The problem is that the namespace hierarchy is static and just as any static hierarchy, no matter how you design it, it is never perfect in every scenario.

**JR** You should use `StringBuilder` when doing several string manipulations. However, it is strange that `String` offers `ToLower`, `ToUpper`, `EndsWith`, `PadLeft`, and `Trim` methods, but `StringBuilder` does not. Hopefully, a future version of the BCL will give greater parity between these two classes.

## Description

This class represents string-like objects that are mutable. After a `System.Text.StringBuilder` object has been created, it can be directly modified by removing, replacing, or inserting characters. This contrasts the `System.String` class, which represents an immutable stringof characters.

The `System.Text.StringBuilder.Capacity` of an instance of the `System.Text.StringBuilder` class is the maximum number of characters it can hold in the currently allocated space. The `System.Text.StringBuilder` will dynamically allocate more space when it is required.

Unlike most types in the Base Class Library, the arguments to `System.Text.StringBuilder` members are assumed to be passed as in/out arguments (passed by reference). [*Note:* Normally arguments are `in` arguments (passed by value) unless explicitly declared as out or in/out.]

[*Note:* An instance of `System.String` is said to be "immutable" because its value cannot be modified once it has been created. Methods on `System.String` that appear to modify a `System.String` instance actually return a new instance containing the modification. The `System.Text.StringBuilder` class provides methods that actually modify the contents of a string-like object. Relational operators only perform reference comparisons (unless overloaded by a particular language compiler). Despite this restriction, relational operators can be used to compare `System.String` objects that are assigned literal values. Their values are immutable and can't change, so a reference comparison is sufficient. Because `System.Text.StringBuilder` instances are mutable, they should not be compared with relational operators. For performance reasons a `System.Text.StringBuilder` might allocate more memory than needed. The amount of memory allocated is implementation specific.]

## Example

```
using System;
using System.Text;

namespace Samples
{
  public class StringBuilderSample
  {
    public static void Main()
    {
      StringBuilder sb = new StringBuilder("Hello");
      Console.WriteLine("Capacity: {0}",
                        sb.Capacity);
      Console.WriteLine("MaxCapacity: {0}",
                        sb.MaxCapacity);
      Console.WriteLine("Length: {0}",
                        sb.Length);
      sb.Append(" world! ");
      sb.Insert(11, " from DAMIEN");
      sb.Replace("DAMIEN", "damien");
      sb.AppendFormat("appended at {0:dd/MM/yy}",
                      DateTime.Now);
      string s = sb.ToString();
      sb.Remove(11, 13);
      Console.WriteLine(s);
      Console.WriteLine(sb);
    }
  }
}
```

The output is

```
Capacity: 16
MaxCapacity: 2147483647
Length: 5
Hello world from damien! appended at 23/06/03
Hello world appended at 23/06/03
```

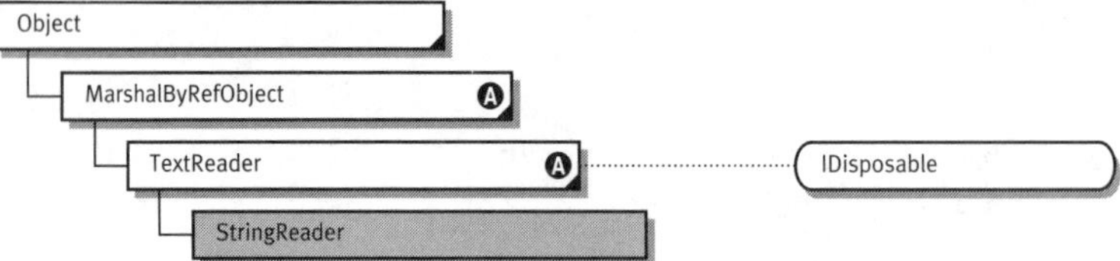




## Summary

Implements a `System.IO.TextReader` that reads from a string.

## Type Summary

```
public class StringReader : TextReader
{
  // Constructors
     public StringReader (string s);

  // Methods
     public override void Close ();
     protected override void Dispose (bool disposing);
     public override int Peek ();
     public override int Read ();
     public override int Read (char[] buffer,
                               int index, int count);
     public override string ReadLine ();
     public override string ReadToEnd ();
}
```

**BG** `StringReader` and `StringWriter` have been some of the harder classes for people to get their heads around in the `IO` namespace. They are roughly similar to C++'s `strstream`. They allow you to read and write to a `String` using the same API's you'd use to write to any `Stream`. Hence, the `TextReader` and `TextWriter` base classes.

## Example

```
using System;
using System.IO;

namespace Samples
{
  public class StringReaderSample
```

```
  {
    public static void Main()
    {
      string s = "damien\nmark\nbrad\n";
      using(StringReader sr = new StringReader(s))
      {
        Console.WriteLine(sr.ReadLine());
        Console.WriteLine((Char)sr.Peek());
        Console.WriteLine((Char)sr.Read());
        Console.WriteLine(sr.ReadToEnd());
      }
    }
  }
}
```

The output is

```
damien
m
m
ark
brad
```

# System.IO StringWriter

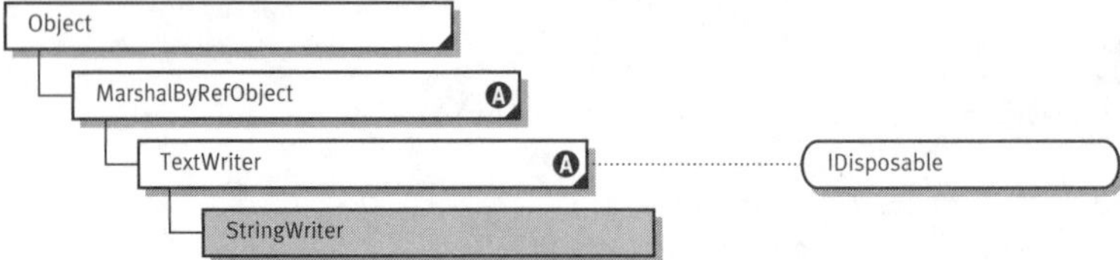




## Summary

Implements a `System.IO.TextWriter` that writes information to a string.

## Type Summary

```
public class StringWriter : TextWriter
{
  // Constructors
     public StringWriter ();
     public StringWriter (IFormatProvider formatProvider);
     public StringWriter (StringBuilder sb);
     public StringWriter (StringBuilder sb, IFormatProvider formatProvider);

  // Properties
     public override Encoding Encoding { get; }

  // Methods
     public override void Close ();
     protected override void Dispose (bool disposing);
     public virtual StringBuilder GetStringBuilder ();
     public override string ToString ();
     public override void Write (char value);
     public override void Write (char[] buffer,
                                 int index, int count);
     public override void Write (string value);
}
```

## Example

```
using System;
using System.IO;

namespace Samples
{
  public class StringWriterSample
  {
    public static void Main()
```

```
    {
      using(StringWriter sw = new StringWriter())
      {
        sw.Write("damien ");
        char[] chars = {'m', 'a', 'r', 'k', ' '};
        foreach(char c in chars)
          sw.Write(c);
        sw.WriteLine("brad");
        Console.WriteLine(sw);
      }
    }
  }
}
```

The output is

```
damien mark brad
```

# System.Threading SynchronizationLockException BCL

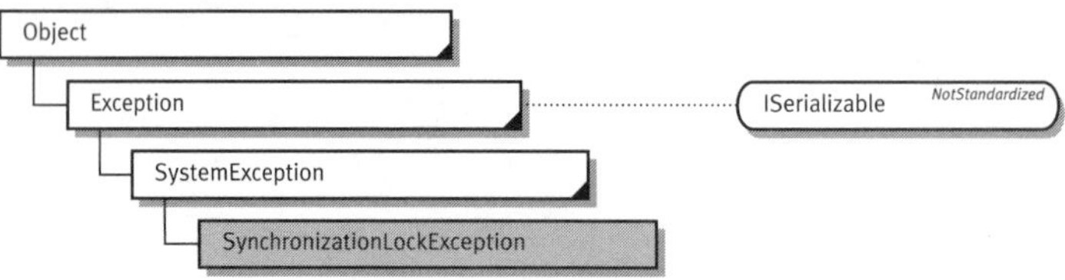


## Summary

Represents the error that occurs when a method requires the caller to own the lock on a given `System.Threading.Monitor`, and the method is invoked by a caller that does not own that lock.

## Type Summary

```
  CF public class SynchronizationLockException : SystemException
  {
    // Constructors
    CF public SynchronizationLockException ();
    CF public SynchronizationLockException (string message);
    CF public SynchronizationLockException (string message,
                                            Exception innerException);
MS  CF protected SynchronizationLockException (SerializationInfo info,
                                               StreamingContext context);
  }
```

## Description

`System.Threading.SynchronizationLockException` is thrown if the `System.Threading.Monitor.Pulse`, `System.Threading.Monitor.PulseAll`, or `System.Threading.Monitor.Wait` methods are invoked for a specified object, but the caller does not own the lock on that object. `System.Threading.SynchronizationLockException` is also thrown when the `System.Threading.Monitor.Exit` method is called to release the lock on an object, but the caller does not own the lock on that object.

To acquire the lock on an object, use `System.Threading.Monitor.Enter`. To release the lock on an object, use `System.Threading.Monitor.Exit`.

## Example

```
using System;
using System.Threading;
using System.Collections;

namespace Samples
{
  public class SynchronizationLockExceptionSample
  {
    private static Object o = new Object();
    public static void Main()
    {
      try
      {
        Monitor.Wait(o);
      }
      catch(SynchronizationLockException e)
      {
        Console.WriteLine("Exception: {0}", e);
      }
    }
  }
}
```

The output is

```
Exception: System.Threading.SynchronizationLockException: Object synchronization
method was called from an unsynchronized block of code.
   at System.Threading.Monitor.ObjWait(Boolean exitContext, Int32
millisecondsTimeout, Object obj)
   at System.Threading.Monitor.Wait(Object obj, Int32 millisecondsTimeout, Boolean
exitContext)
   at System.Threading.Monitor.Wait(Object obj)
   at Samples.SynchronizationLockExceptionSample.Main() in C:\Books\BCL\Samples\
System.Threading\SynchronizationLockException\SynchronizationLockException.cs:line 14
```

# System
# SystemException

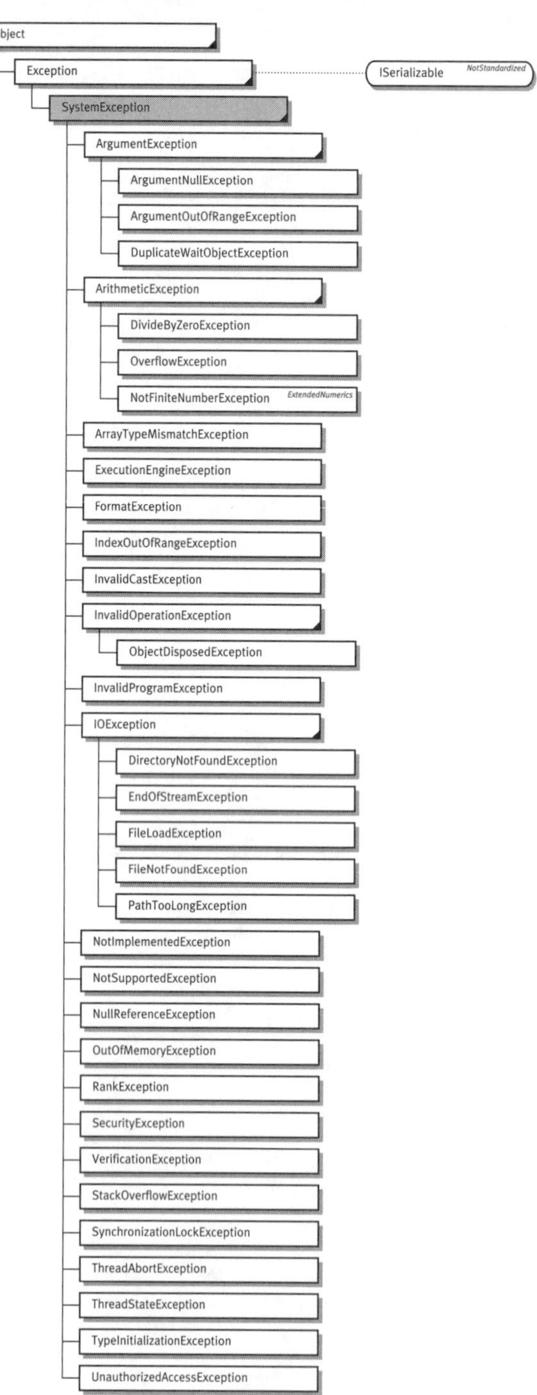

## Summary

`System.SystemException` is the base class for all exceptions defined by the system.

## Type Summary

```
public class SystemException : Exception
{
  // Constructors
     public SystemException ();
     public SystemException (string message);
     public SystemException (string message,
                             Exception innerException);
MS CF protected SystemException (SerializationInfo info,
                                StreamingContext context);
}
```

> **JR** You should not define new exception classes derived from `SystemException`; use `Exception` instead. In addition, you should not write code that catches `SystemException`.

## Description

This class is provided as a means to differentiate between exceptions defined by the system versus exceptions defined by applications. [*Note*: For more information on exceptions defined by applications, see `System.ApplicationException`.]

[*Note:* `System.SystemException` does not provide information as to the cause of the Exception. In most scenarios, instances of this class should not be thrown. In cases where this class is instantiated, a human-readable message describing the error should be passed to the constructor.]

## Example

The following example demonstrates catching an exception type that derives from `SystemException`. There is, however, no valid scenario for catching a `SystemException` type.

```
using System;

namespace Samples
{
  public class SystemExceptionSample
  {
    public static void Main()
    {
```

```
            try
            {
              string s = null;
              Console.WriteLine(s.ToString());
            }
            catch(SystemException e)
            {
              Console.WriteLine("Exception: {0}", e);
            }
          }
        }
      }
```

The output is

```
Exception: System.NullReferenceException: Object reference not set to an instance
of an object.
   at Samples.SystemExceptionSample.Main() in C:\Books\BCL\Samples\System\
SystemException\SystemException.cs:line 12
```

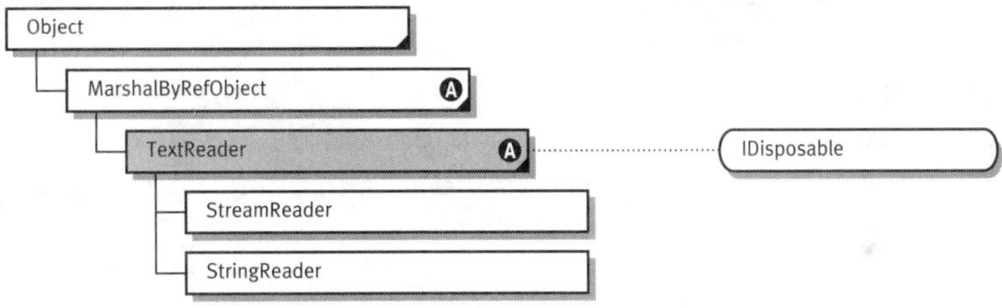


## Summary

Represents an object that can read a sequential series of characters.

## Type Summary

```
public abstract class TextReader : MarshalByRefObject,
                                   IDisposable
{
  // Constructors
     protected TextReader ();

  // Fields
     public static readonly TextReader Null;

  // Methods
     public virtual void Close ();
     protected virtual void Dispose (bool disposing);
     public virtual int Peek ();
     public virtual int Read ();
     public virtual int Read (char[] buffer,
                          int index, int count);
     public virtual int ReadBlock (char[] buffer,
                               int index,
                               int count);
     public virtual string ReadLine ();
     public virtual string ReadToEnd ();
     public static TextReader Synchronized (TextReader reader);

  // Explicit Interface Members
     void IDisposable.Dispose ();
 }
```

## Description

System.IO.TextReader is designed for character input, whereas the System.IO.StreamReader is designed for byte input and the System.IO.StringReader class is designed for reading from a string.

By default, a System.IO.TextReader is not thread safe. For information on creating a thread-safe System.IO.TextReader, see System.IO.TextReader.Synchronized.

## Example

```
using System;
using System.IO;
using System.Text;

namespace Samples
{
  public class TextReaderSample
  {
    public static void Main()
    {
      string s = "textreader.txt";
      using(TextReader tr = new StreamReader(s))
      {
        Console.WriteLine(tr.ReadLine());
        Console.WriteLine((Char)tr.Peek());
        char[] chars = new Char[4];
        tr.Read(chars, 0, chars.Length);
        foreach(char c in chars)
          Console.Write(c);
        Console.WriteLine(tr.ReadToEnd());
      }
    }
  }
}
```

The output is

```
Hello world!
G
Goodbye world!
```

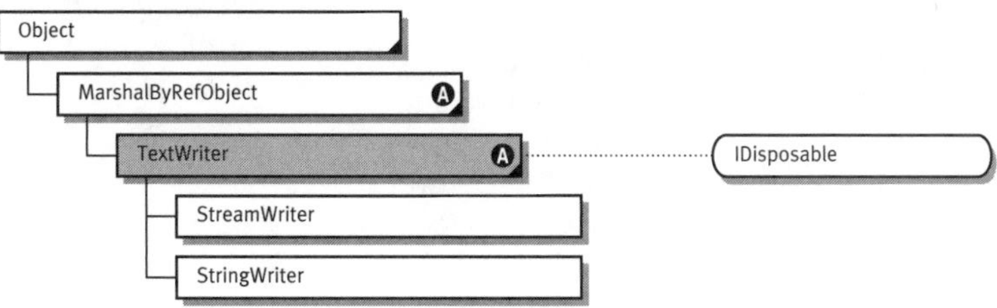


## Summary

Represents a writer that can write a sequential series of characters.

## Type Summary

```
public abstract class TextWriter : MarshalByRefObject,
                                   IDisposable
{
  // Constructors
     protected TextWriter ();
     protected TextWriter (IFormatProvider formatProvider);

  // Fields
  MS protected char[] CoreNewLine = new char [] {'\n'};
     public static readonly TextWriter Null;

  // Properties
     public abstract Encoding Encoding { get; }
     public virtual IFormatProvider FormatProvider { get; }
     public virtual string NewLine { set; get; }

  // Methods
     public virtual void Close ();
     protected virtual void Dispose (bool disposing);
     public virtual void Flush ();
     public static TextWriter Synchronized (TextWriter writer);
     public virtual void Write (bool value);
     public virtual void Write (char value);
     public virtual void Write (char[] buffer);
     public virtual void Write (char[] buffer,
                                int index, int count);
     public virtual void Write (decimal value);
     public virtual void Write (double value);
     public virtual void Write (float value);
     public virtual void Write (int value);
     public virtual void Write (long value);
     public virtual void Write (object value);
```

```
    public virtual void Write (string value);
    public virtual void Write (string format,
                               object arg0);
    public virtual void Write (string format,
                               object arg0,
                               object arg1);
 CF public virtual void Write (string format,
                               object arg0,
                               object arg1,
                               object arg2);
    public virtual void Write (string format,
                               params object[] arg);
    public virtual void Write (uint value);
    public virtual void Write (ulong value);
    public virtual void WriteLine ();
    public virtual void WriteLine (bool value);
    public virtual void WriteLine (char value);
    public virtual void WriteLine (char[] buffer);
    public virtual void WriteLine (char[] buffer,
                                   int index,
                                   int count);
    public virtual void WriteLine (decimal value);
    public virtual void WriteLine (double value);
    public virtual void WriteLine (float value);
    public virtual void WriteLine (int value);
    public virtual void WriteLine (long value);
    public virtual void WriteLine (object value);
    public virtual void WriteLine (string value);
    public virtual void WriteLine (string format,
                                   object arg0);
    public virtual void WriteLine (string format,
                                   object arg0,
                                   object arg1);
 CF public virtual void WriteLine (string format,
                                   object arg0,
                                   object arg1,
                                   object arg2);
    public virtual void WriteLine (string format,
                                   params object[] arg);
    public virtual void WriteLine (uint value);
    public virtual void WriteLine (ulong value);

 // Explicit Interface Members
    void IDisposable.Dispose ();
}
```

## Description

`System.IO.TextWriter` is designed for character output, whereas the `System.IO.Stream` class is designed for byte input and output.

[*Note:* By default, a `System.IO.TextWriter` is not thread safe. See `System.IO.TextWriter.Synchronized` for a thread-safe wrapper.]

## Example

```
using System;
using System.IO;
using System.Text;

namespace Samples
{
  public class TextWriterSample
  {
    public static void Main()
    {
      string s = "textwriter.txt";
      using(TextWriter tw = new StreamWriter(s))
      {
        DisplayInformation(tw);
        tw.WriteLine(DateTime.Now.ToString());
      }
    }
    public static void DisplayInformation(TextWriter tw)
    {
      Console.WriteLine("Encoding: {0}", tw.Encoding);
      Console.WriteLine("Format provider: {0}",
                        tw.FormatProvider);
    }
  }
}
```

The output is

```
Encoding: System.Text.UTF8Encoding
Format provider: en-AU
```

# System.Threading Thread

BCL

A B C D E F G H I J K L M N O P Q R S T U V W X Y Z

## Summary

Represents a sequential thread of execution.

## Type Summary

```
   public sealed class Thread
   {
      // Constructors
         public Thread (ThreadStart start);

      // Properties
MS CF public ApartmentState ApartmentState { set; get; }
MS CF public static Context CurrentContext { get; }
MS CF public static IPrincipal CurrentPrincipal { set; get; }
         public static Thread CurrentThread { get; }
      CF public bool IsAlive { get; }
      CF public bool IsBackground { set; get; }
MS CF public bool IsThreadPoolThread { get; }
      CF public string Name { set; get; }
         public ThreadPriority Priority { set; get; }
      CF public ThreadState ThreadState { get; }

      // Methods
      CF public void Abort ();
      CF public void Abort (object stateInfo);
      MS public static LocalDataStoreSlot AllocateDataSlot ();
      MS public static LocalDataStoreSlot AllocateNamedDataSlot (string name);
      CF ~Thread () {}
      MS public static void FreeNamedDataSlot (string name);
      MS public static object GetData (LocalDataStoreSlot slot);
      CF public static AppDomain GetDomain ();
MS CF public static int GetDomainID ();
      MS public static LocalDataStoreSlot GetNamedDataSlot (string name);
MS CF public void Interrupt ();
      CF public void Join ();
      CF public bool Join (int millisecondsTimeout);
      CF public bool Join (TimeSpan timeout);
 CF 1.1 public static void MemoryBarrier ();
      CF public static void ResetAbort ();
MS CF public void Resume ();
      MS public static void SetData (LocalDataStoreSlot slot,
                                     object data);
```

```
        public static void Sleep (int millisecondsTimeout);
     CF public static void Sleep (TimeSpan timeout);
  MS CF public static void SpinWait (int iterations);
        public void Start ();
  MS CF public void Suspend ();
CF 1.1 public static byte VolatileRead (ref byte address);
CF 1.1 public static double VolatileRead (ref double address);
CF 1.1 public static float VolatileRead (ref float address);
CF 1.1 public static int VolatileRead (ref int address);
CF 1.1 public static long VolatileRead (ref long address);
CF 1.1 public static object VolatileRead (ref object address);
CF 1.1 public static sbyte VolatileRead (ref sbyte address);
CF 1.1 public static short VolatileRead (ref short address);
CF 1.1 public static IntPtr VolatileRead (ref IntPtr address);
CF 1.1 public static UIntPtr VolatileRead (ref UIntPtr address);
CF 1.1 public static uint VolatileRead (ref uint address);
CF 1.1 public static ulong VolatileRead (ref ulong address);
CF 1.1 public static ushort VolatileRead (ref ushort address);
CF 1.1 public static void VolatileWrite (ref byte address,
                                         byte value);
CF 1.1 public static void VolatileWrite (ref double address,
                                         double value);
CF 1.1 public static void VolatileWrite (ref float address,
                                         float value);
CF 1.1 public static void VolatileWrite (ref int address,
                                         int value);
CF 1.1 public static void VolatileWrite (ref long address,
                                         long value);
CF 1.1 public static void VolatileWrite (ref object address,
                                         object value);
CF 1.1 public static void VolatileWrite (ref sbyte address,
                                         sbyte value);
CF 1.1 public static void VolatileWrite (ref short address,
                                         short value);
CF 1.1 public static void VolatileWrite (ref IntPtr address,
                                         IntPtr value);
CF 1.1 public static void VolatileWrite (ref UIntPtr address,
                                         UIntPtr value);
CF 1.1 public static void VolatileWrite (ref uint address,
                                         uint value);
CF 1.1 public static void VolatileWrite (ref ulong address,
                                         ulong value);
CF 1.1 public static void VolatileWrite (ref ushort address,
                                         ushort value);
  }
```

**BA** The `VolatileRead` and `VolatileWrite` methods are a direct result of the standardization work. Many of the committee members felt these were very critical to have for enterprise applications. The product is better for their persistence.

**JM** Notice all of the `Volatile` methods in the `Thread` class. They were not part of the original submission. Thread volatility was discussed at GREAT length within the standardization committee. We brought in outside content experts to discuss the issue. These methods were added as a result of the agreed upon memory model.



## Description

A process may create and execute one or more threads to execute a portion of the program code associated with the process. A `System.Threading.ThreadStart` delegate is used to specify the program code executed by a thread.

Some operating systems might not utilize the concepts of threads or preemptive scheduling. Also, the concept of "thread priority" might not exist at all or its meaning may vary, depending on the underlying operating system. Implementers of the `System.Threading.Thread` type are required to describe their threading policies, including what thread priority means, how many threading priority levels exist, and whether scheduling is preemptive.

For the duration of its existence, a thread is always in one or more of the states defined by `System.Threading.ThreadState`. A scheduling priority level, as defined by `System.Threading.ThreadPriority`, can be requested for a thread, but it might not be honored by the operating system.

If an unhandled exception is thrown in the code executed by a thread created by an application, a `System.AppDomain.UnhandledException` event is raised (`System.UnhandledExceptionEventArgs.IsTerminating` is set to `false`), and the thread is terminated; the current process is not terminated.

## Example

```
using System;
using System.Threading;

namespace Samples
{
  public class ThreadSample
  {
    public static void StartHere()
    {
      Console.WriteLine("Thread starting");
      Thread.Sleep(1000);
      Thread t = Thread.CurrentThread;
      Console.WriteLine("ThreadState within StartHere: {0}",
```

```
                    t.ThreadState);
      for(int i = 0; i < 10; i++)
      {
        Console.Write(".");
        Thread.Sleep(1000);
      }
      Console.WriteLine("\nThread finishing");
    }
    public static void Main()
    {
      Thread t = new Thread(new ThreadStart(StartHere));
      ThreadState ts = t.ThreadState;
      Console.WriteLine("Thread state: {0}", t.ThreadState);
      bool firstTime = true;
      t.Start();
      while(ts != ThreadState.Stopped)
      {
        ThreadState tmp = t.ThreadState;
        if(ts != tmp)
        {
          ts = tmp;
          Console.WriteLine("Thread state: {0}", ts);
          Thread.Sleep(100);
          if(firstTime)
          {
            firstTime = false;
            t.Suspend();
          }
          if((ts & ThreadState.Suspended) != 0)
            t.Resume();
        }
      }
      t.Join();
    }
  }
}
```

The output is

```
Thread state: Unstarted
Thread starting
Thread state: WaitSleepJoin
Thread state: SuspendRequested, WaitSleepJoin
Thread state: WaitSleepJoin, Suspended
Thread state: WaitSleepJoin
ThreadState within StartHere: Running
..........
Thread finishing
Thread state: Stopped
```

# System.Threading ThreadAbortException

BCL

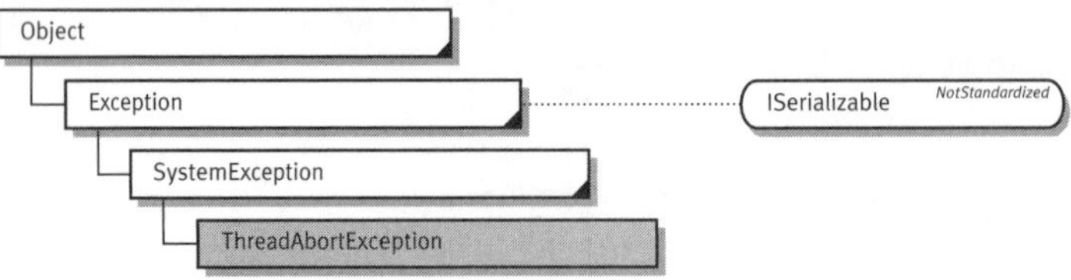




## Summary

Thrown by the system when a call is made to `System.Threading.Thread.Abort`.

## Type Summary

```
CF public sealed class ThreadAbortException : SystemException
{
  // Properties
  CF public object ExceptionState { get; }
}
```

## Description

Instances of this exception type can only be created by the system.

When a call is made to `System.Threading.Thread.Abort` to terminate a thread, the system throws a `System.Threading.ThreadAbortException` in the target thread. `System.Threading.ThreadAbortException` is a special exception that can be caught by application code, but is rethrown at the end of the catch block unless `System.Threading.Thread.ResetAbort` is called. When the `ThreadAbortException` exception is raised, the system executes any `finally` blocks for the target thread. The `finally` blocks are executed even if `System.Threading.Thread.ResetAbort` is called. If the abort is successful, the target thread is left in the `System.Threading.ThreadState.Stopped` and `System.Threading.ThreadState.Aborted` states.

## Example

```
using System;
using System.Threading;

namespace Samples
{
  public class ThreadAbortExceptionSample
  {
    public static void StartHere()
    {
      try
```

```
    {
      Console.WriteLine("Thread starting");
      Thread.Sleep(1000);
      Console.WriteLine("Thread finishing");
    }
    catch(ThreadAbortException e)
    {
      string s  = (string) e.ExceptionState;
      Console.WriteLine(s);
    }
    finally
    {
      Console.WriteLine("In finally");
    }
  }
  public static void Main()
  {
    Thread t = new Thread(
                 new ThreadStart(StartHere));
    Console.WriteLine("Main starting");
    t.Start();
    Thread.Sleep(500);
    t.Abort("Time to go");
    t.Join();
    Console.WriteLine("Main finishing");
  }
 }
}
```

The output is

```
Main starting
Thread starting
Time to go
In finally
Main finishing
```

# System.Threading ThreadPriority Enum



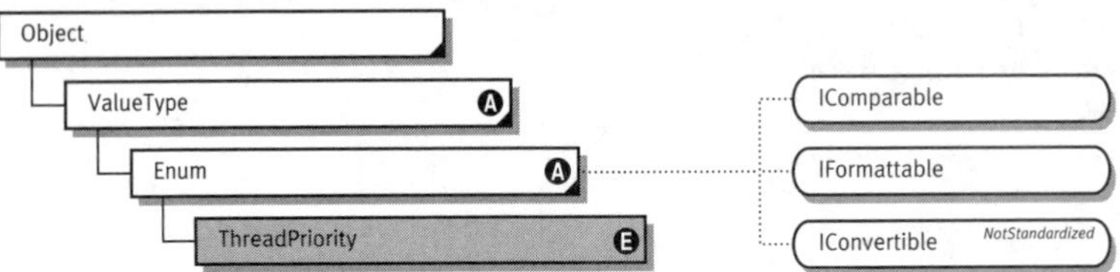


## Summary

Specifies the scheduling priority of a `System.Threading.Thread`.

## Type Summary

```
public enum ThreadPriority  {
      AboveNormal = 3,
      BelowNormal = 1,
      Highest = 4,
      Lowest= 0,
      Normal= 2,
}
```

## Description

`System.Threading.ThreadPriority` values specify the relative scheduling priority of threads.

Operating systems are not guaranteed to support preemptive scheduling. Also, the concept of "thread priority" may not exist at all or its meaning may vary, depending on the underlying operating system. Implementers of this type are required to describe how the notion of thread priority maps to operating system priority. For more information about threads, see the `System.Threading.Thread` class.

The `System.Threading.Thread.Priority` property sets and returns the priority value information for a thread. Applications can request a scheduling priority for a thread by setting the `System.Threading.Thread.Priority` property to the appropriate `ThreadPriority` value. The default thread priority is `System.Threading.ThreadPriority.Normal`.

[*Note:* A thread cannot be scheduled if it is in the `System.Threading.ThreadState.Unstarted` state or the `System.Threading.ThreadState.Stopped` state.]

ThreadPriority Enum

## Example

```
using System;
using System.Threading;

namespace Samples
{
  public class ThreadPrioritySample
  {
    public static void StartHere()
    {
      ThreadPriority[] tps =
                 {ThreadPriority.AboveNormal,
                  ThreadPriority.BelowNormal,
                  ThreadPriority.Normal,
                  ThreadPriority.Highest,
                  ThreadPriority.Lowest};
      Thread t = Thread.CurrentThread;
      foreach(ThreadPriority tp in tps)
      {
        t.Priority = tp;
        Console.WriteLine("ThreadPriority: {0}",
                          t.Priority);
      }
    }
    public static void Main()
    {
      Thread t = new Thread(
                   new ThreadStart(StartHere));
      Console.WriteLine("Main starting");
      t.Start();
      t.Join();
      Console.WriteLine("Main finishing");
    }
  }
}
```

The output is

```
Main starting
ThreadPriority: AboveNormal
ThreadPriority: BelowNormal
ThreadPriority: Normal
ThreadPriority: Highest
ThreadPriority: Lowest
Main finishing
```

# System.Threading ThreadStart Delegate

BCL

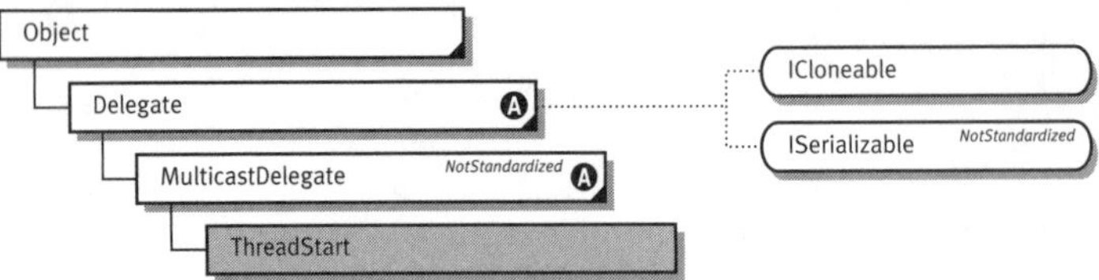


A B C D E F G H I J K L M N O P Q R S T U V W X Y Z

## Summary

Defines the shape of methods that are called when a `System.Threading.Thread` is started.

## Type Summary

```
public delegate void ThreadStart ();
```

**JR** It is a pity that this delegate wasn't defined with an `Object` parameter, allowing the creator of the thread to pass some initialization data into the new thread. To get initialization data into a new thread, you need to define a class, add fields to the class, and add the thread method (whose prototype matches this delegate) to this class. Then, when you want to create a thread, you construct an instance of the object, set the fields to the desired initialization data, and new up the `Thread` object, passing the `ThreadStart` delegate wrapped around the `thread` method that's defined in the class. When the thread starts running, it can access the fields.

## Description

[*Note:* A new instance of the `System.Threading.Thread` class is created using a constructor that takes a `System.Threading.ThreadStart` delegate as its only parameter. When `System.Threading.Thread.Start` is invoked and the thread begins executing, all of the methods in the invocation list of the specified delegate are invoked in the execution context of the thread. If a method in the invocation list receives an unhandled exception, the thread is terminated, but not the process that contains the thread.]

[*Note:* For an example that demonstrates creating a `ThreadStart` delegate, see `System.Threading.Thread.Start`.]

ThreadStart Delegate

## Example

```
using System;
using System.Threading;

namespace Samples
{
  public class ThreadStartSample
  {
    public static void StartHere()
    {
      Console.WriteLine("Thread starting");
      Thread.Sleep(1000);
      Console.WriteLine("Thread finishing");
    }
    public static void Main()
    {
      Console.WriteLine("Main starting");
      Thread t = new Thread(
                   new ThreadStart(StartHere));
      t.Start();
      t.Join();
      Console.WriteLine("Main finishing");
    }
  }
}
```

The output is

```
Main starting
Thread starting
Thread finishing
Main finishing
```

# System.Threading ThreadState Enum

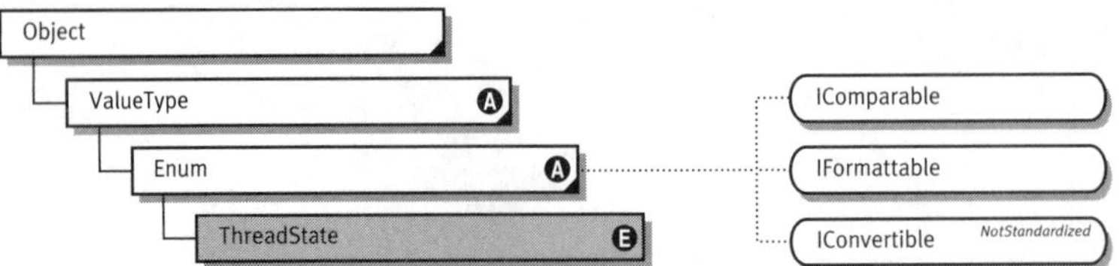


## Summary

Specifies the execution states of a `System.Threading.Thread`.

## Type Summary

```
CF public enum ThreadState  {
  CF Aborted = 0x100,
  CF AbortRequested = 0x80,
  CF Background = 0x4,
  CF Running = 0x0,
  CF Stopped = 0x10,
  CF StopRequested = 0x1,
  CF Suspended = 0x40,
  CF SuspendRequested = 0x2,
  CF Unstarted = 0x8,
  CF WaitSleepJoin= 0x20,
}
```

## Description

`System.Threading.ThreadState` defines the set of possible execution states for threads. Once a thread is created, it is in one or more of these states until it terminates. Not all combinations of `ThreadState` values are valid; for example, a thread cannot be in both the `System.Threading.ThreadState.Stopped` and `System.Threading.ThreadState.Unstarted` states.

The following table shows the actions that cause a thread to change state.

| Action | ThreadState after Action |
|---|---|
| The thread is created. | `Unstarted` |
| `System.Threading.Thread.Start` is invoked on the thread. | `Running` |
| The thread calls `System.Threading.Thread.Sleep`. | `WaitSleepJoin` |

ThreadState Enum

| Action | ThreadState after Action |
|---|---|
| The thread calls `System.Threading.Monitor.Wait` to wait on an object. | `WaitSleepJoin` |
| The thread calls `System.Threading.Thread.Join` to wait for another thread to terminate. | `WaitSleepJoin` |
| The `System.Threading.ThreadStart` delegate methods finish executing. | `Stopped` |
| Another thread requests the thread to `System.Threading.Thread.Abort`. | `AbortRequested` |
| The thread accepts a `System.Threading.Thread.Abort` request. | `Aborted` |

In addition to the states noted above, there is also the `System.Threading.ThreadState.Background` state, which indicates whether the thread is running in the background or foreground.

The current state of a thread can be retrieved from the `System.Threading.Thread.ThreadState` property, whose value is a combination of the `System.Threading.ThreadState` values. Once a thread has reached the `System.Threading.ThreadState.Stopped` state, it cannot change to any other state.

## Example

```
using System;
using System.Threading;

namespace Samples
{
  public class ThreadStateSample
  {
    public static void StartHere()
    {
      Console.WriteLine("Thread: starting");
      Thread.Sleep(1000);
      Thread t = Thread.CurrentThread;
      Console.WriteLine("ThreadState: {0}",
                        t.ThreadState);
      for(int i = 0; i < 40; i++)
        Console.Write(".");
      Console.WriteLine();
      Thread.Sleep(1000);
      Console.WriteLine("Thread: finishing");
```

## ThreadState Enum

```
    }
    public static void Main()
    {
      Thread t = new Thread(
                   new ThreadStart(StartHere));
      Console.WriteLine("1) Thread state: {0}",
                         t.ThreadState);
      t.Start();
      Thread.Sleep(100);
      Console.WriteLine("2) Thread state: {0}",
                         t.ThreadState);
      t.Suspend();
      Console.WriteLine("3) Thread state: {0}",
                         t.ThreadState);
      Thread.Sleep(1000);
      Console.WriteLine("4) Thread state: {0}",
                         t.ThreadState);
      t.Resume();
      Console.WriteLine("5) Thread state: {0}",
                         t.ThreadState);
      Console.WriteLine("6) Thread state: {0}",
                         t.ThreadState);
      t.Join();
      Console.WriteLine("7) Thread state: {0}",
                         t.ThreadState);
    }
  }
}
```

The output is

```
1) Thread state: Unstarted
Thread: starting
2) Thread state: WaitSleepJoin
3) Thread state: SuspendRequested, WaitSleepJoin
4) Thread state: WaitSleepJoin, Suspended
5) Thread state: WaitSleepJoin
6) Thread state: WaitSleepJoin
ThreadState: Running
........................................
Thread: finishing
7) Thread state: Stopped
```

# System.Threading ThreadStateException

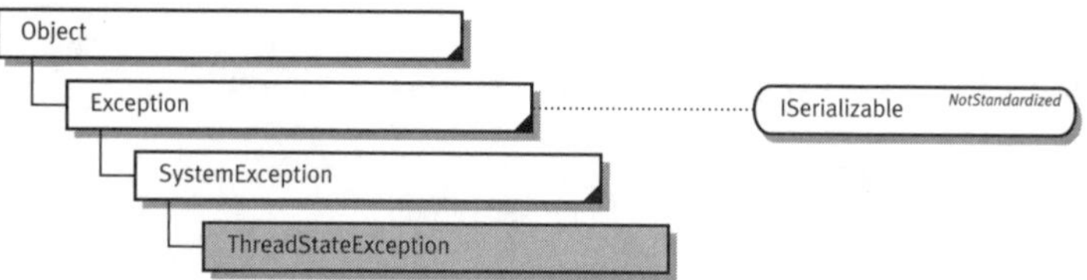


## Summary

Represents errors that occur when a method is invoked on a `System.Threading.Thread` and the thread is in a `System.Threading.Thread.ThreadState` that is invalid for the method.

## Type Summary

```
public class ThreadStateException : SystemException
{
  // Constructors
     public ThreadStateException ();
     public ThreadStateException (string message);
     public ThreadStateException (string message,
                                  Exception innerException);
MS CF protected ThreadStateException (SerializationInfo info,
                                      StreamingContext context);
}
```

## Description

Once a thread is created, it is in one or more states, as defined by `System.Threading.ThreadState`, until it terminates. `System.Threading.ThreadStateException` is thrown by methods that cannot perform the requested operation due to the current state of a thread. For example, calling `System.Threading.Thread.Start` on a thread that has terminated results in a `System.Threading.ThreadStateException` exception.

## Example

```
using System;
using System.Threading;

namespace Samples
{
  public class ThreadStateExceptionSample
  {
    public static void StartHere()
    {
```

A B C D E F G H I J K L M N O P Q R S T U V W X Y Z

```
      Console.WriteLine("Thread: starting");
      Console.WriteLine("Thread: finishing");
    }
    public static void Main()
    {
      Thread t = new Thread(
                   new ThreadStart(StartHere));
      t.Start();
      Thread.Sleep(1000);
      Console.WriteLine("2) Thread state: {0}",
                         t.ThreadState);
      try
      {
        t.Suspend();
      }
      catch(ThreadStateException e)
      {
        Console.WriteLine("Exception: {0}", e);
      }
    }
  }
}
```

The output is

```
Thread: starting
Thread: finishing
2) Thread state: Stopped
Exception: System.Threading.ThreadStateException: Thread is not running; it cannot
be suspended.
   at System.Threading.Thread.SuspendInternal()
   at System.Threading.Thread.Suspend()
   at Samples.ThreadStateExceptionSample.Main() in C:\Books\BCL\Samples\
System.Threading\ThreadStateException\ThreadStateException.cs:line 23
```

# System.Threading
# Timeout

## Summary

Contains a constant used to specify an infinite amount of time.

## Type Summary

```
public sealed class Timeout
{
  // Fields
     public const int Infinite = -1;
}
```

## Example

```
using System;
using System.Threading;

namespace Samples
{
  public class TimeoutSample
  {
    public static void StartHere()
    {
      Console.WriteLine("Thread starting");
      Thread.Sleep(1000);
      Console.WriteLine("Thread finishing");
    }
    public static void Main()
    {
      Thread t = new Thread(
                   new ThreadStart(StartHere));
      Console.WriteLine("Main starting");
      t.Start();
      TimeSpan ts = new TimeSpan(100);
      Console.WriteLine("Joined: {0}",
                        t.Join(ts));
      Console.WriteLine("Joined: {0}",
                        t.Join(Timeout.Infinite));
      Console.WriteLine("Main finishing");
    }
  }
}
```

The output is

```
Main starting
Thread starting
Joined: False
Thread finishing
Joined: True
Main finishing
```

BCL

# System.Threading Timer

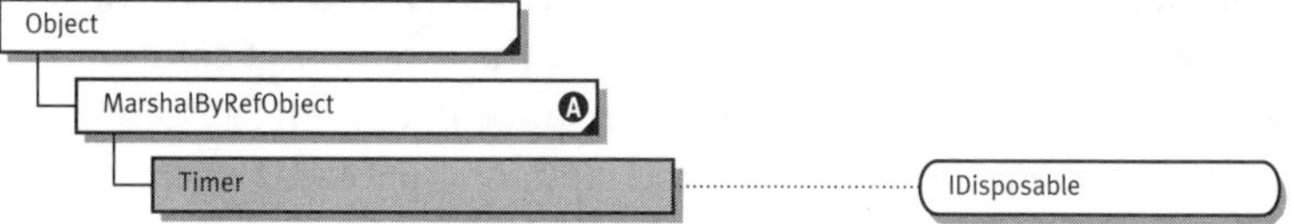


## Summary

Provides a mechanism for executing methods at specified intervals.

## Type Summary

```
public sealed class Timer : MarshalByRefObject,
                            IDisposable
{
   // Constructors
      public Timer (TimerCallback callback, object state,
                    int dueTime, int period);
   MS public Timer (TimerCallback callback, object state,
                    long dueTime, long period);
      public Timer (TimerCallback callback, object state,
                    TimeSpan dueTime, TimeSpan period);
   MS public Timer (TimerCallback callback, object state,
                    uint dueTime, uint period);

   // Methods
      public bool Change (int dueTime, int period);
   MS public bool Change(long dueTime, long period);
      public bool Change(TimeSpan dueTime, TimeSpan period);
   MS public bool Change(uint dueTime, uint period);
      public void Dispose ();
   CF public bool Dispose (WaitHandle notifyObject);
      ~Timer () {}
}
```

**KC** We ended up shipping three timers in the .NET Framework. Luckily only this one got into the CLI Standard. We tried to unify them, but because all three have slightly different design objectives, we decided unification would not be the right thing to do. In general, it's great to unify APIs for similar functionality. In some case, however, one needs to be careful not to take the idea of unification too far.

A B C D E F G H I J K L M N O P Q R S T U V W X Y Z

## Description

A `System.Threading.TimerCallback` delegate is used to specify the methods associated with a `Timer`. The methods do not execute in the thread that created the timer; they execute in a separate thread that is automatically allocated by the system. The timer delegate is specified when the timer is constructed, and cannot be changed.

When creating a timer, the application specifies an amount of time to wait before the first invocation of the delegate methods (due time), and an amount of time to wait between subsequent invocations (period). A timer invokes its methods once when its due time elapses, and invokes its methods once per period thereafter. These values may be changed, or the timer disabled using the `System.Threading.Timer.Change` method.

When a timer is no longer needed, use the `System.Threading.Timer.Dispose` method to free the resources held by the timer.

## Example

```
using System;
using System.Threading;

namespace Samples
{
  public class TimerSample
  {
    public static AutoResetEvent are =
             new AutoResetEvent(false);
    public static Timer t = null;
    public const int number = 9;
    public class StateHolder
    {
      public int counter = 0;
    }
    static void CallMe(Object s)
    {
      StateHolder sh = (StateHolder) s;
      Console.WriteLine("{0}: {1}",
                sh.counter++, DateTime.Now);
      if(sh.counter > number)
      {
        t.Dispose(are);
      }
    }
    public static void Main()
    {
      StateHolder sh = new StateHolder();
      TimerCallback tcb =
                new TimerCallback(CallMe);
```

```
            t = new Timer(
                      tcb, sh, 1000, 1000);
            are.WaitOne();
        }
    }
}
```

The output is

```
0: 24/06/2003 3:26:06 AM
1: 24/06/2003 3:26:07 AM
2: 24/06/2003 3:26:08 AM
3: 24/06/2003 3:26:09 AM
4: 24/06/2003 3:26:10 AM
5: 24/06/2003 3:26:11 AM
6: 24/06/2003 3:26:12 AM
7: 24/06/2003 3:26:13 AM
8: 24/06/2003 3:26:14 AM
9: 24/06/2003 3:26:15 AM
```

# System.Threading TimerCallback Delegate

BCL

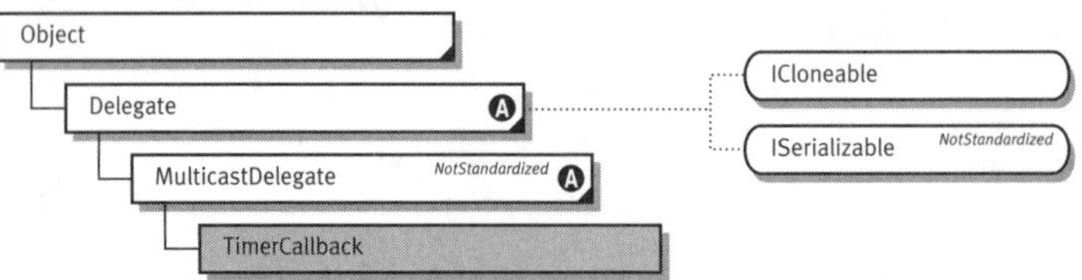


## Summary

Defines the shape of methods that are called by an instance of the `System.Threading.Timer` class.

## Type Summary

```
public delegate void TimerCallback (object state);
```

## Parameters

| Parameter | Description |
|---|---|
| state | A `System.Object` containing application-specific information relevant to the methods invoked by instances of this delegate, or `null`. |

## Description

A `TimerCallback` delegate invokes its methods once after the start time elapses, and continues invoking its methods once per period until the `System.Threading.Timer.Dispose` method is called. [*Note:* The start time for a `System.Threading.Timer` is passed in the *dueTime* parameter of the `Timer` constructors, and the period is passed via the *period* parameter.]

[*Note:* For an example that demonstrates creating and using a `TimerCallback` delegate, see the `System.Threading.Timer` class.]

## Example

```
using System;
using System.Threading;

namespace Samples
{
  public class TimerCallbackSample
```

TimerCallback Delegate

```
  {
    public static AutoResetEvent are =
             new AutoResetEvent(false);
    public static Timer t = null;
    public const int number = 9;
    public class StateHolder
    {
      public int counter = 0;
    }
    static void CallMe(Object s)
    {
      StateHolder sh = (StateHolder) s;
      Console.WriteLine("{0}: {1}",
                sh.counter++, DateTime.Now);
      if(sh.counter > number)
      {
        t.Dispose(are);
      }
    }
    public static void Main()
    {
      StateHolder sh = new StateHolder();
      TimerCallback tcb =
                new TimerCallback(CallMe);
      t = new Timer(tcb, sh, 1000, 1000);
      are.WaitOne();
    }
  }
}
```

The output is

```
0: 24/06/2003 3:38:29 AM
1: 24/06/2003 3:38:30 AM
2: 24/06/2003 3:38:31 AM
3: 24/06/2003 3:38:32 AM
4: 24/06/2003 3:38:33 AM
5: 24/06/2003 3:38:34 AM
6: 24/06/2003 3:38:35 AM
7: 24/06/2003 3:38:36 AM
8: 24/06/2003 3:38:37 AM
9: 24/06/2003 3:38:38 AM
```

# System
# TimeSpan Structure

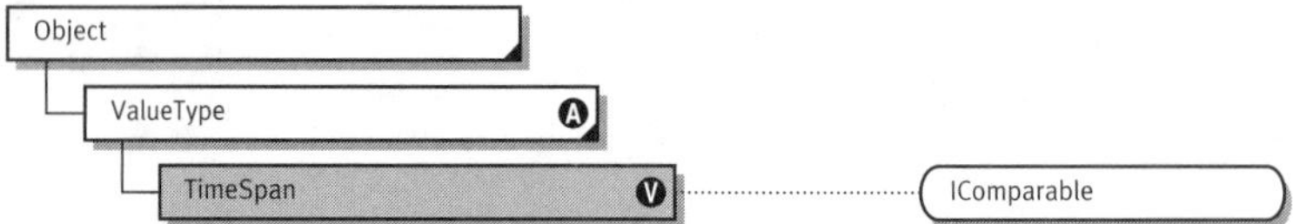




## Summary

Represents an interval of time.

## Type Summary

```
public struct TimeSpan : IComparable
{
  // Constructors
     public TimeSpan (int hours, int minutes,
                      int seconds);
     public TimeSpan (int days, int hours, int minutes,
                      int seconds);
     public TimeSpan (int days, int hours, int minutes,
                      int seconds, int milliseconds);
     public TimeSpan (long ticks);

  // Fields
     public static readonly TimeSpan MaxValue = new TimeSpan (Int64.MaxValue);
     public static readonly TimeSpan MinValue = new TimeSpan (Int64.MinValue);
     public const long TicksPerDay = TicksPerHour * 24;
     public const long TicksPerHour = TicksPerMinute * 60;
     public const long TicksPerMillisecond = 10000;
     public const long TicksPerMinute = TicksPerSecond * 60;
     public const long TicksPerSecond = TicksPerMillisecond * 1000;
     public static readonly TimeSpan Zero = new TimeSpan (0);

  // Properties
     public int Days { get; }
     public int Hours { get; }
     public int Milliseconds { get; }
     public int Minutes { get; }
     public int Seconds { get; }
     public long Ticks { get; }
     public double TotalDays { get; }
     public double TotalHours { get; }
     public double TotalMilliseconds { get; }
     public double TotalMinutes { get; }
     public double TotalSeconds { get; }

  // Methods
     public TimeSpan Add (TimeSpan ts);
```

TimeSpan Structure

```
    public static int Compare (TimeSpan t1,
                               TimeSpan t2);
    public int CompareTo (object value);
    public TimeSpan Duration ();
    public override bool Equals (object value);
    public static bool Equals (TimeSpan t1,
                               TimeSpan t2);
    public static TimeSpan FromDays (double value);
    public static TimeSpan FromHours (double value);
    public static TimeSpan FromMilliseconds (double value);
    public static TimeSpan FromMinutes (double value);
    public static TimeSpan FromSeconds (double value);
    public static TimeSpan FromTicks (long value);
    public override int GetHashCode ();
    public TimeSpan Negate ();
    public static TimeSpan operator +(TimeSpan t1,
                                      TimeSpan t2);
    public static bool operator ==(TimeSpan t1,
                                   TimeSpan t2);
    public static bool operator >(TimeSpan t1,
                                  TimeSpan t2);
    public static bool operator >=(TimeSpan t1,
                                   TimeSpan t2);
    public static bool operator !=(TimeSpan t1,
                                   TimeSpan t2);
    public static bool operator <(TimeSpan t1,
                                  TimeSpan t2);
    public static bool operator <=(TimeSpan t1,
                                   TimeSpan t2);
    public static TimeSpan operator -(TimeSpan t1,
                                      TimeSpan t2);
    public static TimeSpan operator -(TimeSpan t);
 CF public static TimeSpan operator +(TimeSpan t);
    public static TimeSpan Parse (string s);
    public TimeSpan Subtract (TimeSpan ts);
    public override string ToString ();
}
```

**KG** A number of customer requests for `TimeSpan` include the ability to get how many months or years the `TimeSpan` represents. Because `TimeSpan` doesn't have a fixed starting point, it is impossible for us to accurately describe values, e.g., are there 29 days in a month? We could have, however, defined some common behavior for these operations, and included them for the general case. The problem is that every user who cares would probably define their own in order to reflect their needs accurately.

TimeSpan Structure

## Description

The System.TimeSpan structure represents an interval of time with values ranging from System.Int64.MinValue to System.Int64.MaxValue 100-nanosecond ticks.

[*Note:* The value of a System.TimeSpan is represented internally as a number of 100-nanosecond ticks. Both the specification of a number of ticks and the value of a System.TimeSpan can be positive or negative. A System.TimeSpan can be represented as a string in the format "[–]d.hh:mm:ss.ff" where "–" is an optional sign for negative System.TimeSpan values, the "d" component is days, "hh" is hours, "mm" is minutes, "ss" is seconds, and "ff" is fractions of a second. For example, a System.TimeSpan initialized with 1013 ticks would be represented as "11.13:46:40", which is 11 days, 13 hours, 46 minutes, and 40 seconds. Due to a varying number of days in months and years, the longest unit of time that is used by this structure is the day.]

## Example

```
using System;

namespace Samples
{
  public class TimeSpanSample
  {
    public static void Main()
    {
      DateTime start = DateTime.Now;
      Console.WriteLine("MaxValue: {0}", TimeSpan.MaxValue);
      Console.WriteLine("MinValue: {0}", TimeSpan.MinValue);
      Console.WriteLine("TicksPerDay: {0}",
                        TimeSpan.TicksPerDay);
      Console.WriteLine("TicksPerHour: {0}",
                        TimeSpan.TicksPerHour);
      Console.WriteLine("TicksPerMinute: {0}",
                        TimeSpan.TicksPerMinute);
      Console.WriteLine("TicksPerSecond: {0}",
                        TimeSpan.TicksPerSecond);
      Console.WriteLine("TicksPerMillisecond: {0}",
                        TimeSpan.TicksPerMillisecond);
      TimeSpan ts = new DateTime(1973, 9, 25) -
                    new DateTime(1959, 9, 3);
      Console.WriteLine("Damien is older than Brad by: ");
      Console.Write("Days: {0}", ts.Days);
      Console.Write(" Hours: {0}", ts.Hours);
      Console.Write(" Minutes: {0}", ts.Minutes);
      Console.Write(" Seconds: {0}", ts.Seconds);
      Console.WriteLine(" Milliseconds: {0}", ts.Milliseconds);
      Console.WriteLine("TotalDays: {0}", ts.TotalDays);
      Console.WriteLine("TotalHours: {0}", ts.TotalHours);
```

TimeSpan Structure

```
      Console.WriteLine("TotalMinutes: {0}", ts.TotalMinutes);
      Console.WriteLine("TotalSeconds: {0}", ts.TotalSeconds);
      Console.WriteLine("TotalMilliseconds: {0}",
                        ts.TotalMilliseconds);
      Console.WriteLine("MaxValue is: {0} ticks", ts.Ticks);
      TimeSpan diff = DateTime.Now - start;
      Console.WriteLine ("Time to run this program: {0} ",diff);
    }
  }
}
```

The output is

```
MaxValue: 10675199.02:48:05.4775807
MinValue: -10675199.02:48:05.4775808
TicksPerDay: 864000000000
TicksPerHour: 36000000000
TicksPerMinute: 600000000
TicksPerSecond: 10000000
TicksPerMillisecond: 10000
Damien is older than Brad by:
Days: 5136 Hours: 0 Minutes: 0 Seconds: 0 Milliseconds: 0
TotalDays: 5136
TotalHours: 123264
TotalMinutes: 7395840
TotalSeconds: 443750400
TotalMilliseconds: 443750400000
MaxValue is: 4437504000000000 ticks
Time to run this program: 00:00:00.3404896
```

# System
# Type

BCL

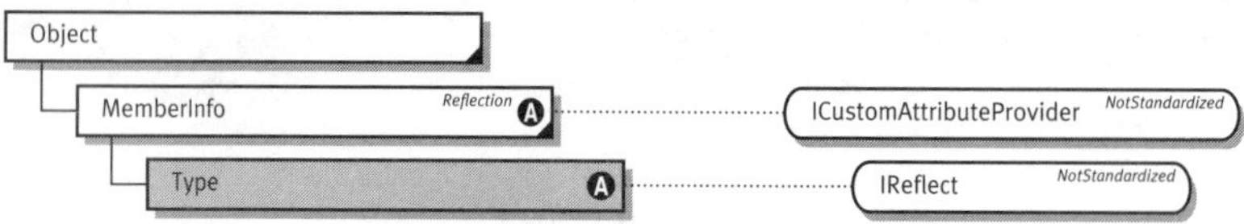




## Summary

Provides information about a type.

## Type Summary

```
   public abstract class Type : MemberInfo, IReflect
   {
     // Constructors
        protected Type ();

     // Fields
        public static readonly char Delimiter = '.';
     CF public static readonly Type[] EmptyTypes = new Type[0];
  MS CF public static readonly MemberFilter FilterAttribute;
  MS CF public static readonly MemberFilter FilterName;
  MS CF public static readonly MemberFilter FilterNameIgnoreCase;
        public static readonly object Missing = Missing.Value;

     // Properties
        public abstract Assembly Assembly { get; }
     CF public abstract string AssemblyQualifiedName { get; }
        public TypeAttributes Attributes { get; }
        public abstract Type BaseType { get; }
     MS public override Type DeclaringType { get; }
        public static Binder DefaultBinder { get; }
        public abstract string FullName { get; }
  MS CF public abstract Guid GUID { get; }
        public bool HasElementType { get; }
        public bool IsAbstract { get; }
     MS public bool IsAnsiClass { get; }
        public bool IsArray { get; }
     MS public bool IsAutoClass { get; }
        public bool IsAutoLayout { get; }
        public bool IsByRef { get; }
        public bool IsClass { get; }
     MS public bool IsCOMObject { get; }
  MS CF public bool IsContextful { get; }
        public bool IsEnum { get; }
     CF public bool IsExplicitLayout { get; }
        public bool IsImport { get; }
```

```
         public bool IsInterface { get; }
      CF public bool IsLayoutSequential { get; }
      CF public bool IsMarshalByRef { get; }
         public bool IsNestedAssembly { get; }
         public bool IsNestedFamANDAssem { get; }
         public bool IsNestedFamily { get; }
         public bool IsNestedFamORAssem { get; }
         public bool IsNestedPrivate { get; }
         public bool IsNestedPublic { get; }
         public bool IsNotPublic { get; }
         public bool IsPointer { get; }
         public bool IsPrimitive { get; }
         public bool IsPublic { get; }
         public bool IsSealed { get; }
   MS CF public bool IsSerializable { get; }
         public bool IsSpecialName { get; }
      MS public bool IsUnicodeClass { get; }
         public bool IsValueType { get; }
      MS public override MemberTypes MemberType { get; }
         public abstract Module Module { get; }
         public abstract string Namespace { get; }
      MS public override Type ReflectedType { get; }
         public abstract RuntimeTypeHandle TypeHandle { get; }
      CF public ConstructorInfo TypeInitializer { get; }
      CF public abstract Type UnderlyingSystemType { get; }

      // Methods
      MS public override bool Equals (object o);
         public bool Equals (Type o);
   MS CF public virtual Type[] FindInterfaces (TypeFilter filter,
                                               object filterCriteria);
   MS CF public virtual MemberInfo[] FindMembers (MemberTypes memberType,
                                                  BindingFlags bindingAttr,
                                                  MemberFilter filter,
                                                  object filterCriteria);
      CF public virtual int GetArrayRank ();
         protected abstract TypeAttributes GetAttributeFlagsImpl ();
   MS CF public ConstructorInfo GetConstructor (BindingFlags bindingAttr,
                                                Binder binder,
                                                CallingConventions callConvention,
                                                Type[] types,
                                                ParameterModifier[] modifiers);
         public ConstructorInfo GetConstructor (BindingFlags bindingAttr,
                                             Binder binder,
                                             Type[] types,
                                             ParameterModifier[] modifiers);
         public ConstructorInfo GetConstructor (Type[] types);
     MS  protected abstract ConstructorInfo GetConstructorImpl (
```

```
                BindingFlags bindingAttr,
                Binder binder,CallingConventions callConvention,
                Type[] types, ParameterModifier[] modifiers);
          public ConstructorInfo[] GetConstructors ();
          public abstract ConstructorInfo[] GetConstructors (
                BindingFlags bindingAttr);
          public virtual MemberInfo[] GetDefaultMembers ();
          public abstract Type GetElementType ();
          public EventInfo GetEvent (string name);
          public abstract EventInfo GetEvent (string name,
                                              BindingFlags bindingAttr);
          public virtual EventInfo[] GetEvents ();
          public abstract EventInfo[] GetEvents (BindingFlags bindingAttr);
          public FieldInfo GetField (string name);
          public abstract FieldInfo GetField (string name,
                                              BindingFlags bindingAttr);
          public FieldInfo[] GetFields ();
          public abstract FieldInfo[] GetFields (BindingFlags bindingAttr);
          public override int GetHashCode ();
       CF public Type GetInterface (string name);
       CF public abstract Type GetInterface (string name,
                                             bool ignoreCase);
    MS CF public virtual InterfaceMapping GetInterfaceMap (Type interfaceType);
          public abstract Type[] GetInterfaces ();
          public MemberInfo[] GetMember (string name);
       CF public virtual MemberInfo[] GetMember (string name,
                                                 BindingFlags bindingAttr);
    MS CF public virtual MemberInfo[] GetMember (string name,
                                                 MemberTypes type,
                                                 BindingFlags bindingAttr);
          public MemberInfo[] GetMembers ();
          public abstract MemberInfo[] GetMembers (BindingFlags bindingAttr);
          public MethodInfo GetMethod (string name);
          public MethodInfo GetMethod (string name,
                                       BindingFlags bindingAttr);
       MS public MethodInfo GetMethod (string name,
                                       BindingFlags bindingAttr,
                                       Binder binder,
                                       CallingConventions callConvention,
                                       Type[] types,
                                       ParameterModifier[] modifiers);
          public MethodInfo GetMethod (string name,
                                       BindingFlags bindingAttr,
                                       Binder binder,
                                       Type[] types,
                                       ParameterModifier[] modifiers);
          public MethodInfo GetMethod (string name,
                                       Type[] types);
```

```
   public MethodInfo GetMethod (string name,
                                Type[] types,
                                ParameterModifier[] modifiers);
MS protected abstract MethodInfo GetMethodImpl (string name,
                                 BindingFlags bindingAttr,
                                 Binder binder,
                                 CallingConventions callConvention,
                                 Type[] types,
                                 ParameterModifier[] modifiers);
   public MethodInfo[] GetMethods ();
   public abstract MethodInfo[] GetMethods (BindingFlags bindingAttr);
CF public Type GetNestedType (string name);
   public abstract Type GetNestedType (string name,
                                       BindingFlags bindingAttr);
CF public Type[] GetNestedTypes ();
   public abstract Type[] GetNestedTypes (BindingFlags bindingAttr);
   public PropertyInfo[] GetProperties ();
   public abstract PropertyInfo[] GetProperties (BindingFlags bindingAttr);
   public PropertyInfo GetProperty (string name);
   public PropertyInfo GetProperty (string name,
                                    BindingFlags bindingAttr);
   public PropertyInfo GetProperty (string name,
                                    BindingFlags bindingAttr,
                                    Binder binder,
                                    Type returnType,
                                    Type[] types,
                                    ParameterModifier[] modifiers);
   public PropertyInfo GetProperty (string name,
                                    Type returnType);
   public PropertyInfo GetProperty (string name,
                                    Type returnType,
                                    Type[] types);
MS public PropertyInfo GetProperty (string name,
                                    Type returnType,
                                    Type[] types,
                                    ParameterModifier[] modifiers);
CF public PropertyInfo GetProperty (string name,
                                    Type[] types);
   protected abstract PropertyInfo GetPropertyImpl (string name,
                                   BindingFlags bindingAttr,
                                   Binder binder,
                                   Type returnType,
                                   Type[] types,
                                   ParameterModifier[] modifiers);
   public static Type GetType (string typeName);
   public static Type GetType (string typeName,
                               bool throwOnError);
```

```
         public static Type GetType (string typeName,
                                     bool throwOnError,
                                     bool ignoreCase);
      CF public static Type[] GetTypeArray (object[] args);
      MS public static TypeCode GetTypeCode (Type type);
   MS CF public static Type GetTypeFromCLSID (Guid clsid);
   MS CF public static Type GetTypeFromCLSID (Guid clsid,
                                              bool throwOnError);
   MS CF public static Type GetTypeFromCLSID (Guid clsid,
                                              string server);
   MS CF public static Type GetTypeFromCLSID (Guid clsid,
                                              string server,
                                              bool throwOnError);
         public static Type GetTypeFromHandle (RuntimeTypeHandle handle);
   MS CF public static Type GetTypeFromProgID (string progID);
   MS CF public static Type GetTypeFromProgID (string progID,
                                               bool throwOnError);
   MS CF public static Type GetTypeFromProgID (string progID,
                                               string server);
   MS CF public static Type GetTypeFromProgID (string progID,
                                               string server,
                                               bool throwOnError);
      CF public static RuntimeTypeHandle GetTypeHandle (object o);
         protected abstract bool HasElementTypeImpl ();
         public object InvokeMember (string name,
                                     BindingFlags invokeAttr,
                                     Binder binder,
                                     object target,
                                     object[] args);
         public abstract object InvokeMember (string name,
                                              BindingFlags invokeAttr,
                                              Binder binder,
                                              object target,
                                              object[] args,
                                              ParameterModifier[] modifiers,
                                              CultureInfo culture,
                                              string[] namedParameters);
      CF public object InvokeMember (string name,
                                     BindingFlags invokeAttr,
                                     Binder binder,
                                     object target,
                                     object[] args,
                                     CultureInfo culture);
         protected abstract bool IsArrayImpl ();
         public virtual bool IsAssignableFrom (Type c);
         protected abstract bool IsByRefImpl ();
         protected abstract bool IsCOMObjectImpl ();
```

```
MS CF protected virtual bool IsContextfulImpl ();
      public virtual bool IsInstanceOfType (object o);
MS CF protected virtual bool IsMarshalByRefImpl ();
      protected abstract bool IsPointerImpl ();
      protected abstract bool IsPrimitiveImpl ();
      public virtual bool IsSubclassOf (Type c);
   MS protected virtual bool IsValueTypeImpl ();
      public override string ToString ();
}
```

**BA** Notice we included only a very cut down version of `System.Type` in the BCL Standard. Just the core members are here to provide for implementations of the standard that could not support the entire reflection system. The rest of the members from `Type` are in the `Reflection` library.

## Description

The `System.Type` class is abstract, as is the `System.Reflection.MemberInfo` class and its subclasses `System.Reflection.FieldInfo`, `System.Reflection.PropertyInfo`, `System.Reflection.MethodBase`, and `System.Reflection.EventInfo`. `System.Reflection.ConstructorInfo` and `System.Reflection.MethodInfo` are subclasses of `System.Reflection.MethodBase`. The runtime provides non-public implementations of these classes. [*Note:* For example, `System.Type.GetMethod` is typed as returning a `System.Reflection.MethodInfo` object. The returned object is actually an instance of the non-public runtime type that implements `System.Reflection.MethodInfo`.]

A conforming CLI program which is written to run on only the Kernel profile cannot subclass `System.Type`. [*Note:* This applies only to conforming programs, not conforming implementations.]

A `System.Type` object that represents a type is unique; that is, two `System.Type` object references refer to the same object if and only if they represent the same type. This allows for comparison of `System.Type` objects using reference equality.

[*Note:* An instance of `System.Type` can represent any one of the following types: The following table shows what members of a base class are returned by the methods that return members of types, such as `System.Type.GetConstructor` and `System.Type.GetMethod`.

| Member Type | Static | Non-Static |
| --- | --- | --- |
| constructor | No | No |
| field | No | Yes. A field is always hide-by-name-and-signature. |
| event | Not applicable | The common type system rule is that the inheritance of an event is the same as that of the accessors that implement the event. Reflection treats events as hide-by-name-and-signature. |
| method | No | Yes. A method (both virtual and non-virtual) can be hide-by-name or hide-by-name-and-signature. |
| nested Type | No | No |
| property | Not applicable | The common type system rule is that the inheritance is the same as that of the accessors that implement the property. Reflection treats properties as hide-by-name-and-signature. |

For reflection, properties and events are hide-by-name-and-signature. If a property has both a get and a set accessor in the base class, but the derived class has only a get accessor, the derived class property hides the base class property, and the setter on the base class will not be accessible.]

## Example

```
using System;
using System.Reflection;

namespace Samples
{
  public class TypeType
  {
    public static void Main()
    {
      Console.WriteLine("Delimiter: {0}",
                        Type.Delimiter);
      Console.WriteLine(
                "Type: object");
      Type t = typeof(object);
      Console.WriteLine("Assembly: {0}",
                        t.Assembly);
      Console.WriteLine(
                "AssemblyQualifiedName: {0}",
```

```
            t.AssemblyQualifiedName);
    Console.WriteLine("BaseType: {0}",
                      t.BaseType);
    Console.WriteLine("DeclaringType: {0}",
                      t.DeclaringType);
    Console.WriteLine("FullName: {0}",
                      t.FullName);
    Console.WriteLine("IsAbstract: {0}",
                      t.IsAbstract);
    Console.WriteLine("IsArray: {0}",
                      t.IsArray);
    Console.WriteLine("IsAutoLayout: {0}",
                      t.IsAutoLayout);
    Console.WriteLine("IsExplicitLayout: {0}",
                      t.IsExplicitLayout);
    Console.WriteLine("IsLayoutSequential: {0}",
                      t.IsLayoutSequential);
    Console.WriteLine("IsClass: {0}",
                      t.IsClass);
    Console.WriteLine("IsEnum: {0}",
                      t.IsEnum);
    Console.WriteLine("IsInterface: {0}",
                      t.IsInterface);
    Console.WriteLine("IsMarshalByRef: {0}",
                      t.IsMarshalByRef);
    Console.WriteLine("IsNestedAssembly: {0}",
                      t.IsNestedAssembly);
    Console.WriteLine("IsNestedFamANDAssem: {0}",
                      t.IsNestedFamANDAssem);
    Console.WriteLine("IsNestedFamily: {0}",
                      t.IsNestedFamily);
    Console.WriteLine("IsNestedFamORAssem: {0}",
                      t.IsNestedFamORAssem);
    Console.WriteLine("IsNestedPrivate: {0}",
                      t.IsNestedPrivate);
    Console.WriteLine("IsNestedPublic: {0}",
                      t.IsNestedPublic);
    Console.WriteLine("IsPublic: {0}",
                      t.IsPublic);
    Console.WriteLine("IsPointer: {0}",
                      t.IsPointer);
    Console.WriteLine("IsPrimitive: {0}",
                      t.IsPrimitive);
    Console.WriteLine("IsSealed: {0}",
                      t.IsSealed);
    Console.WriteLine("IsSpecialName: {0}",
                      t.IsSpecialName);
    Console.WriteLine("IsValueType: {0}",
```

```
                            t.IsValueType);
        Console.WriteLine("Module: {0}",
                            t.Module);
        Console.WriteLine("Namespace: {0}",
                            t.Namespace);
        Console.WriteLine("Members:");
        MemberInfo[] members = t.GetMembers();
        foreach(MemberInfo m in members)
          Console.WriteLine(m);
      }
    }
  }
```

The output is

```
Delimiter: .
Type: object
Assembly: mscorlib, Version=1.0.3300.0, Culture=neutral,
PublicKeyToken=b77a5c561934e089
AssemblyQualifiedName: System.Object, mscorlib, Version=1.0.3300.0,
Culture=neutral, PublicKeyToken=b77a5c561934e089
BaseType:
DeclaringType:
FullName: System.Object
IsAbstract: False
IsArray: False
IsAutoLayout: True
IsExplicitLayout: False
IsLayoutSequential: False
IsClass: True
IsEnum: False
IsInterface: False
IsMarshalByRef: False
IsNestedAssembly: False
IsNestedFamANDAssem: False
IsNestedFamily: False
IsNestedFamORAssem: False
IsNestedPrivate: False
IsNestedPublic: False
IsPublic: True
IsPointer: False
IsPrimitive: False
IsSealed: False
IsSpecialName: False
IsValueType: False
Module: CommonLanguageRuntimeLibrary
Namespace: System
Members:
```

```
Int32 GetHashCode()
Boolean Equals(System.Object)
System.String ToString()
Boolean Equals(System.Object, System.Object)
Boolean ReferenceEquals(System.Object, System.Object)
System.Type GetType()
Void .ctor()
```

# System TypeInitializationException

BCL

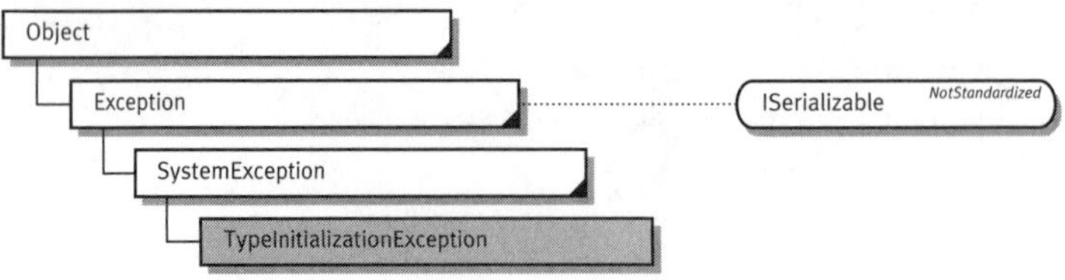


## Summary

Represents the error that occurs when an exception is thrown inside the static constructor of a type.

## Type Summary

```
   CF public sealed class TypeInitializationException : SystemException
   {
     // Properties
     CF public string TypeName { get; }

     // Methods
MS CF public override void GetObjectData (SerializationInfo info,
                                          StreamingContext context);
   }
```

## Description

When a static constructor fails to initialize a type, a `System.TypeInitializationException` instance is created and passed a reference to the exception thrown by the static constructor. The `System.TypeInitializationException.InnerException` property stores the exception that was thrown by the static constructor.

## Example

```
using System;

namespace Samples
{
  public class TypeInitializationExceptionSample
  {
    static TypeInitializationExceptionSample()
    {
      Console.WriteLine("Type Initializer");
      throw new ApplicationException(
                "TypeInitializationException");
    }
    public TypeInitializationExceptionSample()
```

```
    {
      Console.WriteLine("Instance Initializer");
    }
    static public void Main()
    {
      TypeInitializationExceptionSample t =
        new TypeInitializationExceptionSample();
    }
  }
}
```

The output is

```
Type Initializer

Unhandled Exception: System.TypeInitializationException: The type initializer for
"Samples.TypeInitializationExceptionSample" threw an exception. --->
System.ApplicationException: TypeInitializationException
   at Samples.TypeInitializationExceptionSample..cctor() in C:\Books\BCL\Samples\
System\TypeInitializationException\TypeInitializationException.cs:line 10
   --- End of inner exception stack trace ---
   at Samples.TypeInitializationExceptionSample.Main()
```

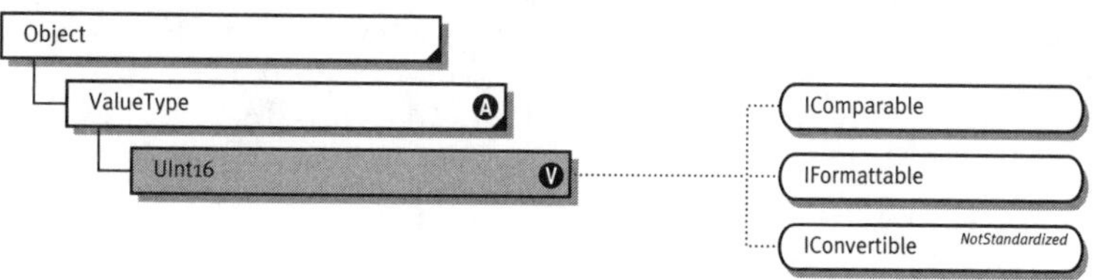


## Summary

Represents a 16-bit unsigned integer. This type is not CLS-compliant.

## Type Summary

```
public struct UInt16 : IComparable, IFormattable,
                       IConvertible
{
  // Fields
     public const ushort MaxValue = 65535;
     public const ushort MinValue = 0;

  // Methods
     public int CompareTo (object value);
     public override bool Equals (object obj);
     public override int GetHashCode ();
  MS public TypeCode GetTypeCode ();
     public static ushort Parse (string s);
     public static ushort Parse (string s, NumberStyles style);
     public static ushort Parse (string s, NumberStyles style,
                                 IFormatProvider provider);
  CF public static ushort Parse (string s, IFormatProvider provider);
     public override string ToString ();
     public string ToString (string format);
     public string ToString (string format, IFormatProvider provider);
     public string ToString (IFormatProvider provider);

  // Explicit Interface Members
  MS bool IConvertible.ToBoolean(IFormatProvider provider);
  MS byte IConvertible.ToByte(IFormatProvider provider);
  MS char IConvertible.ToChar(IFormatProvider provider);
  MS DateTime IConvertible.ToDateTime(IFormatProvider provider);
  MS decimal IConvertible.ToDecimal(IFormatProvider provider);
  MS double IConvertible.ToDouble(IFormatProvider provider);
  MS short IConvertible.ToInt16(IFormatProvider provider);
  MS int IConvertible.ToInt32(IFormatProvider provider);
  MS long IConvertible.ToInt64(IFormatProvider provider);
  MS sbyte IConvertible.ToSByte(IFormatProvider provider);
```

UInt16 Structure

```
    MS float IConvertible.ToSingle(IFormatProvider provider);
    MS object IConvertible.ToType(Type type,IFormatProvider provider);
    MS ushort IConvertible.ToUInt16(IFormatProvider provider);
    MS uint IConvertible.ToUInt32(IFormatProvider provider);
    MS ulong IConvertible.ToUInt64(IFormatProvider provider);
  }
```

## Description

The `System.UInt16` data type represents integer values ranging from 0 to positive 65,535 (hexadecimal 0xFFFF).

## Example

```
using System;

namespace Samples
{
  public class UInt16Sample
  {
    public static void Main()
    {
      ushort max = ushort.MaxValue,
             min = ushort.MinValue;
      Console.WriteLine("MaxValue: {0}", max);
      Console.WriteLine("MinValue: {0}", min);
      Console.WriteLine("Is {0} equal to {1}: {2}",
                        max, max, max.Equals(max));
      Console.WriteLine("Is {0} equal to {1}: {2}",
                        max, min, max.Equals(min));
      Console.WriteLine("{0} has hashcode of: {1}",
                        max, max.GetHashCode());
      Console.WriteLine("{0} has hashcode of: {1}",
                        min, min.GetHashCode());
      string s = max.ToString();
      Console.WriteLine("\"{0}\" parsed from string yields: {1}",
                        s, UInt16.Parse(s));
      s = min.ToString();
      Console.WriteLine("\"{0}\" parsed from string yields: {1}",
                        s, UInt16.Parse(s));
      string[] formats = {"c", "d", "e", "f",
                          "g", "n", "p", "x" };
      foreach(string f in formats)
        Console.WriteLine("{0}: {1}", max, max.ToString(f));
    }
  }
}
```

UInt16 Structure

The output is

```
MaxValue: 65535
MinValue: 0
Is 65535 equal to 65535: True
Is 65535 equal to 0: False
65535 has hashcode of: 65535
0 has hashcode of: 0
"65535" parsed from string yields: 65535
"0" parsed from string yields: 0
65535: $65,535.00
65535: 65535
65535: 6.553500e+004
65535: 65535.00
65535: 65535
65535: 65,535.00
65535: 6,553,500.00 %
65535: ffff
```

# System
# UInt32 Structure

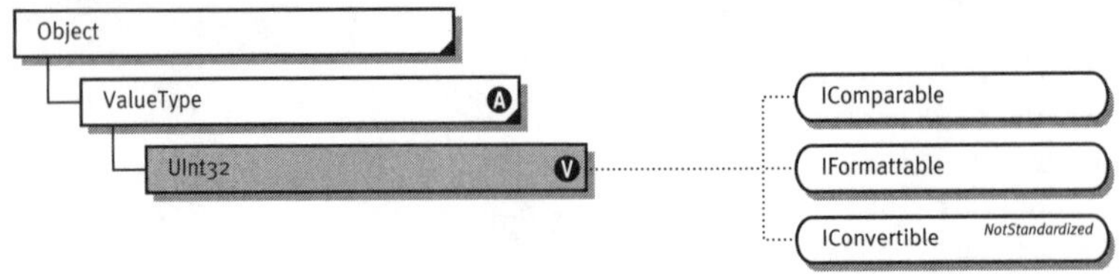




## Summary

Represents a 32-bit unsigned integer. This type is not CLS-compliant.

## Type Summary

```
public struct UInt32 : IComparable, IFormattable,
                       IConvertible
{
  // Fields
     public const uint MaxValue = 4294967295;
     public const uint MinValue = 0;

  // Methods
     public int CompareTo (object value);
     public override bool Equals (object obj);
     public override int GetHashCode ();
  MS public TypeCode GetTypeCode ();
     public static uint Parse (string s);
     public static uint Parse (string s, NumberStyles style);
     public static uint Parse (string s, NumberStyles style,
                               IFormatProvider provider);
  CF public static uint Parse (string s, IFormatProvider provider);
     public override string ToString ();
     public string ToString (string format);
     public string ToString (string format, IFormatProvider provider);
     public string ToString (IFormatProvider provider);

  // Explicit Interface Members
  MS bool IConvertible.ToBoolean(IFormatProvider provider);
  MS byte IConvertible.ToByte(IFormatProvider provider);
  MS char IConvertible.ToChar(IFormatProvider provider);
  MS DateTime IConvertible.ToDateTime(IFormatProvider provider);
  MS decimal IConvertible.ToDecimal(IFormatProvider provider);
  MS double IConvertible.ToDouble(IFormatProvider provider);
  MS short IConvertible.ToInt16(IFormatProvider provider);
  MS int IConvertible.ToInt32(IFormatProvider provider);
  MS long IConvertible.ToInt64(IFormatProvider provider);
  MS sbyte IConvertible.ToSByte(IFormatProvider provider);
```

UInt32 Structure

```
    MS float IConvertible.ToSingle(IFormatProvider provider);
    MS object IConvertible.ToType(Type type,IFormatProvider provider);
    MS ushort IConvertible.ToUInt16(IFormatProvider provider);
    MS uint IConvertible.ToUInt32(IFormatProvider provider);
    MS ulong IConvertible.ToUInt64(IFormatProvider provider);
  }
```

## Description

The `System.UInt32` data type represents integer values ranging from 0 to positive 4,294,967,295 (hexadecimal 0xFFFFFFFF).

## Example

```
using System;

namespace Samples
{
  public class UInt32Sample
  {
    public static void Main()
    {
      uint max = uint.MaxValue,
           min = uint.MinValue;
      Console.WriteLine("MaxValue: {0}", max);
      Console.WriteLine("MinValue: {0}", min);
      Console.WriteLine("Is {0} equal to {1}: {2}",
                        max, max, max.Equals(max));
      Console.WriteLine("Is {0} equal to {1}: {2}",
                        max, min, max.Equals(min));
      Console.WriteLine("{0} has hashcode of: {1}",
                        max, max.GetHashCode());
      Console.WriteLine("{0} has hashcode of: {1}",
                        min, min.GetHashCode());
      string s = max.ToString();
      Console.WriteLine("\"{0}\" parsed from string yields: {1}",
                        s, UInt32.Parse(s));
      s = min.ToString();
      Console.WriteLine("\"{0}\" parsed from string yields: {1}",
                        s, UInt32.Parse(s));
      string[] formats = {"c", "d", "e", "f",
                          "g", "n", "p", "x" };
      foreach(string f in formats)
        Console.WriteLine("Format {0}: {1}", f, max.ToString(f));
    }
  }
}
```

The output is

```
MaxValue: 4294967295
MinValue: 0
Is 4294967295 equal to 4294967295: True
Is 4294967295 equal to 0: False
4294967295 has hashcode of: -1
0 has hashcode of: 0
"4294967295" parsed from string yields: 4294967295
"0" parsed from string yields: 0
Format c: $4,294,967,295.00
Format d: 4294967295
Format e: 4.294967e+009
Format f: 4294967295.00
Format g: 4294967295
Format n: 4,294,967,295.00
Format p: 429,496,729,500.00 %
Format x: ffffffff
```

A B C D E F G H I J K L M N O P Q R S T U V W X Y Z

# System
# UInt64 Structure

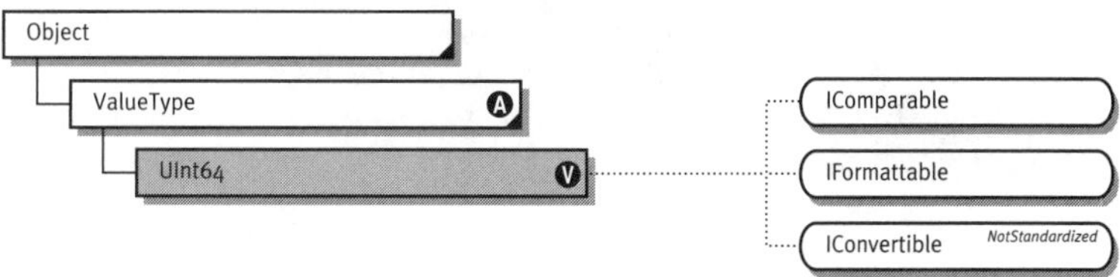


A B C D E F G H I J K L M N O P Q R S T U V W X Y Z

## Summary

Represents a 64-bit unsigned integer. This type is not CLS-compliant.

## Type Summary

```
public struct UInt64 : IComparable, IFormattable,
                       IConvertible
{
  // Fields
     public const ulong MaxValue = 18446744073709551615;
     public const ulong MinValue = 0;

  // Methods
     public int CompareTo (object value);
     public override bool Equals (object obj);
     public override int GetHashCode ();
  MS public TypeCode GetTypeCode ();
     public static ulong Parse (string s);
     public static ulong Parse (string s, NumberStyles style);
     public static ulong Parse (string s, NumberStyles style,
                                IFormatProvider provider);
  CF public static ulong Parse (string s, IFormatProvider provider);
     public override string ToString ();
     public string ToString (string format);
     public string ToString (string format, IFormatProvider provider);
     public string ToString (IFormatProvider provider);

  // Explicit Interface Members
  MS bool IConvertible.ToBoolean(IFormatProvider provider);
  MS byte IConvertible.ToByte(IFormatProvider provider);
  MS char IConvertible.ToChar(IFormatProvider provider);
  MS DateTime IConvertible.ToDateTime(IFormatProvider provider);
  MS decimal IConvertible.ToDecimal(IFormatProvider provider);
  MS double IConvertible.ToDouble(IFormatProvider provider);
  MS short IConvertible.ToInt16(IFormatProvider provider);
  MS int IConvertible.ToInt32(IFormatProvider provider);
  MS long IConvertible.ToInt64(IFormatProvider provider);
  MS sbyte IConvertible.ToSByte(IFormatProvider provider);
```

UInt64 Structure

```
    MS float IConvertible.ToSingle(IFormatProvider provider);
    MS object IConvertible.ToType(Type type,IFormatProvider provider);
    MS ushort IConvertible.ToUInt16(IFormatProvider provider);
    MS uint IConvertible.ToUInt32(IFormatProvider provider);
    MS ulong IConvertible.ToUInt64(IFormatProvider provider);
  }
```

## Description

The `System.UInt64` data type represents integer values ranging from 0 to positive 18,446,744,073,709,551,615 (hexadecimal 0xFFFFFFFFFFFFFFFF).

## Example

```
using System;

namespace Samples
{
  public class UInt64Sample
  {
    public static void Main()
    {
      ulong max = ulong.MaxValue,
            min = ulong.MinValue;
      Console.WriteLine("MaxValue: {0}", max);
      Console.WriteLine("MinValue: {0}", min);
      Console.WriteLine("Is {0} equal to {1}: {2}",
                        max, max, max.Equals(max));
      Console.WriteLine("Is {0} equal to {1}: {2}",
                        max, min, max.Equals(min));
      Console.WriteLine("{0} has hashcode of: {1}",
                        max, max.GetHashCode());
      Console.WriteLine("{0} has hashcode of: {1}",
                        min, min.GetHashCode());
      string s = max.ToString();
      Console.WriteLine("\"{0}\" parsed from string yields: {1}",
                        s, UInt64.Parse(s));
      s = min.ToString();
      Console.WriteLine("\"{0}\" parsed from string yields: {1}",
                        s, UInt64.Parse(s));
      string[] formats = {"c", "d", "e", "f",
                          "g", "n", "p", "x" };
      foreach(string f in formats)
        Console.WriteLine("{0}: {1}", max, max.ToString(f));
    }
  }
}
```

UInt64 Structure

The output is

```
MaxValue: 18446744073709551615
MinValue: 0
Is 18446744073709551615 equal to 18446744073709551615: True
Is 18446744073709551615 equal to 0: False
18446744073709551615 has hashcode of: 0
0 has hashcode of: 0
"18446744073709551615" parsed from string yields: 18446744073709551615
"0" parsed from string yields: 0
18446744073709551615: $18,446,744,073,709,551,615.00
18446744073709551615: 18446744073709551615
18446744073709551615: 1.844674e+019
18446744073709551615: 18446744073709551615.00
18446744073709551615: 18446744073709551615
18446744073709551615: 18,446,744,073,709,551,615.00
18446744073709551615: 1,844,674,407,370,955,161,500.00 %
18446744073709551615: ffffffffffffffff
```

# System UnauthorizedAccessException

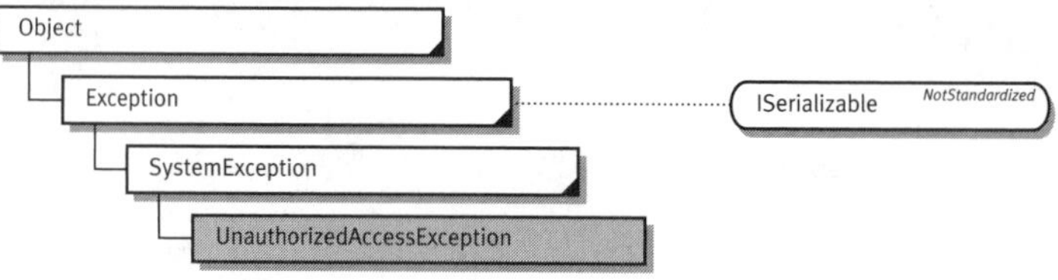




## Summary

Represents the error that occurs when an I/O operation cannot be performed because of incompatible file access levels.

## Type Summary

```
   public class UnauthorizedAccessException : SystemException
   {
     // Constructors
        public UnauthorizedAccessException ();
        public UnauthorizedAccessException (string message);
        public UnauthorizedAccessException (string message,
                                            Exception inner);
 MS CF protected UnauthorizedAccessException (SerializationInfo info,
                                              StreamingContext context);
   }
```

## Description

`System.UnauthorizedAccessException` is typically thrown when a request is made to write to a read-only file, or a file I/O operation is requested on a directory.

## Example

```
using System;
using System.IO;
using System.Security.Permissions;

namespace Samples
{
  public class UnauthorizedAccessExceptionConstructor
  {
    public static void Main()
    {
      try
      {
        string s = "readonly.txt";
        FileStream fs = File.OpenWrite(s);
```

```
      }
      catch(UnauthorizedAccessException e)
      {
        Console.WriteLine("Exception: {0}", e);
      }
    }
  }
}
```

The output is

```
Exception: System.UnauthorizedAccessException: Access to the path
"C:\Books\BCL\Samples\System\UnauthorizedAccessException\readonly.txt" is denied.
   at System.IO.__Error.WinIOError(Int32 errorCode, String str)
   at System.IO.FileStream..ctor(String path, FileMode mode, FileAccess access,
FileShare share, Int32 bufferSize, Boolean useAsync, String msgPath, Boolean
bFromProxy)
   at System.IO.FileStream..ctor(String path, FileMode mode, FileAccess access,
FileShare share)
   at System.IO.File.OpenWrite(String path)
   at Samples.UnauthorizedAccessExceptionConstructor.Main() in C:\Books\BCL\
Samples\System\UnauthorizedAccessException\UnauthorizedAccessException.cs:line 14
```

# System.Globalization UnicodeCategory Enum

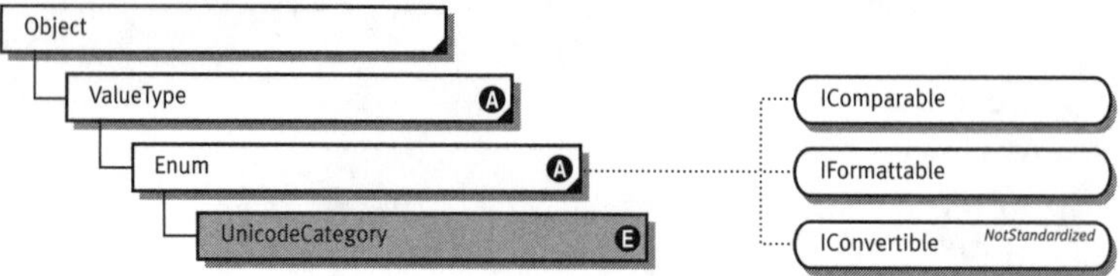


## Summary

Designates the general Unicode category of a `System.Char`.

## Type Summary

```
public enum UnicodeCategory  {
      ClosePunctuation = 21,
      ConnectorPunctuation = 18,
      Control = 14,
      CurrencySymbol = 26,
      DashPunctuation = 19,
      DecimalDigitNumber = 8,
      EnclosingMark = 7,
      FinalQuotePunctuation = 23,
      Format = 15,
      InitialQuotePunctuation = 22,
      LetterNumber = 9,
      LineSeparator = 12,
      LowercaseLetter = 1,
      MathSymbol = 25,
      ModifierLetter = 3,
      ModifierSymbol = 27,
      NonSpacingMark = 5,
      OpenPunctuation = 20,
      OtherLetter = 4,
      OtherNotAssigned = 29,
      OtherNumber = 10,
      OtherPunctuation = 24,
      OtherSymbol = 28,
      ParagraphSeparator = 13,
      PrivateUse = 17,
      SpaceSeparator = 11,
      SpacingCombiningMark = 6,
      Surrogate = 16,
      TitlecaseLetter = 2,
      UppercaseLetter = 0,
  }
```

UnicodeCategory Enum

## Description

These categories conform to Version 3.1 of the Unicode Standard.

[*Note:* For information on mapping specific Unicode characters to categories, see the UnicodeData.txt file in the Unicode Character Database at http://www.unicode.org/Public/UNIDATA/UnicodeCharacterDatabase.html. The UnicodeData.txt file format is described at http://www.unicode.org/Public/3.1-Update/UnicodeData-3.1.0.html.]

This enumeration is used to support `System.Char` methods such as `System.Char.IsLetter`, `System.Char.IsUpper`, etc.

## Example

```
using System;
using System.Globalization;

namespace Samples
{
  public class UnicodeCategorySample
  {
    public static void Main()
    {
      string s = "Pi is (\u03a0)!";
      Console.WriteLine("In string: {0}", s);
      foreach(char c in s)
        Console.WriteLine(
                 "Unicode category of Char '{0}' value: {1} is {2}",
                 c, (int) c, Char.GetUnicodeCategory(c));
    }
  }
}
```

The output is

```
C In string: Pi is ()!
Unicode category of Char 'P' value: 80 is UppercaseLetter
Unicode category of Char 'i' value: 105 is LowercaseLetter
Unicode category of Char ' ' value: 32 is SpaceSeparator
Unicode category of Char 'i' value: 105 is LowercaseLetter
Unicode category of Char 's' value: 115 is LowercaseLetter
Unicode category of Char ' ' value: 32 is SpaceSeparator
Unicode category of Char '(' value: 40 is OpenPunctuation
Unicode category of Char '' value: 928 is UppercaseLetter
Unicode category of Char ')' value: 41 is ClosePunctuation
Unicode category of Char '!' value: 33 is OtherPunctuation
```

# System.Text UnicodeEncoding

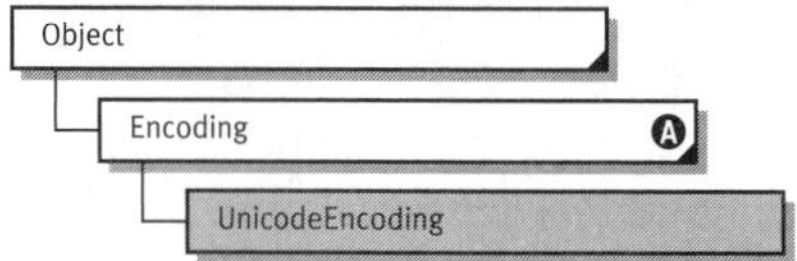




## Summary

Represents a Unicode implementation of `System.Text.Encoding`.

## Type Summary

```
public class UnicodeEncoding : Encoding
{
  // Constructors
     public UnicodeEncoding ();
     public UnicodeEncoding (bool bigEndian,
                             bool byteOrderMark);

  // Fields
  MS public const int CharSize = 2;

  // Methods
     public override bool Equals (object value);
     public override int GetByteCount (char[] chars,
                                        int index,
                                        int count);
     public override int GetByteCount (string s);
     public override int GetBytes (char[] chars,
                                    int charIndex,
                                    int charCount,
                                    byte[] bytes,
                                    int byteIndex);
  CF public override byte[] GetBytes (string s);
     public override int GetBytes (string chars,
                                    int charIndex,
                                    int charCount,
                                    byte[] bytes,
                                    int byteIndex);
     public override int GetCharCount (byte[] bytes,
                                        int index,
                                        int count);
     public override int GetChars (byte[] bytes,
                                    int byteIndex,
                                    int byteCount,
                                    char[] chars,
                                    int charIndex);
```

```
        public override Decoder GetDecoder ();
        public override int GetHashCode ();
        public override int GetMaxByteCount (int charCount);
        public override int GetMaxCharCount (int byteCount);
        public override byte[] GetPreamble ();
    }
```

**JR** Normally, there is no need for your application code to construct an `Encoding`-derived object (such as `UnicodeEncoding`). Instead, you normally obtain an `Encoding`-derived object by calling one of the `Encoding` class's static, read-only properties. Here is an example:

```
UnicodeEncoding unicodeEncoding = Encoding.Unicode;
```

This is more efficient because it returns a reference to a single `UnicodeEncoding` object rather than creating new `UnicodeEncoding` objects.

## Description

`System.Text.UnicodeEncoding` encodes each Unicode character in UTF-16, i.e., as two consecutive bytes. Both little-endian and big-endian encodings are supported.

[*Note:* On little-endian platforms such as Intel machines, it is generally more efficient to store Unicode characters in little-endian. However, many other platforms can store Unicode characters in big-endian. Unicode files can be distinguished by the presence of the byte order mark (U+FEFF), which is written as either 0xfe 0xff or 0xff 0xfe. This `System.Text.Encoding` implementation can detect a byte order mark automatically and switch byte orders, based on a parameter specified in the constructor. ISO/IEC 10646 defines UCS-2 and UCS-4. UCS-4 is a four-byte (32-bit) encoding containing $2^{31}$ code positions, divided into 128 groups of 256 planes. Each plane contains $2^{16}$ code positions. UCS-2 is a two-byte (16-bit) encoding containing the $2^{16}$ code positions of UCS-4 for which the upper two bytes are zero, known as Plane Zero or the Basic Multilingual Plane (BMP). For example, the code position for LATIN CAPITAL LETTER A in UCS-4 is 0x00000041 whereas in UCS-2 it is 0x0041. ISO/IEC 10646 also defines UTF-16, which stands for "UCS Transformation Format for 16 Planes of Group 00". UTF-16 is a two-byte encoding that uses an extension mechanism to represent $2^{21}$ code positions. UTF-16 represents code positions in Plane Zero by its UCS-2 code value and code positions in Planes 1 through 16 by a pair of special code values, called surrogates. UTF-16 is equivalent to the Unicode Standard. For a detailed description of UTF-16 and surrogates, see "The Unicode Standard Version 3.0" Appendix C.]

A B C D E F G H I J K L M N O P Q R S T U V W X Y Z

## Example

```
using System;
using System.Text;

namespace Samples
{
  public class UnicodeEncodingSample
  {
    public static void Main()
    {
      UnicodeEncoding u = (UnicodeEncoding) Encoding.Unicode;
      string s = "Pi is (\u03a0)";
      int count = u.GetByteCount(s);
      Console.WriteLine("In string");
      foreach(Int16 i in s)
        Console.Write("{0}, ", i);
      Console.WriteLine();
      byte[] bytes = new byte[count];
      bytes = u.GetBytes(s);
      Console.WriteLine("Converted to array of bytes");
      foreach(Byte b in bytes)
        Console.Write("{0}, ", b);
      Console.WriteLine();
      count = u.GetCharCount(bytes);
      char[] chars = new char[count];
      u.GetChars(bytes, 0, bytes.Length, chars, 0);
      Console.WriteLine("Converted to array of chars");
      foreach(Int16 c in chars)
        Console.Write("{0}, ", c);
      Console.WriteLine();
    }
  }
}
```

The output is

```
In string
80, 105, 32, 105, 115, 32, 40, 928, 41,
Converted to array of bytes
80, 0, 105, 0, 32, 0, 105, 0, 115, 0, 32, 0, 40, 0, 160, 3, 41, 0,
Converted to array of chars
80, 105, 32, 105, 115, 32, 40, 928, 41,
```

# System.Text UTF8Encoding

## Summary

Represents a UTF8 character System.Text.Encoding.

## Type Summary

```
public class UTF8Encoding : Encoding
{
  // Constructors
     public UTF8Encoding ();
     public UTF8Encoding (bool encoderShouldEmitUTF8Identifier);
     public UTF8Encoding (bool encoderShouldEmitUTF8Identifier,
                          bool throwOnInvalidBytes);

  // Methods
     public override bool Equals (object value);
     public override int GetByteCount (char[] chars,
                                       int index,
                                       int count);
     public override int GetByteCount (string str);
     public override int GetBytes (char[] chars,
                                   int charIndex,
                                   int charCount,
                                   byte[] bytes,
                                   int byteIndex);
     public override byte[] GetBytes (string s);
     public override int GetBytes (string s,
                                   int charIndex,
                                   int charCount,
                                   byte[] bytes,
                                   int byteIndex);
     public override int GetCharCount (byte[] bytes,
                                       int index,
                                       int count);
     public override int GetChars (byte[] bytes,
                                   int byteIndex,
                                   int byteCount,
                                   char[] chars,
                                   int charIndex);
     public override Decoder GetDecoder ();
     public override Encoder GetEncoder ();
```

```
        public override int GetHashCode ();
        public override int GetMaxByteCount (int charCount);
        public override int GetMaxCharCount (int byteCount);
        public override byte[] GetPreamble ();
    }
```

**BA** To adhere to our own guidelines completely, this should have been Utf8Encoding. Unfortunately we closed on the acronym casing rules too late in the product cycle to fix this class.

**JR** Normally, there is no need for your application code to construct an `Encoding`-derived object (such as `UTF8Encoding`). Instead, you normally obtain an `Encoding`-derived object by calling one of the `Encoding` class's static, read-only properties. Here is an example:

```
UTF8Encoding utf8Encoding = Encoding.UTF8;
```

This is more efficient because it returns a reference to a single `UTF8Encoding` object rather than creating new `UTF8Encoding` objects.

## Description

`System.Text.UTF8Encoding` encodes Unicode characters using the UTF-8 encoding (UCS Transformation Format, 8-bit form). This encoding supports all Unicode character values.

[*Note:* UTF-8 encodes Unicode characters with a variable number of bytes per character. This encoding is optimized for the lower 127 ASCII characters, yielding an efficient mechanism to encode English in an internationalizable way. The UTF-8 identifier is the Unicode byte-order mark (0xFEFF) written in UTF-8 (0xEF 0xBB 0xBF). The byte-order mark is used to distinguish UTF-8 text from other encodings. This class offers an error-checking feature that can be turned on when an instance of the class is constructed. Certain methods in this class check for invalid sequences of surrogate pairs. If error-checking is turned on and an invalid sequence is detected, `System.ArgumentException` is thrown. If error-checking is not turned on and an invalid sequence is detected, no exception is thrown and execution continues in a method-defined manner. For more information regarding surrogate pairs, see `System.Globalization.UnicodeCategory`.]

## Example

```
using System;
using System.Text;

namespace Samples
{
  public class UTF8EncodingSample
  {
    public static void Main()
    {
      UTF8Encoding u = (UTF8Encoding) Encoding.UTF8;
      string s = "Pi is (\u03a0)";
      Byte[] bytes = u.GetBytes(s);
      foreach(Int16 i in bytes)
        Console.Write("{0}, ", i);
      Console.WriteLine();
      int count = u.GetCharCount(bytes, 0,
                             bytes.Length);
      char[] chars = new char[count];
      u.GetChars(bytes, 0, bytes.Length, chars, 0);
      foreach(Int16 i in chars)
        Console.Write("{0}, ", i);
      Console.WriteLine();
    }
  }
}
```

The output is

```
80, 105, 32, 105, 115, 32, 40, 206, 160, 41,
80, 105, 32, 105, 115, 32, 40, 928, 41,
```

# System
# ValueType

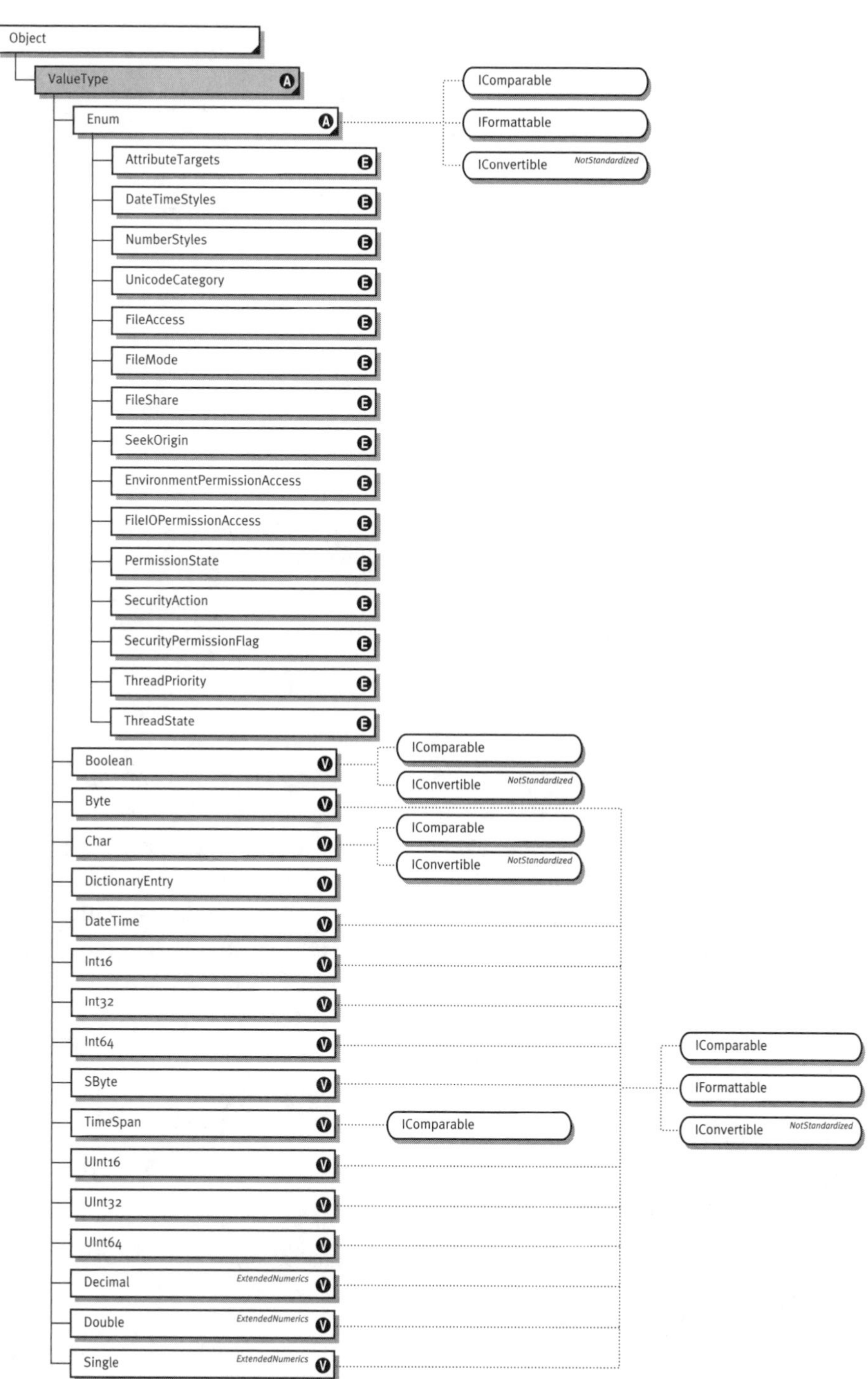

# ValueType Class

## Summary

Provides support for value types. This class is the base class for all value types.



## Type Summary

```
public abstract class ValueType
{
  // Constructors
     protected ValueType ();

  // Methods
     public override bool Equals (object obj);
     public override int GetHashCode ();
  CF public override string ToString ();
}
```

**BA** Notice we override `Equals`, `GetHashCode`, and `ToString` from `System.Object` in this class. We did this because the implementations inherited from `Object` rely on the object's referential identity, so they make no sense for value types. We can also provide slightly more efficient implementations of those methods.

## Description

[*Note:* Data types are separated into value types and reference types. Value types are either stack-allocated or allocated inline in a structure. Reference types are heap-allocated. Both reference and value types are derived from the ultimate base class `System.Object`. In cases where a value type needs to act like an object, a wrapper that makes the value type look like a reference object is allocated on the heap, and the value type's value is copied into it. The wrapper is marked so that the system knows that it contains a value type. This process is known as boxing, and the reverse process is known as unboxing. Boxing and unboxing allow any type to be treated as an object.]

## Example

```
using System;

namespace Samples
{
  public struct ValueTypeSample
  {
    private struct Point
    {
      private int xValue;
      private int yValue;
```

```
        public int X { get { return xValue;} set {xValue = value;}}
        public int Y { get { return yValue;} set {yValue = value;}}
        public override bool Equals(object o)
        {
          if(!(o is Point))
            return false;
          Point p = (Point) o;
          return this.xValue == p.xValue && this.yValue == p.yValue;
        }
        public override string ToString()
        {
          return string.Format("Point: X: {0}, Y: {1}", X, Y);
        }
        public override int GetHashCode()
        {
          return xValue ^ yValue;
        }
      }
      public static void Main()
      {
        Point p = new Point();
        Console.WriteLine("p.ToString(): {0}", p.ToString());
        Console.WriteLine("p.Equals(new Point()): {0}",
                          p.Equals(new Point()));
        Console.WriteLine("p = {0}, p.GetHashCode(): {1}",
                          p, p.GetHashCode());
        p.X = 42;
        Console.WriteLine("p = {0}, p.GetHashCode(): {1}",
                          p, p.GetHashCode());
        p.Y = 42;
        Console.WriteLine("p = {0}, p.GetHashCode(): {1}",
                          p, p.GetHashCode());
        p.X = 0;
        Console.WriteLine("p = {0}, p.GetHashCode(): {1}",
                          p, p.GetHashCode());
        Console.WriteLine("p.Equals(new Point()): {0}",
                          p.Equals(new Point()));
      }
    }
}
```

The output is

```
p.ToString(): Point: X: 0, Y: 0
p.Equals(new Point()): True
p = Point: X: 0, Y: 0, p.GetHashCode(): 0
p = Point: X: 42, Y: 0, p.GetHashCode(): 42
p = Point: X: 42, Y: 42, p.GetHashCode(): 0
p = Point: X: 0, Y: 42, p.GetHashCode(): 42
p.Equals(new Point()): False
```

# System.Security VerificationException

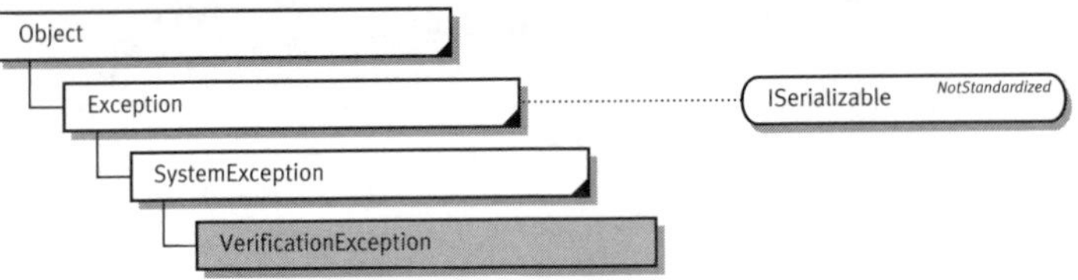


A
B
C
D
E
F
G
H
I
J
K
L
M
N
O
P
Q
R
S
T
U
V
W
X
Y
Z

## Summary

Represents the error that occurs when the security system requires code to be type-safe and the verification process is unable to verify that the code is type-safe.

## Type Summary

```
public class VerificationException : SystemException
{
  // Constructors
     public VerificationException ();
     public VerificationException (string message);
     public VerificationException (string message,
                                  Exception innerException);
MS CF protected VerificationException (SerializationInfo info,
                                  StreamingContext context);
}
```

## Description

[*Note:* The following IL instructions throw `System.Security.VerificationException`]

## Example

```
using System;
using System.Security;
using System.Security.Permissions;

[assembly: PermissionSetAttribute(
             SecurityAction.RequestRefuse,
             Name="SkipVerification")]

namespace Samples
{
  public class VerificationExceptionSample
  {
    unsafe public static void Main(string[] args)
    {
      string s = "damien";
```

```
        fixed(char *ptr = s)
        {
          for(int i = 0; i < s.Length; i++)
            Console.WriteLine(ptr[i]);
        }
      }
    }
}
```

The output is

```
UnhandledException: System.Security.VerificationException: Operation could
destabilize the runtime.
   at Samples.VerificationExceptionSample.Main(String[] args) in C:\Books\BCL\
Samples\System.Security\VerificationException\VerificationException.cs:line 15
```

# System
# Version

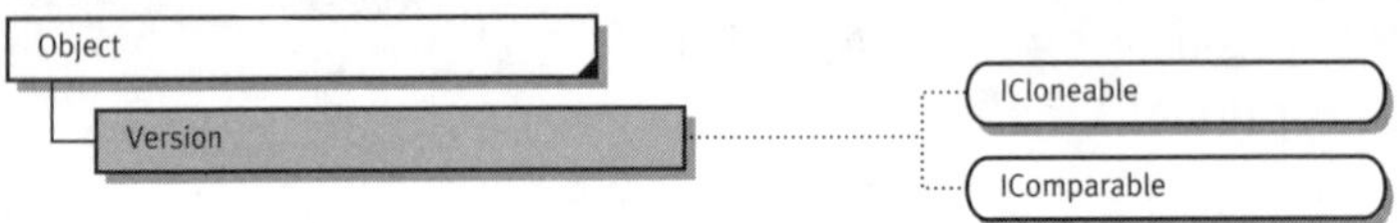




## Summary

Represents the version number of an assembly.

## Type Summary

```
public sealed class Version : ICloneable, IComparable
{
  // Constructors
  CF public Version ();
     public Version (int major, int minor);
     public Version (int major, int minor, int build);
     public Version (int major, int minor, int build,
                     int revision);
     public Version (string version);

  // Properties
     public int Build { get; }
     public int Major { get; }
     public int Minor { get; }
     public int Revision { get; }

  // Methods
     public object Clone ();
     public int CompareTo (object version);
     public override bool Equals (object obj);
     public override int GetHashCode ();
     public static bool operator ==(Version v1,
                                     Version v2);
     public static bool operator >(Version v1,
                                    Version v2);
     public static bool operator >=(Version v1,
                                     Version v2);
     public static bool operator !=(Version v1,
                                     Version v2);
     public static bool operator <(Version v1,
                                    Version v2);
     public static bool operator <=(Version v1,
                                     Version v2);
  MS public override string ToString ();
  MS public string ToString (int fieldCount);
}
```

## Description

`System.Version` numbers for an assembly consist of two to four components: *major, minor, build,* and *revision*. Components *major* and *minor* must be defined. *Build* and *revision* components are optional. Component *revision* may be used if and only if build is defined. All defined components must be a `System.Int32` greater than or equal to zero.

## Example

```
using System;
using System.Reflection;

namespace Samples
{
  public class VersionSample
  {
    public static void Main()
    {
      Type t = Typeof(String);
      Assembly a = Assembly.GetAssembly(t);
      AssemblyName an = a.GetName();
      Version v = an.Version;
      Console.WriteLine("Version: {0}", v);
      Console.WriteLine("Major: {0}", v.Major);
      Console.WriteLine("Minor: {0}", v.Minor);
      Console.WriteLine("Build: {0}", v.Build);
      Console.WriteLine("Revision: {0}", v.Revision);
      v = Environment.Version;
      if(v.Major == 1 && v.Minor == 0)
      {
        Console.WriteLine ("You are running V1");
      }
      else if(v.Major == 1 & v.Minor == 1)
        {
          Console.WriteLine ("You are running V1.1");
        }
        else
          Console.WriteLine ("You are running an unknown version");
    }
  }
}
```

The output is

```
Version: 1.0.3300.0
Major: 1
Minor: 0
Build: 3300
Revision: 0
You are running V1
```

# System.Threading WaitHandle

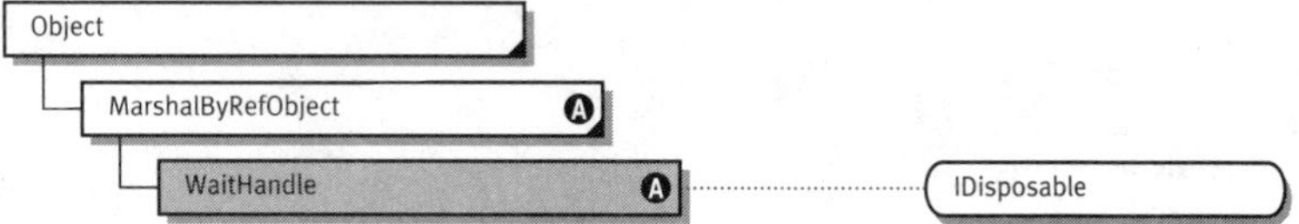


## Summary

Encapsulates operating-system specific objects that wait for exclusive access to shared resources.

## Type Summary

```
public abstract class WaitHandle : MarshalByRefObject,
                                   IDisposable
{
   // Constructors
      public WaitHandle ();

   // Fields
   MS protected static readonly IntPtr InvalidHandle = new IntPtr (-1);
MS CF public const int WaitTimeout = 258;

   // Properties
   MS public virtual IntPtr Handle { set; get; }

   // Methods
      public virtual void Close ();
   CF protected virtual void Dispose (bool explicitDisposing);
      ~WaitHandle () {}
   CF public static bool WaitAll (WaitHandle[] waitHandles);
MS CF public static bool WaitAll (WaitHandle[] waitHandles,
                                  int millisecondsTimeout,
                                  bool exitContext);
MS CF public static bool WaitAll (WaitHandle[] waitHandles,
                                  TimeSpan timeout,
                                  bool exitContext);
   CF public static int WaitAny (WaitHandle[] waitHandles);
MS CF public static int WaitAny (WaitHandle[] waitHandles,
                                 int millisecondsTimeout,
                                 bool exitContext);
MS CF public static int WaitAny (WaitHandle[] waitHandles,
                                 TimeSpan timeout,
                                 bool exitContext);
      public virtual bool WaitOne ();
MS CF public virtual bool WaitOne (int millisecondsTimeout,
                                   bool exitContext);
```

```
MS CF public virtual bool WaitOne (TimeSpan timeout,
                                   bool exitContext);

   // Explicit Interface Members
   CF void IDisposable.Dispose ();
 }
```

**JR** The parameter-less `WaitOne` method will always return `true`. Therefore, there is not a need to test its return value; it should have been prototyped with a `void` return value.

## Description

[*Note:* This class is typically used as a base class for synchronization objects. Classes derived from `System.Threading.WaitHandle` define a signaling mechanism to indicate taking or releasing exclusive access to a shared resource, but use the inherited `System.Threading.WaitHandle` methods to block while waiting for access to shared resources. The static methods of this class are used to block a `System.Threading.Thread` until one or more synchronization objects receive a signal.]

## Example

```
using System;
using System.Threading;

namespace Samples
{
  public class WaitHandle
  {
    static AutoResetEvent threadDone =
             new AutoResetEvent(false);
    public static void StartHere()
    {
      Console.WriteLine("Starting thread");
      Thread.Sleep(1000);
      threadDone.Set();
      Console.WriteLine("Finishing thread");
    }

    public static void Main()
    {
      Console.WriteLine("Starting Main");
      Thread t = new Thread(
                   new ThreadStart(StartHere));
```

```
            t.Start();
            threadDone.WaitOne();
            threadDone.Close();
            Console.WriteLine("Finishing Main");
        }
    }
}
```

The output is

```
Starting Main
Starting thread
Finishing Main
Finishing thread
```

# Annotations Index


**A**

Abrams, Brad 37, 40, 47–48, 57, 60, 65, 68–69, 72, 78, 83, 85–86, 88, 91, 97, 101–102, 112, 118, 122–123, 136, 143, 149, 156, 160, 166, 170, 174, 178, 187, 193, 198, 202, 204, 215, 221, 226–227, 231, 240, 255, 264–265, 267–268, 269, 286–287, 298, 304, 317, 320, 337, 343, 347, 352, 382, 409, 424, 431, 450, 479, 504, 508

**C**

Cwalina, Krzysztof 33, 113, 241, 245, 252, 409, 431, 465

**G**

George, Kit 102, 113, 118–119, 136, 157, 227, 249, 311, 360, 375, 409, 415, 418, 425, 431, 471

Grunkemeyer, Brian 48–49, 54–55, 60, 72, 86, 97, 102, 123, 136, 149, 156–157, 167, 174, 178, 190, 194, 198, 206–207, 227, 231, 240–241, 251, 258, 283, 298, 325, 403, 425, 434

**H**

Hejlsberg, Anders xxii, 91, 102, 112–113, 146, 424

**L**

Lin, Yung-Shin 166

**M**

Marcey, Joel 48, 54, 136, 235, 348, 360, 450

**R**

Richter, Jeffrey 33, 38, 49, 55, 60, 61, 65, 69, 76, 83, 88, 97–98, 113, 119, 136, 143, 146, 167, 175, 187, 194, 228, 235, 245, 248, 252, 255, 262, 265, 298–299, 304, 325, 348, 425, 431, 441, 456, 501, 504, 516

# Index


**A**

Access
  code permissions 90
  environment variables 180
  file security 206
  security actions 185
  System.IO.FileAccess.Enum 204–205
  System.MarshalByRefObject 317–318
Actions
  security 185
  SecurityAction.Enum 384–385
Applications
  console 100–103
  execution 33
  System.ApplicationException 33–34
ArgumentException class 35–36
ArgumentNullException 37–39
ArgumentOutOfRangeException class 40–41
Arguments
  null 41
  System.Event.Args class 187–189
  System.Int32 50
Arithmetic operations 42–43
  *See also* Mathematical functions
  System.OverflowException 356–357
Arrays, System.Collections.ArrayList class 52–56
ArrayTypeMismatchException 57–58
ASCII, Text.ASCIIEncoding class 59–60
Asynchronous operations, objects 245
Asynchronous read and write operations 225–230
Atomic operations, System.Threading.Interlocked 304–306
Attributes 63–67
  FileIOPermissionAttribute 213
  namespaces 4–5
  SecurityPermissionAttribute 395–397
  System.AttributeTarget Enum class 68–70
  System.AttributeUsageAttribute class 71–74
  System.CLSCompliantAttribute 88–89
  System.FlagsAttribute 231–232
  System.ObsoleteAttribute.Class 352–353
  System.Security.Permissions.SecurityAttribute 386–387

**B**

Base classes
  *See also* Classes
  System.ApplicationException 33–34
  System.EventArgs class 187
Base data types, System.Convert class 104–114
Behavior, attributes 71–74
Bit-fields, declaring 231
Blocks of characters, converting into bytes 163
Boolean structure 75–76
Bytes
  characters 163
  structure 77–79

**C**

Callable methods 97
Characters
  bytes, converting into 163
  encoding 164
  System.Char Structure 81–84

System.CharEnumerator 85–87
System.Text.StringBuilder 429–433
Classes
*See also* individual classes
ArgumentException 35–36
ArgumentNullException 37–39
ArgumentOutOfRange 40–41
Array 44–51
DateTimeFormatInfo 122–130
System.ApplicationException 33–34
System.ArithmeticException 42–43
System.Attribute 63–67
System.AttributeTarget Enum 68–70
System.AttributeUsageAttribute 71–74
System.Collections.ArrayList 52–56
System.Collections.Comparer 96
System.Console 100–103
System.Convert 104–114
System.Diagnostics.ConditionalAttribute 97–99
System.Enum 172–176
System.Environment 177–179
System.EventArgs 187–189
System.EventHandler.Delegate 190–191
System.Exception 193–197
System.ExecutionEngineException 198–199
System.IO.EndOfStreamException 170–171
System.ObsoleteAttribute.Class 352–353
System.Security.CodeAccessPermission 90–93
System.Security.Permissions
EnviromentPermission 180–182
EnviromentPermissionAccess.Enum 183–184
EnviromentPermissionAttribute 185–186
SecurityAttribute 94–95
System.Text Encoder 163
System.Text Encoding 164–169
Text.ASCIIEncoding 59–60
Cleanup, resources 264
CLS (Common Language Specification) 66
System.CLSCompliantAttribute 88–89
Code
access permissions 90
CodeAccessPermission class 90–93
security attributes 94
Collections
namespaces 11–12
permissions 367
sorting 258–259
Common Language Specification. *See* CLS
Common mathematical functions 319
Compilers, callable methods 97
Consoles 100–103
Constructors
ExecutionEngineException() 199
Control over resource cleanup 264
Conversion
System.ArrayTypeMismatchException 57
System.Convert class 104–114
Copying arrays 44–51
Customization
collections 258–259
hash functions 283–285
strings 274–282
System.IO.File 202

**D**

Dates
DateTimeFormatInfo class 122–130
System.DateTime structure 115–120
Decimals
System.Decimal.Structure 133–138
System.Double.Structure 155–159
Declarations
bit-fields 231
security actions 185
Defining
attributes 71–74
pre-processing identifiers 97
shape of methods 190
Delegation
namespaces 6
System.Threading.ThreadStart.Delegate 456–457
System.Threading.TimerCallback.Delegate 468–469
Diagnostics
namespaces 14
Dictionaries 146–147
System.Collections.IDictionary.Interface 260–261
System.Collections.IDictionaryEnumerator.Interface 262–263
Directories
security 206
System.IO 148–150
System.IO.Path 359–364
DivideByZeroException 153–154

**E**

Elements 50
System.Security.SecurityElement 388–389
ToString() method 391

Encoding
  object security 388
  StreamReader 414–416
  Text.ASCIIEncoding class 59–60
  UTF8 characters 503–505
Entries, dictionaries 146–147
Enumeration
  System.Enum class 172–176
  System.IO.File 202
Enumerators
  System.AttributeTarget Enum class 68–70
  System.CharEnumerator 85–87
Environment, System.Environment class 177–179
Errors
  *See also* Troubleshooting
  execution engines 198
  streams 100, 170
  System.Exception class 193
Events, System.EventArgs class 187–189
Exceptions
  ArgumentException 35–36
  ArgumentNullException 37–39
  ArgumentOutOfRange 40–41
  ArrayTypeMismatchException class 57
  DirectoryNotFoundException 151
  DivideByZeroException 153–154
  FileLoadException 215–217
  FileNotFoundException 220–222
  namespaces 7–8
  NotFiniteNumberException 331–332
  PathTooLongException 365–366
  StackOverFlowException 406–407
  System.ApplicationException 33–34
  System.ArithmeticException class 42–43
  System.DuplicateWaitObjectException 160–161
  System.Exception class 193–197
  System.ExecutionEngineException class 198–199
  System.IndexOutOfRangeException 292–293
  System.InvalidCastException 307–308
  System.InvalidOperationException 309–310
  System.InvalidProgramException 311
  System.IO.EndOfStreamException 170–171
  System.IO.IOException 312–313
  System.NotImplementedException 333–334
  System.NotSupportedException 335–336
  System.NullReferenceException 337–338
  System.ObjectDisposedException 350–351
  System.OutOfMemoryException 354–355
  System.OverflowException 356–357
  System.RankException 378–379
  System.Security.SystemException 390–391
  System.Security.VerificationException 510–511
  System.SystemException 441–442
  System.Threading.SynchronizationLockException 438–439
  System.Threading.ThreadStateException 461–462
  System.UnauthorizedAccessException 496–497
  SystemFormatException 233–234
  ThreadAbortException 452–453
  TypeInitializationException 484–485
Execution
  engines, troubleshooting 198
  environments 177
  System.Exception class 193
  troubleshooting 33
Explicit conversion, System.InvalidCastException 307–308
Extended numerics
  System.Decimal.Structure 133–138
  System.Double.Structure 155–159
  System.NotFiniteNumberException 331–332
  System.Single.Structure 402–405

## F

Fields
  bit-fields 231
  FileMode.Append 219
FileIOPermissionAttribute 213–214
FileLoadException 215–217
FileMode.Enum, Append field 219
FileNotFoundException 220–222
Files
  opening 218–219
  security 206
  sharing 223–224
  System.IO File 201–203
  System.IO.FileAccess.Enum 204–205
  System.IO.Path 359–364
Finalizers 236
Flags, System.FlagsAttribute 231–232
Formatting
  arrays 44–51
  services 271–272
  System.FormatException 233–234
  System.Globalization.NumberFormatInfo 339–342
  System.Globalization.NumberStyles.Enum 343–346

**G**

Garbage Collector, System.GC 235–237
Globalization
  namespaces 15

**H**

Hash functions, customizing 283–285
Hashtables, System.Collections.HashTable 239–243

**I**

I/O operations
  namespaces 17–19
  System.IO.IOException 312–313
Identifiers, pre-processing 97
Implementation of System.Collections.IComparer interface 96
Indexes 50
  System.IndexOutOfRangeException 292–293
Input streams 100
Instances
  iteration over 267
Int16 294–296
Int32 297–300
Int64 301–303
Integers
  byte structure 77–79
  System.Int16.Structure 294–296
  System.Int32.Structure 297–300
  System.Int64.Structure 301–303
  System.SByte.Structure 381–383
  UInt16.Structure 487–489
  UInt32.Structure 490–492
  UInt64.Structure 493–495
Interfaces 245–247
  namespaces 6
  System.Collections.ICollection.Interface 251–253
  System.Collections.IComparer.Interface 96, 258–259
  System.Collections.IDictionary.Interface 260–261
  System.Collections.IDictionaryEnumerator.Interface 262–263
  System.Collections.IEnumerable.Interface 267–268
  System.Collections.IEnumerator.Interface 269–270
  System.Collections.IHashCodeProvider.Interface 283–285
  System.Collections.IList.Interface 286–291
  System.FormatProvider.Interface 271–272
  System.ICloneable.Interface 248–250
  System.IComparable.Interface 255–257
  System.IDisposable.Interface 264–266
  System.IFormattable.Interface 274–282
  System.Security.IPermission 314–315
Internal errors 198
Iteration
  over instances 267
  System.CharEnumerator 85–87

**L**

Length of arrays 50
Logarithmic functions 319
Lower bound of dimensions 50

**M**

Mathematical functions 319–320
Memory
  System.IO.MemoryStream 321–324
  System.OutOfMemoryException 354–355
Methods
  callable 97
  shape of, defining 190
  System.IO File 202
  troubleshooting 35–36
Modification of arrays 44–51

**N**

Namespaces
  attributes 4–5
  collections 11–12
  delegates 6
  diagnostics 14
  Exceptions 7–8
  globalization 15
  I/O operations 17–19
  interfaces 6
  permissions 22
  security 21–24
  System 3–4
  text 25
  threading 27–30
  utility objects 5
Nanosecond units 119
Null arguments 41
Null methods, troubleshooting 37–39
NumberFormatInfo 339–342
Numbers
  System.Globalization.NumberFormatInfo 339–342
  System.Globalization.NumberStyles.Enum 343–346
  System.Random 375–377

Numeric type, converting 114
Numerics. *See* Extended numerics

**O**
Objects
  asynchronous operations 245
  security, encoding 388
  services 271–272
  strings 274–282
  System.MarshalByRefObject 317–318
  System.Object 347–349
  System.ObjectDisposedException 350–351
  utility 5
Opening files 218–219
Operations
  System.InvalidOperationException 309–310
  System.IO File 201–203
  System.IO.IOException 312–313
  System.NotImplementedException 333–334
  System.NotSupportedException 335–336
Output streams 100
Overflows, StackOverflowException 406–407

**P**
Paths
  System.IO.Path 359–364
  System.IO.PathTooLongException 365–366
Permissions
  *See also* Security
  code access 90
  namespaces 22
  SecurityPermission 392–394
  SecurityPermissionAttribute 395–397
  System.Security.IPermission.Interface 314–315
  System.Security.Permissions.Permission-State.Enum 373–374
  System.SecurityPermissionSet 367–372
Pre-processing identifiers, defining 97
Priorities, System.Threading.ThreadPriority.Enum 454
Programming
  *See also* Code
  System.GC 235–237
Programs, System.InvalidProgramException 311
Pseudo-random numbers 375–377

**R**
Random numbers 375–377
Ranges, ArgumentOutOfRange class 40–41
Rank of arrays 50
Reading
  end of streams 170
  strings. *See* StringReader class
Read-only access, System.CharEnumerator 85–87
Resources, cleanup 264

**S**
Scheduling System.Threading.ThreadPriority.Enum 454
Searching arrays 44–51
Security
  actions 185
  CodeAccessPermission 90–93
  environment variables 180
  FileIOPermissionAccess.Enum 211–212
  files 206
  namespaces 21–24
  SecurityAttribute 386–387
  System.Security.Permissions.FileIOPermissions 206–210
  System.Security.SecurityElement 388–389
    ToString() method 390–391
SecurityAction.Enum 384–385
SecurityException 390–391
SecurityPermission 392–394
SecurityPermissionAttribute 395–397
Seeking references 400–401
Sequential threads. *See* System.Threading.Thread class
Services, formatting 271–272
Shape of methods, defining 190
Sharing files 223–224
Signed integers, System.SByte.Structure 381–383
Single-precision floating-point number 402
Sorting
  arrays 44–51
  collections 258–259
StackOverflowException 406–407
StreamReader 414–416
Streams 408–413
  *See also* System.IO.MemoryStream
  reading 170
StreamWriter 417–419
StringBuilder 429–433
StringReader 434–435
Strings
  customizing 274–282
  System.String 420–428
StringWriter 436–437

Structure, System.Char Structure 81–84
Synchronous read and write operations 225–230
System namespace 3–4
System.ApplicationException class 33–34
System.ArithmeticException class 42–43
System.Array class 44–51
System.ArrayTypeMismatchException. *See* ArrayTypeMismatchException
System.AsyncCallback Delegate 61–62
System.AsyncResult.Interface 245–247
System.Attribute class 63–67
System.AttributeTarget Emun class 68–70
System.AttributeUsageAttribute class 71–74
System.Char structure 81–84
System.CharEnumerator 85–87
System.CLSCompliantAttribute 88–89
System.Collections
  ArrayList class 52–56
  Comparer class 96
  DictionaryEntry structure 146–147
  Hashtable 239–243
  ICollection.Interface 251–253
  IComparer.Interface 258–259
  IDictionary.Interface 260–261
  IDictionaryEnumerator.Interface 262–263
  IEnumerable.Interface 267–268
  IEnumerator.Interface 269–270
  IHashCodeProvider.Interface 283–285
  IList.Interface 286–291
System.Console class 100–103
System.Convert class 104–114
System.DateTime structure 115–120
  DateTimeFormatInfo class 122–130
System.Decimal.Structure 133–138
System.Delegate 142, 145
System.Diagnostics.ConditionalAttribute class 97–99
System.DivideByZeroException 153–154
System.Double.Structure 155–159
System.DuplicateWaitObjectException 160–161
System.Enum class 172–176
System.Environment class 177–179
System.EventArgs class 187–189
System.EventHandler.Delegate class 190–191
System.Exception class 193–197
System.ExecutionEngineException class 198–199
System.FlagsAttribute 231–232
System.FormatException 233–234
System.GC 235–237
System.Globalization
  DateTimeStyles 131
  NumberStyles.Enum 343–346
  UnicodeCategory.Enum 498–499
System.ICloneable.Interface 248–250
System.IComparable.Interface 255–257
System.IDisposable.Interface 264–266
System.IFormatProvider.Interface 271–272
System.IFormattable.Interface 274–282
System.IndexOutOfRangeException 292–293
System.Int16.Structure 294–296
System.Int32.Structure 297–300
  arguments 50
System.Int64.Structure 301–303
System.InvalidCastException 307–308
System.InvalidOperationException 309–310
System.InvalidProgramException 311
System.IO
  Directory 148–150
  EndOfStreamException class 170–171
  File 201–203
  FileAccess.Enum 204–205
  FileLoadException 215–217
  FileMode.Enum 218–219
    Append field 219
  FileNotFoundException 220–222
  FileShare.Enum 223–224
  FileStream 225–230
  IOException 312–313
  MemoryStream 321–324
  Path 359–364
  PathTooLongException 365–366
  SeekOrigin.Enum 400–401
  Stream 408–413
  StreamReader 414–416
  StreamWriter 417–419
  StringReader 434–435
  StringWriter 436–437
  TextReader 443–444
  TextWriter 445–447
System.IO.Directory
  NotFoundException 151
System.MarshalByRefObject 317–318
System.Math 319–320
System.NotFiniteNumberException 331–332
System.NotImplementedException 333–334
System.NotSupportedException 335–336
System.NullReferenceException 337–338
System.Object 347–349

System.ObjectDisposedException 350–351
System.ObsoleteAttribute.Class 352–353
System.OutOfMemoryException 354–355
System.OverflowException 356–357
System.Random 375–377
System.RankException 378–379
System.SByte.Structure 381–383
System.Security
  CodeAccessPermission class 90–93
  IPermission.Interface 314–315
System.Security.Permissions
  EnvironmentPermission class 180–182
  EnvironmentPermissionAccess.Enum class 183–184
  EnvironmentPermissionAttribute class 185–186
  FileIOPermission 206–210
  FileIOPermissionAccess.Enum 211–212
  FileIOPermissionAttribute 213–214
  PermissionState.Enum 373–374
  SecurityAction.Enum 384–385
  SecurityAttribute 386–387
  SecurityAttribute class 94–95
  SecurityPermissionAttribute 395–397
  SecurityPermissionFlag.Enum 398–399
  SecurityPermissions 392–394
System.Security.PermissionSet 367–372
System.Security.SecurityElement 388–389
  ToString() method 390–391
System.Security.SecurityException 390–391
System.Security.VerificationException 510–511
System.Single.Structure 402–405
System.StackOverflowException 406–407
System.String 420–428
System.SystemException 441–442
System.Text
  ASCIIEncoding class 59–60, 167
  Decoder 140
  Encoder class 163
  Encoding class 164–169
  StringBuilder 429–433
  UnicodeEncoding 167, 500–502
  UTF8Encoding 167, 503–505
System.Threading
  Interlocked 304–306
  Monitor 325–329
  SynchronizationLockException 438–439
  Thread 448–451
  ThreadAbortException 452–453
  ThreadPriority.Enum 454–455
  ThreadStart.Delegate 456–457
  ThreadState.Enum 458–460
  ThreadStateException 461–462
  Timeout 463–464
  Timer 465–467
  TimerCallback.delegate 468–469
  WaitHandle 515–517
System.TimeSpan.Structure 470–473
System.Type 474–483
System.TypeInitializationException 484–485
System.UInt16.Structure 487–489
System.UInt32.Structure 490–492
System.UInt64.Structure 493–495
System.UnauthorizedAccessException 496–497
System.ValueType 508–509
System.Version.Class 512–513

## T

Text
  namespaces 25
  System.Text.Encoder class 163
  System.Text.Encoding class 164–169
  System.Text.UTF8Encoding 503–505
  UnicodeEncoding 500–502
Text.ASCIIEncoding class 59–60
TextReader 443–444
TextWriter 445–447
Threads
  namespaces 27–30
  System.Threading.Interlocked 304–306
  System.Threading.Monitor 325–329
  System.Threading.SynchronizationLockException 438–439
  System.Threading.Thread 448–451
  System.Threading.ThreadState.Enum 458–460
  ThreadAbortException 452–453
  ThreadPriority.Enum 454–455
  Timeout 463–464
  Timer 465–467
  Timercallback.Delegate 468–469
Ticks 119
Time
  System.DateTime structure 115–120
    DateTimeFormatInfo class 122–130
  System.TimeSpan.Structure 470–473
Timeouts 463–464
Timers 465–467
  TimerCallback.Delegate 468–469
Trigonometric functions 319

Troubleshooting
  applications 33
  arguments 35–36
  arithmetic operations 42–43
  ArrayTypeMismatchException class 57
  execution engines 198
  null arguments 41
  null methods 37–39
  streams 170
  System.Exception class 193
Type
  enumeration 175
  System.Type 474–483
  System.TypeInitializationException 484–485
types of values, System namespace 3

**U**

UnauthorizedAccessException 496–497
Underlying type 175
Unicode characters, System.Char Structure 81–84
UnicodeCategory.Enum 498–499
UnicodeEncoding 500–502
Unsigned integers
  byte structure 77–79
  UInt.16.Structure 487–489
  UInt.32.Structure 490–492
  UInt.64.Structure 493–495
UTF8Encoding 503–505
Utility objects, namespaces 5

**V**

Validation 35–36
Values
  dates and times 119
  System namespace 3
ValueType 508–509
Variables
  environments 180
  System.Threading.Interlocked 304–306
Vectors 50
VerificationException 510–511
Versions, System.Version.Class 512–513

**W**

WaitHandle 515–517
Wrappers, StreamWriter 417–419
Writing strings. *See* StringWriter class

**X**

XML (Extensible Markup Language), SecurityElement 388–389

**Z**

Zero, DivideByZeroException 153–154

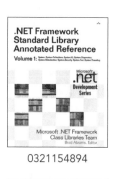

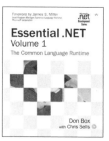

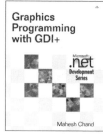

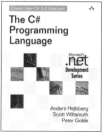

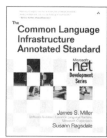

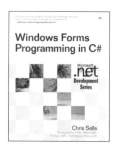

# CD-ROM Warranty

Addison-Wesley warrants the enclosed CD-ROM to be free of defects in materials and faulty workmanship under normal use for a period of ninety days after purchase (when purchased new). If a defect is discovered in the CD-ROM during this warranty period, a replacement CD-ROM can be obtained at no charge by sending the defective CD-ROM, postage prepaid, with proof of purchase to:


Disc Exchange
Addison-Wesley Professional
Pearson Technology Group
75 Arlington Street, Suite 300
Boston, MA 02116
Email: AWPro@aw.com


Addison-Wesley makes no warranty or representation, either expressed or implied, with respect to this software, its quality, performance, merchantability, or fitness for a particular purpose. In no event will Addison-Wesley, its distributors, or dealers be liable for direct, indirect, special, incidental, or consequential damages arising out of the use or inability to use the software. The exclusion of implied warranties is not permitted in some states. Therefore, the above exclusion may not apply to you. This warranty provides you with specific legal rights. There may be other rights that you may have that vary from state to state. The contents of this CD-ROM are intended for personal use only.

More information and updates are available at:

http://www.awprofessional.com/

**NOTE:** To ensure optimal performance of the PDF files on this CD, you first need to configure your Web browser to open PDF files in a separate Adobe Acrobat window. For more information, see "Important Information About Viewing the eBook" in the eBook Instructions on the CD.